MW01119813

PERFORMING GREEK COMEDY

Alan Hughes presents a new complete account of production methods in Greek comedy. The book summarizes contemporary research
and disputes, on such topics as acting techniques, theatre buildings,
masks and costumes, music and the chorus. Evidence is reinterpreted,
and traditional doctrine overthrown. Comedy is presented as the
pan-Hellenic, visual art of theatre, not as Athenian literature. Recent
discoveries in visual evidence are used to stimulate significant historical revisions. The author has directly examined 350 vase scenes of
comedy in performance and actor-figurines, in 75 collections, from
Melbourne to St Petersburg. Their testimony is applied to acting
techniques and costumes, and women's participation in comedy and
mime. The chapters are arranged by topic, for convenient reference
by scholars and students of theatre history, literature, classics and
drama. Overall, the book provides a fresh practical insight into this
continually developing subject.

ALAN HUGHES is Professor Emeritus, University of Victoria, a theatre historian and professional who has operated his own repertory
company. Published research includes *Henry Irving, Shakespearean*, an
account of the actor-manager's productions, and his edition of *Titus
Andronicus* in the New Cambridge Shakespeare series. In 2006 the
T.B.L. Webster Fellowship recognized his contributions to the archaeology of Greek theatre, leading to the completion of *Performing Greek
Comedy*.

PERFORMING GREEK COMEDY

ALAN HUGHES
University of Victoria

CAMBRIDGE
UNIVERSITY PRESS

CAMBRIDGE UNIVERSITY PRESS
Cambridge, New York, Melbourne, Madrid, Cape Town,
Singapore, São Paulo, Delhi, Tokyo, Mexico City

Cambridge University Press
The Edinburgh Building, Cambridge CB2 8RU, UK

Published in the United States of America by Cambridge University Press, New York

www.cambridge.org
Information on this title: www.cambridge.org/9781107009301

First published 2012

Printed in the United Kingdom at the University Press, Cambridge

A catalogue record for this publication is available from the British Library

Library of Congress Cataloguing in Publication data
Hughes, Alan, Ph.D.
Performing Greek comedy / Alan Hughes.
p.   cm.
Includes bibliographical references and index.
ISBN 978-1-107-00930-1
1. Theater – Greece – History – To 500.   2. Greek drama (Comedy) – History
and criticism.   I. Title.
PA3201.H84   2011
792.2′30938 – dc23   2011027499

ISBN 978-1-107-00930-1 Hardback

Contents

v

Contents   ix

Illustrations

Preface

The need for a book like this one became apparent shortly after I was appointed as the theatre historian in a university Department of Theatre. Qualified for the job only because I had written a book about the theatre in nineteenth-century London, I was expected to teach the history of theatre from Greeks to Grotowski. This was, and still is, the normal state of affairs wherever there are broad studies of classical or western literature and drama, history of the theatre, ancient or western art. Few instructors in any of these disciplines command the leisure to master the current state of knowledge in a succession of fields of study which are no more than contiguous with their own. Three or four weeks are allocated to the Greeks; then one must get on to the Romans, Middle Ages, Renaissance. Teaching theatre history, my students and I needed a book which would summarize the state of contemporary research on the performance practice of Greek theatre, arranged systematically by topic. Since nothing of the sort was available, I was obliged to turn to the relevant chapters of Bieber's obsolete *History of the Greek and Roman Theatre*, first published in 1939. For many instructors and students, it remains the last resort.

That was why I conceived the notion of writing a book that would supersede Bieber. I am an historian of the theatre, not a classicist. It may be asked, where I found the temerity to write about Greeks. I approach the subject pragmatically, as a working theatre not unlike others. I examine it as a composite art, in which the text is only one component. For costume, masks, music, theatre buildings and equipment, acting style, I turn to the visual sources provided by archaeology. And to interpret what I see, I refer to a lifetime of experience in the living theatre and a working knowledge of how things are done, and made.

Research on eighteenth-century acting showed me that pictures are more reliable evidence than texts. While descriptions of style degenerate into assertions that the acting of the writer's time is 'more natural' than that of the previous generation, painters are fellow-artists, sympathetic and observant. Eighteenth-century artists faithfully document actors, costumes, stage sets, theatres and audiences of their time. When I turned to the Greek theatre, however, there seemed to be little equivalent evidence.

Tragedy dominated the reading list, in which comedy was represented only by *Frogs*, which is about tragedy. In practice, 'Greek theatre' seemed to mean 'Athenian tragedy in the fifth century', for which surviving material evidence is inadequate. There was not one statue of a tragic actor, but some lively terracotta figurines seemed to be comic actors, masked and indecently costumed; and a handful of pots and fragments offered blurred and broken glimpses of comedy.

The breakthrough came in 1986, at my Faculty Club. Since nobody wanted to be seen lunching with the acting Dean, lest they be suspected of currying favour, I was free to look through a new issue of *Phoenix*. Thus I read Eric Csapo's account of a vase in Würzburg, with a detailed picture of a performance of a scene in Aristophanes. Yet the vase had been painted in Italy, in the fourth century. It was 'new' evidence, because its relevance had not hitherto been understood.

Many similar scenes were known, but they had been dismissed because they were thought to show crude Italian farces known as *phlyakes*. Now it seemed likely that many represented fourth-century performances of Athenian comedy, or something similar. And indeed, so it proved. More scenes have come to light, and their relevance to comedy has become widely accepted.

As far as possible, I have examined the primary material evidence, the vases and figurines, rather than photographs. This practice avoids mistakes, when smudged paint is interpreted as horns on a mask, a mysterious pyramid turns out to be cracks in the fabric, or an incised inscription is overlooked. I have never examined a comedy vase without learning something new. For research of this kind, a good deal of travel is required: I have visited 75 museums and private collections, and studied 350 artifacts.

This book deals only with comedy, for which vase painters used a highly realistic technique; tragic subjects were idealized. Most of the vases were painted in the Greek cities of southern Italy and Sicily, in the fourth century BCE. No doubt many of the comedies were written in Athens, but some may have been composed in Syrakousai or Taras, cities with a native dramatic tradition.

The Würzburg scene was painted many years after Aristophanes wrote the comedy it represents, and vases twenty years apart have scenes from the same comedy: evidently these were either local or touring performances of old plays. By the fourth century, Athenian comedy was performed every-where Greek-speakers lived; it had truly become 'Greek theatre'. Encour-aged by the acknowledged relevance of *phlyax* scenes to 'legitimate' comedy, I have taken into account associated pictures from some of the same work-shops, to extend the meaning of 'theatre' beyond the three official genres of the Athenian festivals. These feature performers in dramatic entertain-ments like the 'mime' described by Xenophon. These too may be termed Greek theatre; and its performers extend those boundaries farther still, because many are women.

Colleagues, curators, students and friends have assisted and advised me in the twenty-five years since I began the research leading to this book. I have accumulated a continuing debt to Sarah Stanton of Cambridge University Press, for concealing her consternation when an author she knew as a Shakespearean proposed a book about Greek comedy, and persevering in her faith that I would somehow bring it to a conclusion.

Richard Green, the master of this discipline, has been unfailing with advice and encouragement. I owe an equal debt to Grigoris Sifakis, for his wisdom and guidance as I ventured upon ground sometimes reserved for Classicists, and for helping me to win a T.B.L. Webster Fellowship, for which I am grateful to Michael Edwards and the Institute of Classical Studies. Jeffrey Rusten has been most generous with his assistance, and Eric Csapo encouraged me to press on, and to add New Comedy to my topics.

My research has been supported by the Social Sciences and Humanities Research Council of Canada, ICS and the University of London. The University of Victoria provided preliminary faculty research grants, which brought me the aid of research assistants Ereca Hassell, Sylvia Diaz-Denz and Don DeMille.

This work has benefited from the generosity of private collectors Guido and Giovanna Malaguzzi Valeri, William Knight Zewadski, Alessandro Ragusa, Leonardo and Paula Mustilli, and George Ortiz, all of whom have graciously permitted me to examine and publish their treasures; and of James Ede, who provided me with two antiquities which illustrate this book.

Curators and superintendents of public collections have admitted me to the close examination of the unique artifacts which are the founda-tion of this book, and granted permission to publish them. Amongst the most helpful have been Giuseppi Andreassi and Teresa Cinquantoquattro, Puglia; Elena Lattanzi, Calabria; Amalia Curcio, Siracusa; Elio Galasso,

Benevento; Antonio De Siena, Metaponto; Maurizio Sannibale, Vaticano; and Francesco Valenti, Lentini. In Athens, Nikolaos Kaltsas and Irini Papageorgiou; Mary Louise Hart in Malibu, Elena Ananich in St Petersburg and Ursula Kästner in Berlin. In the midst of a devastating earthquake, Penelope Minchin-Garvin in Christchurch far exceeded the call of duty.

I owe two of the illustrations to the talents of my daughter Katie. And the debt I owe to my wife Mary cannot be adequately acknowledged here. She has lived with Greek pots as long as she has lived with me. She accompanied every research trip, to Caltanissetta where the lights went out, and into the roof at Naples where she discovered a picture of one of the women whose acrobatic feats are exceeded only by Mary's feats of patience.

Finally, please note that dates are BCE, and approximate, unless otherwise indicated.

CHAPTER I

Comedy in art, Athens and abroad

Theatre is a mimetic art, composite and ephemeral. Directed by an underlying aesthetic, conscious or intuitive, theatrical imitation may be culturally determined or intellectually constructed. Performers deliberately imitate the 'other', whether human or animal, divine or spirit, allegory or force of nature. This *mimesis* is a compound, a variable array of associated arts, which may include music, dance, song and speech, supported by oral or literary composition. And every performance occurs in a unique, irrecoverable moment of time. Greek theatre is no exception. Ancient performances cannot be revived, but we have learned a good deal about their form and circumstances.

This is a book about performance practice, the art of comic theatre in classical Greece. Historically, comedy has been examined less thoroughly than tragedy, in part perhaps because the extant texts are fewer and less representative, and documentary evidence comparatively scarce. While thirty-three extant tragedies are attributed to the three most celebrated poets, we have only eleven comedies by Aristophanes, and one by Menander, with some substantial fragments. The works of their rivals have disappeared. The extant tragedies represent continuous development during the greater part of the fifth century, while the comedies yield little more than snapshots of two widely separated eras.[1]

Archaeology has contributed evidence of comic performance, but much of it refers to performance beyond Attica, principally in the western Greek cities of Sicily and Megale Hellas – southern Italy – during the fourth century. Traditionally, this is neither the place nor the period in which we were most interested, because the great Attic tragedies of the fifth century became established as essential Greek literature, in much the same way as we have adopted Shakespeare's plays as literature. Nevertheless, in the working theatre of their time, Greek play-texts, like Shakespeare's manuscripts, were simply one component in the creative array. They were 'scripts', composed to support theatrical speech and choral song. And if the fourth century has not endured in memory as a Golden Age of tragic liter-ature, it may yet be perceived as the first great age of theatrical art, when an innovative actors' theatre disseminated Athenian culture wherever Greek was spoken. The surviving texts and fragments of comedy and commentary are essential primary resources for the study of Greek theatre. With their testimony, this book will consider extensive archaeological evidence, much of it recently discovered, or newly interpreted. While fragments of Menan-der still come to light in Egypt, the sands have yielded neither Eratos-thenes' lost treatise on Old Comedy nor the seventeen-volume *History of the Theatre* by King Juba II of Mauretania. Until that happens, our best evidence for comedy performance is found in vase painting and terracotta figurines.

The significance of these materials has been underappreciated. Black-figured vase scenes showing men costumed as birds and knights seemed to foreshadow Aristophanes' choric titles, but they were painted much too early.[2] A few pictures, including another bird-chorus, can be dated closer to the lifetime of Aristophanes, but most are damaged, controver-sial, or show children dressed up as actors. The only scene that included a stage was not available for study between 1935 and 2005.[3] Vases painted in Greek cities of Sicily and Megale Hellas in the fourth century were usually acknowledged to be both Greek and theatrical, but most scholars denied any relevance to Athenian comedy. They were believed to repre-sent *phlyakes*, a type of 'low-class Italian farce'. When terracotta figurines of comic actors were excavated in the Greek west, they too were dis-missed as *phlyakes*. Those with an undeniably Athenian provenance were a conundrum which only Webster dared to address. If the style and type of mask, the padded costume and outrageous artificial *phallos* were demon-strably identical with those worn by the *phlyakes*, he asked whether the latter might represent Attic comedy instead. The reaction was swift, and negative.[4]

Almost forty years later, Csapo and Taplin positively identified the pic-ture on a newly published Apulian *phlyax* vase by the Schiller Painter as the scene in Aristophanes' *Thesmophoriazousai* in which Euripides' Kinsman threatens to stab the wineskin-baby, which is represented complete with the 'booties' to which the text refers. Taplin proposed more identifications of vase scenes with Attic comedies, and most scholars have subsequently come round to the view that both *phlyax* vases and terracottas represent Athenian comedy, west Greek performances in the Athenian manner, or blended variations of both.[5]

THE EVIDENCE

Vases

The earliest fabrics of red-figured pottery in the west were probably established by immigrants from Athens. The first was a workshop in Metapontion (Metaponto), where production began before the end of the fifth century; a shop in nearby Taras (Taranto) opened a decade later. Most vase scenes are either Dionysian, with the god accompanied by maenads and satyrs, or mythological narratives, sometimes apparently connected to tragedy. Following Athenian practice, the painters avoid representing tragic scenes literally, as they would have appeared in the theatre. Instead, they show a 'further reality' of the myth, where some artists may have been influenced by direct experience of the theatre. Comedy called for a different convention, because neither the characters nor their story had any previous, independent existence. They were entirely invented by the author, and therefore neither comic characters themselves nor the actors who presented them consistently pretended that they were real. Old Comedy was 'metatheatre', in which all were 'aware of their own theatricality', and shared that consciousness with the audience. While Athenian artists could not agree how to represent a comic scene, their western colleagues understood comedy's self-referentiality, and adopted conventions which were the diametric opposite of those used for tragic-mythical scenes. 'It is not quite true that there is a total lack of dramatic illusion', says Green, 'but depictions of comedy are of men dressed up being funny'.[6] The actor is shown literally, the details of his mask, costume and gestures as accurate as the painter can make them.

The earliest scenes from Metapontion show actors 'stage-naked', no doubt to exploit the novelty of their wrinkled and padded tights, the grotesque, sometimes identical masks, and their attitudes of laughably exaggerated dignity (Figure 1).[7] The first pictures of complete comic scenes on a stage were painted in Taras, by the artists we know as the Tarporley and Choregos Painters.[8] From the first half of the fourth century, Tarentine workshops have left us more than seventy complete scenes with two or more actors, including *Thesmophoriazousai* and three different moments in an unknown comedy, each by a different artist. About thirty more are portraits of actors in character.[9] The earliest red-figured fabric in Sicily seems to have commenced operations in Syrakousai (modern Siracusa) shortly after the defeat of the Athenian expedition in 413, but theatrical subjects do not appear until *c.*380, when several mythological scenes, which may be 'informed' by tragedy, are attributed to the Dirce Painter.[10] The same artist furnished one known comic scene, the earliest Sicilian example, but in view of Sicily's theatrical sophistication, it is remarkable that few similar pictures have come to light until forty years later, when the Lentini-Manfria Group began illustrating novel stage conventions.

Towards the middle of the fourth century, a generation of artists emigrated from Sicily, perhaps to escape political turmoil and civil war. Some set up shop in distant Campania, and one seems to have fetched up in Albania. Asteas had been an established painter somewhere in Sicily when he moved to Poseidonia (Paestum), where comedy was rarely if ever seen. Establishing a workshop, he found a ready market for Dionysian scenes, often autographed by the painter. These show the god as a *komast*, frequently attended by comic actors wearing distinctive costumes which Asteas may have seen in Sicily before he emigrated. After Timoleon imposed a comparative peace in 338, Sicily experienced a revival of comedy and painting. Vigorous scenes began to appear, with up to four actors performing on a new type of stage. In some instances, the conventions of New Comedy masks and costumes seem to have been emerging, but before the transition was complete, artists turned from red-figure to new styles.[11]

Figurines

Terracotta figurines of actors are another valuable resource, particularly for the costumes worn in comedy. A few have long been recognized as Athenian, but scholars who denied that Aristophanes tolerated the artificial *phallos* preferred to relegate the earliest figures to a date after his death, which safely quarantined them in the Middle Comedy period. Today, the 'New York Group' is believed to date from the end of the fifth century. These skilful figurines, said to have been found in a single grave in Athens, represent the essential character types of comedy: old men, slaves, young women of ambiguous virtue, Herakles, a foolish youth, the nurse and crone. Cast in moulds, they were mass-produced for domestic and export markets, perhaps as souvenirs. They were copied and adapted by local coroplasts in many Greek towns, notably on Lipari, an island near the north-eastern coast of Sicily. Local types were also made in widespread workshops, no doubt reflecting regional styles of comedy. Production in Athens continued to develop through the New Comedy period, with lively new figures still appearing in the first century BCE.[12]

Much of this book is based upon the evidence of more than 200 comic vases, and many other scenes of tragedy, *symposion* entertainers and related subjects. Almost 400 terracotta figurines have been consulted, in 250 different character types and poses.[13] Like the vases, many were made in western Greek workshops during the fourth century. Together, these two types of visual evidence are the foundation of chapters which analyse acting and acting style, costumes and masks, theatre structures and performances involving women. While formal comedy is central, 'classical Greek theatre' is taken to refer to a variety of performances, wherever Greeks lived, during the fifth and fourth centuries. The author does not pretend to offer significant new perspectives on dramatic literature. An account of the poets and their plays is provided, with suggestions of scenes and figures which might illustrate performance of different types of comedy, and sometimes, specific plays. In the same spirit, chapters on the chorus, music and New Comedy outline contemporary thinking on these topics, from a viewpoint informed, and illustrated, by the visual evidence.

Is this evidence reliable?

The material evidence of vase scenes must be used with discretion, compounded of basic understanding of the material, and common sense. We should recognize that each artist's accuracy depended upon the individual skills which he brought to his craft, his opportunities to observe his subjects, and his objectives. Neither vase scenes nor figurines are photographs, and while most painters aspired to a measure of naturalism for human figures, few recorded contexts or peripheral details with photographic fidelity. It is unlikely that they sat in the theatre with a sketch-pad; painters and the coroplasts who made actor-figurines probably copied from memory, rather than from life.

Scenes of tragedy were presented as myth by Athenian painters; as Csapo points out, 'no matter how directly inspired by the theatre, [they] drew not masks, but faces, not stages, but palaces or temples, not messengers narrating, but the concrete actions reported by their narratives'. Apulian artists sometimes modified this convention by alluding to stage costume and properties; for example, a humble messenger could be shown wearing elaborate tragic costume and boots (*kothornoi*). Nevertheless, it is frequently difficult to distinguish scenes related to tragedy from those representing pure myth.[14]

The painters' treatment of comedy could be inferred by comparing the shapes of pots. While most mythic-tragic scenes are found on large, prestigious vessels such as volute *krater*s, a comic scene typically decorates a modest bell *krater* or small jug (*oinochoe*), used to serve wine at a drinking party (*symposion*): the former is heroic, the latter, Dionysian. As in tragedy, the circumstances, objectives and skills of artists working in different fabrics determine the value of their testimony. Classical Athenian sculpture strove for naturalism, tempered by an ideal of beauty. Seeking a convention for the display of a relative novelty such as comic actors, a few Athenian artists experimented with naturalistic detail. For example, the Nikias Painter plainly shows that an actor as a slave wears an oversized *phallos* and wrinkled, droopy tights; but in the same scene, the artist withholds from Herakles and Nike any comparable sign of theatrical contrivance (Figure 18).[15] The Athenian painter of the Perseus Dance scene was adept at depicting human bodies and their drapery, but he had no established convention to follow when he composed the earliest surviving picture of a stage, muddling perspective and the compression needed to depict such a large object on a small pot. Indeed, the techniques needed to produce a creditable picture of a building seem to have baffled many vase painters. Long after artists in the west had adopted a consistently realistic convention for an actor's costume, mask and gestures, the majority continued to approach structures with crude draughtsmanship and extreme dimensional compression.[16] When exceptional artists took the trouble to learn how to represent the way in which a structure was actually built – a stage or the stairs linking it to ground, *skene* doors or the porch that sheltered them – the structural details make sense to a modern carpenter, and suggest how the pictures of the less accomplished vase painters should be interpreted. The most sceptical critics acknowledge that artists mutually confirm the details of stage structures, costumes and masks, while denying their utility in attempts to reconstruct lost plays.[17]

Athenian comic scenes of this period are as uneven in quality as they are rare, but the coroplasts who moulded the original statuettes of the New York group show an attention to detail which must have been carefully observed from comic theatre practice. For several decades, painters in Metapontion and Taras confirm the authenticity of these images, notably in the exact correspondence between no fewer than nine details in the dialogue of *Thesmophoriazousai* and the Schiller Painter's picture. The most determined of sceptics admits that the scene must be connected with the comedy, while our leading authority on the vases affirms, 'There can be nowadays no doubt that most of them show Athenian comedy.'[18] The accuracy of their testimony is verified by agreement between independent artists. Actors with the same distinctive mask and walking-stick show up in scenes by three different artists, two of which involve geese.[19] Numerous painters in several different cities arrived at the same fundamental convention, which amounted almost to inversion of the way heroic scenes of myth and tragedy were represented. For scenes of comedy, artists took pains to avoid idealization and illusion. Tragedy refashions the characters and narratives of myth, but comic stories and their characters have no separate existence. Artists had no reason to depict them as other than they really were, actors in costume, performing on a platform. Indeed, had comedy tacitly invited the audience to suspend disbelief, pretending that masks were real faces, tights were bare skin, padded bodies and a grotesque *phallos* were real, artists invariably showed, in detail, the utter failure of that illusion. Of course, there was no such attempt; the clumsy artifice was self-referential, an essential part of the humour. Tights were noticeably wrinkled, and sagged over the actor's feet; there were visible seams at the cuffs, and sometimes down the legs. Artists delighted in displaying actors as 'stage-naked', permitting the viewer to see how the arms and legs of tights (fleshings) were fastened to the torso, and how the latter was lumpily padded.[20] The *phallos* was manifestly unreal, and the mask was clearly shown as a false face, sometimes inhumanly grotesque.

After Asteas reached Paestum about mid-century, new circumstances altered his objectives. Now his actors appeared exclusively in male parts, and rarely in dramatic scenes, but they continued to wear metatheatrical tights in which a dark torso contrasted with skin-coloured fleshings and breasts.[21] Since several other painters show similar costumes, we may suppose that Asteas began to illustrate a new trend in tights shortly before he emigrated, and in isolated Paestum he continued to paint from memory what he had seen in Sicily. His costumes, therefore, and perhaps the masks and gestures, are useful for comedy in Sicily *c.*350, but we cannot rely upon him for evidence of comic practice at a later date or another location. This is partially confirmed by the 'Manfria Group' of painters who emerged in Sicily a decade after his departure. Their scenes show a new configuration of stage and *skene*, naturalistic masks for actors playing young characters, and costumes that decently hide the *phallos*. Evidently, production methods continued to evolve.

FESTIVAL AND COMPETITION

Growing awareness of archaeological evidence has renewed interest in early vase scenes, which may help to unravel an obstinate problem. The origins of comedy are even older and more elusive than those of tragedy. Tradition attributed the 'invention' of comedy to a certain Sousarion, who was said to have competed for a prize of figs in Ikarion, coincidentally the same

Attic deme in which Thespis, the similarly legendary inventor of tragedy, was said to have competed for a goat. Remarkably close to Sousarion's traditional dates, black-figured vases show men wearing fanciful costumes, who dance to a piper's music. From these it is inferred that a prototype comedy-chorus may have existed in Attica by *c.*560.[22]

Seven hundred kilometres to the west, a parallel development was occurring independently. We know nothing of the origin of Sicilian comedy, or whether Epicharmos, its earliest named poet, called his plays 'comedies'. Fragments do not tell us whether he used a chorus, but his mythological plots may have been related to some of the earliest Athenian comedies. Epicharmos' career probably began before the end of the sixth century, in Megara Hyblaia; perhaps when that city was destroyed in 483, he moved to nearby Syrakousai. The extent of early intersection between Sicilian and Attic comic traditions is unknown, but fragments by later poets show that distinctive Sicilian comedy was still being composed after 450.[23] No doubt the relationship between the traditions was more intricate than we can discern, or hope to disentangle. While some circumstances of performance in Attica are well documented, we are remarkably ignorant of practices in Sicily and the Italian peninsula, particularly in the fifth century. Vases and figurines show that by the fourth century, comic costumes, masks and stages were much the same everywhere, but western Greeks do not seem to have shared the Athenian impulse to commemorate public events and responsible personalities with stone inscriptions.

From the earliest times, Athenians celebrated their festivals with competitions, in athletics, music, poetry – and drama. Greeks revelled in *agon*, the relentless competition from which we derive 'agony': these people devised the Olympic Games. As Revermann observes, 'the agonal spirit pervades Greek social practices: if there is no competition, Greeks are sure to create one'. Competition took place in the presence of an audience, which gathered in a *theatron* or 'watching place' to take part in the *agon*. The nature of audience participation has been explored as ritual, as an expression of the Athenian *polis*, or as critical and judgemental. Its fundamental character was probably far from passive: theatre can only occur when performers and audience interact. Poets and performers continually courted spectator approval, as they do today, and because Old Comedy was metatheatrical, this manipulation could be either direct or subtle.[24] Moreover, competition made consequences more tangible and immediate: the judges sat in broad daylight, where actors could see how they were taking it.

Greeks had neither the Judaeo-Christian Sabbath nor the 'weekend' that grew out of it in the nineteenth century. Work carried on every day, except when a festival enabled whole communities to make holiday together. The most important Athenian festival was the mid-summer Panathenaia, which honoured the city's tutelary goddess with a procession, followed by musical and athletic competitions. Late in the sixth century, a minor festival was transformed into a showcase for the *polis*. The City or Great Dionysia was celebrated in the month of Elaphebolion (March/April), when winter gales had subsided, permitting visitors from overseas to attend. Proceedings began with demonstrations of Athenian wealth and power, and the image of Dionysos was carried into the theatre, where it stood in the front row near his chief priest.[25]

Competition for tragedy was introduced about 528, in the time of the tyrant Peisistratos; twenty years later, an *agon* was added for dithyrambic choruses representing the ten new 'tribes' organized by Kleisthenes. Comic choruses participated unofficially on the 'fringe' until 486, when comedy was formally admitted to the festival programme. The first victor may have been Chionides, with a chorus costumed as dolphin-riders.[26]

Every Dionysia in the fifth century was a festival of new plays. The responsible *archon* determined who would be 'granted a chorus', assigning a wealthy citizen to serve as *choregos*, who financed and organized a comedy as a 'liturgy', a combination of tax and public service. Five comedies were performed, either all on one day or on each of five days otherwise devoted to dithyrambs and tetralogies, which comprised three tragedies and a satyr play.[27] Competition was keen, and audiences expressed their opinions energetically; care was taken to ensure that the five judges were selected impartially. First, second and third prizes were awarded to the victorious *choregos* and poet, who competed as director of the chorus (*didaskalos*). Compared to dithyramb, a comic or tragic liturgy was modest, and prizes were more symbolic than substantial.[28]

A second Dionysian festival was transferred to the Theatre of Dionysos *c*.444–441. Celebrated in the month of Gamelion (January/February), when hazardous weather discouraged travel by sea, the Lenaia was well suited to satirical comedy because a poet could not be accused of 'defaming the city in the presence of foreigners'. Comic poets entered one play, while tragedians entered two rather than a trilogy, as they did at the Great Dionysia. Because it is uncertain whether Sophokles or Euripides ever competed, it has been suggested that the Lenaia was 'less highly regarded' than the Great Dionysia, or that the poets were 'on a lower level'.[29] In fact, the best comic poets took part: Aristophanes, Kratinos and Eupolis all competed in 425, and it was at the Lenaia that Aristophanes enjoyed the unique honour of a second performance of *Frogs* following his victory in 405.

A prize for a tragic *protagonist* was offered for the first time about 449, at the Great Dionysia, and by 432 an actor's *agon* in each genre had been established at the Lenaia. This acknowledged a significant change in emphasis. Early poets were members of a literate elite, whose private means allowed them to write, compose, choreograph and even to lead the chorus or act, if they chose. In the best sense of the word, they were amateurs, who sought only the honour symbolized by the victor's wreath. Aischylos and Sophokles withdrew from acting, recruiting their *protagonists* from an emerging class of specialists in the distinctive new craft of actor. With their help, a poet had a better chance of victory. For similar reasons, Aristophanes found an experienced *didaskalos* like Kallistratos to direct his plays; when Platon the poet tried his hand at directing his own comedy, he placed fourth.[30]

THE PROFESSION OF ACTOR

Specialization signified an advance in theatrical quality. Production standards had to improve, because, like the Parthenon, begun in 447, the Great Dionysia became a showcase of Athenian culture, imperial prestige and power. Early comedy had been primarily choric, but two or more actors were essential for a new type of narrative comedy, which had a unified plot. Now *protagonists* competed for a prize of their own, and some began to emerge as professionals. Like the Parthenon's architect, Iktinos, actors learned that they could make a living by practising their art beyond the city, first in the Attic demes, and subsequently abroad.

At least five of Attica's 139 demes had theatres by the end of the fifth century, and there is evidence of theatrical activity in many more. It has been assumed that dramatic performances at their 'rural' Dionysia were 'shoddy, derivative, late, lumpish and short'; but if that was the case, it is strange that Plato should refer to enthusiasts who 'run about to all the Dionysia, never missing one'. Moreover, inscriptions name Aristophanes, Kratinos, Sophokles and Euripides as victors at deme festivals. Aelian says Sokrates went to Peiraeus to see performances of Euripides, Parmeno the celebrated comic actor was said to have acted at Kollytos and a fourth-century inscription from Thorikos probably commemorates a victory by Theodoros, the great *protagonist* of women's roles, who is praised by Aristotle.[31]

The Athenian festivals offered no more than two opportunities each year for theatre artists to compose, act, direct or dress a new play. Restrictions or custom may have deterred poets from presenting more than one comedy a year, at least in their own names, and plays were performed only once: the revival of *Frogs* in 404 was unique.[32] Deme festivals provided fresh opportunities of celebrity for poets, but for actors, *didaskaloi* and the musicians who accompanied a chorus, they could offer more: independence and a living wage. Late in the fifth century, theatre was becoming a profession, open not only to the elite, but to any free man with ability. Plato's theatre fans pursued their enthusiasm in 'country-villages', but also in *poleis*, which should refer to cities other than Athens.[33] For professionals, performance abroad reached a wider audience and extended the rehearsing and acting season, which in Attica was confined to four consecutive months. By some miracle of co-operation, the demes apparently scheduled their local Dionysia during the month of Poseideon (December/January), and the season ended with the City Dionysia, in early April.[34] After that, troupes were free to travel, but where could they go?

The ancient theatre seen by visitors to Syrakousai took its present, impressive form in the third century, under Hieron II, but construction on the site in the 'New City' (Neapolis) probably began no earlier than the middle of the fourth century. Nevertheless, fifth-century Syrakousai must have had appropriate facilities for the performance of the indigenous comedies of Epicharmos, probably in the 'Old City' on the island of Ortygia. This theatre was probably compatible with Athenian production methods, because it was able to accommodate performances of Aischylos' *Women of Aitna*, written to commemorate the 'foundation' of Katana (modern Catania) in 475, and of his *Persians*, our earliest extant tragedy. No doubt Syrakousai subsequently became a significant destination for touring companies from Athens and elsewhere. The poet Phrynichos was disgruntled when his comedy, *Muses*, was defeated by *Frogs* at the Lenaia in 405; he died in Sicily, seeking a more receptive audience amongst the western Greeks.[35] We do not know whether other Greek cities built similar theatres, but by the early fourth century travelling actors would find permanent theatres in Argos, Corinth and neighbouring Isthmia, Chaeroneia in Boiotia, Salamis and Eretria on Euboia, and perhaps Thasos in the northern Aegean.[36] Early theatres have not always left traces, but inscriptions commemorate fourth-century dramatic performances at Delphi, Delos and Cyrene in far-away Libya. Neither Taras nor Lipari has yielded evidence other than their enormous output of comedy vases and figurines, which proves that the citizens of both places enjoyed comedy.

Most evidence of travelling actors links 'stars' who made their reputations in Athens with powerful patrons who invited them to perform abroad, and rewarded them lavishly. Alexander celebrated his victories with festivals of music and drama, performed by the most celebrated artists; on one such occasion, he gave the comedian Lykon 10 talents for making a good joke. Theodoros was able to contribute 70 drachmas to rebuild a temple at Delphi. Such men were frequently in demand as ambassadors between Greek cities, partly because of their eloquence and presence, but also because as servants of Dionysos they enjoyed safe-conduct throughout the Greek lands.[37]

It is doubtful whether the Athenian pattern of *choregia*, *agon* and adjudication was followed in many other cities, but evidence is scanty. While the term '*choragoi*' in a Sicilian document seems to mean 'chorus-leaders', it may nevertheless suggest the use of choregic liturgies there. According to Hezychios, there were five judges of comic choruses, 'not only in Athens but in Sicily', and a fragment of Epicharmos refers to a decision that 'rests on the knees of the five judges', which seems to confirm that adjudication in fifth-century Syrakousai followed the Athenian pattern. A century later, Plato condemns 'the present law in Sicily and Italy' for 'entrusting the decision to the spectators, who award the prize by a show of hands'. Alexander admired Athens, and several of his royal dramatic festivals were organized as competitions adapted from the Athenian model, once with Cypriot kings as *choregoi*. Ironically, the Athenian *choregia* was abolished by a Macedonian-appointed governor shortly after Alexander's death.[38]

TOURING

Athenian practices accidentally shaped acting troupes that were ideal for touring. At the Dionysia, each comedy was allocated a *protagonist*, who was said to 'act the play', and engaged a *deuteragonist* (assistant) and a *tritagonist*, who 'doubled' several small parts. Because Aristophanes sometimes calls for more than three speakers, and some vase scenes show four costumed figures on a stage, it has been argued that festival rules permitted additional actors in comedy.[39] For a tour, it is unlikely that any such rules applied. It was business, and the *protagonist* was boss. He could recruit whomever he chose, but salaries, expenses and profits were affected by the size of the troupe. An ordinary company might comprise three actors, an *aulos*-player and, perhaps, an experienced *chorodidaskalos* who could lead a local chorus, or take small 'fourth actor' parts as required.[40] A Greek company could 'travel light'.

'Light' does not mean 'haphazard'. Travelling troupes are sometimes described as casual strollers, 'rogues and vagabonds' who aimlessly 'wandered around', paradoxically carrying their properties and even a 'temporary stage with backwall' and porch, which they would then 'set up on the market-place' or theatre.[41] This fantasy takes no account of geographical, theatrical or historical reality. The alternating mountains and dry water courses of the Greek mainland, southern Italy and Sicily were unsuitable for travel by heavily laden wayfarers. When Greeks travelled, they went by sea. Actors called at towns that could furnish a theatre with an appropriate *skene* building, equipped with entrance doors opening onto a raised stage. Stages of this type may be seen in many of the vase scenes (Figures 8, 9, 10). Because they were constructed of wood, it has sometimes been thought that they were temporary, improvised and portable. This cannot have been the case: the stages were much too large and heavy to be transported. Elizabethan playhouses had wooden stages, but nobody has supposed that Shakespeare's company annually dismantled the Globe's stage and hauled it around the country with them.[42] A Greek touring company needed to carry little more than their masks, costumes, the walking-sticks used for male characterization and a *skeue ton hypokriton* (property basket); most 'props' shown in vase scenes are domestic articles that would be available anywhere.[43]

Safe passage depended upon careful planning. War was the natural state of a Greek *polis*. A prudent leader would keep abreast of events in the area where he hoped to tour. Akragas in 406/5 would have been an awkward destination, where a company might turn up to find the city under siege by Carthaginians, or be caught in the subsequent sack. A date at Thebes in 382, if carelessly chosen, risked arrival just as the Spartans seized the city. The south coast of Italy became hazardous when the native peoples rose against the Greek colonies in 343. Perhaps the most ambitious tours employed an advance agent, who travelled ahead to make suitable arrangements; or *protagonists* may have maintained contacts in their principal destinations.

Touring actors seldom leave enduring evidence in their track, but there are signs that they diffused Athenian drama and theatrical practices throughout the Greek world, supplanting local styles. The earliest known Sicilian actor-figurine is dated 450–440, when Epicharmos' successor Deinolochos and his rivals were probably still active (Figure 2). Its distinctive mask and rhetorical gesture reflect those of a fifth-century figure from Corinth, the mother city with which Syrakousai retained ties into the fourth century. Corinthian figurines and a scene of comic cooks retain distinctive characteristics as late as 375–350 but even Megara Hyblaia,

Epicharmos' birthplace, yields only copies of Attic types. By mid-century, Athenian style prevailed everywhere, except perhaps in Cyprus, where figurines with marked local characteristics were still being made after 350.[44]

Uniformity of style is no guarantee that actors were Athenian. Vase scenes imply that in the west, Attic plays were sometimes performed long after their Athenian *premières*. The Tarentine *Thesmophoriazousai* scene was painted thirty years after the comedy was staged at the City Dionysia in 411. Perhaps the artist had recently read a script, but it is more likely that a tour or successful local revival of the old comedy had created a market. A recent 'hit' in Athens, perhaps with a comedy about *choregoi*, might encourage a *protagonist* to exploit his success with a tour of the west. And we can do no more than guess how it came to pass that within a period of thirty years three Tarentine painters independently illustrated moments in a comedy we know only as the 'Goose Play'. A stage-naked character with a distinctive, beardless mask appears in all three, and a dead goose in a scene painted about 400 is alive again in another, which was painted thirty years later. The most elaborate scene, now in New York, has dialogue-balloons in Attic dialect, implying that the play was Athenian.[45]

By the end of the fourth century, old theatres were being remodelled, and many new ones constructed. The Theatre of Dionysos in Athens had been rebuilt in stone, its round *orchestra* and high *proskenion* setting the pattern in Greek *poleis* everywhere. Communities defined themselves as Hellenic by their temples of the Olympians, and by their theatres, where comedies in the new style of Menander, Diphilos and Philemon were first performed by touring troupes from Athens and other, emerging theatrical centres. Menander's Greek is less specifically Attic than that of Aristophanes, facilitating export.[46]

We can conjecture touring circuits. Taras was the greatest city of Megale Hellas, with a population estimated at a quarter of a million. Most of the surviving comic vases were painted there, but the earliest come from Metapontion, only 40 kilometres along the coast to the south-west. The first Attic troupes to visit Megale Hellas may have performed in its fifth-century *ekklesiaterion*, and in Taras the actors soon found a notoriously theatre-loving audience. While significant finds near Bari and Ruvo suggest that actors visited the Adriatic coast,[47] overland travel to Taras and the west is hampered by mountains, and the long sea voyage round the 'heel' of Italy risks the hazards of Capo Otranto and Sta Maria di Leuca. Two new southern colonies were more accessible by sea: Herakleia (Policoro) was established from Taras in 433/2, and Thurii was populated largely from Athens in 446/5. Southward lay hazardous Cape Colonna, and a lee shore relieved only by Kroton, once prosperous but largely depopulated after the death of Dionysios I in 367. An audience could be expected in the 'toe' of Italy, at Lokroi, or in Rhegion (Reggio Calabria), until it was destroyed in 385.

It is unlikely that many troupes ventured north, 250 kilometres up the Tyrrhenian coast to Poseidonia and the Greek towns of the Bay of Naples, to Neapolis (Napoli) and Cumae, or inland to Capua, which were controlled by native Lucanians for most of the fourth century. Instead, they would cross the turbulent currents of the strait to Messana (Messina), the starting-point of a Sicilian tour, beginning with Meligunis, the theatre-loving town on the island of Lipari, an easy 60 kilometres west of Cape Pelorus, and the great city of Syrakousai to the south, with stops at (Giardini) Naxos, Katane (Catania) and Leontinoi (Lentini). West of Syrakousai to Kamarina, Gela, Manfria, Akragas (Agrigento), Herakleia Minoa and Selinunte, the south coast became increasingly unstable as one travelled.

Voyaging east from the Greek mainland, it is unclear what routes would have been followed. Many *poleis* on the Aegean islands and the coast of Asia Minor built permanent theatres only in the third century or later. We know of no tradition of theatrical vase painting like that of Apulia, and while theatrical artifacts in several forms have been found throughout the region, most are Hellenistic in date, like the theatre buildings in the area. The Aiolian town of Myrina is a rich source of New Comedy figurines, perhaps manufactured in Pergamon.[48] The cities of the Aiolian and Ionian coasts, together with the chief towns on Samos, Chios and Lesbos, would comprise a coherent circuit; the Kyklades another; and Olynthos in Chalkidike could be combined with the northern Aegean islands, Lemnos, Samothrace and Thasos.[49]

Instability following Alexander's death threatened this intense touring activity, prompting itinerant performers and associated craftsmen to form guilds, the *technitai* (artists) of Dionysos. Membership included actors, musicians and *choreutai*, scenic artists, mask-makers and costumers; mimes and pantomime dancers were not admitted until the second century. Like modern trade unions, the guilds sought to ensure their rewards by collective bargaining, and their safety by solidarity and their religious status; they wore the insignia of Dionysos as Elizabethan players wore the livery of a powerful lord. Their solidarity enabled them to withhold labour from any *polis*, Macedonian kinglet or miscellaneous warlord too parsimonious to pay their price. They demanded guaranteed freedom to travel, and exemption from taxation or prosecution for debt in the places they passed through. The *technitai* were truly pan-Hellenic and supra-national, behaving in some respects like a state with a government and ambassadors. Professionalism could hardly become more complete.

Alexandria supplanted Athens as the dramatic metropolis in the reign of Ptolemy II (309–246). The *didaskaliai* and victor lists commemorating the Athenian Dionysia come to an end in the mid-second century BCE, but the *technitai* persisted, retaining their Greek character in spite of Roman domination. They had a long run. A reference by Aristotle *c.*330 to 'self-styled' *technitai* of Dionysos may be the earliest, and we last hear of them in the third century CE.[50]

CHAPTER 2

Poets of Old and Middle Comedy

The names of more than fifty Old Comedy 'poets', as dramatists were called, are known to us, but their plays are lost. Of Aristagoras, Aristomenes and Aristonymos, Menekrates, Metagenes and Myrtilos, Theopompos, Xenophilos and Xenophon, we have no more than titles, and random fragments. Since every comedy entered for competition at the annual Great Dionysia and Lenaia was a new play, we can calculate that in the fifth century alone, five or six hundred comedies must have been performed, but only nine survive, all by Aristophanes. From the entire fourth century we have three, with substantial fragments of four more.[1] Aristotle knew little about early comedy 'because no serious interest was taken in it', an attitude he transmitted to the Renaissance. Consequently, we have no authoritative ancient account of the history of comedy, and surviving works that touch upon the subject are either focussed elsewhere or are so late that they must rely upon lost sources whose trustworthiness it is difficult to estimate.[2]

ARCHAIC COMEDY

The earliest period of Attic comedy corresponds chronologically with the style in painted pottery which art historians call 'late Archaic'. Beginning in the second quarter of the sixth century BCE, when Athenian black-figure supplanted Corinthian ware in prestige and for export, this Archaic phase is conventionally understood to end with the Persian invasion in 480. By that time, black-figure had given way to the red-figure style of the classical period. The earliest period of Attic comedy is contemporary with Archaic vase painting, and sometimes provided its artists with subjects. Artists of this period have left us twenty-four lively scenes of comic choruses, all but one painted in black-figure, on *sympsion*-vessels. After *c.*480, artists turned to other subjects; when they returned to comedy fifty years later, the novelty of actors in costume seems to have attracted their attention.[3]

According to a reliable inscription, the first comic chorus was staged by citizens of Ikarion, and 'invented' by Sousarion, between 582 and 560. This approximate date of the earliest comic choruses seems to be confirmed by two black-figured vases with groups of men wearing co-ordinated costumes, but without masks, who dance to a piper's music: both are dated 560–550.[4] Whether Sousarion is historical or mythical, the inscription does not claim that he was the first poet of comedy. In fact, we do not know so much as the name of any Attic comic poet who was active before the fifth century. Consequently, we can only reconstruct Archaic comedy and its development from the vase paintings, and what we know of contemporary conditions in Attica.

Archaic comedy was primarily a choral spectacle, with agricultural roots. Whether it was the invention of a single artist, or evolved from ritual, festive dances or other folk-customs, it must have originated in agrarian villages. The seasons impose their rhythms upon agricultural societies, which mark spring planting and the harvest with celebrations. Groups from neighbouring Attic villages may have gathered in market towns like Ikarion, to dance and sing; and because they were Greeks, these village choruses competed for a prize. When people celebrate, they like to dress up; it is easy to imagine that the best-dressed village chorus tended to win. The earliest vase scenes suggest that *choreutai* began by wearing animal ears; later they turned to dressing as foreigners, walking on stilts and riding simulated exotic animals, ostriches or dolphins. No doubt they sometimes wore masks, which are clearly visible in a scene of dancers as birds.[5]

Aristotle seems to imply that comic choruses were performed at the Great Dionysia as an unauthorized sideshow in the forty years that elapsed between the first competition for tragedies and official recognition of comedy, with its own *agon* and prize.[6] We can only guess how comedies were composed before that date. Individual dancers and singers can improvise, but a chorus requires co-ordination: someone devised their dances and songs, but the only reliable information refers to the end of the period. A biographical note names Chionides as a comic poet, who competed 'eight years before the Persian Wars', which probably means that the first comic *agon* took place in 486. The plural form of his titles, *Heroes*, *Assyrians* or *Persians*, and *Beggars*, suggests the identity of the chorus, including foreigners, as in some early vase paintings. The note also refers to Chionides as *didaskalos* and *protagonist*. As *didaskalos* he would have composed verses and dance figures, teaching them to the chorus, most of whom would have been illiterate.[7] In this early period, however, '*protagonist*' is anachronistic.

Later in the fifth century, this term referred to the actor who led a support-ing cast of two or three; but Chionides may have been the only actor in his comedies, an *hypokrites* (answerer) who could engage in dialogue with the chorus or its leader. Apart from a small figure in one vase scene, this is our only hint that an actor ever took part in Archaic comedy (Figure 24).[8]

OLD COMEDY AND FESTIVAL

With its inclusion in the Great Dionysia, comedy participated directly in the urban life of the *polis*. It was admitted to Athenian history, the victors' names inscribed in the official records we call *Fasti*. The earliest inscriptions show that poets were officially awarded the prize as *didaskalos*, as Chionides and earlier poets must have been. The system of *choregia*, which had been developed for competition in tragedy, was adapted for the financing and adjudication of comic performances. Presiding over each year's festival was an eponymous *archon*, the elected official for whom the year was named in the Attic calendar. We do not know how he selected comedies; five were chosen and granted a chorus, which was financed by a citizen-*choregos*. At a later date, each comedy was assigned a *protagonist* from a 'pool' of qualified actors, but the early poets were gentleman-amateurs, retaining the right to act in their own plays if they wished.

Magnes

It is not certain that Chionides continued to present comedies after 486, but Aristotle links his name with a successful new poet named Magnes, who won eleven times, only one of which can be dated. The title of his victorious comedy in 472 is unknown, but it was probably named for the collective identity of the chorus, like other comedies attributed to him, *Lyre-players*, *Fig-flies*, *Lydians*, *Birds* and *Frogs*. Aristophanes offers a significant clue to the character of Magnes' comedies: 'he ended up getting booed off the stage, veteran that he was, because his powers of mockery had deserted him' (*Knights* 524–5). Aristotle refers to 'iambic poets' who 'write about a particular person'; this metre was used for personal invective, 'when they lampooned one another'. If early choruses with plural identities, such as *Beggars* or *Fig-flies*, attacked or ridiculed individuals, perhaps his audience rejected Magnes' experiments with a new type of comedy. Singular titles, such as *Grass-cutter*, *Dionysos* and *Pykatides*, may refer to dramatic characters in a narrative type of comedy, with actors.[9]

We do not know when his audience drove Magnes from the stage, but when *Knights* was produced at the Lenaia in 424 it seems to have been within living memory, and therefore cannot have occurred much before 455–450, when two new poets began a rivalry in contrasting comic styles. Kratinos, who first competed *c*.453, was the earliest of the triad established by posterity as the Old Comedy equivalent of the tragic Big Three; like the younger Aristophanes and Eupolis, he was probably selected for this distinction because of his rich vein of political and personal invective.

Krates, who turned poet *c*.450 after acting for Kratinos, rejected personal satire: Aristotle says he was 'the first to relinquish the iambic manner (*iambikes ideas*), and to create stories and plots with an overall structure'. Plot is the significant development, an essential component of mature Old Comedy. Aristotle believed that 'the composition of plots originally came from Sicily', by which he seems to attribute it to Epicharmos, whom he calls 'a much earlier figure than Chionides and Magnes'.[10]

THE SICILIAN CONNECTION

Epicharmos

Educated Romans, who learned history from Thucydides and classical Attic from Aristophanes, handed both down to us, with an Athenocentricity that is difficult to shake. We know little about Sicilian comedy, not because it was inconsiderable or provincial, but because Rome preserved the Athenian article instead. Therefore, we do not know enough about Epicharmos to form an accurate assessment of his influence upon Attic comedy. For this purpose, it is of little consequence whether he began writing late in the sixth century. His extant fragments belong to the period when the arts flourished in Syrakousai with the encouragement of Hieron, 478–467/6.

As the tyrant's guest in 471–469, Aischylos must have met Epicharmos, who would ensure that the Athenian celebrity saw or read some of his plays. More than half the attributed titles suggest burlesques of mythological stories about personages like Herakles and Odysseus, who could be depicted respectively as gluttonous, or too clever for their own good: *Herakles' wedding, Odysseus deserter, Herakles' quest for the belt, Kyklops*. The tragedian would understand how these differed from the choral Attic comedies he had seen at the same Dionysia as his own trilogies. The Sicilian plays probably had a narrative form, with plots that were propelled by the interaction between dramatic characters. Perhaps Aischylos returned to Athens bearing examples of Sicilian comedy, and showed them to his comic colleagues. Magnes began constructing plots; and Kratinos took up mythological burlesques, two of which had titles identical with Epicharmos' *Bousiris* and *Dionysoi*; the Kyklops of *Odyssey* IX loomed as large in his *Odysseis* as in Epicharmos' play.[11] Nevertheless, influence in either direction had a great way to travel. Without leaving home, any Athenian comic poet could learn a good deal about plots by watching how his colleagues in tragedy managed three actors. After his victory in 472, Magnes can scarcely have failed to attend the performance of Aischylos' *Persians* at the same festival.

Influences may have been more complex than Aristotle suggests, and no doubt they were reciprocal, like the traffic between Athens and Syrakousai. At an early period, each city evolved a distinctive dramatic form, independent in origin and consequently dissimilar in style and spirit. Epicharmos would not have referred to his plays as 'comedies', and whereas Athenian comedy was primarily choric, it is unlikely that Syrakousan plays employed a chorus at all, as long as they continued as a distinctive type. But how long was that? Phormis was probably a younger rival of Epicharmos, and Deinolochos a successor. Prose 'mimes' attributed to Sophron, and the younger Xenarchos, are bawdy scenes of everyday life which take place indoors, suggesting private performance, like Xenophon's fictional *symposion* mime; presented by a man from Syrakousai, it is set in 421.[12]

MATURE OLD COMEDY

While influences are difficult to measure, it is evident that Attic comedy at mid-century resembled the Syrakousan type more closely than hitherto. When Kratinos and Krates first competed in Athens, Magnes had experimented with a narrative form, employing a plot and several actors. It is significant that Krates had been an actor before he turned poet; the functions were separating, and emphasis was shifting from choruses to actors. This was acknowledged when prizes were awarded to tragic actors at the Great Dionysia (*c*.449) and comic actors at the Lenaia (*c*.432). Artists began to make pictures of comic actors, evolving a realistic convention to represent the peculiarities of their new costumes. Innovative poets at mid-century each developed distinctive objectives and plots. Kratinos' thinly veiled attacks on public figures suited an era dominated by Perikles; Aristophanes and Eupolis directed their attacks at demagogues during the wartime years. After the war was lost, political satire fell out of favour, to be replaced by new types which were subsequently called, for want of a better term, Middle Comedy.

Kratinos

We do not know whether Kratinos' language was compared with that of Aischylos because it was rich and inventive, or simply because he was the senior canonical poet of Old Comedy, as Aischylos was of tragedy. Many of his titles are mythological, but accounts of their incidents show that some were caustic allegories directed at Perikles, whom the poet identified with Zeus because of his personal power, ridiculing the statesman's large head as a symbol of his pride. *Ploutoi* celebrated Perikles' temporary suspension from power in 430, or perhaps his death. Rejoicing in the fall of tyrant Zeus, the chorus of Titans revived Ploutos in order to restore the Golden Age of Kronos (Kimon, Perikles' predecessor). *Nemesis* parodied a well-known myth, in which Zeus made love to Nemesis in the guise of a great swan. She gave her egg to Leda, who put it in a chest until Helen was hatched from it.[13]

A papyrus plot-summary (*hypothesis*) of *Dionysalexandros* shows how Kratinos used heroic parody to attack Perikles, for beginning the war with Sparta in the first place, and then for cowardly failure to stand up and fight. The anti-hero was Dionysos (Perikles), who impersonated Paris (Alexandros) as judge of the famous divine beauty-contest. He chose Aphrodite, who rewarded him with possession of Helen, whom he carried off to Troy. When the Greeks followed, seeking Alexandros and setting fire to the Troad, Dionysos became frightened and transformed himself into a ram. The satire is indirect, but inescapable. Perikles is accused of bringing war upon his city. The Spartans marched into Attica, destroying farms and burning crops in the hope that the Athenian citizen-soldiers could be provoked into giving battle, only to be destroyed by the terrible Spartan phalanx. Perikles anticipated this traditional tactic. His Long Walls connected Athens to Peiraeus harbour, securing the city's food supply, while he kept his citizen-army safe behind the city walls. Many perceived this prudent strategy as cowardice. The papyrus says Helen was hidden in a basket, but a vase scene in which a small, ithyphallic figure with a ram's head is discovered in a wicker *kiste* shows that it must have been Dionysos/Perikles who hid, behind his basket/walls. This picture, and another of the hatching-scene in *Nemesis*, both painted in Taras (Taranto) between 380 and 360, suggests that Kratinos' mythological burlesque remained popular after time and distance had drawn the teeth of his political satire.[14] This characterization of Dionysos may have introduced a stock character type to comedy; another cowardly Dionysos appears in *Frogs*. Kratinos may have found the greedy, muscle-bound Herakles in Epicharmos, and transmitted the stereotype to grow hungry again in *Birds*, a dozen vase scenes (Figures 18, 34, 45), and as the most popular of all terracotta actor-figurines (Figure 29).

Kratinos won the last of his nine victories in 423, a year after Aristophanes wrote him off as 'an old man doddering about . . . wearing a withered crown and perishing of thirst' (*Knights* 533–5). This thirst refers to the poet's fondness for the bottle, which is the title of his last comedy, *Pytine* (*Flask*). Here the poet is the target of his own satire; his wife, Comedy personified, threatens to divorce him if he does not reform. In a fragment he protests, 'You'll never create anything brilliant by drinking water.'[15] Aristophanes placed third, with *Clouds*.

Krates

Perhaps an innovative comedy with a 'universal' plot gave Krates victory in 450, at a time when Athenians could hope that a Thirty Years' Peace guaranteed them leisure to laugh at the antics of ordinary citizens. However, neither the peace nor the poet's comic style yielded prolonged success: in the next twenty years, he won only twice more. New wars abroad, and Perikles' disputed measures at home, revived an atmosphere that must have been more hospitable to political satire than domestic comedy, if that was really Krates' style. Most of his titles are plural, which is usually thought to refer to the chorus; *Neighbours* and *Games* sound domestic, but titles can be misleading. *Theria* (*Beasts*) leads us to expect an old-fashioned chorus masked as miscellaneous animals, but a long fragment reveals that this comedy was a Utopian fantasy, in which animals refuse to be eaten and no man works, because utensils and tools are automatic: grain-sacks knead dough for bread, and the wine cup washes itself.[16]

There is little evidence that Krates' innovations were successful enough to instigate a distinctive 'Sicilian' type of comedy in Athens, as Sidwell suggests.[17] On the contrary, the young Aristophanes speaks of him with the condescension a rising star can afford to offer a has-been. His 'inspired comic poesy was some hearty fare', which raised a 'chuckle' and 'used to send you home with a low-cost snack, baking up witty ideas from his dainty palate'; but he had to endure 'violent rebuffs'. This may refer to frequent defeat, but one attributed title hints at a different cause. Samos revolted in 440; Perikles led an expedition to retrieve the reluctant ally, and spoke eloquently at the state funeral for the Athenian dead. One title attributed to Krates is *Samioi* (*Men of Samos*). Written before the revolt, it might have made good-natured fun of a chorus of quaint provincials; performed soon afterwards, any ill-timed humour may have given offence. Its date, alas, is unknown.[18]

Pherekrates

Like Krates, Pherekrates began as an actor, winning his first poet's victory in 437. He was 'inventive in stories', some of them fantasies. In *Agrioi* (*Savages*), men abandoned society to seek freedom; Plato deplores its chorus as 'a kind of wild folk', misanthropes reared without society or laws. *Myrmekanthropoi* (*Ant-Men*) were ants transformed into men in order to repopulate the earth after Deukalion's flood. Pherekrates seems to have avoided political satire, but one fragment of dialogue disparages the lyre-players Meles and Chairis, and in a monologue from *Cheiron*, a female personification of music uses sexual conceits to mock practitioners of the New Music.[19] Some of Pherekrates' titles are the names of *hetairai*, *Petale* (*Leaf*), *Thalatta* (*Sea*) and *Korianno* (*Coriander*). While these women must have been the focus of sex-intrigues, it is doubtful that they saw much action as characters. In a fragment of *Korianno* a father and son quarrel over a woman, but she says nothing: as the casting director said to the starlet, 'I'm afraid you have no lines, but *they talk about you a lot*.' These plays had characteristics of the urban comedies of intrigue which became dominant by the middle of the fourth century. Apulian vases may show scenes from late productions of *Cheiron* and *Korianno*.[20]

Eupolis

Despite his enduring fame, we have no intact comedies by Eupolis, who was a near-contemporary of Aristophanes. Only seventeen titles are known, but he won seven victories. He first competed with *Prospaltioi* (*Men of Prospala*) in 429, apparently at the age of 17. Eupolis wrote no parodies, but his necromantic fantasies were famous. In *Taxiarchoi*, General Phormion returns from the dead to train Dionysos as a soldier and rower in a warship. *Demoi* (*Demes*) was amongst the most renowned and frequently quoted of Old Comedies. Disgusted with misgovernment in general and Athens' defeat at Mantinea (418) in particular, the comic hero Pyronides raises four wise men from the Underworld – Aristides, Perikles, Solon, Miltiades – to advise the city.[21] Other comedies satirized prominent citizens or political figures. In *Kolakes* (*Toadies*) Kallias, historically the richest man in Athens, squanders his inheritance on a banquet attended by sycophants (amongst them the sophist Protagoras) who end by looting his house. *Autolykos* (420) may be the first title to name an individual, the *eromenos* of this same Kallias: the comedy's occasion is a victory feast following the youth's Panathenaic victory in the ferocious *pankration*. No doubt Kallias was the poet's real target, but the athlete's mother is also abused in one fragment.[22] *Marikas* (421), on the other hand, attacked the demagogue Hyperbolos thinly disguised as a Persian slave of bad character; Aristophanes accused Eupolis of imitating *Knights* (424), where Kleon received similar treatment. In *Baptai* (*Dippers*) it was Alkibiades' turn. Eupolis' language was called 'abusive and coarse', but also 'imaginative and attractive'.[23]

Eupolis' death at sea, perhaps in a naval engagement in 411, generated the myth that Alkibiades had pitched him overboard on the way to Syrakousai (415).[24] After that, the story went, fear made the comic poets abandon political attacks against prominent individuals. They did no such thing, of course. Political satire continued, criticizing Athenian policy through the personalities of its proponents. Personal attacks became less virulent after the war was lost; but when Platon (active *c.*421–380) turned his attention from demagogues to other subjects, he probably responded to the changes in public taste that ushered in Middle Comedy, rather than to any threat.

Aristophanes

In a long career (427–*c.*386), Aristophanes was not remarkably productive. We have eleven comedies, and the titles of twenty-nine more. Like Kratinos and Eupolis, he produced an average of one play each year, a modest output when compared with the enormous activity of Menander or Alexis in the next century. If Aristophanes performed a liturgy, or served in his city's forces, we have not heard of it, but he is known to have represented his tribe as councillor. No doubt he lacked the means to fit out a warship or chorus, but some scholars believe he was sufficiently prosperous to be socially and sympathetically aligned with the *equites* (knights).[25] A citizen of his class who was either idle or employed in trade was held in contempt by his peers. His natural career was the service and government of the *polis*; and while Aristophanes held public office, and displays an appropriate familiarity with the Assembly and juries, his comedies were his public service. The responsibility of a poet, he reminds his audience, is to advise and instruct the citizens: 'For children the teacher is the one who instructs, but grown-ups have the poet' (*Frogs* 1054–5). This sense of public responsibility may have been common to poets of Old Comedy; Kratinos said, 'let the prize go to him who gives the best advice to this city'.[26]

The comic poet advised through laughter, which went beyond entertainment, but not yet beyond Athens. The teaching implicit in tragedy applied to universal questions, and consequently Athenian tragedies 'travelled well': numerous vases with scenes related to Euripides show that he had readers, and perhaps a theatre audience as well, in the Greek cities of southern Italy and Sicily. In the fourth century, when comic poets began to address domestic questions that applied to every Greek, they became professionals. Aristophanes was a poet for Athens alone. His wartime comedies advise the citizens to save the city by making peace. Like Demosthenes, he might have hammered away at his point in a series of speeches in the Assembly; instead, Aristophanes' weapons were fantasy, and comic attacks upon demagogues or citizens whom he regarded as bad influences.

The most famous example of the latter is *Clouds* (423), which attacks Sokrates – not the philosopher as Plato's dialogues show him, but a composite of the nonsense which conservatives have always pinned on eccentrics. Everyone had it in for sophists, because everyone knew they were hypocrites who subverted the values that made the city great, for personal gain. Kratinos mocked sophists in *Panoptai* (*All-Seers*), Sokrates was part of a sophist chorus in Ameipsias' *Konnos*, which defeated *Clouds*, and Eupolis made Protagoras the chief parasite in *Kolakes* two years later. Aristophanes' most conspicuous target was Kleon, who almost succeeded in persuading the Athenians to massacre the rebellious Mytileneans (427).[27] We do not know how the young poet's lost comedy *Babylonians* (426) stung the demagogue, but because it was performed at the Great Dionysia, Aristophanes was charged with 'slandering the city before foreigners'. *Knights* (424) repaid Kleon in full, transparently presenting him as a Paphlagonian slave, who hoodwinks and robs his master Demos (the people). After Kleon persuaded the Assembly to reject favourable peace terms, the poet turned to shrill abuse in *Wasps* (422), calling his enemy a monster with 'the voice of a death-dealing torrent, the smell of a seal, the monstrous unwashed balls of a Lamia, and the arsehole of a camel' (1030–5). There was no retribution, suggesting either that comic freedom of speech was unlimited or that the citizens did not take Aristophanes seriously.[28]

In any case, had the citizens wished to act upon the poet's advice, Kleon forestalled them by dying in battle that summer, leaving Aristophanes bereft of an habitual target. Perhaps it is not stretching a point to say that he missed the old rascal. Hyperbolos succeeded Kleon as leading demagogue, but Eupolis chastised him so thoroughly in *Marikas* that Aristophanes gave up demagogue-comedy, and turned to Euripides.[29] There was nothing new in tragic burlesque. In *Acharnians*, the poet had primed the audience with a parody of Euripides' old tragedy *Telephos* and brought its author onto the stage as a comic character; but *Thesmophoriazousai* (411) and *Frogs* (405) are all about Euripides. The poet burlesques his own tragedies, and is defeated by Aischylos in an *agon* which demonstrates the faults which Aristophanes condemns. His language is clever and trivial, where it ought to be wise and noble; it promotes idle chatter and sophistry. His beggar-heroes and wicked women are bad examples who encourage degeneracy:

And what evils can't be laid at his door? Didn't he show women procuring, and having babies in temples, and sleeping with their brothers, and claiming that 'life is not life'? As a result, our *polis* is filled with assistant secretaries and clownish monkeys for politicians forever lying to the people, and for lack of physical fitness there's nobody left who can run with a torch (*Frogs* 1078–87).

Contempt for degeneracy underlies much of Aristophanes' satire. Kallias is his synecdoche for idle profligacy. The effeminate Kleisthenes is the butt of fourteen jokes and a special appearance amongst the women at the Thesmophoria; and after a certain Kleonymos threw away his shield in battle, Aristophanes mocked him for cowardice, seventeen times. Any Athenian could attend a comedy and learn too late that he was singled out for ridicule. Let us for a moment put ourselves in the place of Archedemos, attending the Lenaia in 405. Watching *Frogs* and no doubt enjoying the poet's gibes at others, he abruptly heard the entire chorus of twenty-four men sing (416–17):

> So what say we get together
> and ridicule Archedemos.

The song continues, while the victim tries to sink beneath the earth.

Aristophanic comedy

Aristophanes is not all satire. Nine of the extant comedies are fantasies Webster called 'comedy of the dominant idea': all begin with a whimsical supposition. Suppose one Athenian made a separate peace (*Acharnians*)? What if someone were to fly to Olympos on a giant dung-beetle, find Peace and set her free (*Peace*)? What if all Greek women united to proclaim a sex-strike until the men halted the war (*Lysistrata*)? Or took over the Assembly (*Ekklesiazousai*)? Suppose someone organized the birds, to block the gods' sacrifices: what then (*Birds*)? Imagine, what if Wealth dwelt only with those who deserve it, rather than with the wicked (*Wealth*)?

The comedies are short, with slightly more than half as many lines as Shakespeare's average. Much of their structure is shaped by the chorus. Each play opens with a *prologos*, which is a dramatic scene rather than the short address to the audience we sometimes call a 'prologue'. In Aristophanes, the situation is established here: Lysistrata organizes the women, Peisetairos and Euelpides go in search of the land of the birds, Dionysos and his slave Xanthias embark for the Underworld. The *prologos* can comprise almost a quarter of the play.[30]

Next, the chorus enters, singing the *parodos*, the entrance-song named for the broad ramp by which they enter the *orchestra*. As a group with an attitude, the chorus interacts with the characters on stage, sometimes in conflict. The conservative Acharnian farmers long to destroy Dikaiopolis for making his separate peace; the Knights attack Paphlagon/Kleon; the Clouds, however, enter only as Sokrates' new-fangled gods. In *Ekklesia-zousai*, the Athenian women's chorus impersonate men in preparation for their *coup*. There is no immutable pattern, but before the end of the scene, the conflict (*agon*) is somehow resolved. This concludes the play, in New Comedy and the tradition descended from it via Terence, Molière and Sheridan.

Not so in most Aristophanic comedies. The actors leave the stage, but the chorus remains to address the audience in the *parabasis*, the 'stepping-forward'. The *koryphaios* (leader) begins in anapaestic verse, bragging about the poet in the first or third person (*Acharnians*, *Peace*, *Clouds*), or speaking in chorus-character about the superiority of birds or women (*Birds*, *Thesmophoriazousai*). Chorus and leader then sing alternately, usually satirizing a variety of people. A series of humorous 'episodes' follows, punctuated by choral odes: because the plot, as we would understand it, has ended with the *agon*, narrative is scarce. Character types and individuals are ridiculed, punished and dismissed. There are exceptions. *Knights* and *Clouds* retain a greater measure of narrative unity, because the chief villain is not expelled until the end; and in *Thesmophoriazousai*, Euripides' stratagems to liberate his Kinsman comprise a separate *agon*, resolved only at the *exodos*.

The comedy ends in a spirit of affirmation, usually with a wedding or feast to be celebrated offstage. In practical terms, a crowd's *exodos* from a large playing area is not easily managed without becoming anticlimactic. Actors and extras went first, with the chorus bringing up the rear. There was no Victorian-style curtain, or quick blackout. Perhaps some conventional signal showed the audience that it was time to applaud, when the chorus alone remained in the *orchestra*: the prize was theirs, after all. The signal may have been some sort of stage business, often independent of words.

At the end of *Wasps* someone – the *koryphaios*, or Karkinos – declares that, whatever it is, it has never been done before. After that, the *auletes* could lead the chorus down the *parodos*, singing and dancing no doubt, but largely unheeded.

Lost Aristophanes

We know a little about Aristophanes' first comedies, because he tells us himself. A certain Kallistratos served as *didaskalos* for the young poet. *Banqueters* (427) contrasted the educations of two young men, one naughty and one nice; a year later, *Babylonians* attacked Kleon, earning first prize, and the demagogue's reprisal. For the next thirty-five years, we can only guess the subjects of lost comedies from their titles and fragments. *Farmers* and *Anagyros* (an Attic deme) may have invoked the country folk against the war, in the manner of *Acharnians*. *Phoenissai*, *Polyidos* and *Danaids* burlesqued tragedies by Euripides, who may also have felt the bite of satire in *Proagon*, which refers to the opening ceremony of the Dionysia, where it won first prize in 422. Fragments show that *Gerytades* was fantasy, with a descent into the Underworld, as in *Frogs*, this time by three poets, possibly to bring back a personified Poetry.[31] *Women claiming tent-sites*, about women camping out at a festival, and a play we might call *Thesmophoriazousai*, the sequel again exploited what could happen if women took the lead. No doubt the female chorus of *Merchant Ships* (423) was ingeniously contrived to recall the talking triremes of the second *parabasis* in *Knights* the year before. These plays seem to have been not unlike the Aristophanic comedy we know, but others are difficult to assess. Did *Storks* have a spectacular, theriomorphic chorus like *Birds*? That seems unlikely, because it belongs to the post-war period, when spectacle was rare. Perhaps the title is an allegory on the Law of the Storks, whereby children provide for their parents, rather than beating them.[32]

Late in Aristophanes' career, his son Araraos was *didaskalos* for the lost comedies *Kokalos* (387) and *Aiolosikon* (c.386). Aischylos condemns Euripides' *Aiolos* in *Frogs* (1081), and a character of Aristophanes' protests against its shocking theme of incest (*Clouds* 1371–2). It is not easy to imagine how such a subject could have been parodied; perhaps the incestuously married siblings made up semi-choruses. Somehow the character of Aiolos was assumed by Sikon, the slave-cook who later became a stock character, who is depicted and named on a Campanian vase, and appears in Menander's *Dyskolos*. Conflict was inevitable when a gluttonous Herakles arrived. The title of *Kokalos* suggests that the comedy was related to Sophokles' lost

Kamikoi, in which Daidalos hid with King Kokalos until Minos caught
him by using the stratagem of the spiral seashell. If Aristophanes' comedy
was a burlesque of that story, it seems an unlikely place to have introduced
'rape and recognition and all the other things Menander emulated'.[33] Nevertheless, it won first prize at the Great Dionysia.

MIDDLE COMEDY

Middle Comedy is often defined by what it is not, or simply ignored.
Textbooks skip nimbly from Aristophanes to Menander, or dismiss Middle
Comedy as 'feeble' and full of 'false starts'. Sidwell argues that it never
really existed. In Norwood's conceit, 'Between the excitingly varied land-
scape of Old Comedy and the city of Menander stretches a desert: therein
the sedulous topographer may remark one or two respectable eminences,
and perhaps a low ridge . . . but the ever-present foreground of his journey
is sand, tiresome, barren and trickling.' Tragedy of the same period 'survived only in a weak and negligible form'. A generation after the death
of Aischylos, his status was firmly established, and in *Frogs* (405) Sophokles and Euripides – both recently dead – are already canonized alongside
the 'big bombastolocutor'. Regardless of Aristotle's willingness to discuss
the tragedies of Astydamos, Theodektes and Dikaiogenes on equal terms
with the canonical three, posterity dismissed them. Their defeat by Sparta
is supposed to have left Athenians 'fatigued, disheartened, depressed, or
otherwise on the skids'.[34] Therefore, their tragedies no longer grappled
with great ethical issues, and the comic chorus declined. We cannot judge
for ourselves, because only fragments remain; nevertheless, while admitting
that 'no specimens have been preserved', Haigh assures us that 'poets of the
fourth century never rose above mediocrity'.[35]

Professional theatre

Alexandrian scholars studied and preserved Old and New Comedy, but
they allowed Middle Comedy to perish. According to the author of *De
comoedia*, its poets 'did not pretend to poetic style'; scholars understood
plays as literary texts, but these comedies were acting scripts which, in
theatrical parlance, would probably 'read badly, but play well'. From his
literary viewpoint, Aristotle deplored this state of affairs: nowadays, he
grumbled, 'actors have greater influence on the stage than poets'.[36] No
doubt that was true. If Middle Comedy was not great literature, that was
never its purpose. It was the written component of the evolving art of

the theatre, significant primarily for a comic repertoire that propelled the first great actors' theatre in history. Middle Comedy was a pan-Hellenic cultural phenomenon, best defined by its dates, beginning with the defeat of Athens in 404, and ending with the death of Alexander in 323.

Defeated in war, Athens turned to cultural conquest, emerging as the theatrical metropolis of the Hellenic world during the Middle Comedy period. Athens alone provided Old Comedy with its matter and audience, but before Menander's time Attic drama was performed wherever Greek was spoken, opening an extended market to Athenian dramatic products, and drawing many who aspired to become actors and poets to Athens. By exploiting the proliferation of production opportunities far beyond the borders of Attica, poets could become highly professional, and consequently prolific: one ancient source mentions 57 poets and 607 plays, and Athenaios of Naukratis claims to have read 800 Middle Comedies.[37]

Navigating Middle Comedy

Attempts to trace a linear evolution are frustrated by lack of evidence. Within the defining dates, only *Ekklesiazousai* and *Ploutos* (*Wealth*) are extant. Few fragments convey much about the plays they come from. Athenaios is the source of more than half, but his peculiar focus on the pleasures of the table seems to distort and trivialize Middle Comedy.[38] References in later literature can yield glimpses, but we must be wary: surviving commentaries are late, and sometimes questionable, like the anonymous *Life* of Aristophanes, several versions of a *Prolegomena*, *On the distinctions among comedies* attributed to the otherwise unknown Platonios, and assorted scholiasts. These writers may draw upon valuable sources which have been subsequently lost, but they also crib from each other and assert demonstrable nonsense.[39]

Alexandrian scholars developed an evolutionary interpretation of comedy. On the analogy of Aristotle's account of the development of tragedy, comedy attained its natural and best form while Athenian democracy flourished, expressing freedom of speech in political satire. Its most political, satirical and hence democratic poets were Kratinos, Eupolis and Aristophanes; consequently, they were canonized as the best.[40] With the fall of Athenian democracy, comedy declined. The chorus was suppressed because *choregoi* were not democratically elected, or were afraid to come forward. Poets were intimidated by oligarchic decrees against satire, or the alleged murder of Eupolis. Satire became 'enigmatic', hidden beneath the characterization and narrative of mythological burlesques. These gave way in

turn to situation-comedies of everyday life. Stylistically, the poets 'pro-
ceeded through familiar speech, and their virtues are those of prose – there
is in them little work of the poet. They are all careful of their plots.'[41]
This development led at last to New Comedy, which was apolitical – this
time, for fear of the Macedonians – but it had the virtue of elegance.
This approach oversimplified the character of Middle Comedy, much as
excessive emphasis upon democracy, satire and the canonical poets misrep-
resented the Old.

Aristophanes' Middle Comedies

As Magnes had lingered in the early days of Kratinos and Krates, Aristophanes continued to write in the first years of the new era. His *Aiolosikon*
and *Kokalos* were myth-burlesques, but the extant late plays are both 'what-
if' fantasies in his old manner. In *Ploutos* (*Wealth*), the personification of
Wealth comes to live with a poor farmer. *Ekklesiazousai* is a Platonic utopia;
after Praxagora abolishes private property, there will be universal feasting,
free love and no work. The novelty is the relative absence of personal
satire. Towards the end of the war, Platon had taken lampoon to personal
extremes in his demagogue comedies, *Hyperbolos*, *Periandros* and *Kleophon*.
Afterwards, he turned to burlesque in *Laius*, *Phaon* and *Zeus in trouble*.
While comedies like these signalled new directions for their poets, they
were not innovations. Mythological burlesque in Athens was as old as
Kratinos, and it had enjoyed a revival since the Peace of Nikias: nearly half
the titles dated between 420 and 400 imply parodied tragedy or myth,
and almost the same frequency remained until the middle of the fourth
century, after which they decline abruptly. It is more significant that both
poets abandoned satire.[42]

Decline of the chorus?

Traditional accounts emphasize the 'decline' of the chorus in Middle Comedy. Its erosion is said to begin in Aristophanes' last plays, and to conclude
with its detachment from the action in Menander. In the texts as we have
them, neither *Ekklesiazousai* nor *Wealth* has a *parabasis*. After the *prologos* of the former, when the women prepare to pack the Assembly, the
chorus has little to do until the *exodos*. The chorus is present throughout
Wealth, but does even less. Where odes might be expected, '*chorou*' has
been inserted in the manuscripts, as in Menander's texts. However, this may
signify only that our texts have been cut for touring.[43] Choral spectacles

disappeared with the fifth century, and while some plural titles may still refer to the composition of a chorus – *Wreath-sellers* (Euboulos), *Scythians* (Antiphanes), *Dionysiazousai* (*Women at the Dionysia*, Timokles) – others do not. The chorus of Eupolis' *Poleis* consisted of women as allied *cities*, but in a fragment of a Middle Comedy with the same title, the 'cities' were evidently represented by actors as Greek and Egyptian citizens. Few choral fragments are preserved, but in Athens at least choruses continued to be an indispensable part of the Dionysian festivals. Indeed, the odes sung and danced by comic choruses may have been performed so skilfully that only separation prevented the chorus from overwhelming the play.[44]

POETS AND TYPES OF MIDDLE COMEDY

If posterity had seen fit to name three canonical poets of Middle Comedy, the triad might have been composed of Antiphanes, Euboulos and Alexis, with Anaxandrides and Timokles as runners-up. Antiphanes is the earliest; his career began soon after 384, ending in the 330s. Euboulos was the leading poet of mid-century, flourishing from *c.*360 to 340. Alexis began writing about 355, and did not stop until New Comedy was past its prime; he may have retired for a time *c.*300, but returned to the theatre before he died sometime in the 270s, when he was about 100 years old.[45] Anaxandrides, who flourished from 376 to 340, won ten victories – Alexis won no more than four, at the Lenaia; and Timokles was the youngest, competing between the 340s and *c.*317.

Only Euboulos is said to be Athenian, but allegations of foreign origins were no longer used as a slur, as they were against Aristophanes. If Alexis came from Thurioi to make his name in Athens, that attested to the city's splendour. Demand abroad was so great that these poets became full-time professionals, their productivity exaggerated beyond credibility in our sources. Antiphanes was credited with a comedy for every day of the year. Verifiable titles remain impressive in number: 141 by Antiphanes, and 57 attributed to Euboulos.[46]

Myth and tragedy upside-down

A fragment by Alexis suggests how a novel type of myth-burlesque was practised in Middle Comedy. In legend, Herakles was studying music with Linos, when he lost his temper and brained the tutor with his own lyre. Here, 'literary anachronisms' are the instrument of travesty. Linos tells the hero to choose a book from his library; of course Herakles chooses a cookbook, which may soon become a weapon in his hands. Private libraries were a novelty in the fourth century, and Linos' culinary manual was a current fashion. In comedies of this type, gods and heroes were characterized irreverently, as though they were contemporary oafs who were *phaulos* and *geloios* (inferior and laughable).[47] Vase scenes leave the viewer in no doubt about what this meant in the theatre.

Anachronous burlesque was much favoured by Euboulos, half of whose known titles refer to myth. A scene from his *Kerkopes* may be shown on an Apulian vase, where Herakles delivers two cages containing small, ape-like creatures to a king (Eurystheos). Both actors wear grotesque masks, and the customary undercostume with its dangling *phallos*.[48] Some of these titles suggest full-scale tragic parody. Aristophanes ridiculed climactic scenes from *Telephos* and *Andromeda* in *Acharnians* and *Thesmophoriazousai*, but when Euboulos' titles are identical with those of Sophokles (*Nausikaa*) and Euripides (*Auge*, *Medea*), we may guess that each comedy was a sustained parody, which could only succeed if his audience were familiar with the old plays, either in contemporary productions or through reading.

A fragment of Antiphanes that contrasts comic with tragic writing shows that he is thinking about an entirely different type of comedy. Speaking for the poet, an actor says tragedy is easy because audiences already know the plots. One need only say 'Oidipous' or 'Alkmaion' and everyone remembers the whole story. Comic poets 'have to invent everything: new names ... and then what happened previously, the current situation, the conclusion (*katastrophe*), and the introduction (*eisbole*). If some Chremes or Pheidon omits even one of these points, he's hissed off the stage, but they let Peleus or a Teucer get away with it.'[49] Antiphanes exaggerates, of course. The characters of the ever-popular burlesques did not need to be invented: poets borrowed stories from myth and tragedy, and turned them upside-down.

City comedy

Handley points out that 'alongside their development of mythological comedy, the fourth-century dramatists were powerful innovators in the drama of everyday life, in the creation of comic *fiction*'. For this new, realistic comedy, Aristotle says, 'the poets construct the plot on the basis of probability, and only then supply arbitrary names'.[50] Titles often refer to character types like *Ship's Captain*, *Adulterers*, *Boor*. Others, which subsequently reappear in New Comedy, are *Parasite*, *Pimp*, *Soldier*. Comedy observed Athenian custom by refraining from referring to citizen women by their names. Play titles that allude to a woman by her foreign origin, in Ephesos, Ambracia, Lemnos, Boiotia, Corinth, Samos, may conclude by revealing that she is Athenian-born, like the *Andria* of Terence; but as Menander's *Samia* shows, there are no guarantees. Other titles are simply *hetaira*-names, like *Agonis*, *Neottis* (*Chick*), *Kynagis*.[51] What manner of comedy was this?

We have little to guide us, beyond titles and a few of the New Comedies that developed from these earlier 'comedies of everyday life'. Plays with type-characters are often called 'comedies of manners', those with love affairs 'comedies of intrigue' and those with independent young women may be known as 'recognition' comedies, because the woman or her children turn out to be respectably born (free, Athenian). A clever slave may carry out the intrigue, a nurse may save the exposed child: Alexis' *Titthe* (*Nipple* or *Nurse*) is named for this important character. Perhaps all of these related kinds of comedy, with their sex-intrigues and urban settings, are best gathered under the name coined for the similar comedies of Ben Jonson, 'city comedy'.

If 'the first identifiable New Comedy was hatched out of its egg during the period of Middle Comedy', there is reason to believe that the egg was fertilized by Pherekrates. Perhaps the *hetairai* of his titles never spoke, but the sex-intrigues which inevitably swirled around them contained the seeds of city comedy. Aristophanes' *Life* is certainly wrong to claim that *Kokalos* taught Menander all he knew, but if Anaxandrides began writing about 'love-stories and seductions of virgins' near the time of his first victory (*c.*376), themes we associate with New Comedy were explored before Menander was born. Perhaps that is why Anaxandrides' *Treasure* (*Thesauros*) was revived at the Dionysia in 311. Was the 'treasure' a girl?[52]

City comedy largely replaced burlesque before the accepted beginning of New Comedy, but most Middle Comedy poets were at home with both types. Euboulos turned aside from his mythological speciality in *Pamphilos*, where a lover exploited an old nurse's greed for wine in order to seduce her charge, a virgin (*parthenos*) of the citizen class. Athenaios quotes a conventional lover's conceit about Eros in the same poet's *Kampeleion*, and a clever slave's description of a sex-intrigue in Antiphanes' *Hydria*:

The lad of whom I speak saw an *hetaira* who lived in a neighbour's house and fell in love with her; she was of the citizen class, but destitute of guardian and kinsmen; she had a character of golden excellence, a real *hetaira* [companion]. For all the other women of her profession spoil by their manners the name that is really so fair.[53]

Satire

Middle Comedy never completely abandoned satire, but concentrated attacks upon politicians ceased. At first, their favoured targets were sophists and philosophers. Plato is mentioned frequently, and the Pythagoreans of Taras were notorious enough that both the younger Kratinos and Alexis could present comedies entitled *Tarantinoi*. Unlike the savage attacks of Old Comedy, as in *Clouds*, this satire was not unfriendly, but slightly contemptuous of philosophers in general and the Academy in particular. Personal invective recovered its edge only later in the century, when Timokles revived it with something like the vigour of a century before. He attacked demagogues in *Demosatyrs* and pederasts in *Orestautokleides*, a title with a play on one man's name. Many real-life *hetairai* are named in Middle Comedy, but Timokles makes a title of *Neaira*, who was prosecuted by Demosthenes. The orator was also a target, though less frequently than Kallimedon, a politician attacked for his gluttony. In a time when Philip of Macedon's agents combated Demosthenes' warnings against his imperial ambition, it is ironic that Timokles abused the orator for corruption, and as a warmonger, taking advantage of democratic freedom of speech to attack the leading spokesman for Athenian independence. Perhaps the poet was himself corrupted by Philip's agents, but it is more likely that he simply resented Demosthenes' influence. Timokles lost no opportunity to ridicule his eccentric diction.[54]

THE ARCHAEOLOGICAL RECORD

The foregoing analysis of change and development in Middle Comedy is based upon literary records, and extant titles. It seems to offer a coherent roadmap, but is it accurate? Titles have been lost, and many that survive may be misleading. For want of context or narrative, fragments have been selected for their subjects. Everything we know about the comedy of an entire age is founded upon hearsay and scraps from literary middens; inevitably, 'for the lack of continuous Greek texts, we tend to think in terms of survivals from the age of Aristophanes and anticipations of Menander'.[55] More and better evidence is needed; it would be convenient if a papyrus entitled 'Best Middle Comedies' were to turn up in Egypt. Failing such a literary windfall, we can consider archaeological evidence, visual records of Middle Comedy, made by people who saw it for themselves. These may tend either to confirm or contradict impressions deduced from literary sources. The evidence of popular art has limitations peculiar to its media, but it offers new perspectives when it is accurately interpreted.

Archaeology, uses and limitations

In vase scenes, characters' names are sometimes painted beside them; otherwise, attributes can identify mythical figures. Zeus has his eagle sceptre, Herakles his club. Relationships between characters can suggest a mythical narrative, even when it is parodied. Where clues like these are absent, we can usually recognize a scene that represents city comedy: a wife scolds her husband, a slave who carries cakes is waiting upon a dinner-party, or a madam bargains at her door with a client's slave.[56] Nevertheless, identification can be uncertain, and archaeological accident can distort our view of the relative frequency of character types: one pot is found, while another remains underground. Accepting these reservations, what do the scenes suggest about varieties of Middle Comedy, and their development?

Vases, changing comic styles

More than 150 scenes directly representing comedy have been dated between the end of the Peloponnesian War and the death of Alexander.[57] About one-third are portraits of an actor in character, but the rest show a scene in progress. Approximately one-third of those are burlesqued myth or tragedy. For example, a pot-bellied Zeus ineptly manoeuvres a ladder, in order to court Alkmene with the aid of Hermes. Neoptolemos, his long *phallos* dangling, is on the point of killing Priam on an altar where the old king has sought sanctuary. No doubt some absurd accident will save the old fellow at the last moment; after all, this is comedy. Two-thirds are scenes from city comedies of manners and intrigue, like a Sicilian picture of a handsome young couple and a bald and bearded slave dressed in women's clothing who gestures elegant surprise towards a young couple. We are uncertain what is happening, but we recognize the comic style (Figure 39).[58]

Before *c.*360, burlesque accounts for nearly half of the scenes, but by mid-century almost three-quarters are urban comedies. Later in the century, burlesques decline and sex-intrigues become more frequent.[59]

	Mythological burlesque	Tragedy burlesque	City comedy	Sex-intrigue	Total
Total %	42 35.6	(6)	76 64.4	(8)	118
404–360 %	27 43.5	(5)	35 56.5	(2)	62
After 360 %	15 26.8	(1)	41 73.2	(6)	56

Evidence of development in a different direction is found in vases with pictures of a single actor. Most are depicted as characters in action, running away, baking cakes, speaking and gesturing to someone just outside the frame. All play male characters, usually slaves, shown in profile. Around mid-century, artists in Taras introduced a new, colourful style of vase painting, known today as 'Gnathia'. These usually have frontal portraits showcasing an actor in a favourite character, like Victorian tuppence-coloured engravings: 'Mr. T.P. Cooke as Roderick Dhu'. Some project a stage personality possessed of considerable charm, like the toper 'Philopotes' (Figure 3); one is a portrait of Konnakis, perhaps the first woman performer whose name is known to history.[60]

These portraits show that towards the middle of the fourth century, 'stars' were emerging; comic actors were achieving popular recognition. One of them made Philopotes so popular that he turned up in several plays. This goes beyond the emergence of a new character stereotype like Sikon or Herakles, because Philopotes was a vehicle for a popular actor. These Gnathia portraits, like most scenes of single actors in action, evidently refer to city comedy, but a few of the latter have attributes linking them to burlesque. Two show Herakles, and a Hermes seated on an altar is identified by his *kerukeion* (a herald's winged staff wound with serpents) and traveller's hat (*petasos*). A parody-Telephos may refer to Aristophanes' *Acharnians*, and I like to think that a cook at a tripod is Peisetairos grilling renegade birds (1583–5), but most figures are popular character types which might belong to any kind of comedy, the slave and the old man.[61] Three dozen portrait vases, however, cannot tell us much about the relative popularity of characters, or of changes in popular response to Middle Comedy during its eighty-year history. For this, terracottas offer a broader database.

Figurines, stage characters

The first comedy figurines were manufactured in Athens near the end of the fifth century. They were exported and imitated throughout the Greek world for more than two centuries, with new characters and poses frequently reflecting developments in comedy in Athens and abroad. Unlike the actors in a vase scene, most figurines are static, their body-language rarely suggesting engagement in a scene. Sometimes a man carries a burden, or a woman unveils herself seductively, but most merely stand still and express personality or state of mind by physical attitude and self-reflective gesture (Figures 35, 41d).[62] If a vase painter wanted his customers to interpret a comic scene, he knew it was necessary to portray all of the participating characters, the passive virgin along with the funny slave; but terracottas were souvenirs, which people bought because they liked particular characters. Indeed, the figures were so treasured that people took them to their graves, where we have found them. Their frequency and date are useful measures of popularity and its fluctuations.

The analysis by J. R. Green of 700 Middle Comedy figurines shows that slave characters were the most popular (35 per cent), followed by old men (25 per cent). Young men, old women and Herakles, taken together, have a smaller share of popularity than old men, but young women are twice as popular as old ones (16 per cent). Wives were regarded as 'generally boring, if not unpleasant' and are seldom encountered: less than 1 per cent. As a young wife who is also a charismatic leader, Praxagora (*Ekklesiazousai*) is exceptional in Middle Comedy. From the subjects of vase scenes, we can infer that forms of city comedy became dominant after mid-century, and Green's census of figurines confirms this; there are fewer old men, but the cheeky, manipulative slaves who drive the plot are more numerous, as are the young women who represent the love-interest.[63]

Because figurines are not contextual, mythical personalities are sometimes identifiable only by their attributes: Herakles has his lion's skin and club. Six early figurines seem to represent characters in a mythological burlesque, because they were discovered with a Herakles manufactured in the same workshop. Aside from these, no more than twenty figurine types can be recognized as probably mythical. A dejected woman might be Niobe; Kadmos is identified by his blanket roll and jug, and a traveller on an ithyphallic ass is probably Hephaistos. A comic actor as an old man may be linked to burlesque by his gesture, which signifies 'alas' in scenes linked to tragedy (Figure 4). Strangely, the most frequent attribute for men is a baby. Green shows that old women are frequent in the late fourth century because they nurse the foundlings who are central to many intrigue *dénouements*, but only two actually hold a baby, whereas seven different male figures carry an infant. A vase from Capua shows an actor gesturing surprise at a swaddled infant at his feet; like some of the figurines, this parodies a foundling myth like Oidipous and the herdsman, and one scene certainly burlesques a Telephos-tragedy.[64]

BEYOND ATHENS

Epicharmos of Syrakousai influenced Attic comedy; his successor Deinolochos, as well as Sophron, Xenarchos and other writers of prose mime, kept independent Sicilian dramatic forms alive while Old Comedy flourished in Athens. When demand for Attic drama spread abroad, what became of these, and similar comic forms, elsewhere in the Hellenic world?

Artists were drawn to Athens, seeking fame and fortune. Like many illustrious Boiotian musicians in the later fifth century, poets and actors migrated from abroad, in the fourth. The poet Alexis and Aristodemos the tragic actor were said to have come from Thourioi and Metapontion in Megale Hellas, the poets Antiphanes and Anaxandrides from Rhodes or points east, Neoptolemos the tragic *protagonist* from the island of Skyros, and his comic counterpart Satyros from Olynthos.[65] Of the three canonical New Comedy poets, only Menander was a native Athenian; Philemon came from Syrakousai or Soli, and Diphilos from Sinope on the Black Sea. It is unlikely that their success in the theatrical metropolis was achieved without first acquiring experience closer to home. Because most of our sources for this period are Athenian, there is little documentation of theatrical activity on the part of non-Athenians, beyond Attica, but archaeology offers some inferences.

A few cities built theatres, or meeting places that may have doubled as theatres, before troupes from Athens took to the road. After touring became common, however, Greek cities everywhere began building new theatres, or modifying older ones, on the Athenian pattern. No doubt these were used for local festivals and performances, but these theatres cannot tell us whether they retained distinctive conventions, or followed Athenian models.[66] Most fourth-century images of comedy performance, from the Greek west or elsewhere, show Athenian methods of staging, regardless of whether they represent a touring company, or local productions of comedies. Athenian conventions for masks and costumes were adopted throughout the Greek world.

Nevertheless, a few images show something different. In the hands of a skilful artist, some adapt comic techniques to a cartoon, like the 'Rape of Diomedes' by Asteas, or a reader's imaginative realization of a play like *Pytine*. Other scenes are provincial work by painters who may have seen, but misunderstood, pictures of comedy.[67] However, a few small finds hint at performances in other styles. A portrait on a vase from Nola may be an actor in a comic Oscan play; he wears the mask of an old slave, but his costume lacks the artificial *phallos* of Middle Comedy. Two scenes by one of a group of artists whom we know as accurate illustrators of Athenian-style comedy show a drunken Herakles and a man who wears a crown, *kothornoi* and a transparent *chiton*, who dances on a low stage. The masks and costumes are entirely unlike those of Attic comedy.[68]

Some Corinthian figurines use an unique convention, with a simplified rendering of mask and costume (Figure 31). Others from Cyprus have an uncommonly wide-mouthed mask and a bow-legged stance that marks a different acting style, although other details reflect Athenian practice. It is possible that a set of three figurines from Ortygia, the *città vecchia* of Siracusa, are no more than inept imitations, but their grotesque masks, body-attitudes and uniquely formed appendages vary sufficiently from the New Comedy standard of their time that we may find in them a survival from the early comic plays of Epicharmos and his successors. Perhaps they connect that fifth-century tradition with a new, local variant at the end of our period, when we find one more literary reference to a comic poet, Rhinthon of Syrakousai or Taras, who wrote 'tragic *phlyakes*' or 'comedy-tragedy' in Doric dialect.[69]

42

1 Stage-naked actor, in an attitude of mock-dignity. Su concessione del Ministero per i Beni e l'Attività Culturale: Direzione Regionale per i Beni Culturali Paesagisticci della Basilicata, Soprintendenza per i Beni Archeologici della Basilicata.

2 Distinctive early Sicilian actor-figurine. Museo Archeologico Regionale 'Paolo Orsi', Siracusa, su concessione dell'Assessorato per i Beni Culturali e dell'Identità Siciliana della Regione Sicilia.

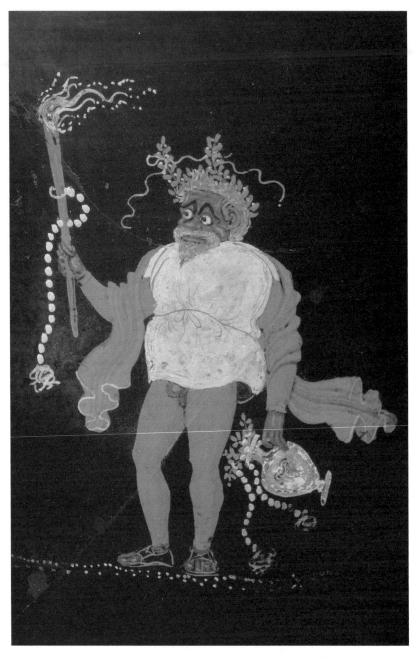

3 Portrait of actor as Philopotes, 'he who loves to drink'. © Musée d'art et d'histoire, Ville de Genève.

4 Comic actor as an old man, gesturing dismay in the tragic manner. Collection Allard
Pierson Museum, Amsterdam.

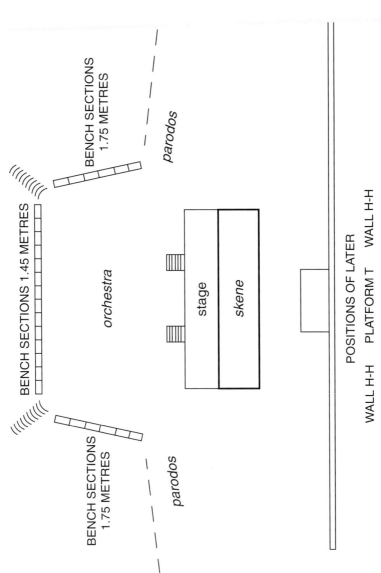

BENCH SECTIONS 1.45 METRES

BENCH SECTIONS 1.75 METRES

BENCH SECTIONS 1.75 METRES

parodos

parodos

orchestra

stage

skene

POSITIONS OF LATER

WALL H-H   PLATFORM T   WALL H-H

5 *Orchestra* and *skene*, Theatre of Dionysos, Athens: conjectural ground-plan of the second stage of the *theatron*, 446–440. Drawing: A. Hughes.

6 Performance of a comedy, probably in Taras *c*.380–370; the stage is drawn in a form of perspective. © The State Hermitage Museum. Photo: Vladimir Terebenin, Leonard Kheifets, Yuri Molodkovets.

7 An early fourth-century stage as represented in scenes painted in Taras, showing conjectural construction. Model: A. Hughes.

8 A comic scene performed on a stage in Taras *c.*350–340, with swan entrance 'porch', perhaps indicating a *paraskenion*. Soprintendenza Speciale per i Beni Archeologici di Napoli e Pompei.

9 A performance of a tragedy in an Apulian theatre with *paraskenia*. Martin von Wagner Museum der Universität Würzburg. Photo: K. Oehrlein.

50

10 Comic scene by Asteas; an old man struggles with thieves. The artist's view compresses the stage. Antikensammlung. Staatliche Museen zu Berlin – Preussischer Kultur. Photo: Jutta Tietz-Glagow.

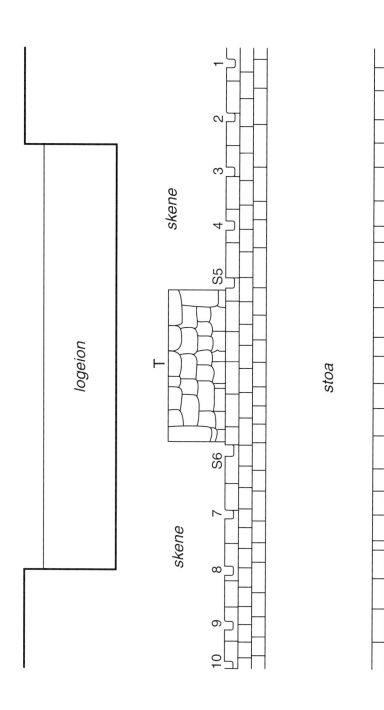

11 *Skene*, Theatre of Dionysos, Athens: ground-plan showing extent of *breccia* used in foundations of the *skene*, *c*.325. Drawing: A. Hughes, after E. Reisch.

12 Theatre of Aphrodisias, with colonnade supporting the Hellenistic *logeion*. Grooves and sockets in the pillars may have supported changeable scenic units. Photo: A. Hughes.

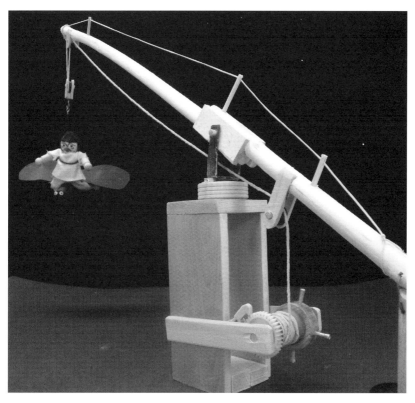

13 The *mechane*, reconstruction showing the windlass, stepped spars with standing
rigging, Trygaios and his mount. Model: A. Hughes.

14 Attic *komastai* or 'fat men', 600–550. Musée du Louvre © RMN/Hervé Lewandowski.

15 Giants, an Archaic chorus on stilts; tall hats enhance their height. The James Logie Memorial Collection and the University of Canterbury.

16 One of an Archaic chorus of armed men carrying severed heads. © The Trustees of the British Museum.

17 Archaic dolphin-rider, perhaps representing a victorious chorus in the first competition for comedy at the Great Dionysia, *c.*486. Image: Katherine Esther Hughes.

18 Herakles in a centaur-chariot driven by Nike; the torch-bearer is costumed as a comic
actor. Centaurs may be members of a chorus. Musée du Louvre © RMN/
Hervé Lewandowski.

19 Stage-naked figures on a large potter's wheel, perhaps members of small, touring comic chorus.

CHAPTER 3

Theatres

On a hot afternoon in 1968, a dusty road in the Peloponnesian back-country led me to a traditional Greek threshing-floor, circular and built into a hillside. Imagination populated the slope with a multitude draped in white linen, who watched the graceful dance of an Aischylean chorus: 'Sing sorrow, sorrow; but good win out in the end.' My fancy confirmed all I had read about the evolution of the Greek *orchestra* from just such a floor, and of the *theatron* (watching place) from a hollow hillside (*koilon*). It was thoroughly logical, plausible and seductive. Forty years later, the same account is repeated in handbooks and classrooms; but 'Zeus, who guided men to think' has also driven archaeologists to dig, and scholars to question received history, no matter how symmetrical. Subsequent research shows that the earliest Athenian *orchestra* was roughly rectilinear, and the earliest seating was composed of wooden grandstands erected upon level ground.[1]

The Theatre of Dionysos in Athens may be neither the oldest nor the best preserved of Greek theatres, but none has been so thoroughly dug or exhaustively discussed. Much of the stone structure that visitors see is Roman in date, the last in an accumulation of alterations which have obliterated most traces of the fifth-century theatre, whose 'meagre remains have been buried under an endless heap of commentaries'.[2] At the risk of adding to the pile, this chapter will attempt a synthesis of contemporary interpretation; irreconcilable disputes are too numerous to permit consensus.

ATHENS: THE EARLIEST THEATRE

Choric comedies may have been performed in or around Athens as early as 560 BCE, dithyrambs earlier still, and some prototype of the tragic chorus certainly existed before a contest for tragedies was incorporated in the Great Dionysia *c*.528. These performances required open space, sufficient to accommodate choruses of fifty dancers in dithyrambs, as well as spectators. Most scholars locate that space in the *agora*, which was the administrative centre of the *polis*, the citizens' customary gathering place on festive occasions, and probably the only broad, reasonably level space within the city's walls. About 500, the Dionysia was transferred to the sanctuary of Dionysos Eleutherios, at the south-eastern end of the Akropolis, initiating the first stage in the development of the Theatre of Dionysos.

The *agora* seen by visitors to modern Athens lies to the north-west of the Akropolis. This was the market-place of the Periklean age, but some scholars believe it was not established until the beginning of the fifth century. If that is correct, it cannot have been the site of the early Dionysian performances. Archaeological discoveries imply that an 'archaic' *agora* occupied a site 200 metres north-east of the theatre, to which it was connected by the Street of the Tripods, where trophies were later erected by victorious dithyrambic *choregoi*. Others argue that it should be located north of the Akropolis, east of the Tower of the Winds in the modern Plaka district.[3] No remains of a sixth-century theatral area have been identified in any of these locations, but incidental remarks in two of Plato's dialogues seem to point to the classical *agora*. Sokrates refers to books for sale 'in the *orchestra*'; and in Plato's ideal commonwealth, touring actors will apply to perform in the *agora* of the ideal *polis*, which apparently lacks a permanent theatre. Therefore, it has been assumed that booksellers used the area where the original *orchestra* had once been, and that in Plato's time (fourth century) this was in the *agora*. It is proposed that the early *orchestra* adjoined the Panathenaic Way where it crosses the *agora*, near the altar of the Twelve Gods.[4]

Wherever choruses were to perform, provision for an audience was necessary. Vases painted between 580 and 550 show people seated on wooden benches, or bleachers, called *ikria* by ancient lexicographers. There is a tradition that seating of this type collapsed beneath the press of spectators, and that the performances were consequently transferred.[5] This accident is frequently dated 499–496, because according to ancient authority it occurred during a performance of a tragedy by Pratinas, who competed against both Aischylos and Choirilos in the seventieth Olympiad (499–496). However, there is no implication that these events were simultaneous; they are simply two things the author knew about Pratinas. Moreover, the collapsing-bleachers story is the kind of anecdotal cause cooked up by ancient commentators to explain an important result. We need no anecdote to explain why the Athenians constructed a new place of assembly on the Pnyx early in the fifth century. Their motive is easily found in the Kleisthenic reforms, which established a democratic Assembly. Likewise, if the Great Dionysia was reorganized *c*.502–501, no disaster was needed to demonstrate the need for a suitable building. While the seventieth Olympiad is not in itself a useful date, early fifth-century pot-shards in landfill at the theatre confirm that work was carried out at about that time, on the southern slope at the east end of the Akropolis.[6]

Orchestra *and* theatron

When the hillside overlooking the Dionysian precinct was made ready for spectators, the sloping ground at the bottom would have to be prepared for choric dance. Earth and rubble on the high side were dug away and used to raise the low ground, where a retaining wall was constructed, to keep the fill in place. The shape of this early *orchestra* was probably accidental, directed more by topography than by a deliberate aesthetic or ideology. The site was irregular, and so no doubt was the wall. The *orchestra* was simply the available space between the sloping hillside and the retaining wall.

Archaeology has revealed masonry – a total of about twenty worked stones – and a cutting in the bedrock. Since there is no stratigraphic evidence, these remains are difficult to date, but comparison with similar work elsewhere has suggested that a straight wall, west of the present *orchestra*, may have been put in place *c*.550, and a longer, curved wall at a later date, perhaps 500–490. The former may precede the theatre, having been built to prevent the hillside's soil from washing down into the sanctuary; or it might be part of a retaining wall for a *parodos*. The later, curved wall is 4.25 metres long, and describes a slightly irregular arc of a little more than 20 degrees. Dörpfeld recognized that the circular *orchestra* could be dated no earlier than the fourth century, but he reasoned that it should have followed the configuration of the original *orchestra*. Therefore, he projected the wall's curvature more than sixteen times to form a circle, defining an *orchestra* 27 metres in diameter. Ever since, round *orchestras* of various dimensions and in several positions have been promoted, revised and endowed with symbolism. As Csapo says, belief in the original circle 'will be a hard habit to shake'.[7] Elsewhere in Attica, the roughly rectilinear *orchestra* at Thorikos seems to have preceded the Theatre of Dionysos. Similar configurations have been found in other Attic demes, as well as in Isthmia, Argos and Corinth on the Greek mainland, and Neandria in the Troad.[8] No *orchestra* is certainly known to have been distinctly defined as a circle before the reconstruction of the Theatre of Dionysos in the later fourth century, or the great theatre at Epidauros, whichever came first.

Perhaps the audience in the original theatre simply sat on the hillside, but anyone who has watched a lengthy spectacle while seated upon a steep slope will understand why Athenians would have agitated for benches before very long. The early fifth-century landfill probably indicates that the slope was graded to accommodate wooden *ikria*.[9] These were erected for each festival, after which they were dismantled and securely stored by the *theatrones* (contractor) who leased the theatre from the state, and charged spectators admission to watch the show from his benches. Temporary seating like this could be readily altered, leaving no permanent traces.

Skene

So long as tragedy and comedy remained primarily choral, there was no need for a stage building or any entrance other than the *parodoi*. Moretti shows that the early deme theatres at Thorikos and Ikarion lacked space for a *skene* beyond the *orchestra*. Perhaps their form was influenced by the new theatre in Athens, where the *skene* with entrances, which was firmly established by 458, need not have been incorporated in the original configuration.[10] On the contrary, it has been suggested that a *skene* in the strict sense of the word, a tent or booth, was set up for festivals in the *agora*, and that this practice continued in the fifth century. If such a prototype-*skene* was ever built, its form is unknown; no doubt it was modest, but not necessarily crude. Indeed, if it was used only at an annual festival, and was stowed out of the weather until next year, there is no reason it should not have been as splendid as a Spanish Easter *pasos* (float).

Aischylos' tragedies require a more substantial *skene*, which combined three functions. It served as a dressing-room for changing masks and costumes; it offered an alternative to the *parodoi* by which actors, and sometimes a chorus, could quickly enter or exit the playing area; and it visually defined dramatic space as a specific location, several places simultaneously, or nowhere in particular. In fact, the *Oresteia* uses the *skene* with such sophistication and authority that it cannot have been a novelty in 458. Attention is focussed upon a single door, compelling the audience to imagine dreadful deeds within; the door gathers thematic significance as it becomes, in turn, the portico of Agamemnon's palace, Klytemnestra's house and the sanctuary of Apollo, where the Furies awaken to pursue Orestes. Nothing in the trilogy implies the presence of a raised stage, but *Agamemnon* calls for a practicable roof for the Watchman, and all three tragedies may have required some means of displaying interior *tableaux*, either by means of a device subsequently known as *ekkyklema* or simply by opening large stage doors.[11] It is probable, therefore, that by 458 the booth-*skene* had been replaced by a larger and better-equipped building, which may nevertheless have been partially temporary because it was still needed only for one springtime festival. If it stood vacant for the remainder of the year, the *skene* would be subject to deterioration and theft. As a practical compromise, a framework of heavy timbers would be capable of withstanding weather and thieves, and of bearing a tile roof, which could be removed piecemeal for safekeeping between festivals: tiles are the property of the contractors in a Peiraeus theatre lease. A façade of movable decorative panels and door units could be rearranged as required for each day's performances.[12]

SECOND PHASE, 446–440

The twenty-five years following Aischylos' death in 456/5 saw many changes in Athenian theatrical practice, which probably contributed to alterations in the physical theatre. Now, the dominant tragic poet was Sophokles, and Euripides competed for the first time in 455; each had his unique stagecraft, and from *c*.453 the innovative comedies of Kratinos and Krates may have intensified the strain upon ageing facilities.[13] Perikles began his monumental building programme with the Parthenon, but another project, usually identified as the Odeion, encroached upon the *theatron*. As a consequence, extensive alterations were undertaken between 446 and 440.[14] To compensate for the surrender of space on the *koilon*'s eastern slope, the builders filled more of the hillside to the west. Permanent stone benches replaced some of the wooden *ikria*, probably in the front row: ten marble sections, recycled in subsequent alterations, have been identified as belonging to this period. Cut square, these can only have been connected as straight benches. Those on the east were aligned with the wall of the Odeion as it intersected the eastern side of the *theatron* at an angle of approximately 75 degrees to the centre section (Figure 5).[15] If corresponding benches were similarly aligned on the opposite side, the *orchestra* would have been clearly defined as trapezoidal, and the wings would probably accommodate more spectators than hitherto. The benches behind these first-row seats were probably still made of wood: Kratinos and Aristophanes use '*ikria*' as though the word were synonymous with '*theatron*'. This seating arrangement remained essentially unchanged until its reconstruction in stone, in the latter half of the fourth century.[16]

These alterations extended the *theatron*, where estimates of capacity vary from 3,700 to 15,000. In any case, supply cannot have been adequate to satisfy demand: the free population of the citizen and metic classes was greater than 200,000.[17] Victim of its own success, next to the Panathenaia the Dionysia had become the most important festival in the Athenian calendar. While performances were occasionally repeated in deme theatres, no enterprising *archon* offered the urban overflow crowd a 'Best of the Dionysia' day. Each *agon*, with its inevitable judgement, was the genuine event; repetition was as unthinkable as repeating a World Cup match. It is not known when Athens took the extraordinary step of charging admission to a religious festival. The price for each day's performance was 2 *obols*, equal to a day's wage. No doubt the money was needed to compensate the *theatrones*, but it must have reduced the demand for seats. However, every citizen who was present in the city at the time of the festival was eligible to receive a modest subsidy (*theorikon*), which would partially defray the admission.[18]

The dramatic components of the Lenaia were transferred to the Theatre of Dionysos soon after its reconstruction. The exact date is unknown, and the festival's previous location is disputed, but motives must have been improved seating and public accessibility. Celebrated two months earlier than the Great Dionysia, the Lenaia extended the theatrical 'season', intensifying wear and tear on the old *skene* and its temporary façade. An *agon* for tragic *protagonists* established at the Dionysia *c.*449 acknowledged the growing importance of actors, and when the Lenaia offered prizes for both tragic and comic actors *c.*332, the festival recognized a significant shift in dramatic emphasis, from the traditional citizen-chorus, to the specialized *hypokrites*.[19]

Changes in the configuration of theatres have historically followed changes in performance methods.[20] While no trace remains of the earliest *skene*, the stagecraft implicit in Aischylos' texts never requires an elevated stage: even his chorus of Furies seems to enter the *orchestra* directly from the *skene*. In 422, when Aristophanes won second prize at the Lenaia with *Wasps*, a stage seems to have been in use, with at least one entrance from the interior of the *skene*. Near the end of the comedy, Philokleon returns home from a *symposion* with an abducted *auletris*: 'Come up this way, my little blonde cockchafer. Grab hold of this rope with your hand ...' (1341–3). He has ascended the steps from the *orchestra* to the stage, and offering his stage *phallos* as a rope, assists her to climb up beside him. He exits into his 'house', soon returning to the stage to challenge the sons of Karkinos to a dance *agon*.

Close to the same date, an Attic vase painter attempted the earliest known picture of a stage. A comic dancer as Perseus is depicted competently, but the artist has bungled the stage, as though struggling to represent a novelty. Nevertheless, it is clear that the structure was made of wood, and that it was less than 1 metre high. The pot's provenance and curved benches in the background suggest that this was the stage of a deme theatre, where performances from the city's festivals were sometimes repeated. In order to accommodate such transfers, the low stage and its steps would duplicate the facilities in the Theatre of Dionysos.[21] By 410, Athenian actors were beginning to extend this practice beyond rural Attica to other Greek cities on the mainland and overseas, exploiting a growing appetite for Attic comedy and tragedy.

THEATRES OUTSIDE ATTICA

Argos, Chaeroneia, Megara and perhaps Eretria built theatres before 400, Corinth and Isthmia soon afterwards. Hippokrates mentions a theatre on the Aegean island of Thasos, and, in remote Campania, a 'primitive' phase of the theatre at Velia was built in the late fifth century.[22] King Archelaos of Macedonia probably provided a theatre for the tragedians Euripides and Agathon, his guests until their deaths in 407/6 and 401, but no fifth-century remains have been found at Aigai (modern Vergina).[23] The pace of construction accelerated early in the fourth century, with new theatres at Olynthos and Mantinea, and in small *poleis* such as Herakleia Minoa in Italy, Morgantina in Sicily, Lato in Crete, Samos and Lemnos in the Aegean, Sikyon near Corinth and Priene in Ionia. An archaic building at Cyrene (Libya) was converted into a theatre. Pausanias reports that when several Arcadian towns amalgamated as Megalopolis, they built the largest theatre in Greece.[24]

It is not easy to determine what most of these theatres were used for. Like a temple, a monumental theatre was prestigious, and useful as well: it could accommodate local festivals of music and dance, or serve as a *bouleterion*. Itinerant theatrical troupes are not documented until the third century, when inscriptions at Delos and Delphi began to record *choregoi* and contestants in festivals: but these were exceptional sites, centres of pan-Hellenic cults.[25] Visual evidence can sometimes show how and by whom theatres were used, or what a stage or *skene* looked like. Ironically, the archaeological quest for fourth-century theatre buildings has been frustrated in those sites where contemporary visual evidence is most abundant. Most significant of these are the great cities of the western Greeks, Syrakousai and Taras.

Lost theatres

The comic poets Epicharmos and Phormis flourished in Syrakousai during the reigns of Gelon and Hieron I (485–467/6). A theatre of some sort must have been available for their performances, and those of their successors, who wrote in a variety of local dramatic forms. No doubt the same theatre was available *c.*476 for Aischylos' *Women of Aitna*, and it was probably modernized for the tragedies of the tyrant-poet Dionysios I, who died after celebrating his Lenaian victory in 367. Tourist guides tell visitors that the great *koilon*, carved into the Epipolai escarpment in suburban Neapolis (New City), is the ancient 'theatre of Demokopos', the fifth-century *architekton* who distributed perfume (*myron*) to 'his fellow citizens' at its inauguration, according to a mime fragment attributed to Sophron.[26] However, if Demokopos ever built a theatre, it is more likely to have stood in the old city than the new one.

In a hasty post-war study of the Epipolai site, Carlo Anti uncovered cuttings in bedrock which he assigned to the early fifth century. Conveniently, this date coincided with Aischylos, and agreed with the *myron* story. Reviewing Anti's book, Bieber found 'his arguments as to the date of holes . . . impossible to follow', and Pickard-Cambridge declared that his 'account of the "theatre of Epicharmos" is almost entirely imaginary'. Archaeologists have subsequently dated the earliest remains to the second half of the fourth century. Consequently, the Epipolai theatre can be associated with neither Aischylos nor Demokopos.[27] What has become of their theatre?

When Syrakousai was founded in the eighth century, the city was confined to Ortygia, a narrow island 1,600 metres long. Apollo's temple was built there in the sixth century, and the *duomo* (cathedral) incorporates part of Gelon's great temple of Athene, erected in 480. A coroplast's workshop in the Piazza Duomo has yielded comic figurines of distinctively Sicilian type, implying that the theatre, and no doubt the city's administrative centre, were not far away.[28] The city expanded across a causeway onto the immediate shore and, later, inland to Neapolis. As the population approached 250,000, demand for space on Ortygia, and a growing audience, must have called for a new theatre. No doubt the suburban site was selected because, like the Dionysian precinct in Athens, its hillside could accommodate ample seating. No architectural remains of the old theatre have been found. Lightly built on relatively level ground, it would have been demolished and its site overlaid, to lie somewhere beneath the labyrinthine *città vecchia*.

Syrakousai had a distinctive tradition of Sicilian comedy, but until the third century nothing of the kind is known in Taras, the metropolis of Apulia.[29] While a few comic figurines and theatrical vases have turned up in the Sicilian capital, most of the extant comic scenes were painted in Taras. Many show a stage, with steps or elements of a *skene*. Before the earliest of these could have been painted, *c.*400, there must have been a theatre somewhere in Taras, but archaeology has so far failed to uncover its material remains. Colonists from Sparta founded the city upon a narrow peninsula, smaller than Ortygia, where the first theatre was probably built. Unlike Syrakousai, Taras backed upon an open, level hinterland to the south-east, which offered space for urban expansion, but lacked a suitable hillside for a *koilon*. An account of conflict with a Roman fleet early in the third century implies that the theatre remained inside the old city, within sight of the sea. That area has been heavily overbuilt in modern times.[30]

We may wonder why the greatest cities of the Greek 'new world' failed to participate in the first phase of theatre construction, at a period when vase painters and coroplasts were producing tangible evidence of intense dramatic activity, particularly in comedy. Historical literature provides no direct answers, but significant clues may be sought in the Apulian comic scenes. Many show a simple stage with wooden boards, like the Perseus Painter's rural Attic platform, and the adjacent *skene* was probably no more substantial. Such structures are easily altered or demolished, and all traces of their perishable materials erased. Significantly perhaps, while stone benches identify most excavated theatres of this period, none of the vase scenes acknowledges a *theatron*. On the evidence, the theatres on Ortygia and the Tarentine peninsula may have consisted of no more than a stage, a *skene* and an *orchestra* that shared the level ground with standing room.

This interpretation is circumstantially confirmed in two smaller towns. Thirty kilometres west of Taras, Metapontion may have been the first western *polis* to welcome Athenian comic actors. Before the end of the fifth century, scenes of comedy were painted in a workshop near the archaic *ekklesiaterion*, which was briefly used as a theatre.[31] Built upon level ground, its circular embankment supported benches for 8,000 spectators, surrounding a level space like a rectangular *orchestra*. Evidently the building was unsuitable; within a decade it was abandoned and stripped of its stone-work, but the stone benches were not used to build a permanent theatre. Later scenes related to tragedy, and illustrations of comedy, suggest that Metapontion continued to provide performing facilities, but no theatre earlier than the third century has been found, either in the relatively undisturbed townsite, or in a hinterland that has been surveyed with uncommon thoroughness.[32] If a fourth-century theatre was constructed, its materials must have been perishable, like those at Syrakousai and Taras. And because the stone seating on the embankment of the *ekklesiaterion* was dismantled, it may be inferred that this type of *theatron* was not required at Metapontion, or at the other sites. The case of Meligunis on Lipari may suggest why.

Situated in the volcanic 'Aiolian' islands, Meligunis is characterized by its archaeology as the most theatre-loving of Greek towns. Excavation has revealed comic vases, notably a famous scene by Asteas, but terracotta figurines and masks seem to have been amongst the island's chief products. Manufactured in the second half of the fourth century, some adapt Athenian models, but most are local types representing theatrical practices that differed significantly from those of Syrakousai and Taras fifty years earlier.[33] Since the figurines were not exported, local demand for mementoes of comedy must have been intense, suggesting that Meligunis was a regular stop on the western touring circuit, in spite of apparent disadvantages. Lipari was accessible only by sea, half a day's sailing from Mylai (Milazzo), the nearest Sicilian port. The population, and consequently the potential audience, was small in comparison with Syrakousai and Taras. No literary or archaeological evidence explains the island's apparent success as a touring destination. We know nothing about the local theatre, because no material remains have been found anywhere on the island's 37 square kilometres. It may be, however, that the island's apparent shortcomings as a destination for actors were of little consequence to an Athenian *protagonist* who planned a western tour.

Comic actors on vases have been described as though they were mediaeval strolling players who 'wandered around' performing 'impromptu' farces on 'makeshift' stages.[34] If we delete all mediaeval anachronism, add the Athenian origin of many productions and apply Greek modes of travel to Italian topography, new probabilities emerge. A *protagonist* and his troupe toured in pursuit of fortune, and of wider fame. Because Greeks normally travelled by sea, Lipari was no less accessible than Taras, but neither destination was a casual speculation. Itinerant acrobats might perform in an *agora* and pass the hat, but an eminent *komodos* owed it to himself to play only at established festivals, by invitation. Little is known about western festivals, but Greek practice elsewhere suggests that they were expressions of the body politic, in which everyone participated. Visiting artists received an honorarium from the *polis*, in consideration of which they competed in an *agon*. No doubt Meligunis offered a modest fee, but victory might generate an invitation from Syrakousai, and ultimately perhaps from Alexander, who invited Lykon of Skarphe to perform at his wedding.[35]

The *agon* was probably performed on a stage and *skene* that were compatible with those in Taras and Syrakousai, substantial, but constructed of perishable materials. A town on a seismic island had no need of a monumental stone *theatron* to accommodate an annual festival, and traces of wooden *ikria* have inevitably been lost. If the stage were near the present citadel, some spectators could have found space on the hillside, while others stood.

FOURTH-CENTURY STAGES IN THE GREEK WEST

Scholars have taken notice of the Perseus Dance scene, far in excess of its significance. Widely illustrated and discussed since its first publication in 1935, its picture of a stage is distinguished from at least seventy others by little more than its Attic provenance. Painted in Sicily and Megale Hellas, these images are significant documents in the history of a theatre that was no less Greek than that of Athens. Most are better-preserved, and some artists developed a practicable convention for representing a stage.[36]

The painters who decorated *symposion* ware with scenes of comedy sought to earn a living by meeting a demand. They were trained to represent the human body, its drapery and accessories; heroic subjects were idealized, and artists quickly learned to invert the ideal for scenes of comedy. They explicitly recorded gesture, mask and undercostume, complete with *phallos*, seams and wrinkles, exposing their artificiality with skill and humour. Gods and heroes were identified by their attributes, and their mythical stories could be recognized with a minimum of scenic or architectural context: stylized rocks or trees, a chariot for Medea, a temple door for Iphigeneia. Comedy was a different matter. Actors were carefully drawn, because clients were interested in them; if the action required stairs or a door, the artist put them in. The scale of human subjects, and minor tokens of their context, are well suited to the inherent limitations of vase painting, but even a good-sized *krater* offers a small picture frame, which is far from flat. The most skilful artists had trouble drawing a respectable tree, and large buildings presented difficulties that were never entirely overcome. When a scene's narrative required any building larger than a shrine, most painters lacked the necessary skills. In a famous scene, two slaves help their arthritic master to climb a flight of steps onto a stage, and in another a traveller mounts stairs for an interview with Zeus Ammon.[37] The stage must be shown because the narrative requires that the viewer understand where the stairs lead. This is hard on a painter who lacks an established technique for representing a stage; if he reduces such a large structure to fit his little frame, human figures drawn to the same scale must be impracticably small.

Baroque artists drew their frame around the human figures which were their real subjects, enclosing only enough of the background structure to identify the setting. Thus, the scale of the architecture corresponded to that of the people who inhabited it, and a small part of a great temple could represent the whole. Apulians never discovered this simple synecdoche, turning instead to an unstable mixture of realism and conventional shortcuts. Attempts to apply a primitive form of perspective to comic scenes were less than triumphant.[38] Drawing the height of the stage to the same scale as the actors, most painters distorted its lateral dimension by compressing it until it was forced to fit inside the frame. At the same time, they adopted something not unlike the baroque convention by making three or four of the posts that supported the stage stand for many more.

In spite of their shortcomings, the independent testimony of many artists yields data about fourth-century Greek theatres which excavation has been unable to provide. As in Athens, stage and *skene* were built of perishable materials that were easily modified and demolished. From pictures by local artists, it is evident that the stage in Taras underwent several alterations between 400 and 350, and we can deduce how Sicilian stages were adapted to new trends in drama, from a few years before mid-century to 330. Therefore, painters in Taras, Paestum and Sicily provide us with a continuous series of pictures of working theatres in the Greek west for most of the fourth century.

The Perseus Dance scene includes two spectators and some curious lines in the background which may represent benches. None of the western pictures shows any part of a *theatron*, or members of an audience. They also omit the façade of the *skene*, leaving a plain black-glazed background for the reserved red figures of actors and stage properties. Sometimes small objects such as a mask, a wine-jug or a sash seem to hang in mid-air, probably not because such things actually decorated the *skene*, but to fill a vacant space. Functional features such as entrances, windows and slim columns are used sparingly, as needed for the artist's narrative. Analysed cumulatively, these pictures provide valuable clues to the structure and development of the *skene* in the Middle Comedy period.

Taras

Taking these conventions into account, we can form an approximate picture
of an Apulian stage, which resembled the platform with a ladder in the
Perseus scene, painted no more than twenty years earlier. The wooden
stage stands between 0.7 and 1.6 metres high, measured against an actor
of average stature, and judging by the number of steps connecting it
to the ground in eight Apulian scenes. At first, these are lightly built,
perhaps movable rather than temporary, but in later pictures they are more
substantial. Most viewpoints are frontal, the stage appearing to be no more
than 2.5 to 4.25 metres. wide. This is manifestly distorted, but since four
actors may share the stage with large properties such as furniture, a width
of no less than 9 or 10 metres seems likely. Three early artists adopt a point
of view near one end of the stage, compressing its apparent depth to little
more than 1 metre; however, allowing for entrances, the actual depth can
be estimated at 3.5 to 4.5 metres.[39]

While their evidence of height and depth is fairly consistent, painters
have different methods of portraying structural details. Columns supporting the stage, for example, are represented as plain and square, Doric or
Ionic.[40] If most or all of the Apulian pictures represent the Taras stage,
their apparent disagreement need not invalidate their testimony. These
scenes were painted over a period of fifty years, during which alterations
in a wooden stage must be expected.[41] In scenes painted later than *c*.370,
the stage platform and supporting posts seem impossibly heavy, apparently
up to 40 centimetres thick. A close examination of the artist's black-glazed
lines, superimposed on red clay to represent the angles of posts, beams and
the boards of the stage, shows that some painters were attempting a crude
perspective (Figure 6). Whereas earlier artists aligned the viewer's eye with
stage level, a higher point of view simultaneously shows us the front of the
stage and its surface, and two vertical planes of each rectangular post.[42]
This viewpoint offers some hints about structure. Boards aligned with the
long axis of the stage must have been nailed across stout joists at intervals
of about 0.5 metres. Since the downstage ends of the joists are never shown,
they were probably hidden by a fascia board. Joists could be borne by stout
longitudinal beams, supported by posts or columns at intervals of up to
2 metres (Figure 7).[43]

While these scenes use a new idiom to display the Taras stage, significant
alterations may have waited until *c*.360, when fluted Ionic columns replaced
plain supporting posts.[44] Slender matching columns stood upon the stage,

sometimes supporting a sloping roof above double entrance doors, which usually stand ajar.[45] This 'porch' appears in the earliest scenes, and some of the latest as well, with variations which may represent several renovations. The roof is sometimes supported by a plain buttress which springs from the door-post, but in two scenes gracefully curved buttresses end in swan-heads (Figure 8).[46] These entrances seem to be placed either at stage left or stage right, never at centre; perhaps this is not significant, but it is possible that the 'porches' were *paraskenia*, and that there was no central stage entrance. In a fragmentary tragic scene dated after 350, double doors are certainly set within a *paraskenion* at stage right; the slim Ionic columns that support its roof are linked to a colonnade across the *skene* façade (Figure 9).[47]

Paestum

Some of the liveliest comic scenes were painted in Paestum by Asteas, the first western Greek painter to sign his work, and by his pupil Python. Asteas learned his trade in Sicily, where his early pictures have been attributed to him as the 'Painter of Louvre K240'. Emigrating to Paestum shortly before the middle of the fourth century, he mass-produced scenes of Dionysos attended by satyrs, maenads and comic actors. It is unlikely that Paestum had a theatre, or frequent visits by touring actors: the artist probably drew upon memories of Sicily when he depicted the appearance and behaviour of comic actors, with highly metatheatrical costumes which may have been worn by a Sicilian troupe. Similarly, perhaps his five scenes in a theatre recall a type of stage used in Sicily before his departure.[48]

Unlike other artists, Asteas avoids structural compression; instead, he frames part of the stage, which the viewer's imagination extends beyond the frame (Figure 10). His stage appears to be close to 1 metre high, supported in one instance by Doric columns about 60 centimetres on centre, which makes structural sense; in other scenes, supports are concealed by hangings pinned at approximately the same intervals. Our viewpoint is directly before the front edge of the stage, which is decorated with a frieze of circles, or a maeander pattern.[49] Two pictures show unroofed double doors at stage left, conceivably a *paraskenion* entrance in a *skene* that lacks a central door.[50] In several pictures, the *skene* has a distinctive window, high in an otherwise blank façade. Occupied by birds or women, these windows frequently fill vacant space in Paestan scenes. The women look like cardboard cut-outs, but since actors sometimes woo them with ladders and lamps, it is likely that windows were a real feature of the theatre Asteas remembered. His most detailed picture has two of them, occupied by actors wearing the white masks of women.[51]

If Asteas painted stages from memory, his originals must have been in use somewhere in Sicily. If he emigrated in order to avoid the disturbances that followed the assassination of Dion in 354, it is likely that he remembered the lost theatre of Ortygia, because he had settled in Paestum before the great *koilon* was hewn from the rocky slope of Epipolai. His *skene* with two practicable windows, however, was found on Lipari, and it is tempting to suppose that Asteas paused there long enough to leave us our only glimpse of that drama-loving island's lost theatre.[52]

Sicily

The latest images of Greek stages were painted *c.*340–30 by Sicilian artists known as the Lentini-Manfria Group, for the widely distributed provenances of their pots. These scenes show a novel type of stage which differed significantly from the structures Asteas remembered. The group has left us a number of comedy scenes and two of tragedies, one of which is unidentified; the second is a recognizable moment in *Oidipous Tyrannos*.[53] All depict the same stage, using a peculiar reverse perspective which makes the platform seem to be narrower downstage than 'up'. Its construction is difficult to interpret, because it is apparently enclosed on all sides, like a big packing-case. The front of the platform and vertical edges of the enclosure beneath it are highlighted by a band of white, as though the ends of the box were closed by slabs as thick as the stage itself. It is likely that its front was panelled, and in one instance it is decorated with painted incense-burners (Figure 45). As usual the *skene* is not shown, but slender columns with Doric or Ionic capitals usually seem to support the decorated upper border of the picture, as though it were a roof. In two scenes, double doors at stage right have neither a roof nor associated columns; if there was an entrance at each side, there is no sign of *paraskenia*.[54] As in the Apulian scenes, the stage is compressed to fit the frame, its apparent breadth varying from 2.2 to 3.7 metres. In several scenes, it is reached by one or two flights of six or eight steps, suggesting that the platform may have been as high as 1.8 metres above the ground, anticipating the lofty *logeion* (stage) of the Theatre of Dionysos in Athens as it was soon to be reconstructed.

ATHENS: THE STONE THEATRE

After the alterations of 446–440, no evidence of structural work has been reliably dated earlier than the second half of the fourth century. In western

Greek cities, vase paintings document continuous development of stage and *skene*, no doubt reflecting changes in dramaturgy and stagecraft. Since these must have originated in Athens, that is where we would look first for corresponding structural innovations; however, neither Athenian painters nor its perishable materials have left traces of the working stage and *skene*, until they were rebuilt in stone.

This monumental reconstruction is reminiscent of the architectural achievements of the Periklean age, the Parthenon and, next to the theatre, the Odeion. Like them, the marble theatre was a monument to the glory of Athens and, consequently, archaeologists formerly assigned a date in the fifth century. Excavations in the 1960s, and comparison with other sites, show that the massive foundations of the new *skene* could not have been laid before the middle of the fourth century. In fact, the reconstruction may have begun *c*.343. No doubt the work was interrupted following the defeat at Chaeoneia in 338, resuming under the administration of Lykourgos, the city's financial manager from 338 to 326.[55]

Lykourgos initiated a secular and religious programme of Athenian affirmation, on the Periklean model.[56] The navy was rebuilt, with new ship-sheds and an armoury at Peiraeus, and the military training of young citizens (*epheboi*) was reformed. Lykourgos rehabilitated sanctuaries and renewed the city's festivals, building a new *stadion* for the Panathenaia and transforming the theatre to accommodate the Dionysia, with fundamental changes in each of its constituent parts: *theatron*, *orchestra* and *skene*. Structure usually reflects use, but New Comedy was becoming the dominant dramatic form when the stone theatre was completed; the broad outlines of its configuration had been laid out twenty years earlier. Consequently, it was not designed specifically for the requirements of the plays of Menander and his rivals; indeed, 'old tragedy' was better served than New Comedy.

Theatron *and* orchestra

The old *theatron* was extensively rebuilt, its wooden *ikria* replaced by marble benches, which could not be removed and stored between festivals: the theatre was now managed by the *architekton*, an elected public servant.[57] The hillside was graded and filled, adding new rows at the rear, and extended rows were supported by masonry retaining-walls, perhaps doubling capacity to as many as 15,000. This was a calculated response to demand, which had exceeded capacity for a century. Stairways divided the benches into thirteen wedges (*kerkides*), and marble chairs (*prohedria*) in the front row accommodated dignitaries, such as the priest of Dionysos and the *archon*.[58]

Seating was arranged to define the new *orchestra*, which was round, and much larger than its rectilinear predecessor. Concentric tiers of stone benches curved through an arc of 200 degrees, focussing attention upon the circular *orchestra*. This physical relationship between *theatron* and *orchestra* seems to have been designed primarily for dithyrambic performances. In New Comedy, 'the *logeion* belonged to the actors and the *orchestra* to the chorus', but sightlines to the *orchestra* were better than to the stage where actors played comedies, and the new *orchestra* was too big for a comic chorus of twenty-four. Moreover, its shape was best suited to dithyramb, which was a 'circular dance' by fifty members of a single competing tribe, whose 'fans' may have sat together in their own *kerkis* to cheer for their home team.[59]

Skene

The foundations of the new, permanent *skene* were constructed of *breccia*, a distinctive conglomerate rock. The rear of the *skene* was supported by a retaining wall, more than 60 metres long, which separated the theatre from a *stoa* associated with the sanctuary on the lower level to the south. Ten sockets in the masonry are believed to have supported heavy wooden posts, which formed some part of the building (Figure 11).[60] Foundations are the principal evidence for the configuration of the *skene*, and of the narrow *proskenion* beneath the *logeion*. The stage was more than 20 metres in width, and approximately 3 metres deep. Comparison with better-preserved theatres suggests that the *logeion* stood at least 2 metres above the ground, and that it was supported at the front by a colonnade of wooden posts facing the *orchestra*. Behind the *logeion*, a second storey of the *skene* may have served as the background for dramatic action, which might sometimes call for more than one entrance; but there is no evidence for the appearance of the façade, and no material remains testify that it existed at all. Therefore it may have had a central door, an open colonnade, movable scenery, or any combination of the three. Projections at each end of the foundations are believed to have supported *paraskenia*, stage entrances like the 'porches' in vase scenes from Taras, where double doors were protected by a small roof sustained by columns or buttresses.[61]

Because the Athenian theatre is likely to have been the prototype of the well-preserved Hellenistic theatres at Priene and Aphrodisias, its *proskenion* was probably not unlike theirs, in form and function (Figure 12). Entrances

through the colonnade opened directly into the *orchestra*, facilitating interaction between actors and chorus. This was not useful in New Comedy,
where the two estates never communicated, but it would have suited the
'old tragedies' that were regularly revived at the Great Dionysia after 341.[62]
Spaces between the posts could also accommodate movable, painted panels, and even perhaps the mysterious *ekkyklema*, which, like the *mechane*,
provided special effects in fifth-century tragedy, and was ridiculed by the
comic poets.

SPECIAL EFFECTS

Ekkyklema

A stone platform projects from the retaining wall at the rear of the
proskenion.[63] It has been suggested that this supported an '*ekkyklema*',
the name used by Pollux in the second century CE for a theatrical device
that 'looks down on unspeakable deeds behind the *skene*'. This is often
thought to refer to a low, mobile rostrum that could be wheeled out of
the *skene* to reveal interiors. Commentators assert that Aischylos used it, to
display Klytemnestra exulting over the corpses; Sophokles, to reveal Ajax
amongst the slaughtered sheep; and too frequently by Euripides, who may
have used it to display mad Herakles with his dead family. However, the
only textual references are found in comedy. When Aristophanes 'rolled
out' Agathon and Euripides onto the stage, his audience understood that
the tragic poets were being mocked for using a rolling contraption like the
ekkyklema.[64]

If tragedies like these were revived in the reconstructed theatre, something of the sort may have been required. Nevertheless, it is unlikely that the
builders constructed a platform from some thirty blocks of ashlar masonry
merely to support one 'special-effects' machine when it was not in use. In
order to carry its dismal cargo out of the *proskenion* and into the light,
the *ekkyklema* had to roll almost 10 metres, but the platform extends no
more than 3 metres towards the *orchestra*. And if the wagon's dimensions
approximated those of the platform, it must have been close to 7 metres
wide. One-third of the colonnade would have to be removed to make way
for its passage, resulting in the collapse of the *logeion*. Instead, explanations
of the *breccia* platform as a place to park the *ekkyklema* must collapse,
opening the way for a more practical conjecture.

Because *breccia* was used in the foundations of the *skene*, it is likely
that the platform served as a foundation. If that is correct, it supported
an interior structure which, since it was at the rear of the *skene*, cannot

have been a permanent part of the façade, such as a monumental central entrance. Its position and dimensions suggest that it might have been a stair-well, connecting ground level, *logeion* and, perhaps, a *theologeion* on the roof of the *skene*.

Mechane

The *mechane* is better documented than the *ekkyklema*; it seems to have been a derrick which simulated the unassisted flight of gods, or of heroes like Perseus, with his winged footwear, and Bellerophon, riding upon Pegasos. The convention of illusion, however, ensured that tragedy texts never acknowledge the *mechane*, rarely so much as implying that a speaker is airborne. Jason swears that Medea cannot escape his revenge unless she hides beneath the earth, or, ironically, on wings. When she enters, Medea merely explains that a vehicle (*ochema*) provided by her grandfather Helios protects her from Jason's attack. Nothing in the text justifies the editor's stage direction that she flies in a chariot drawn by dragons. We know of the dragons from vase paintings, and her flight is confirmed by Aristotle, who complains that the conclusion comes *apo mechanis*, out of a machine. According to Plato, this is the common practice of tragic poets who, 'whenever they are stuck, take refuge in machines and raise up the gods'.[65]

Unlike tragedy, Old Comedy delights in calling attention to theatrical artifices like the *mechane*, and their frequent use by Euripides. At the conclusion of *Thesmophoriazousai* (1098), the tragedian assumes the role of Perseus, flying to the rescue of his Kinsman, who impersonates Andromeda. Dialogue shows that Sokrates in *Clouds* (218–27) dangles overhead, in a basket. *Peace* burlesques Euripides' *Bellerophon*, with Trygaios flying to heaven on a dung-beetle. He directly addresses the *mechanopoios*, operator of the 'machine': 'if you aren't careful I'll be feeding the beetle' (174). From the evidence of Menander's extant texts, the Lykourgan theatre might not have been equipped with a *mechane*; editors refer to his airborne prologues, but 'stage level . . . fits the confidential tone of such gods', and only Pan (*Dyskolos*) accounts for his movements, entering from his shrine in the *skene*.[66]

Regrettably, we have no vase-painter's memento of a flying scene. If the conventional realism such artists used for costumes were applied to the *mechane*, we might be less obliged to rely upon inferences and literary scraps. We infer from Aristophanes' dialogue that the 'machine' could hoist an actor, and transport him to the stage, from some point out of sight. Several clues to its mechanism can be deduced. Like Plato, Antiphanes claims that tragic poets 'lift the crane just like a finger' when they run short of ideas. In a fragment, a speaker calls it a *krade*, meaning a branch of a tree, and refers to the operator's *trochos*. If this word is translated as 'windlass', it explains a vocal stunt of Theodoros, who was celebrated for his ability to imitate the sound of the *mechane*, at the end of a tragedy.[67]

In structural terms, this suggests that the *mechane* comprised a fixed base, surmounted by a long boom that pivoted through an arc, and was counterweighted so as to raise the tip from the horizontal to a steep angle, like a finger. If no single spar of sufficient length was available, a second spar may have been stepped, like a ship's topmast, and the joint stiffened by standing rigging. A line at the tip of the spar raised and lowered its load, probably with a double-purchase tackle. The line was paid out by a windlass at the base which, according to Pollux, 'stands beside the left *parodos*'. While it is unclear whether this refers to stage or house left, it must signify that the base was located off-centre, no doubt in order to permit the long boom to reach centre stage (Figure 13).[68]

Classical Athenian audiences brought an elastic collective imagination to their theatre. With every *eisodos*, they tacitly adapted to the world of the play, laughing with the *komodoi* in the afternoon at the tragic illusions they had accepted in the morning. Today, we cannot readily share their complacency with effects that seem crude. Perhaps we are incredulous that a crowd could contain its mirth as the *ekkyklema* bumped along with its cargo of bouncing corpses and swaying heroes, or that spectators could ignore the thick rope and jutting boom of the *mechane*. Having persuaded ourselves that they saw things much as we do, we prefer our prejudices to the evidence. Surely, illusion would be better served if the derrick were out of sight behind the *skene*; therefore, in spite of Pollux' evidence that it stood beside the *parodos*, and Theodoros' mimicry of its rattling windlass, that is where we place it.[69]

Skene *painting*

The legacy of Italian Renaissance efforts to apply perspective to Vitruvian principles led early scholars to confound 'painting the *skene*' with illusionist 'scene painting'. The 'invention' of scene painting has been attributed to a certain Agatharchos with such assurance that in 1920 a scholar reconstructed the artist's perspective design for the towers of Thebes, in Aischylos' *Seven against Thebes* (467). 'How amazing must have been the first sight of it to the Athenians, who had never seen the like', the author exclaims, and concludes, 'the fame of Agatharchos will live' for painting a scene 'that revolutionized art for ever'.[70]

Those towers were founded on nothing more substantial than a sentence in Vitruvius, which has been described as 'probably the most obscure and problematical of all the ancient texts on art'. It seems to say that Agatharchos made, built or executed a *scaena*, a word Vitruvius uses elsewhere in the sense of a comic, tragic or satyric 'setting', but it can also mean a stage, or the façade of a *skene*. The connection with Aischylos is indeterminate, but it is unlikely to mean that the artist collaborated with him during the poet's lifetime, because Agatharchos was probably very young when the poet died.[71]

A terse passage in *Poetics*, attributing *skenographia* to Sophokles, may be spurious.[72] Should it be authentic, Aristotle probably does not refer to 'scenery' or 'backdrops' representing battlemented towers or landscapes.[73] Judging by vase paintings, Greek artists were not at their best with trees. When Lysistrata's chorus of women invoke Nike (321), there is no need for a painted temple beside the *skene* door that stands for the Propylaia. Most locations, named or implied by the comic poets, are urban exteriors; action takes place before 'the house of Zeus' (*Peace* 178), Sokrates' Thinkery (*Clouds* 128), or the semi-detached houses of Demeas and Nikeratos (*Samia*). If the fifth-century *skene* was enclosed with panels, these may have been painted with a neutral decorative theme that would serve for an entire festival, rather than a new scheme for every play. The Lykourgan *skene* was the background for the first performances of most New Comedies, which are frequently set in a city street. Greek houses usually faced inwards, upon a courtyard; passers-by saw only a continuous wall, pierced at intervals by double doors and an occasional window at a safe height. This is how the *skene* appears on Apulian and Paestan vase scenes.

Dialogue names a few exceptional locations, such as Tereus' thicket (*Birds* 207) and Knemon's isolated farmhouse (*Dyskolos* 2–6). Several large paintings that represented scenes in Menander's comedies were publicly displayed in Athens during the poet's lifetime. They seem to have been admired, because many copies have survived, in a variety of small media that may distance them from the originals. Amongst those that appear to be most authentic are a relief and two mosaics, all in the Museo Archeologico Nazionale in Naples.[74] Behind the actors, one mosaic shows only a plain background and part of a tall door (Figure 54). In the relief, a more elaborate door and a wall with pilasters suggest that the mosaic may be simplified in order to highlight the actors. The door should be a practicable element of the *skene* rather than a painted panel or 'flat' (Figure 52). The second mosaic shows actors as women, seated within what appears to be a simple 'box set' representing a room, with furniture and steps. An attempt to locate such a three-dimensional scene anywhere in the theatre could only be conjectural; and if this was a painted panel, it was not 'scenery' (Figure 55).

Greek scene painting remains 'an opaque subject'.[75] We cannot be sure that scenery was ever used as a visual substitute for the imagination of the audience. Like Elizabethans, Greeks beheld performances in daylight. It was only when the English players moved indoors at the Blackfriars that artificial lighting opened the way to illusion. Like groundlings at the Globe, Greeks were good listeners. When it mattered, dialogue told which door in an unchanging façade was to be understood as Knemon's front door, a palace gate or a dung-beetle's stable – for the moment. When the moment passed, it could become conventionally invisible once more.

CHAPTER 4

The comic chorus

At the onset of one of those outbreaks of antiquarian enthusiasm with which western culture is periodically stricken, a friend confided to Thomas Gray his ambition to write a tragedy with a chorus. The poet's response was not encouraging:

A greater liberty in the choice of the fable, and the conduct of it, was the necessary consequence of retrenching the Chorus . . . The soft effusions of the soul, Mr. Mason, will not bear the presence of a gaping, singing, dancing, moralizing, uninteresting crowd. And not love alone, but every passion is checked and cooled by this fiddling crew . . . Could Hamlet have met the Ghost, or taken his mother to task in *their* company? If Othello had said a harsh word to his wife before *them*, would they not have danced to the window and called the watch?

Gray objected to the chorus because he found it unbelievable and, hence, preposterous. Ironically, realism is a significant legacy of Greek art. The development of sculpture from archaic *kouroi* to Praxitelean naturalism was a manifestation of the same aspiration to realism that led to the separation of the chorus from dramatic action in New Comedy. Western culture absorbed Greco-Roman realism with the Renaissance, applying it relentlessly to drama of all kinds, only countenancing a chorus within the surreal conventions of opera and ballet.

   Realism in drama is always relative and conditional, depending upon how far an audience can extend what Coleridge called 'That willing suspension of disbelief for the moment, which constitutes poetic faith'. Film and ballet are equally conventional, but film's pretension to realism encourages passive illusion, regardless of its fundamental artificiality. Similarly, in Greek tragedy nothing was permitted to fracture convention; even Euripides' metatheatrical moments are veiled communications between the poet and a discerning minority in his audience. In comedy, however, the same spectators were enthusiastically complicit in metatheatrical conventions, in which a fantastical world was inflated like a balloon, for the pleasure of exploding it with a self-referential pin.[1] For illusion or poetic faith, comedy substituted the fantasy of 'what if', where laws of reason and nature were suspended until a sudden return to extra-theatrical reality exploited the shock of incongruity, both to make the *polis* laugh, and to prepare the citizens to accept the poet's admonishments.

In Old Comedy the chorus was the agent of fantasy, and also of its subsequent deflation. It is difficult for us to appreciate the impact of its first entrance, the *parodos*, with its extravagant costumes, poetry, music and dance. Such an assault upon the senses was to be experienced only rarely; the *parodos* was fantasy made manifest, transforming the comedy's 'what if' into 'what is'. In the *parabasis*, the chorus punctured the fantasy by 'stepping forward' to address the audience directly, upon topics that varied between personal invective, the good taste of the poet's jokes and the fun a man could have if only he could fly.

EARLY COMEDY IN WRITING

We know something of the early development and form of tragedy, because seven plays by Aischylos survive, including a complete trilogy, the *Oresteia* (458). Of comedy before Aristophanes' *Acharnians* (425), only fragments remain. Consequently, scholars have searched literary sources for clues to its origin and early character. These can tell us less than we should like; the circumstances of comedy's origin were mostly forgotten in Aristotle's time, two centuries later. Seventy years ago, classical scholars turned to an anthropological approach, comparing cultures to propose how Attic drama might have developed from ritual. After all, it was performed in honour of Dionysos. Cultural analogy could not proceed beyond speculation, however; and while these studies produced plausible results for tragedy, no theory of comic origins achieved consensus. Today a new generation of 'ritualists' has arisen, concentrating principally upon tragedy, but sometimes seeking to link ritual with comedy.[2]

Two unique documents offer brief accounts of comedy's origin. The 'Parian marble' is an inscription which was found in three fragments; in the seventeenth century, two of these were transported to England, where one part was lost, though fortunately not before it was recorded. The other is now in Oxford. The third piece subsequently turned up in Paros. Taken together, the fragments form a chronological list of significant events related to Athens, beginning with legendary kings, and ending in 264/3, when the marble was inscribed by persons and for reasons unknown.[3] The brief reference to comedy says a chorus was established in Athens, the people of Ikarion first produced it, Sousarion invented it, and the first prize consisted of figs and wine. The date is illegible, but has been calculated as *c.*581–560 BCE. The source of this inscription may be folklore, but independent evidence suggests that the date, at least, may not be far wrong.

The inscription seems to mean that the first competition between comic choruses was sponsored by the demesmen of Ikarion, in Attica, who provided the rustic prize. However, there are grounds for scepticism about Ikarion and Sousarion. Tradition has Thespis 'invent' tragedy in the same place, and while it is one of a handful of Attic demes which had a theatre at an early date, the coincidence is suspicious. Nevertheless, someone composed the first comic choral songs and dances; unlikely as it may be that his name was Sousarion, no alternative is known.[4]

The second significant document is the *Souda*, an encyclopaedia of 30,000 entries on a great variety of ancient topics. Compiled in the tenth century CE, nevertheless it draws upon sources of which we would otherwise know nothing.[5] Its biographical note on the poet Chionides says he competed as *protagonist* of Old Comedy in 486, and that he instructed or directed (*didaskein*), presumably the chorus. This suggests that, like other early poets, he composed all aspects of his comedy, verse, dance and music, instructed the chorus, and then either led them as *exarchos* or acted the leading role. No doubt the occasion was the first competition for comedy at the Great Dionysia, and the *Souda* singles out Chionides because he was the first victor.[6]

Aristotle's terse references to early comedy apply to this period. From an 'improvisatory origin' with the 'leaders (*exarchontes*) of the phallic songs (*phallika*)', comedy was not at first seriously practised, but 'performed by volunteers' as an unofficial event outside the Great Dionysia; at a later date than tragedy, it was 'granted a chorus'. Comic plots were first devised by Epicharmos, the Sicilian poet who was 'much earlier' than Chionides; and in Athens, Krates 'was the first to relinquish the iambic manner and to create stories and plots with an overall structure'.[7] This suggests that Chionides' principal business was iambic lampoon, sung either by the chorus or by an actor.

The context of the first competitions was probably a rural festival, which would have been controlled and probably financed by the local landed aristocracy. As a matter of policy, the tyrant Peisistratos sought to weaken local power by centralizing festivals in Athens. When he introduced the competition for tragic poets at the Great Dionysia about 528, some early form of the *choregia* liturgy may have been devised in order to transfer patronage and financing from landed aristocrats to the wealthy urban citizens who were the tyrant's power base. It remained for the Kleisthenic democracy to reorganize the festival in 502–501, and to apply a reformed *choregia* to comic competitions in 486.[8]

For the origins of drama, this pragmatic and secular emphasis has been balanced by renewed attempts to establish an historical or archaeological link between ritual and drama, justifying Aristotle's reference to the 'phallic songs'. It has been argued that he did not know what he was talking about, admitting as he does that 'comedy's early history was forgotten because no serious interest was taken in it'; on the other hand, his claim that the *phallika* 'remain even now a custom in many cities' in the fourth century has encouraged some scholars to interpret 'phallic songs' as Dionysian 'processions', or to seek an archaeological link to ritual in images of 'padded dancers', *komastai* or 'fat men'.[9]

EARLY COMEDY IN PICTURES

Fat men

Two types of painted pottery show groups of dancers, frequently accompanied by an *auletes*, which should constitute choruses. Dancing 'fat men' first appear in the seventh century, on Corinthian black-figured ware, which was subsequently imitated in other cities, and on Athenian ware until *c.*550 (Figure 14). Debate about their relevance to comedy is continuous but inconclusive.[10] Black-figure conventions inhibit most artists from showing the viewer whether the dancers' protuberant stomachs and buttocks are artificial or real, or if they are masked, and therefore whether the scenes depict a real *komos*, a dancing crowd of drunken revellers who all happen to be overweight, or a chorus *imitating* a crowd of drunken revellers and dressed up as fat men. Although '*komos*' is associated with 'comedy', without *mimesis* (*role*-playing) a connection is difficult to sustain. In a few of these scenes, apparent *role*-playing has suggested comparisons between archaic *komos*-dancers and the comic actors of the later fifth century, but similarities are insufficient to establish a link. The obvious distinction is the *phallos*, with which the comic actor's undercostume is always equipped, while the fat men are rarely phallic. Moreover, while the ritual *phallos* may be erect and fertile, the comic article is invariably flaccid and impotent.[11]

The term 'padded dancers' is often applied in an attempt to connect the appearance of the archaic dancers with the comic actor through his undercostume, but with 'no clear evidence that that they are normally or even ever really "padded"' we must attribute the comparison to 'hindsight', by which Smith means 'looking back from our more complete knowledge of the theatrical costuming of later periods . . . to explain the dress of Archaic *komasts*'. This requires us to look back rather too far, because our first picture of an actor wearing undercostume was painted 120 years after the last Athenian fat men.[12] The genuine connection between the fat *komastai* and the comic actor is nothing less than an aesthetic ideal that all Greeks shared. Both types invert the beautiful and the good, with their physical ugliness and laughable absurdity. Inversion of the admirable is the philosophical bedrock of comedy. We encounter the same theme in every aspect of comic theatre, its masks, costumes and acting style.[13]

Archaic choruses

The earliest examples of the second type of pottery appeared in small numbers between *c*.560, shortly before the komastic scenes disappeared, and around the time of the first comic *agon* in 486. Most are painted on *symposion* paraphernalia: the *amphora* for storing wine, *oinochoe* for serving it, the deep-bowled *skyphos* and shallow *kylix* for drinking and playing *kottabos*, a game in which lees were thrown at a target. The painters have depicted groups of men dressed in strange garments and behaving unconventionally, usually accompanied by a musician playing double pipes (*aulos*). These are certainly choruses, and they are disciplined: unlike the disorderly *komastai*, their movements are co-ordinated, and each group has a collective identity conferred by similar costumes and uniform movement.[14] Csapo notes that they cannot represent comedy 'as we know it' from Aristophanes, in spite of the coincidence of theriomorphic choruses of men 'dressed up as animals, or riding on animals' that seem to suggest his *Birds* or *Knights*, but neither can they represent phallic songs, hypothetical Dionysian processions, or dithyramb as we know it. While some early dithyrambic choruses may have been spectacular, there is no evidence that masks or theriomorphic costumes were worn, or that spectacle ever went beyond golden crowns and opulent but conventional robes. These archaic scenes are the genuine stuff of comedy, fancifully depicting old men standing on their heads, exotically costumed, stilt-walking 'giants', riders mounted upon men costumed as horses, or on pantomime-dolphins and ostriches, and vigorous dances by men masked and costumed as fowl or cattle. It would be strange if scholars failed to regard them as crucial evidence of comic origins.[15]

At present, we know of twenty-four scenes on twenty vases painted before *c*.480, when production abruptly ceased, for reasons unknown. Painters or their customers may have simply lost interest, or perhaps we have failed to dig in the right places. Chronologically, most of the vases fall into two clusters. Perhaps significantly, the earlier group has five scenes dated *c.*560 to 530, not long after the innovation attributed to Sousarion. The two earliest show men dancing to the music of an *auletes*; the same step is danced in each, arms akimbo, one knee up and toes pointed. In each chorus there is an alien element: dancers wear headgear of conventionally Asian types, some with feathers, or headbands with animal ears. Two slightly later scenes are fanciful, with men walking on stilts, and cavalrymen who wear alien helmets and ride other men with horse-masks and tails. Again, non-Greek costumes mark each chorus as outsiders (Figure 15).[16]

Four intermediary scenes develop the taste for fantasy and spectacle, which seems to supplant the foreign costumes of the earlier scenes. Men in Greek armour ride dolphins around the body of a *psykter* so that, as it floated in a *krater* of cool water, the dolphins seemed to swim: the riders sing '*epi delphinos*' ('on a dolphin'). Men in feathered tights with wings fastened to their arms wear half-masks with avian features and crests. Two artists have painted a chorus of men in bull-masks, with tights and tufted tails; they may represent the rivers, sons of Oceanus.[17]

The latest cluster has sixteen choric scenes, most with a piper, on thirteen vases. A *skyphos* has two scenes of an old men's chorus who enter running in single file, carrying torches and wearing voluminous mantles. On the reverse, they have stripped to their shirts, and are standing on their heads. Like the bull-men, several choruses were chosen as subjects by more than one artist. Two vases show men with long beards and crested helmets, who hold spotted cloaks before their faces. In a third scene the same men appear without their *himatia*, dancing with castanets. A chorus of young men with crested helmets on the reverse similarly dances with castanets; the same chorus may be identified in another scene in which armoured men carry swords in one hand and, in the other, severed heads wearing helmets like their own.[18] Did one half of the chorus simulate the decapitation of the other half (Figure 16)?

No fewer than six different painters chose a chorus of dolphin-riders for their subject: identical in essential details, all must surely refer to the same performance (Figure 17).[19] Nothing in the pictures explains why this chorus attracted more attention than the one depicted in the *epi delphinos* scene twenty-five years earlier, when comedy was still a 'fringe' event at the Great Dionysia. An explanation may be found in the dating of the six later dolphin scenes, which were all painted close to 486, when Chionides won the first comic *agon* at the Great Dionysia. It is tempting to suppose that his victorious chorus entered riding upon dolphins, perhaps representing the mythical founders of Taras.[20]

Presenting the chorus

Some Archaic vase scenes contain clues to production practices which may have continued in the time of Aristophanes. Verbal stage directions show that the semi-chorus of old men in *Lysistrata* remove their cloaks before battle, like the Wasp-chorus and the chorus of Acharnians before the *parabasis*. It has been suggested that choruses habitually removed cloaks early in a comedy, which implies that it was the convention to wear them for their first entry, the *parodos*. The dolphin-riders on the *psykter* wear no cloaks, but those in five of the six later scenes are heavily wrapped. Indeed, no cloaks are worn by any of the choruses in the earlier cluster and transitional scenes, but almost every chorus in the later cluster is wrapped in *chlanis* or *himation*. The *auletes* often moves ahead of them, showing that this is the *parodos*. When the cloaks have been removed – when the old men stand on their heads – the piper turns to face the chorus, or takes his place in their midst. It is likely that at about the time when comedy was officially granted a chorus, a spectacular choral entry, cloaked and led by the *auletes*, became the convention. Casting off their mantles, the 'calculated surprise' when spectacular costumes were revealed could help a chorus to win the prize.[21]

There are two more scenes of choral *parodos*, cloaked and theriomorphic, with men in cock-masks, behind a piper, and a chorus of ostrich-riders.[22] It might be supposed that pictures of men riding beasts are products of the painter's imagination, but it is easier to reconstruct the means by which such a stage spectacle was achieved than to explain why six different painters had identical fantasies. The riders astride ostriches and dolphins have disproportionately small legs and feet hanging down, of course without stirrups. The ostriches are shown with long, thin legs and big bird feet; the dolphins seem to float through the air. Stage animals must have been constructed like 'hobby-horses', with small false legs attached to their sides, and an opening in the back. The 'rider' stepped through this opening and lifted the 'hobby-ostrich' to waist level, securing it with straps over his shoulders. His cloak concealed the joint. His legs were dressed to resemble those of a bird, or, in the case of a dolphin, the rider's real legs were conventionally invisible, perhaps hidden by sea-blue hangings. The paintings show, not what the spectators actually saw, but what they were meant to imagine with suspended disbelief. This conforms with normal practice in scenes derived from tragedy, where 'Attic artists generally ignored drama's signifiers in direct contemplation of what it signified: it is the impact of the dramatic illusion, not the performance, that one can detect on many hundreds of mythological scenes in Attic art'.[23]

With its inclusion in the Great Dionysia, comedy entered history. Reliable if fragmentary records replace the unverifiable and meagre. Official procedures for the production of comedies were adapted from the system which had been established for tragedy when the festival was reorganized in 502–501. Soon after his election eight months before the festival, the responsible *archon* 'granted a chorus' for five comedies, appointing a *choregos* to produce each play. Criteria and methods of selection may have varied. Perhaps access was more direct for established poets than for rookies, and for last year's victor than for the poet who had finished fifth. Judges awarded prizes to the *choregos* and poet of the three best comedies.[24] Titles were frequently derived from the composition of the chorus – *Fig-flies* (Magnes), *Cities* (Eupolis), *Dionysiazousai* (Timokles) – and the audience must have eagerly anticipated the herald's cry of *Eisage ton choron*, 'Bring on your chorus.' How would flies or cities be staged? How would two dozen women of Dionysos behave?

We do not know how *choreutai* were recruited, but visual evidence suggests that comic choruses were largely composed of young men, perhaps *epheboi* between 18 and 20 years old. This seems likely, given the physical demands of chorus work. If so, they must have been temporarily exempted from military service.[25] Their leader (*koryphaios*) was an important figure in comedy; he is the centre of attention in the Aristophanic *parabasis*, speaking directly to the audience on behalf of the poet. His role is greater than Euelpides in *Birds*, or Lamachos in *Acharnians*.[26] Such a part could not be left to an amateur of 20. Before the end of the fifth century, the increasing professionalism of actors would have shown amateur choruses to disadvantage, unless an experienced instructor (*chorodidaskalos*) was engaged to drill the young men, 'knock them into shape', and then provide experienced leadership in performance as *koryphaios*. As actors and narrative plots gradually displaced the chorus at the centre of comedy, experience may have replaced youthful energy as the essential attribute of a *choreut*. Writing near the middle of the next century, Aristotle takes it for granted that a chorus could perform comedy on one occasion, and tragedy on another. If this is taken literally, it means that a class of habitual *choreutai* had emerged in Athens, and perhaps in other cities as well. These could not have been raw *epheboi*; essentially, many of them may have been as accomplished as the professional actors of their time.[27]

ENTER THE ACTOR

A skilful poet or *chorodidaskalos* exploited the spectacle and originality of his chorus at their first entrance, making the maximum impact upon spectators, judges and, incidentally, vase painters. In all of the archaic scenes, only one figure is neither *choreut* nor *auletes*. A little man who faces the chorus of ostrich-riders may be our first glimpse of the *hypokrites*, the 'answerer' who engages a chorus in dialogue and, sometimes, in conflict. Art shows us no more actors for fifty years.[28] It seems likely that the first comic poets to compose dialogue for actors were following the initiative of their tragic counterparts, who were developing tragedy into a narrative form. Aischylos, who won his first victory two years after comedy's *début* at the Dionysia in 486, is said to have introduced the second actor; the third is attributed to Sophokles, perhaps in 467.[29] We have no similar attributions with respect to comic actors, but it is probable that the narrative type of comedy, which required several actors, was becoming established when Krates and Kratinos began their careers about 450. It is uncertain whether the number of actors allocated to a comedy was officially restricted, but the comic actor's increasing importance was recognized when the Lenaia offered the first comic actor's prize *c*.432. Nevertheless, the comic chorus was never overshadowed by actors during the fifth century, retaining its significance in Aristophanes' plays until we reach *Ekklesiazousai* and *Wealth*. Even there, its decline may be more apparent than real.

As early vase painters expected their customers to recognize a comedy by the identity of its chorus, so the titles of most fifth-century comedies refer to that identity. Three-quarters of the titles attributed to the poets who followed Chionides are plural; they name groups, as presented by the chorus. Lost comedies by Magnes, Kratinos, Krates and Hermippos have such titles as *Cheirons*, *Seasons*, *Gods*, *Satyrs*, *Birds*, *Beasts* and *Frogs*. Titles continued to identify the chorus in Aristophanes' time; of his extant comedies, only *Lysistrata*, *Peace* and *Wealth* have titles with different themes. Half of his lost plays and two-thirds of those by his rivals, Eupolis and Kratinos, follow the same practice: *Banqueters*, *Merchant Ships*, *Herdsmen*, *Laws*, *Demes*, *Cities*.[30] Titles of this type become less frequent in the fourth century, but not until *c*.380 do they dwindle into a minority, largely supplanted by the names of individuals, often from myth and legend: *Io*, *Theseus*, *Pasiphae*, *Atalanta*, *Medea*. These subjects were probably burlesqued.

THE CHORUS IN LATER ART

Many plural titles sound as though the chorus must have been spectacular and visually exciting, but despite their interest in the first comic choruses at the Great Dionysia, Athenian vase painters soon turned away from comedy. Between *c*.480 and the early fourth century, no more than five scenes have been interpreted as representing part of a comic chorus. This loss of interest cannot have taken place because actors were supplanting choruses in the collective visual imagination; pictures of comic actors at work do not begin to appear until the last thirty years of the century. Indeed, painters scarcely returned to comedy at all; we have a dozen scenes of actors, or children playing at actors, but the market was essentially left to the coroplasts, who mass-produced terracotta statuettes of popular character types. However, none of these seems to be a comic *choreut*.[31]

A small, rather crudely painted *krater* with two ithyphallic bird-men dancing to the music of an *auletes* has been difficult to date accurately. Green has argued that it refers to Aristophanes' *Birds* (414), but many scholars now believe that it should be dated to 430 or even earlier. The discovery of an Attic *pelike* with an almost identical bird-man, who dances in a similar style to the music of an *auletes*, confirms the later date. Two different artists have been independent witnesses of the costumes, masks and dance of *choreutai* in the same, unknown comedy.[32]

A polychrome scene from the Athenian *agora* shows a man rowing a turquoise fish. His only costume is the actor's flesh-toned suit of tights, without a visible *phallos*. Like single figures in the dolphin-rider series, one man can stand for a chorus. The fish-rider sits atop his mount rather than astride, suggesting that it may be a wheeled device propelled by the oars, rather than a hobby-fish. The entry of a full chorus, rowing a shoal of these vehicles, would have presented a formidable spectacle. No doubt the *choreutai* would dismount in order to dance.[33]

An intriguing red-figured vase, vividly painted by the Athenian Nikias Painter at about the same date as the piscine oarsman, was found at Cyrenaica in Libya. Herakles rides in a chariot driven by Nike (Figure 18). A torch-bearer leads the way, stage-naked but for a cloth worn like a shawl across his shoulders; his wrinkled tights and dangling *phallos* mark him unmistakably as a comic actor. He looks back towards the four centaurs who draw the chariot. Their identical, ill-natured faces are evidently slave-masks. This scene is not to be dismissed as a theatrically impossible artist's fantasy.[34] Technicians whose grandfathers had been capable of devising ostrich-riders would scarcely blench at the challenge of fabricating another theriomorph. The title of Kratinos' *Cheirones* (436) suggests that stage centaurs were not a novelty, and the artist provides enough details to permit us to guess how they were achieved. Each centaur wears a belt where the horse-body meets the human torso, and another just behind the beast's forelegs. While these must belong to the *choreut* wearing the centaur-mask, they were certainly rendered as equine as ingenuity could compass, while the hindquarters either belonged to a second *choreut*, as in a 'pantomime horse', or they were supported by the straps which the painter has shown crossing the human shoulders and fixed to the belts. Equipped like this, a chorus of twenty-four men could have drawn enough chariots to transport half a dozen deities.

Painted early in the fourth century, an Attic scene shows one *choreut* as a woman, who is enveloped in a voluminous, spotted robe (*enkuklon*) with a fringe; it passes respectably over her head like a hood (*kalymma*). Opposite 'her', a young man dances energetically, wearing a *himation*, his chest and right shoulder bare. A mask is pushed to the top of his head; like his partner's mask, it is that of a young wife. The first figure must be a man as well, but the body-language is feminine. Perhaps the painter contrasts this with the fully costumed man's more restrained movement in order to show the viewer that one *choreut* is in character and the other is not, which should signify that the chorus is rehearsing 'offstage', rather than performing before an audience.[35]

Other pictures show choruses costumed identically and dancing in unison. Fragments of a *chous* in the Benaki Museum (380–360) have six men wrapped in a short cloak (*tribon*) and masked as identical middle-aged citizens. At centre is an *aulos* played by a pair of white hands, a painter's convention indicating that the musician is a woman. The *agora* reliefs (350-325) show files of dancing men, who wear the actor's padded tights with a short *chiton*. If their high-stepping dance conceals an artificial *phallos*, these choruses are costumed in the same fashion as comic actors. One scene is evidently a *parodos*, since the chorus follows a piper. Because the reliefs were probably commissioned to commemorate choregic victories, it is possible that they are conventional pictures of a generic chorus. If they are specific, however, little distinguished one fourth-century chorus from another: masks represent either citizens or slaves, but never birds, minotaurs or even foreigners. Lacking the opportunity for fantasy and surprise that Archaic comedy once offered, Aristotle's 'vulgar man' could only dress his comic chorus in purple cloaks, as though they were performing a tragedy, hoping to impress the audience by means which no artistic medium could reproduce.[36]

CHORIC DANCE

The chorus-men in the *agora* reliefs perform the same lively dance step, in knees-up, foot-stamping unison, with heads and bodies swivelling to maintain a vigorous equilibrium. It is tempting to identify this as the *kordax*, which ancient writers name as the characteristic dance of comedy, lascivious, ignoble and obscene. Aristophanes repudiates it in the same *parabasis* in which he deprecates the leather *phallos*. Comic choruses danced other *schemata*, some of which parodied serious dance: the women in *Thesmophoriazousai* dance a tragic *diple*, and in *Wealth* the chorus of old farmers burlesque a dithyramb.[37]

Formation and size

Our evidence for the size and formation of dithyrambic and tragic choruses is probably sound, but sources for comedy are questionable. The theatrical practices described by Iulius Pollux were as remote from his time as Shakespeare is from ours, and to Ioannis Tzetzes, more ancient than Justinian is for us. They had access to authors now lost, but we cannot know how accurately they followed their sources, or how reliable those might have been. Both assert that a comic chorus consisted of twenty-four men, who entered in a formation which, according to Pollux, consisted of six files, four to a file, and four rows, six to a row.[38] Reality can hardly have been this simple. It is unimaginable that two centuries of *chorodidaskaloi* tolerated restriction to an immutable formation.

No doubt the chorus was two-dozen strong in 414, because that is the number of species named in the text of *Birds*. However, we have reasonably good evidence that the tragic chorus changed in size, from twelve to fifteen, early in the fifth century. Literary sources have nothing to say of developments in comedy, but it would be surprising if there were no variations in practice. Were twenty-four dancers the standard for archaic comedies? Here the vases cannot help, because the painters used various numbers, from one to eight, to stand for the whole.[39] Perhaps an original Athenian chorus was sometimes retained for two or three performances in the Attic demes, but touring companies must have devised various alternatives to the difficulty of travelling with two dozen young men.[40] Some cities would have been capable of providing a local chorus, if the visitors brought an experienced *koryphaios* to lead them. This would be easier in the later fourth century, when poets no longer wrote odes that were specific to a particular comedy, merely allowing for choral interludes (*embolima*). This was a practical response to the realities of touring; it made sense to separate the functions of actors and chorus, as a precaution against whatever might befall during a tour. If no local chorus could be found, ready to provide whatever odes they happened to know, the chorus could be altogether omitted.[41]

The chorus in the Greek west

If indigenous Sicilian comedies of the Epicharmos tradition did not employ a chorus, visiting Athenian troupes may have been unable to perform comedies like *Thesmophoriazousai*, in which the chorus is indispensable; but it seems that Taras was able to accommodate them by *c.*370.[42] However, there is little evidence that even the major western Greek cities developed their choral capabilities as more tours passed through. No more than half a dozen vase scenes have figures we can interpret as members of a comic chorus. Scarcely distinguishable from an actor, a fourth-century chorus-man is difficult to recognize. Only when a painter shows several dancers, or an *auletes*, can we be reasonably confident. Artists may have been reluctant to sacrifice narrative space in their economical compositions, except when the chorus itself was the story.

Two Apulian scenes probably show chorus members on a stage, inter-acting directly with actors. Wearing identical costumes, but masked as an old citizen and a younger man, two actors labelled ΧΟΡΗΓΟΣ (*chore-gos*) stand on either side of Pyrrhias (ΠΥΡΡΙΑ), a slave who seems to be declaiming. Aigisthos (ΑΙΓΙΣΘΟΣ), in tragic costume, has entered from the *skene*, surprising the older man. The scene may be a dispute between the leaders of two semi-choruses, who remain in the *orchestra*. In the other scene, two identical men dance vigorously about an altar, their short cloaks flying (Figure 22). They pretend to play *auloi*, while the official piper plays behind a property-tree. Watching from stage right, an actor masked as an old man makes a 'ring' sign. The gesture is enigmatic, except that it is clearly conspiratorial: whatever message it communicates to the piper is not meant for the dancers' eyes.[43]

Two lost vases showed groups of three *choreutai*. Photographed in 1912, one has three old men dancing as a group, but with different steps and gestures. The other scene had identical stage-naked slaves who are grouped symmetrically on an enormous potter's wheel: two face each other in mirror-image, while the third sits in the centre, playing a single *aulos* towards his neighbour's *phallos*, like a snake-charmer. It is uncertain whether these groups stand for larger choruses, or a group reduced for

touring (Figure 19).[44] These scenes were all painted in Taras. Evidence
from other fabrics is scantier still. Neither Sicily nor Paestum has left us
a choric scene or a figurine which has been identified as choric. Campanian artists show little understanding of the theatre, save for the Libation
Painter, but if the pipers in his lively comic scenes accompany a chorus, he
excludes the *choreutai* from his frame.[45]

DECLINE OF THE CHORUS?

In a progressive interpretation of history, matters are always either improv-
ing or going to pot. As often as we read about the 'emergence' or 'rise' of
the chorus, we hear of its 'decline'. If a time came when there were no more
Greek choruses, there was another time when the chorus was yet to come. It
is wiser to understand that in art, there is neither progress nor decay, there
is merely change. No doubt the earliest comedies were entirely choric. Narrative plots, and consequently actors, altered the balance, blending fanciful
fictions with anapaestic social criticism in Aristophanic Old Comedy. It is
folly to pretend that, at that point, comedy had 'achieved its own nature'
and should, or could, have remained as it was. Comedy was engaged with
Athens, and the city itself was changing rapidly as it reacted to defeat, oligarchy and revolt. It is true that in the form in which we have his last two
plays, Aristophanes' chorus has fewer lines than hitherto, but the quanti-
tative role of the chorus in *Ekklesiazousai* (*c.*392) and *Wealth* (388) is partly
attributable to scribal omission of one ode in the former and six in the
latter. Qualitatively, the chorus is as important in *Ekklesiazousai* as it is in
Thesmophoriazousai, and *Wealth* is a different kind of comedy. When next
we encounter comedy scripts, integrated odes have given way to *embolima*,
which were deplored by Aristotle because he believed that the chorus should
be an actor.[46] Had these choral interludes been truly deplorable, audiences
in Athens and throughout the Greek world would have rejected them, but
audiences continued to grow. Texts have not been preserved, and no doubt
few *embolima* were great literature. Neither are Verdi's *libretti*. At their
best, they may have become performance art, blending music, lyrics and
dance, performed by polished *choreutai* and accompanied by distinguished
musicians. That is neither improvement nor decline: it is simply change.[47]

CHAPTER 5

Music in comedy

'Now listen to me', Dionysos tells the shades of Aischylos and Euripides in the Underworld, 'I came down here for a poet. Why? So our city could survive and continue her choral festivals' (*Frogs* 1417–19). The chorus and its music were central to the life of the *polis* and the public events that defined it, and the *choreutai* were its citizens. The chorus was fundamental to comedy, tragedy and satyr play, no less than to dithyramb. 'Bring on your chorus', the herald cried to start the play. And when a chorus sang and danced, it was invariably accompanied by the *aulos*. Greeks used a variety of musical instruments. At the *symposion* an educated man was expected to sing, and play the *barbitos*, the small lyre associated with Dionysos.[1] Apollo's lyre was the *kithara*, a large concert instrument, which could be played alone, or to accompany a soloist. In spite of their divine connections, stringed instruments lacked the power and mobility required to accompany a chorus in a large theatre.

THE AULOS

The *aulos* consisted of a pair of tubular pipes, made of bone, ivory or wood. Unlike a flute, which is played by blowing across a column of air, the *aulos* had a mouthpiece fitted with a double reed, as in an oboe; finger holes governed the length of the air column that vibrated when the musician blew through the reed. The double pipe migrated to Greece from Phrygia by way of Thrace, gaining popularity as festivals multiplied. Easily made and highly portable, it was not difficult to play, although to play it really well required virtuosity. It became ubiquitous, accompanying public sacrifices and processions, private ceremonies like weddings and funerals, and exercise at the *palaistra*; soldiers marched to the *aulos*, and it gave the stroke for rowers on warships.[2] Musicologists believe that the two pipes 'spoke together, perhaps in unison'. Because its tone was 'brilliant and exciting', Plato and Aristotle distrusted the irrational Dionysian emotions the *aulos* aroused. 'Loud and penetrating', it obliged choruses to sing lustily in order to be heard distinctly, but the *aulos* could conveniently hide an occasional mistake. The instrument's range was limited until late in the fifth century, when technical innovations by Pronomos extended its capabilities.[3]

Musicians at festivals

At Athenian festivals, every chorus in dithyramb, tragedy or comedy was accompanied by the *aulos*. Therefore, as many as eighteen musicians would have been needed for the annual Great Dionysia. The *auletes* was linked so closely to choral song and dance that an Attic painter could identify a group of dancers or dolphin-riders as a comic chorus simply by including him in a vase scene. Fifty years before comedy was officially admitted to the Great Dionysia, a beardless piper wearing a striped mantle plays the *aulos* for the Berlin 'knights'; a century later, a heavily bearded man in a *chiton* decorated with mythical beasts plays between ithyphallic bird-men.[4]

Competition between choruses was central to the Great Dionysia and Lenaia in Athens, and to similar festivals wherever there were Greeks. Theirs was a 'militant festival culture', in which a festival inevitably implied *agon*, competition.[5] Musicians were at first paid by the poets, but, according to Plutarch, the dithyrambist Melanippides introduced difficult 'New Music', which could overwhelm choric poetry. Since victory or defeat could depend upon the skill and commitment of the *auletes*, the Assembly passed a law requiring the presiding *archon* to 'allocate a piper to each by lot'.[6] This implies that a pool of musicians was somehow established, and that they submitted to allocation. Moreover, an Athenian vase on which the illustrious *auletes* and composer Pronomos is identified as accompanist to a satyr chorus suggests that the most distinguished *auletai* were not always assured of an assignment within their musical specialities. Perhaps they accepted because victory in Athens could bring fame, which was a marketable commodity for an itinerant musician. It has been suggested that pipers were not named on the commemorative inscriptions (*Fasti*) because they were aliens, who played for hire.[7]

Pipers like Pronomos and musician-composers like Melanippides were prosperous and widely respected, but the work of ordinary musicians was too close to manual labour to earn much respect. Women who played the *aulos* to accompany entertainers such as acrobats, or at the *symposion*, stood low on the social scale. Many were slaves or foreigners, because a male drinking-party was no place for a respectable woman. However, a well-known Athenian *auletris*, or the women whose portraits were painted by Apulian artists in the fourth century, may have been able to perform in public and yet be treated respectfully. If troupes toured with comedies or tragedies that required a chorus, they would be obliged to find one in each town; perhaps the *tritagonist* could double as a *chorodidaskalos*, but an expert piper would be an indispensable colleague.[8]

Musicians and convention

The *auletes* shown in a picture of choral performance often wears a leather harness called a *phorbeia*, which held the mouthpieces of the *aulos* in place, and prevented the musician's lips from parting and releasing the pressure of his breath during strenuous playing. In myth, Athene either invented or found the *aulos*, but she discarded it in disgust at the unsightly way it puffed out her cheeks. In the light of that, it is remarkable that in art the *phorbeia* is worn principally by men. It has been suggested that women used a softer reed because they usually played indoors, and consequently had no need of the harness. However, some women certainly played in the open, with a chorus or at public events. A charming picture on a *krater* painted in Metapontion shows a young *auletris* with cheeks puffed out like balloons, soft reeds notwithstanding. Perhaps the men harboured a larger share of Athene's vanity than their female colleagues (Figure 20).[9]

The piper's special costume was the *xustis*, described as 'a long soft robe of ornately decorated purple fabric, worn by both sexes'. Many pictures, from Athens and the Greek west, show what this official gown looked like: floor-length, long-sleeved and often decorated with a pattern, dyed in rich colours which could not be duplicated in the colour-scheme of a red-figured vase (Figure 21). This splendid garment has much in common with the costume of tragic actors; Plutarch repeats an account of Alkibiades' return to Athens from Samos in 408, in a sumptuously appointed ship, with Chrysogonos, a Pythian Games victor, playing his *aulos* while Kallipides the tragic *hypokrites* called the rowers' stroke. Each wore the *xustis* of his profession. In *Clouds* (70), Pheidippides' indulgent mother envisions him wearing a *xustis* while driving a chariot in the procession of the Panathenaia; the chorus in *Lysistrata* (1190) names it as a rich gown appropriate to the four noble maidens who 'carried a basket' on the same occasion. The *xustis* was thus a ceremonial, festive garment.[10]

Wearing his distinctive costume, an *auletes* must have been conspicuous in the *orchestra* with any comic chorus, no matter how colourful. Little dramatic illusion was expected in comedy, and consequently the source of musical accompaniment did not have to be conventionally invisible, like stagehands (*kuroko*) in Kabuki theatre, who dress in black. When a splendid figure like this made music, in the street outside Philokleon's house, or with the chorus of Acharnian farmers, a literal mind might perceive some incongruity; but Old Comedy was not for the circumscribed imagination. Conventional invisibility could be contrived in special circumstances, as in the scene on a stage in which two dancers pretend to play *auloi*, while the real piper plays his instrument behind a slender tree (Figure 22). Of course the tree is incapable of concealing him, but the gesture of sitting behind it sends the audience a signal that they are to receive him as temporarily invisible. Metatheatre like this is characteristic of Old and Middle Comedy, and the vase painter has participated in its spirit by showing the transparency of its artifice. In the same spirit, painters showed the wrinkles in the actors' 'fleshings' and the seams where they were attached to the 'torso'.[11]

The spatial relationship between chorus and piper fluctuated during the performance of a comedy, and it would be surprising if practice did not change in the course of two centuries. Most pictures show an early stage of development, often with the *auletes* leading the chorus in a dramatic *parodos*, when surprise and delight at novelty and spectacle could make a favourable first impression on audience and judges. The piper may have been the last to leave the stage at the *exodos*, playing the chorus off. In the scenes between, he faced the chorus.[12] This was the most practical position, because they could take visual cues from the accompanist, whose back would be turned to a substantial proportion of the audience, which meant that he could not easily divert their attention from the chorus. This traditional musical relationship remained the proper one in the minds of everyone involved except, perhaps, some virtuoso *auletai*. No doubt comic poets, chorus instructors (*chorodidaskaloi*) and leaders (*koryphaioi*) agreed wholeheartedly with the early tragic poet Pratinas: the *aulos* should be subordinate. 'The muse made song queen; let the pipes dance in her train! The pipe is a servant!'[13]

In some instances, the official piper was openly acknowledged. An old woman asks the *auletes* to accompany her in *Ekklesiazousai* (891). A comic actor on a Campanian vase, who stands upon a low stage, apparently rebukes an *auletris* in the *orchestra*, and someone instructs a girl to play her *aulos* in a fragment of Eupolis. Bdeleklleon recognizes and names Dardanis, the *auletris* who made a special appearance in *Wasps* (1371), and participated in the action.[14] In *Birds*, the chorus refers to the official piper as Chairis and Peisetairos calls him a *phorbeia*-wearing raven (858).[15]

In *Birds*, the role of the *aulos* is unique. In other comedies, the official piper is neither heard nor seen until he leads the chorus into the *orchestra*, playing the entrance song. However, the first music in *Birds* precedes the *parodos*, when Tereus the hoopoe calls upon Prokne the nightingale to awaken, and she summons the birds with her song. Since the *aulos* must represent and then accompany the hoopoe's complex monody, the *auletes* probably either entered earlier than usual or played 'offstage' until the time came to lead the bird-chorus into the *orchestra* (297).[16] Then he seems to have remained in the *orchestra*, in order to accompany the three instalments of a choral song that punctuate the long scene that follows.[17] Next, Tereus presents the nightingale to his guests:

PEISETAIROS God almighty [Zeus], what a beautiful chick! So tender and fair!
EUELPIDES Know what? I'd be glad to spread those drumsticks!
PEISETAIROS She's got quite a [gold] choker, like a debutante [*parthenos*].
EUELPIDES Me, I think I'd also like to give her a kiss.
PEISETAIROS Look, you screw-up, she's got a couple of skewers [spits] for a beak!
EUELPIDES OK, it's like an egg: we'll just have to peel that shell off her head and
    kiss her that way (667–74).

The actors exit into the *skene*, leaving the *orchestra* to the chorus, who address Prokne as 'weaver of springtime tunes on the fair-toned *aulos*', asking her to 'lead off our anapaests' in the *parabasis*.[18]

How was this staged? Prokne may appear as an opulently dressed young woman, probably an *auletris*: the 'spits' were her pipes, and the 'egg-shell' her *phorbeia*. Nevertheless, it was unnecessary to hire a genuine *auletris*, or even to make a Prokne-mask, unless she was to be ironically ugly: she was not required actually to play. The text offers the official piper no cue to leave the *orchestra*, and for a musician capable of accompanying Tereus' complex monody, the anapaests can have presented little challenge. Perhaps this was another metatheatrical scene, in which an 'extra' mimed Prokne and her music, while the *auletes* played, and the audience pretended he was invisible.[19]

MUSICAL LANGUAGE

The metre of spoken dialogue was iambic trimeter, which closely resembled the language Athenians used in the street.[20] Its alternating short and long syllables have a walking rhythm, ta-*dum*, ta-*dum*, ta-*dum*, like Shakespeare's longer pentameters:

The *time* is *out* of *joint*. O *cursèd spite*,
That *ever I* was *born* to *set* it *right*.[21]

Attic Greek differed from English, however, in that syllables were not
simply stressed, but also marked by the musical pitch of the voice. While
in English the stress falls on a long syllable, the Greek 'pitch-accent may
fall on a long or short syllable'.[22]

The chorus leader exchanged spoken dialogue with actors, but because
our manuscripts lack speech headings, it is uncertain whether the whole
chorus, smaller groups or individual *choreutai* were ever assigned a few lines
of spoken dialogue. Choral passages are frequently anapaestic tetrameters,
each foot comprising two short followed by one long syllable – ta-ta-*dum*.
Its eight feet are longer and, consequently, slower than the trimeters of
dialogue.[23] Metre was not as simple as it seems, because voice pitch varied
the relative values of syllables, but the rhythmic effect must have been
subtler, and less like a doggerel, than some English translations. The chorus
often performed the *parodos* and *exodos* in a 'marching' anapaestic rhythm,
but in comedy this metre became associated so closely with the *parabasis*
that, according to Pollux, its verses were known as anapaests, even when
composed in other metres. Thus, the *koryphaios* or the chorus introduce the
parabasis as 'our anapaests' in *Acharnians*, *Knights* and *Birds*.[24] Evidently
the Athenian audience was alert to prosody. The chorus delivered their
anapaests in a manner somewhere between rhythmic speech and outright
song, accompanied by the *aulos*. This was known as *parakataloge*, which has
been interpreted as 'chant' or 'recitative'.[25] It may have consisted of a simple
musical line subordinated to the sense of the words, while maintaining the
anapaestic rhythm. As in Verdi's *recitativo*, passions such as Aristophanic
indignation against Kleon may have permitted some dramatic dynamics,
in which case 'chant' would be the less appropriate term.

Choral passages of lyric, often with complicated and varied metres, were
sung as we understand singing. Some lyrics must have been as complex
and dramatic as tragic odes, because comedies could burlesque myth and
tragedy. Between the *parodos* and the *parabasis*, the chorus could engage in
debate or conflict, with the comic hero (*Acharnians*, *Birds*), his opponent
(*Knights*, *Wasps*) or itself (*Lysistrata*). After the resolution, choral lyrics
sometimes alternate with the leader's anapaests. Later in the comedy, the
chorus might be called upon to perform a variety of lyrics, which were
frequently cast in a familiar and relatively simple mould. West suggests
that some are close to popular music: 'they give us a distinct impression
of genuine forms of popular song, for example in the wedding hymns at
the end of *Peace* and *Birds* and the amorous serenades in *Ekklesiazousai*'.[26]

Aristophanes confirms this in the *parabasis* of *Knights*, where he reminds the audience that the lyrics of his older contemporary Kratinos had been favourites of the *symposion*. 'At a party there was no singing anything but "Goddess of bribery with shoes of impeach wood" and "Builders of handy hymns", so lush was his flowering! But now you see him drivelling around town, his frets falling out . . .' (529–32).

Choral music

Vocally, there was much for the young men in the chorus to learn. Like any choir they had to control their breathing, which is difficult when simultaneously singing and dancing. Large theatres demand voice projection, particularly in the open air; and there was no guarantee that audiences would maintain a respectful silence. A smooth blend of voices was important, but their words had to be audible over the piercing note of the *aulos*, and clear enunciation was expected: Greeks were attuned to the smallest errors in diction.[27] While none of this can have been easy, the demands did not exceed the capabilities of generations of young *choreutai*. Harmony had not yet been invented. While the chorus sang in unison, the *aulos* would 'duplicate the vocal melody' and the metre dictated by the verse. Greek choral singing does not seem to have required a special, acquired voice tone, as for example in Chinese classical opera, but did *choreutai* simulate women's voices when they sang the odes in *Lysistrata* or *Ekklesiazousai*? Theodoros changed his voice to play tragic women, but he was a specialized impersonator. The high-pitched *aulos* was capable of providing 'registers and tones not easily available to the singing adult male voice', but did it? Praxagora tells the women how to behave like men, but not how to sound like them. Reporting events at the Assembly, Chremes says the strangers were pale, but fails to mention their voices. If the chorus sang baritone, perhaps the audience was accustomed to it and did not care.[28] Song was still queen, verse trumped music.

THE NEW MUSIC

A prize for comic actors was first awarded at the Lenaia about 432, which is very near the date of our earliest extant picture of an actor wearing comic undercostume.[29] Both are signs that this new type of performer was changing comedy as Athenians had known it for half a century. A primarily choric form was in the process of transformation into narrative drama. Dithyramb remained strictly choral, which may explain why musical innovations began there. A significant proportion of our information

about these developments comes from comic poets, who unanimously
loathed the New Music. 'Exaggeration is a truth that has lost its temper',
said Khalil Gibran; perhaps the poets exaggerated, but here we are only
concerned with music insofar as they perceived it, and as it affected comedy. Pherekrates has left us a field guide to New Musicians in a fragment
of his comedy *Cheiron*. It is a speech by Music, whose exponential abuse
by several lovers in succession she describes in musical terms with sexual
overtones. They were Melanippides of Melos, Kinesias the Athenian, who
turns up in Cloudcuckooland as a rejected pretender to birdliness (1373–
1408), Phrynis of Lesbos, who carries his lyre on a comic vase painted in
distant Paestum halfway through the next century (Figure 23), Timotheos
of Miletos and Philoxenos of Kythera.[30]

These men were all dithyrambic poets and composers, and all were
foreigners except for Kinesias who therefore, Pherekrates implies, ought to
have known better. They were true professionals, drawn to Athens by the
fame and prizes offered at the great festivals. Dissatisfied with simple music
which aspired only to accompany, they sought liberation from the tyranny
of words. New Music was difficult and showy; like Tereus the hoopoe's
aria, it required musicians whose superior skills were beyond the reach of
an amateur chorus.[31] Melanippides substituted an instrumental *intermezzo*
for part of the traditional sung dithyramb. His choral music 'ignored the
natural tonal accent and the vowel quantities of spoken Greek, thereby
liberating itself from the hegemony of the poet's words'.[32] Novelties like
this drew public attention to the musician, whose virtuosity could excite
an audience when the chorus could not.

Dithyramb led the way in musical innovation; tragedy followed, and
comedy jeered. Dikaiopolis says he 'died on the rack' when the New
Musician Chairis played a tune (*Ach.* 15–16). Aristophanes accused both
Euripides and the younger Agathon of indulging in new-fangled musical
stunts. In the course of their competition in the Underworld, Aischylos
mocks Euripides for stretching the same vowel over many notes: 'ei-ei-ei-ei-
ei-ei-lissete', in both his choruses and monodies.[33] Again, Aischylos suggests
that the accompaniment leads the poetry by needlessly repeating words:

> But he flew up to the sky
> on the lightest of wingtips,
> leaving me but woes woes,
> and tears tears from my eyes
> did I shed in my misery.
>   (1352a–5)

Clouds is about conflict between generations. Inevitably, father and son squabble over tastes in music. Strepsiades has included Pheidippides in a banquet with his friends, and called upon his son to take a turn in the traditional after-dinner singing. 'First of all I asked him to pick up his lyre and sing a song by Simonides', as an elderly parent today might ask for a 'golden oldie' like 'White Cliffs of Dover'. With a sneer, the boy substituted the fifth-century equivalent of 'rap': 'he tossed off some speech by Euripides about how a brother, god save me, was screwing his sister *by the same mother*!'[34] New Music is frequently compared to creepy-crawlies, burrowing, twisting and 'wi-i-i-nding'. In *Thesmophoriazousai*, Agathon is overheard rehearsing a new choral *stasimon*. 'What's that he's vocalizing,' asks Euripides' Kinsman, 'ant tracks or something?' (100) Later, Euripides calls for a 'Persian dance tune' from a piper named Teredon, whose name means 'shipworm' (1175). Pherekrates' character Music complains of Timotheos' 'winding paths of anthills', and that Philoxenos filled her with caterpillars, like a cabbage, very much as teredos riddle a ship's hull.

The comic poet Strattis called Kinesias 'chorus-killer' because young citizen-amateurs could not cope with the New Music. The poet Platon recalled that in his youth, 'if anyone danced well . . . it was a good show, but now they don't do anything but stand stock-still as if stunned, and howl'.[35] At the same time, actors were becoming more professional, which highlighted choral ineptitude. Inevitably, the chorus was marginalized.

SONG AND DANCE

Plutarch quotes an epigram of Phrynichos, an early tragic poet who boasted, 'As many figures Dance gives me as baleful night makes waves upon a stormy sea.' Athenaios says Aischylos 'created many dance-steps himself and passed them on to the members of his choruses', and the comic poet Kratinos was one of those 'called "dancers" because not only did they integrate their own dramas with choral dancing, but, quite apart from their own compositions, they taught anyone who wanted to learn to dance'.[36] It is likely that Aristophanes participated in the composition of music and dance; in passages of lyric verse and implicit stage directions he often requires actors to dance as well as sing.

Tereus' monody in *Birds* was exceptionally difficult; but most of Aristophanes' solos are parodies of tragedy, which require expert mimicry rather than mellifluousness. In the course of the poetic *agon* in the Underworld, the Euripides-actor mocks Aischylos' verse by assuming a pompous and monotonous delivery, 'thratto-thratto-thratto-thrat', and Aischylos in his

travesty of Euripides must squeak and quaver over the crawly spiders which
'wi-i-i-i-nd' through New Music (*Frogs* 1283–95, 1309–22). When playing
Agathon, an actor could parody the awkward capering of an entire chorus
of gawky youths, as they tried to be tragic maidens, as well as the falsetto
voice of their young *koryphaios*; as the poet's slave, the same actor would
have to find a third style of parody (*Thes*. 101–29, 39–58). Versatility in
modes of clowning, rather than vocal refinement, could pull off such a
tritagonist's tour de force.[37] Mockery aside, *protagonist*s are seldom called
upon to sing anything more difficult than straightforward hymns and folk-
songs in ceremonial scenes like Dikaiopolis' Acharnian Dionysia, Trygaios'
sacrifice to Peace, and his wedding, where he sings and dances with the
chorus (*Ach*. 263–79, *Peace* 974–1015, 1320–59).[38]

The Spartan Ambassador begins the celebration at the conclusion of
Lysistrata with a 'two-step' (*dipodia*, 1243), while he sings to Artemis. The
auletes, or perhaps a specialist musician, accompanies him on the bagpipes,
which suggests this was a Lakedaimonian folk-dance. The disputed distribution of roles in this scene precludes certainty, but it seems likely that the
protagonist was the dancer. The title role offers him excellent opportunities,
except the chance to demonstrate versatility. As Lysistrata he could only
watch the dance; therefore Aristophanes sends the actor into the *skene* for
fifty-five lines, to change his mask and costume, returning in the role of
the Spartan to cut a caper that might clinch the *protagonist's* prize. The
deuteragonist gets his chance in *Wealth*, when Cario leads the chorus of
poor farmers in celebration of their future affluence. This takes the form of
a dialogue, sung and danced: he mimes the Cyclops, then Circe, while the
Chorus mime lambs, goats and pigs. This scene parodies a dithyramb by
Philoxenos, who filled Music with caterpillars; but it is also an opportunity
for the actor to display his versatility.[39]

It should come as no surprise if we were to learn that *choregoi* tried
to avoid producing Aristophanes because he made expensive demands.
As though twenty-four bird-costumes and -masks were not enough, his
script requires four bird-extras in extravagant plumage, richly costumed
Prokne and a specialized singer to stand in for Tereus in the monody. The
conclusion of *Thesmophoriazousai* could not have been performed without
a 'guest artist', a dancer whose stage name was Elaphion. And the poet's
choregos at the Lenaia in 422 was obliged to pay half a dozen specialized
dancers to perform one spectacular scene.

Wasps concludes with a dance *agon*. Old Philokleon has abandoned his
crankiness, and attends a *symposion*, where he is charmed by the *auletris*

and her music. He gets drunk, abducts her and brings her home, where she plays for him. Rejuvenated, he dances in the style of Phrynichos:

> Look here,
> the opening steps – where you bend the torso vigorously,
> how the snout snorts, and
> the spine cracks! Phrynichos crouches like a rooster –
> kicking his legs sky high.
> The arsehole splits
> because now my hip joints
> roll smoothly in their sockets!   (1484–95)

Three dancers enter, each in succession challenging him to an *agon*, no doubt dancing to a parody of New Music as used by their father, Karkinos the tragic poet: and the old man defeats them all.

Since no ordinary actor could dance that scene, Aristophanes used a device that he later repeated in *Lysistrata*: he sent the *protagonist* into the *skene* for thirty-three lines, just long enough to remove his mask and costume, and for a specialist dancer to put them on. Perhaps the challengers were hired to play themselves; Karkinos was a real poet, who may have joined his defeated sons in the *exodos*. The scene was a ballet within a play. The chorus could only stand and watch.[40]

CHAPTER 6

Acting, from lyric to dual consciousness

The dominant choric poetry of the sixth century was lyric: hymns, dithyrambs, or songs of praise for a patron or an athletic victor. The earliest poets are too legendary for strict credibility. Herodotus' claim that Arion invented dithyramb is not strengthened by his anecdote of the poet's rescue from pirates by a friendly dolphin, contradictory tales about Alkman are almost as numerous as his surviving fragments and Stesichoros was allegedly buried in several places.[1] Lyric poets of the later sixth and early fifth centuries, however, are more reliably documented, and significant portions of their works have survived. Composing songs for the ruling classes in much of the Greek world, Simonides, Pindar and Bacchylides were itinerants. An aristocratic native of Boiotia, Pindar enjoyed a celebrity that took him to Macedonia, Asia Minor, Cyrene and Sicily: like Aischylos, Pindar and Simonides both sojourned at the court of Hieron of Syrakousai (478–467/6). The poets taught their lyrics to choruses of young men and personally led their public performances. In a fragment, Archilochos boasts that he knows how to lead the 'beautiful dithyramb of the lord Dionysos' while appropriately drunk with wine. He refers to the poet as *exarchos*, where he improvised verses, and they answered with a refrain.[2]

While other lyric forms declined along with noble patronage, dithyramb was co-opted by the Athenian democracy. The city emerged as a rewarding market for poets, developing its Great Dionysia and the *choregia* as expressions of the *polis*. Competition between dithyrambic choruses of men and boys was pursued as enthusiastically as were athletics, because everyone was eligible to compete. Tragedy and comedy were fresh choral forms, which arose in the Attic countryside; composed by citizen amateurs, and performed by well-drilled citizens, the new choral forms shook off their rustic origins and took their place beside dithyramb as public dance-poetry. Performed in the competitive context of the Dionysia, comedy evolved rapidly, transforming itself into dramatic art. As poets strove to devise innovations that might bring victory, they turned to actors for their potential as the instruments of narrative, dramatic conflict and its resolution.[3]

BEGINNERS ON STAGE

'Now, tragedy's stages of development, and those responsible for them, have been remembered', says Aristotle, 'but comedy's early history was forgotten because no serious interest was taken in it.' In his own time, he complains, 'actors have greater influence on the stage than poets'.[4] The Greek actor had come a long way rather quickly: it is unlikely that the first *komodos* took the stage much earlier than 450, but by the middle of the fourth century he had become a 'star'. His development followed a trajectory that is well documented in the later national theatres of France and England, where actors transformed the plays of great poets – Racine, Shakespeare, Molière, Jonson – into classics. Their first audiences went to see Shakespeare's new tragedy, or Jonson's new comedy, but once *Hamlet* and *The Alchemist* had become canonical, a new generation of spectators wanted to see how Mr Garrick interpreted Hamlet or Abel Drugger. For this purpose, the actor had become more important than the poet. Garrick interpreted these parts some 130 years after they were created, and Aristotle's complaint followed Aischylos' first victory at about the same interval of years.[5] Perhaps there is a natural rhythm to these events, beginning and culminating with actors.

Greeks felt compelled to name an 'inventor' of phenomena of all sorts: Dionysos of wine, Kadmos of the alphabet, Alkman of love poetry; both the anchor and the potter's wheel were attributed to Anacharsis, a Scythian poet. According to the Parian marble, the comic chorus was invented by Sousarion and produced by the people of Ikarion at some date between 581 and 560. Thespis, the inventor of tragedy, came from 'Ikarios', and the same village is named as home to both Chionides and Magnes. Athenaios ironically attributes this concentration of creativity in one village to wine, but while we may share his sceptical view of this coincidence and, indeed, of Sousarion himself, early vase scenes are tangible evidence that comic choruses were performing in Attica near the date given by the Parian inscription.[6]

Between 560 and 530, Athenian painters discovered a fresh Dionysian subject for their *symposion* vessels. These black-figured scenes show groups of men in alien costumes, dancing, walking on stilts or riding other men masked as horses. Most are accompanied by an *auletes*, which confirms that these groups are choruses.[7] Archilochos leaves us in no doubt that dithyramb was associated with Dionysos, but while it was not incorporated in the Great Dionysia until *c.*509–507, it was performed before the middle of the sixth century. These new choruses are potentially outrageous; the dancers' disguise as foreigners or animals freed them from Hellenic constraints. They must be the 'volunteers' (*ethelontai*) who performed comedies on the festival's fringe before they were admitted to compete in an official *agon.*[8] Their performances are likely to have been brief, comprising an *eisodos* in costume, a *parabasis* with topical satire and vulgar jokes at the expense of well-known individuals, concluding with a swift and prudent exit. This type of performance could not sustain a narrative, because the necessary characterization would be interrupted and subverted as soon as the chorus turned to address their fellow-citizens. Their masquerade as aliens or animals was transparent; everyone knew who they were.

From poet to actor

Like the professional lyric poets, the citizen-poet of Old Comedy taught his chorus the verse, music and dance-*schemata* he had composed. He led them in performance as *exarchos*, and if, like Archilochos, he was emboldened by a cup or three of wine, that counted as an offering to the god. He probably delivered much of his satire as a solo.[9] Since there is unlikely to have been either conflict or dialogue between chorus and leader, we need not scrutinize the archaic poet-*exarchos* for the origins of the comic actor. It is more likely that comedy subsequently adapted the idea of the actor from tragedy, Epicharmos the Sicilian, or both.

Whether his name was Thespis, Choirilos or Aischylos, one man cannot have 'invented' tragedy from scratch. Like comedy and dithyramb, it must have begun as a folk-chorus, perhaps lamenting the downfall of a legendary hero. No doubt the poet led the chorus until somebody broke with tradition and began the transformation of tragedy from choric threnody into dramatic narrative. Handing over the leadership of the chorus, perhaps to a senior *choreut*, the poet put on a *prosopeion*, the mask which embodied the hero's identity, and engaged the chorus or its leader in dialogue. With that first dialogue, our poet became an *hypokrites* (answerer), an 'actor' as we understand the word.[10]

The fundamental relationship between a chorus, its leader and the *hypokrites* remained unchanged until a second actor was introduced, which enabled dialogue between actors without participation by the chorus. Aristotle credits Aischylos with this innovation, which took place no later than 472, when he produced *Persians* with two actors. Such a novelty might account for his first victory in 484.[11] However, the second actor may be another 'invention' arbitrarily linked to a famous name, which could have been attributed to one of the poet's predecessors or rivals, Choirilos, Phrynichos or Pratinas. In any case, it is likely that the Kleisthenic reorganization in 502–501 modified the choregic rules to allow each *protagonist* an assistant, a *deuteragonist*. By 458, three actors were permitted in tragedy.[12]

First comic actors

There is no similar account of the comic actor's origin. Sousarion is linked with the chorus, which was given a distinctive collective identity, as suggested by vase scenes and titles like *Persians*, *Beggars* (Chionides), *Lydians* and *Birds* (Magnes). Comedy must have remained a musical spectacle until the first actor assumed a separate character. We can only guess when or how this happened. If tragedy was admitted to the Great Dionysia only after the first actors gave it dramatic form, perhaps comedy followed its lead before participating officially in the festival. Perhaps it is not coincidental that the earliest picture which may, conceivably, show a comic actor, was probably painted to commemorate that first comic *agon* in 486 (Figure 24). One side shows a chorus of dolphin-riders, popular with artists that year and possibly victorious. The reverse has a chorus of ostrich-riders. Between these and the tall *auletes* stands a diminutive figure who wears a half-mask. Below the mask's black glaze the little man's beard protrudes, painted in applied light brown. Although he meets Csapo's iconographic criteria identifying an *exarchos*, Sifakis is surely right to suggest that he is also the 'ancestor of the actor', because he assumes a character. Confronting the chorus, his body-language expresses an attitude, signalling confident authority with arm akimbo, his chin thrust defiantly towards the leading *choreut* upon his lofty mount. Their dialogue is our earliest example of dramatic conflict in comedy. The mask may convey a clue to his character, which has been interpreted as Pan: some photographs seem to show horns, but direct study resolves these into a crest of hair, with some dark, worn spots in the fabric. The mask lacks the grotesque features found on Old Comedy masks towards the end of the century, which were regarded as base and inferior (*phaulos*); it is noble, with the high forehead and straight nose which contemporary art attributed to a god or hero. Perhaps his diminutive stature identified his part in a comic treatment of a myth with an Egyptian setting, as the ostriches seem to imply. Whatever his character, the artist directs the viewer to perceive the *exarchos*/proto-actor as secondary; on a vase, the chorus was 'the obvious and in practice probably the only way to represent the play'.[13]

PLOT AND THE RISING ACTOR

If the little man is the first recorded comic actor, the composers of comedies were beginning to adopt tragic practices, experimenting with actors and, consequently, with plot. Poets and actors could hardly fail to learn by watching each other at each year's Dionysia. In 472, Magnes won his first victory; he may have taken a lesson in plot construction by attending Aischylos' *Persians* at the same festival. Plot, and the actors who propel it, were essential to the emerging dramatic comedy. Comic plots are fundamentally different from tragic, of course, and by the 470s the Sicilian Epicharmos was writing plotted comedies for several actors. Aristotle refers to him when he says 'the composition of plots originally came from Sicily'.[14] Aischylos may have met him or seen his work at Hieron's court. Frequent travel between Athens and Syrakousai was the principal means by which poets in both cultural centres became aware of each other. No doubt influence was exchanged in both directions, and perhaps as a consequence, after a 'dark age' (*c*.480–450) during which we have no direct knowledge of its development, Athenian comedy emerged as a narrative form, with plots that employed several actors. The mythological burlesques of Kratinos probably owed something to Epicharmos, who favoured this type of comedy: both poets wrote a *Bousiris* and a *Dionysoi*.[15]

A prize for acting in tragedy was at last established *c*.449, and between 444 and 441 the ancient festival of Lenaia was, for the first time, celebrated in the Theatre of Dionysos and began to award a prize for comic poets. Like the Great Dionysia, it was financed by a *choregia*, and by 432 there were prizes for actors in both genres, recognizing them as specialists and setting them on the path towards professionalism. The poet's withdrawal from performance was now complete because, as Slater points out, 'separation of poets from actors is a natural result as the latter's part in the drama increased in both size and complexity'.[16] Poetic and histrionic talent are seldom found in equal measure in the same person. Sophokles' weak voice is said to have persuaded him to relinquish acting in favour of Tleptolemos, who 'continually acted for him'. The wisdom of his withdrawal became clear the first time a 'best actor' award was won by the *protagonist* in a losing play. In comedy, the inevitable was clearer, and may have come earlier: the funniest writer, set upon his feet before an audience, can be disastrous. Krates acted, but only before he became a poet.[17]

During most of the fifth century, the successful pursuit of dramatic poetry required a level of education, and an expenditure of time, that were available only to the Athenian elite.[18] Therefore, the first poet who decided to give up acting would have to search for a substitute amongst his own class. The only experienced actors available must have been his rivals, other poets. Perhaps he approached one of these, whose comedies were less successful than his performances in them. Failing that, he could take a chance with a novice, someone who was always the life of the *symposion*. Evidently the experiment succeeded, because a distinct class of actors emerged, specialists who were not poets. As professionalism developed, and an actor could hope to earn a living wage, the three-actor structure probably encouraged an informal system of apprenticeship and promotion through the ranks, opening the field to talented recruits of diverse origins, some of whom came from abroad. Mynniskos of Chalkis is said to have served as *deuteragonist* for Aischylos, becoming one of the first victorious *protagonists*.[19]

Near the date of the first actor's prize, some vase painters returned to comic subjects. Now most of the subjects were actors, instead of the choruses of fifty years before:

The fact of their appearance, despite the continuing existence of the convention of identifying comedies by their choruses, is a sign that the public recognized an important change in the nature of comedy. The part played by actors in the totality of a performance is seen as increasingly crucial and interesting. They are something the public can now relate to. The implication is that coherent plots were becoming normal.[20]

The renewed interest on the part of Athenian painters was limited, and they failed to establish a convention for representing comic actors. While scenes based upon tragedy show figures as though they were the actual people of myth, some comic scenes painted in Athens between 430 and 400 are inconclusive experiments with realism.

These vases tell us little about acting in the time of Aristophanes, because none shows a dramatic scene in progress, although some yield glimpses of a performance. An actor as Perseus dances on a stage, watched by judges. Slaves carry a loaf on a spit, a beardless man runs with a large wine-jug, and a slave with torches leads a spectacular entrance by Herakles and Nike, who ride in a chariot drawn by centaurs. Children costumed as actors seem to be posed, static.[21] Other pictures are fragmentary or worn. In all we have fifteen reasonably distinct pictures of actors, with eighteen masks, all male except for Nike. The masks and costumes show that one fundamental principle had already been established: the comic character is *phaulos* and *geloios* (inferior, laughable), and his appearance violates the classical ideal. However, at this period there is no consensus as to the *manner* of the violation. Most of the actors are depicted as stage-naked, perhaps because the comic undercostume was an interesting novelty. Wherever the artificial *phallos* is shown, it is already grotesquely large, but in scenes earlier than *c.*415 the torso is not yet padded. In similar fashion, while some masks have the bridgeless nose which became the conventional inversion of the ideal 'Grecian profile' of heroic sculpture, others display jutting noses, tubular or aquiline, under a bulging forehead, whereas the high forehead of an ideal profile is directly aligned with the nose (Figure 25).[22]

ACTORS IN SOCIETY

We know little about individual comic actors in the classical period. The *Fasti* omit their names, and other inscriptions are fragmentary. References in literature are brief. Poets attacked each other, and ridiculed tragic actors, but in all of Aristophanes there is only one joke about a *komodos*.[23] There are more anecdotes of *tragodoi*, in part because some became transnational stars in the fourth century. Several were chosen to undertake diplomatic missions, and Alexander gathered them about him.[24] Comedy and the actors who performed in it were less well regarded, perhaps because of a cultural preference for high seriousness. There is little evidence of prejudice against actors in the far-flung Greek lands, but segregation by genre was more complete than in any theatre in subsequent European tradition: neither actors nor poets crossed genre lines. This was not mere specialization, nor was it legislated. Comedy and tragedy were sealed environments according to custom.[25]

Neither poets nor actors were regarded as bohemian. The theatre sometimes ran in families, but 'theatre people' were never a subculture. Heredity was customary in other callings and pursuits, both humble and exalted. Alkibiades was nephew and ward of Perikles, Speusippos succeeded his uncle Plato at the head of the Academy. Aristophanes' son Araros became a poet, and an actor named Philippos may have been a descendant. Names also ran in families. Euphorion son of Aischylos son of Euphorion of Kolonos was a successful *didaskalos* for revivals of his father's plays. One Kallippos, who acted in a comedy at Delos in 268 and his brother Kallias, three times Lenaia victor, were probably sons of Kallippos son of Kallias who acted in the *Heniochos* of Menander at the City Dionysia in 312.[26]

CASTING

How many actors?

Tragedy 'achieved its own nature' with three actors, says Aristotle. Perhaps nature was more flexible in Old Comedy. Three actors could not sustain the principal roles in *Peace* and *Birds*, while somehow 'doubling' the succession of minor characters who make brief appearances after the *parabasis*. One or two small-part players were indispensable; perhaps they were 'apprentices', novices beginning their training.[27] Several vase scenes show four masked and costumed figures, but since the plays are unidentified, we cannot be sure that all represent speaking characters. Extant New Comedy scripts never call for more than three actors, but most are too fragmentary to be certain.[28] Thus, we cannot be sure that a 'rule of three actors' always applied to comedy, either as a regulation of the Athenian *choregia* or simply a custom. The *archon* assigned the *protagonist* to 'act the play', with the assistance of a *deuteragonist* and *tritagonist*, whom he may have paid from his own purse. Perhaps mute extras, small-part actors and special appearances by celebrity dancers or pipers were the responsibility of the *choregos* who authorized them.

Doubling opportunities

It is frequently assumed that actors and poets were hampered by restrictions which obliged them to resort to awkward expedients like doubling and role-splitting. For example, one practicable doubling scheme for *Birds* assigns nine parts to the *deuteragonist*. A role like Theseus in *Oidipous at Kolonos* must be played by two actors, in different scenes. A device like this is deplored as clumsy work on the part of Sophokles, unbelievable for the audience and destructive of the actor's 'identification' with his character. Sifakis shows, on the contrary, that this could be deliberately contrived as an opportunity for an actor. When Sophokles wrote with the *physis* of his actors in mind, we should understand that he created opportunities for his leading man to display his best abilities. Thus, the *protagonist* who played Antigone would have taken his assistant's place after the *katastrophe*, when the shattered Kreon's great aria would offer him 'ample scope for a full exhibition of histrionic virtuosity'. After all, there was no prize for 'best supporting actor'.[29]

Similar practices were normal in comedy. It was physically possible for one actor to play Peisetairos (*Birds*) throughout, but a *protagonist* could hardly overlook the opportunity of cameos like Herakles or Poseidon (1565–1693). An assistant would double as Peisetairos while his chief got the laughs. Meanwhile, an apprentice could learn about comic timing by playing the barbarian god. While the *protagonist* in *Frogs* would certainly play Dionysos before the *parabasis*, in the Underworld scene (830–1481) he could choose either Aischylos or Euripides, according to his *physis*: here, Dionysos becomes at best a *tritagonist*'s role. Lysistrata appears to be conceived for a single actor, but she fails to preside over the reconciliation she has brought about. Perhaps the poet, mindful of a particular *protagonist*'s peculiar accomplishment, freed him to show off his Dorian singing and dancing as the Spartan delegate (1242–72). When we grow accustomed to the notion that doubling and part-splitting were opportunities for the actor, fresh openings for *tours de force* by *protagonist*s become apparent. To do that, we must abandon inappropriate assumptions, and recognize that the Athenian audience had no expectations inherited from the nineteenth-century Theatre of Illusion, that subordinate actors had no expectation of equal opportunity and that nobody had heard of Stanislavsky.

Nothing to do with Stanislavsky

If some Greek theatrical practices seem to us to imperil the dramatic illusion of tragedy, we need feel no anxiety for Old Comedy, which is intensely metatheatrical and self-referential, and almost entirely disregards illusion. At any moment a quip may draw attention to an individual in the audience, and the *parabasis* addresses the citizens directly, simultaneously drawing attention to the poet. Xanthias asks whether he is to begin *Frogs* with the usual jokes. Even when the actor who plays Trygaios (*Peace*) leaves off calling upon the operator of the crane to be careful, the manifest unreality of his mask and costume reminds the viewer that he is only a man 'dressed up being funny'. Comedy cannot violate, rupture or breach illusion, because it creates none: we must inflate a balloon before we can prick it. Tragedy seeks to bind actors and audience in a tacit contract, exchanging willing suspension of disbelief for *katharsis*, but comedy establishes complicity in a comic response to life which, in Aristophanes, can approach conspiracy.[30] These objectives are so diverse, we scarcely need to wonder why no actor practised both genres.

   It is sometimes said that tragic acting was representational, and comic, presentational. Stanislavsky and Brecht are invoked, together with fragments of their theories of 'building a character' from within, or 'demonstrating the stranger' from a distance. Modern theory can sometimes illuminate ancient practice without fatal anachronism, but these two processes were designed to address perceived flaws in acting methods which were specific to their time, and inevitably alien to classical Greece. Moreover, while the means of achieving the Brechtian *Verfremdungseffekt* was conceived as the antithesis of Stanislavsky's system (he never referred to a 'Method'), Greek actors in both genres had much in common. Their physical techniques, in particular, were founded upon a shared aesthetic, which the tragic actor sought to embody, and the comic actor to invert.

VOICE, SPEECH, MOVEMENT

An actor attended carefully to his vocal technique, because his voice was assessed and evaluated by audiences and judges alike. He needed to know how to project without shouting; theatres were large, and few can have been as acoustically perfect as Epidauros. It was partly for the cultivated beauty of their voices, and their skill in delivery, that tragic actors were chosen to carry out diplomatic missions; but according to Plutarch, Demosthenes turned to the comic actor Satyros when he wanted to learn 'delivery and disposition of his words'.[31]

We do not know how much characterization – gender, age, class, region – actors introduced into their speech at the time of Aristophanes. When playing a woman, did an actor change his voice? That seems likely, in view of the emphasis upon speech. Perhaps this is what Aristotle means when he says that other actors sounded artificial when one compared them with Theodoros, who specialized in tragic women's roles. He created the illusion that his voice was that of his character. When he won his first victory *c.*390 this would have been an innovation; but Csapo argues that, by the time of Menander, vocal characterization was 'systematic and extensive'.[32]

An actor could show off his vocal versatility by playing a variety of character types in a single performance. Tragedies offered the opportunity to excel in three distinct modes of delivery: song, unaccompanied speech and, between these, *parakataloge*, usually translated as 'recitative', which was accompanied by the *aulos*. Comedy has a greater variety of verse-forms, and may consequently have required even more versatility; many of its songs were simple, and ordinary comic dialogue is relatively idiomatic, but actors had to be able to imitate tragic modes as well. Thus, mimicry was an important accomplishment, as reflected in anecdotes about Parmeno, whose pig's squeal was proverbial, and Theodoros, who could mimic the windlass of the *mechane*, the derrick that 'flew in' a god to conclude some tragedies.[33] Audiences were alert to distinctions between verse-forms, and attuned to subtleties of speech. Aristophanes' chorus leader could refer to the anapaests of the *parabasis* without puzzling them. And when the tragic actor Hegelochos slightly 'fluffed' one word, so that 'calm' sounded like 'weasel', at least three comic poets were able to make the audience laugh at the memory. Little wonder that Hermon, intent upon his vocal exercises, missed an entrance cue.[34]

Comic speech sometimes parodied tragic declamation, which was regarded as beautiful and elevated. Demosthenes attributed the excellence of Aischines' speaking voice to his previous career as a tragic actor, but we cannot know what qualities were considered effective. We have no means of discerning the aesthetic standard of beauty in speech, or its opposite, but we can deduce more about the visual style of acting, relative to the shared aesthetic which Greeks derived from *sophrosyne*, the ideal of 'control of emotions and refinement of manners' evolved by the same social class that produced the first poets and actors. The characters of tragedy are *spoudaios*, *beltion*, serious and better than ordinary people, while comic characters are base and laughable. Thus, the deportment of the former should be formed by *sophrosyne*, and the latter by its reverse. In everyday life, *sophrosyne* was expressed by emotional restraint, and the behaviour which went with it. Grace was cultivated, gesticulation and grimace avoided. A gentleman never hurried.[35] Conversely, comic behaviour was unrestrained and graceless. Tragic events, of course, are unlike everyday life. Verbal stage directions require actors to perform unusual actions, or to express strong emotions. Pleading with Achilles for Iphigeneia, Klytemnestra's words describe what the actor must do: 'I am not ashamed/to clasp your knees.' Similarly, Iocaste's actions must justify the words of the chorus, 'Why has the queen gone, Oedipus, in wild/grief rushing from us?' It is not easy to imagine how an actor should kneel, rush and express wild grief or other powerful emotions with *sophrosyne*. Indeed, how did he sit or stand?[36]

AESTHETICS, PROCESS

Actors and visual artists often share an aesthetic, because all art is one. Aristotle draws a parallel between the characters of tragedy and comedy, and the art of the painters Polygnotos and Dionysios. Serious art and tragedy depicted the same personages, performing the same actions. The paintings of Polygnotos are lost, but vase scenes from Athens and Apulia can offer a reliable picture of how tragic actors must have moved and gestured in the fifth and fourth centuries respectively. J.R. Green warns against taking these scenes as accurate representations of tragedy.[37] Nevertheless, wherever we can identify the characters and deduce what they are doing, we can be reasonably sure that a tragic actor would try to behave in much the same way. For example, the faces of serious figures in sculpture and vase painting of the classical period never show emotion, even in violent action. The same evidence of *sophrosyne* is found in the lofty deadpan of classical tragic masks. The audience could only understand the significance of a comic actor's awkward, excited and rapid actions with reference to the aesthetic which governed tragedy.

Visual art was informed by the same ideal, which directed a simple act like sitting, where a god or hero gracefully advances one foot, drawing the other back to rest lightly on the toes.[38] Because it idealized emotional behaviour and even violence, which are the business of tragedy, the style of movement and bodily attitude that we see in heroic art was the physical vocabulary that a tragic actor had to learn. Actors in every age have always assimilated physical and vocal techniques, which are necessarily conventional. This does not imply that Greek acting was exaggerated or artificial. The understatement of film acting is no less conventional than ballet. Genuine naturalism is as unattainable as it is undesirable; as Henry Irving said, 'To act on a stage as one really would in a room would be ineffective and colourless.'[39] Art is art because it is not life.

Believing characters

Like any actor, a Greek *hypokrites* had to persuade an audience to believe in his character. It is never enough simply to speak the lines and walk through the 'blocking'. Audiences quickly see through the amateur who stands apart from his role, communicating 'He's very silly, isn't he? And am I not a funny fellow?' They cannot believe unless the actor believes as well, but does this mean that Greek actors necessarily 'identified' with a role? Pictures of men studying masks have been taken to show that they did. However, at least one of these figures is a poet and another, Dionysos. Since neither the poet nor the god is likely to have submerged his identity in a character, we cannot be sure what either they or the actors were seeking in the mask.[40] Indeed, there is little evidence of actors identifying with a character before the nineteenth century, but many are known to have shared their characters' feelings: that is quite another matter. Perhaps there is no literal truth in the anecdote of Polos, when as Elektra he brought his son's ashes on stage in the urn supposed to contain the remains of Orestes. It does not matter. The story was not repeated in order to show that the actor 'became' Elektra, but that he felt as she would at a particular moment, consequently expressing 'genuine grief and unfeigned lamentation'.[41] Other performers arrived at an emotional pitch by less drastic methods; Ion, Plato's rhapsode, shared emotion with the people in his narrative, Theodoros made a hardened tyrant weep, he and Kallipides both took pride in their emotional effect upon an audience. These were tragic actors, but Aristotle says Parmeno (of pig-squeal fame) habitually suffered from thirst as a consequence of great emotional strain. Evidently there were occasions when comedy too could evoke strong feeling.[42]

How did actors achieve the emotional intensity which was needed to carry spectators along with them, believing in their characters, sharing their feelings? While ancient writers say little about the actor's mental process, discussions of the related art of rhetoric suggest that a vivid imagination was essential. A successful actor cultivated the ability to visualize his character and events by focussing upon them those developed powers of concentration which are central to actor-training today. In private life, many actors belonged to the Athenian elite, sharing its ideal of *sophrosyne*; for them it would come more naturally to imagine tragic superiority than to project oneself into comic characters, who were inferior. Given the status of women in Athens, playing a female role in comedy must have stretched the imagination even farther. It would be remarkable if a novice never took the easy route, 'hamming' a woman's role to meet the crude stereotypes of a (notionally) male audience. The hags in *Ekklesiazousai* may seem to invite that sort of treatment, and some figurines have masks that scarcely seem human; but audiences quickly weary of superficiality, which could not in any case be applied to characters like Praxagora or the young women of New Comedy, whose femininity must seem secure for the sake of the plot. When a responsible actor played a woman, he had to approach the character as he did Xanthias, Herakles or the Sausage-seller of *Knights*, who were equally alien to his own personality. Instead of looking at the mask from the outside, he allowed it to endow him with the character's own self-image. Then he could represent her attitudes and appetites with conviction, perceiving as justified her indignation, lust or greed. This was not subtle characterization. Most roles were conceived as types, whose mental and physical characteristics, manner of speech, gesture and movement, could be learned as a distinct subset and assumed with the appropriate mask.

Transitions

When doubling parts, an acquired focus enabled the actor to shift his imagination between the behavioural subsets belonging to 'characters of different social status, age, gender, emotional fibre', as well as mental and emotional state.[43] Moreover, Old Comedy as we know it is metatheatrical; the actor moves in and out of character. These rapid transitions required mastery of techniques for characteristic movement and voice, which the actor selected to suit each successive character. This was not so difficult as it may appear, because a Greek *protagonist* probably had no conception of 'building a character' as a unique, imaginary individual. The basic repertoire of types was stored in his imagination, to be brought forward at a moment's notice. None of this process was too deliberate and rational to be compatible with emotional acting. Modern theatre practice shows that training, rehearsal and concentration enable actors to make these transitions swiftly and completely. Acting schools with formal instruction in the techniques of movement and speech are a twentieth-century phenomenon; actors from Thespis to Irving have learned by observation, apprenticeship and experiment. By repetition, in the theatre and in rehearsal, actors have always assimilated technique, so that it becomes 'second nature'. As practised in conformity with the prevailing aesthetic as applied to Old Comedy, the style of movement of a young wife or an old slave were not at all like the movement natural to a young citizen, who happened to be an actor. He had to learn them so well that he adopted them at need. We make similar transitions in a triathlon; running, we move naturally, but in our transitions to cycling and thence to swimming we adopt unnatural modes which we have assimilated so thoroughly that they have become automatic. And we do not have to think about it very much; if we rehearse the triathlon for a month, we do not have to think at all. Neither does the trained and well-rehearsed actor.

Granted, a Greek comic actor's task was more complex, because he made more transitions, and each one required techniques in several modes, voice, gesture, the style of movement proper to each character. It may have been as though he rode a bicycle while singing *Voi che sapete*, then backstroked while speaking a parody of Olivier in *Henry V*. To do this, he must have cultivated the concentration that promotes the mental technique François Joseph Talma called 'dual consciousness': while the 'inspiring and directing self' believes and feels, the 'executive self' remains detached, controlling speech and gesture.[44]

20 *Auletris* playing without a *phorbeia*, her cheeks puffed out. Su concessione del Ministero per i Beni e le Attività Culturali: Direzione Regionale per i Beni Culturali e Paesaggistici della Puglia, Soprintendenza per i Beni Archeologici della Puglia.

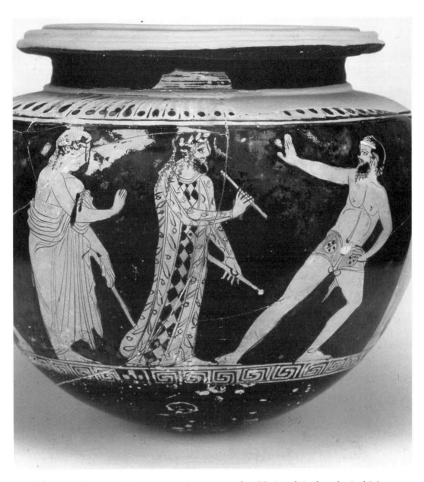

21 *Auletes* wearing a *xustis*, accompanying a satyr play. National Archaeological Museum, Athens © Hellenic Ministry of Culture and Tourism/Archaeological Receipts Fund.

22 Conventionally invisible behind a property-tree, an *auletes* accompanies dancing *choreutai* who pretend to play. Courtesy of the collector, and the J. Paul Getty Museum, Los Angeles. Photo: Vincenzo Pirozzi.

23 Phrynis the New Musician is restrained by fiery Pyronides. Direzione dei Musei Provinciali, Salerno.

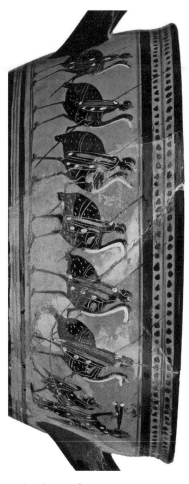

24 Archaic chorus of ostrich-riders confronted by their *exarchos*, prototype of the actor.
Photograph © 2011 Museum of Fine Arts, Boston.

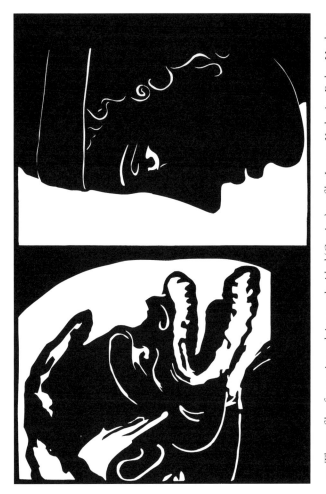

25 The profile of a comic mask inverts the ideal 'Grecian' profile. Image: Katherine Esther Hughes.

26 The awkward gait of the running slave was part of the actor's characterization. With permission of the Royal Ontario Museum © ROM.

27 Behaviour inappropriate to a citizen's *sophrosyne* causes him to lose control of his *himation*. National Museum, Copenhagen, Department of Classical and Near Eastern Antiquities.

128

28 A slave with a grievance finds sanctuary on an altar. © The Trustees of the British Museum.

29 A popular figure in comedy, Herakles is characterized by his lion's skin, club and crossed legs. © The Trustees of the British Museum.

30 Groups of figurines are rare: two actors as *komastai*, old rowdies on the spree. Antikensammlung. Staatliche Museen zu Berlin – Preussischer Kultur. Photo: Johannes Laurentius.

31 Corinthian in style, this figurine shows a comic actor in a rhetorical attitude, implying the presence of listeners. © The Trustees of the British Museum.

32 Sitting at ease, an actor as an old man gestures conversationally.

33 Portrait of an actor as a black man; his *himation* is style α. Gift of Barbara and Lawrence Fleischman, The J. Paul Getty Museum, Villa Collection, Malibu, California.

34 Herakles eats the offerings he has brought for little Zeus, who threatens him with his thunderbolt. © The State Hermitage Museum. Photo: Vladimir Terebenin, Leonard Kheifets, Yuri Molodkovets.

134

35 An actor's body-attitude defines his characterization of a crone. © The State Hermitage Museum. Photo: Vladimir Terebenin, Leonard Kheifets, Yuri Molodkovets.

36 Stage-naked, an actor as an old citizen labours for a younger overseer.
Courtesy of the collector.

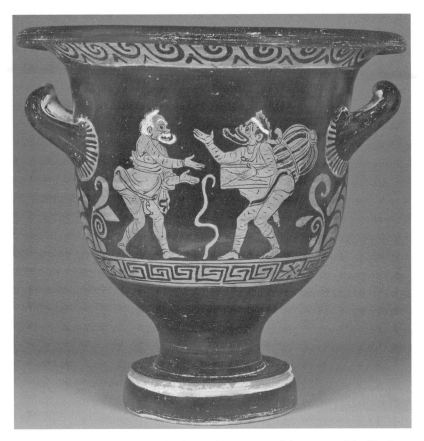

37 Returning from a journey with a *kiste*, a slave argues with his master. Gift of Barbara and Lawrence Fleischman, The J. Paul Getty Museum, Villa Collection, Malibu, California.

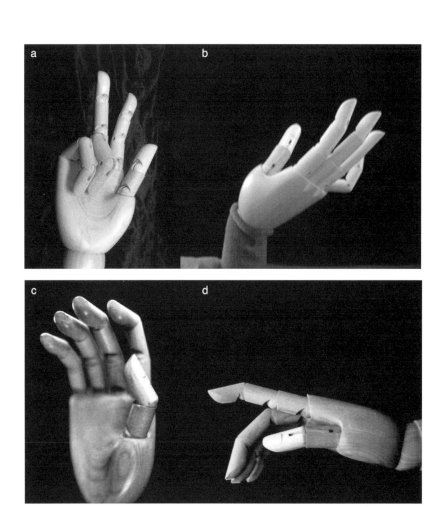
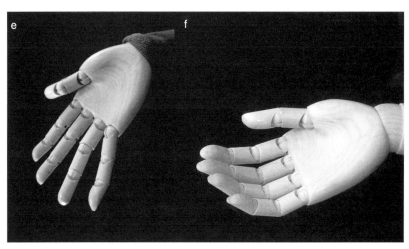

38 Hand gestures used in comedy: (a) admonitory, (b) stop, (c) ward, (d) rebuke, (e) rejection, (f) significance uncertain. Photos: A. Hughes.

39 Comic rapture of an old man; the permanently beatific expression and closed eyes of
his mask may be less probable than his gesture. National Museum, Copenhagen,
Department of Classical and Near Eastern Antiquities.

40 Ladylike gesture of an old transvestite. Courtesy Servizio Soprintendenza per i Beni Culturali e Ambientali, Messina.

41 Types of young women in comedy: (a) *hetaira*, (b) *kore*, (c) *pseudo-kore*, (d) virgin.
Photos: (a) Antikenmuseum der Universität Heidelberg, (b, c) © The State Hermitage
Museum. Photos: Vladimir Terebenin, Leonard Kheifets, Yuri Molodkovets,
(d) A. Hughes.

42 A wife in comedy rebukes her husband with an admonitory gesture. Courtesy of the
Nicholson Museum, University of Sydney.

43 Actor as a crone; her body-attitude is aggressive. © 2009 Musée du
Louvre/Anne Chauvet.

44 A *hetaira* helps a young symposiast to be sick. Archaeologisches Institut der Universität Göttingen. Photo: Stephan Eckardt.

144

45 A comic exploit of Herakles, with a young woman wearing tragic dress, at a shrine. Assessorato dei Beni Culturali e dell'Identità Siciliana, Servizio Parco Archeologico di Leontinoi.

46 Comic parody of the Boiotian Hermes, goat-bearer. Musée du Louvre
© RMN/Hervé Lewandowski.

CHAPTER 7

Technique and style of acting comedy

PHYSICAL CHARACTERIZATION

Tragic acting was governed by the ideal of *sophrosyne*, which comedy turned upside-down. 'The physical appearance of the actor was fundamental to the presentation of comedy', Green explains, because his face and figure are 'anti-types of the ideal, free, citizen male'. From vase scenes and figurines, we can reconstruct the comic actor's preposterous appearance. Apparently taking it for granted, the play-texts rarely refer to it. He was usually represented as a man with a fat stomach, protuberant buttocks and grotesquely oversized *phallos*, all simulated by a metatheatrically artificial 'undercostume' representing his naked body which was inadequately covered by an indecently short *chiton*. For female roles the undercostume was hidden beneath normal contemporary dress, but until the later fourth century many female masks, and virtually all males, were grotesque inversions of society's ideals, both of regular features and imperturbability. Bulging eyes, a gaping mouth and flattened nose, large ears, warts, wrinkles and disordered hair all suggested inferior human types in states of extravagant excitement: 'given their physical appearance, they could not be expected to behave properly, within society's normal codes'.[1]

Dramatic dialogue often contains verbal stage directions that tell an actor what must be done:

CHARON Sit to the oar . . . Hey you, what do you think you're doing?
DIONYSUS Who me? Just sitting on the oar, right where you told me.
CHARON No, sit over here, fatso . . . Now put out those hands and stretch your
    arms . . . Put your feet against the stretcher and start rowing, gung-ho!

(*Frogs* 197–204)

It is explicit that Dionysos must sit upon an oar, sit on a thwart, reach for the oar, brace his feet: but *the manner* of doing these things is left to the actor. Examples of Greek musical notation survive, but we have no corresponding treatise or transcription describing how the *komodos* sat, stood, walked, gestured – or rowed. For his style of movement, our best resource is the static figurines and pictures on vases that show actors in characteristic action. Because these media normally observed a realistic convention, we can be reasonably confident that they depict the generalized *style* of body-language used by actors, although photographic accuracy is not to be expected. In broad terms, these pictures show that a comic actor's acquired, fictional 'second nature' subverted the behaviour which society expected of him in his real life as a citizen. He learned to gesture on a generous scale, flinging his arms high and wide, and in parts like Philokleon (*Wasps* 1482ff) to caper and dance extravagantly.[2]

The most specific manifestation of *sophrosyne* is the gait appropriate to an Athenian citizen, calm, unhurried, dignified.[3] The running slave of comedy is the antithesis of this ideal. He is *phaulos*, beneath consideration, running in the street, often in a manner that is *geloios*, laughable. In retreat, running *away* from something, such as an angry master, his movement is inefficient, awkwardly unbalanced; he kicks up his heels or runs stiff-legged (Figure 26). He may swing his arms stiffly, or too high; or he fails to co-ordinate arms with legs, swinging left arm with left leg, right with right: 'goon-walking'. When he is not running in outright terror of a pursuer, he strives furtively against his fat body to tread upon egg-shells. Hurrying *towards* a destination, his awkwardness is less pronounced, perhaps because he is performing his proper function, delivering food, an announcement, or the *kottabos*-stand for a *symposion*.[4]

It would be inconsistent with a citizen's dignity either to chase a transgressing slave or, having caught him, to administer punishment. This is the distasteful task of a slave-overseer. In an early Lucanian scene, a senior slave tethers a miscreant, beating him with the master's staff: overhead, a third holds his nose. Behaviour appropriate to a citizen was linked to his dress. In the eyes of the conservative Athenian whom we know as the 'Old Oligarch', citizens in his time were 'no better dressed than the slaves and metics', an exaggeration which approaches truth in comic vase scenes and terracottas where, for every three citizens wearing the *himation*, it is worn by two slaves.[5] It was a practical symbol of citizenship, because it would betray the citizen who forgot his dignity. Since the wearer was obliged to hold his *himation* in place, inappropriate activity disarranged it. Thus, when an old thief runs, his cloak opens, spilling his booty; when a man crouches to gawk sharply upwards, it falls off his shoulder (Figure 27). An angry master runs with the same awkward gait and outstretched hand as the slave he pursues; they chase each other around a small *askos*, which implies that there is nothing to choose between them. In fact, they are dressed alike, because the old man has stripped to his *exomis*.[6] Movements like these are undignified and ugly, because they are unbalanced.

The running slave and his vengeful master arrive at a predictable climax when the fugitive finds sanctuary on an altar. This is a popular subject in terracotta, perhaps because a single figure could remind viewers of a common comic situation. Significantly, the earliest example was made towards the middle of the fourth century, when Middle Comedies of everyday life became popular. Two vases have the same subject. When Athenian coroplasts made their first series of comic figures (the New York Group *c*.400), four of the twelve male figures were seated, but the two on altars are not slaves, while the slaves sit on draped stools. Apparently the 'slave on the altar' theme was not yet familiar. Subsequently, two of these types were imitated and adapted to the new subject, which remained popular in New Comedy as late as the second century BCE. Variants have been found in sites as widespread as Lipari, Egypt, Libya, Cyprus and around the Black Sea. The earlier figures sit in a variety of attitudes. Some hug themselves, in a gesture of lonely self-comfort. In several popular types, the slave holds his hand to one ear, as though his master has struck him (Figure 28). One holds a baby, and another has a sack on his shoulder, perhaps because he has packed his meagre possessions and fled to sanctuary. A lively figure recently excavated in Sicily shows the slave before he runs away: kneeling, he hugs himself, right hand to left shoulder, no doubt affirming his innocence.[7]

It is not always clear how absurd these figures were meant to appear. The altar is rarely so high as to oblige the slave to sit with his legs dangling, like a risible little Zeus perched on his own altar, or a comic Priam seeking sanctuary from Neoptolemos. Towards the end of the fourth century, most seated slaves casually cross their legs at the ankle, but none has the *sophrosyne* to display 'god feet', an attitude favoured in classical art for its harmonious asymmetry, with one foot advanced and the other tucked under the seat, lightly resting on tip-toe. This is how Sicilian and Paestan painters usually depict a seated Dionysos, and Hera, the only identifiable goddess on a comic vase. Even when playing divinities, comic actors seldom sit gracefully. As Zeus Ammon in his shrine, an actor is enthroned on a stool that is too low for him, knees up and spread with *phallos* dangling between, clutching his royal eagle by the throat. Dionysos squats, his *phallos* dangling almost over the front of the stage. Rare exceptions defy explanation: perhaps a lost fragment showed why an actor with an inverted lyre sits with 'god feet', but an intact context fails to explain why the 'Rio fish-eater' sits in the same attitude as Aura, the sea breeze personified.[8]

THE EVIDENCE

The coroplasts of the New York Group knew terracotta was too fragile to represent actors in vigorous action. Poses are less kinetic than those in vase scenes. At first the figurines may have represented characters from specific comedies, but they are not easily combined in small groups to form a coherent scene, and individual figures were subsequently duplicated or adapted in places where the original plays cannot have been known. Self-contained images like these evolved into portraits of character types. Aristophanes' major characters are individuals: Lysistrata or Peisetairos could never become stereotypes, but the hungry Herakles in *Birds* became a stock figure in Middle Comedy. Comedy borrowed the hero's crossed legs from serious art, transforming them into an attribute, like his lion skin and club (Figure 29). These made him immediately recognizable, the subject of the most widely distributed comic figurines; he also takes part in eleven vase scenes. At rest with ankles crossed, he usually leans upon his club.[9] When another comic character leans with crossed legs, his attitude may be intended as a Herakles-reference.

Paired figures are rare, but easily interpreted: a *komast* supports his drunken crony (Figure 30), two slaves fight and a comic Telephos threatens baby Orestes on an altar. Single figures may imply an invisible second: a slave on an altar implies a master, an angry man threatens to strike someone, a young woman veils her face against scrutiny, men gesturing rhetorically imply the presence of an audience (Figure 31).[10] The media complement each other. As city comedy displaced fantasy, character types marked social distinctions, identified by masks and costumes. The body-language of figurines expresses temperaments and moods, while vase scenes usually show comic characters reacting to the stimulus of other temperaments, either in conflict or combination; they participate in scenes, which are our best evidence for style, but we also have more than forty pictures of individual actors. Few are simple portraits. The medium allows more movement than clay, and most are engaged in some action which might refer directly to another character in a play, running, conversing with gestures, carrying food, beating a donkey, gesturing a reaction.[11] Many of these confirm the impression conveyed by the statuettes, that comic actors moved, stood or sat in attitudes quite distinct from those used in tragedy.

Red-figured vase portraits show actors engaged in activities expressive of their character types, such as the running slave. A lively picture shows a white-haired, senior slave, who briskly prepares for a *symposion*; with a flourish, he carries a tray of sweetmeats in his right hand and a *kottabos*-stand in the crook of his left arm. A slave approaches a shrine, indicated by a laurel; his wreath and the sprig in his hand show that his basket and *situla* contain offerings. His master has sent him on this journey, judging by the bedroll on his back. An old citizen leans forward on his stool, knees apart, feet firmly planted, walking-stick over his arm; he holds forth, his speaking gesture directed towards an invisible listener (Figure 32).[12]

Portraits from Taras show how, within the comic convention of inverted ideals, actors could set their individual stamp on old types, and introduce new ones. Two pictures show an old citizen returning home from a party; his torch indicates the late hour, and his empty wine-jug illustrates his name, Philopotes – 'Loves-drink' (Figure 3). With his stick tucked jauntily under his arm, an old fellow named Derkylos dances a 'soft shoe', gracefully pointing his toes. A charming figure with black mask and tights seems to shrug, looking over his shoulder as he sidles, one hand open at his thigh, palm downward, fingers spread, as though supplicating the earth beneath his feet (Figure 33). That unique gesture cannot be translated into words. It is part of an actor's physical expression of a personality.[13] Characters like these must have been identified with the actors who created them, as Theodoros' voice was always recognizable in tragedy, and the comic actor Hermon fulfilled audience expectations with his well-known 'slapstick' stage business.[14]

Action propels comedy, whether it is fantastic, mythological burlesque, or city comedy of intrigue. The extant texts and fragments seem to be full of sex and violence. Peisetairos threatens to rape Iris, Strepsiades climbs on Sokrates' roof to set fire to the Thinkery, the terrified Dionysos transforms himself into a ram. There must certainly have been a great deal of scurrying about, but Green points out that only one small vase fragment shows 'someone with their arms round someone else' and the naked figure perched upon a slave's shoulder in a vigorous fragmentary scene is not a costumed actor.[15] A search for scenes of comic violence yields little. As in the texts, threats are common, but physical contact of any sort is rare. We have five scenes of coercion: a robbery, a father and son hauling a *hetaira* back and forth, two with men who pull others by the arm and a guard with a prisoner. While there is light hand-contact in each, one conventional gesture is used to symbolize restraint: the captor sets his foot upon the foot of his captive (Figure 23). Friendly contact is found in three scenes, in which Cheiron's comrade and Xanthias push and pull him upstairs, a woman holds a sick man's head (Figure 44) and an old man helps ram-masked Dionysos to emerge from the basket.[16]

Contact seems imminent when men are boxing, others fight with spears, or a master raises his walking-stick to beat his slave, but no contact is shown to occur. A nocturnal lover climbs a ladder to offer a wreath to a woman in a window, and Herakles reaches towards a young woman, but neither completes the gesture (Figure 45). When a market-woman demands that an old man be trussed up, he seems to be bound by a magic spell rather than a rope.[17] Nor is there any evidence that the sexuality or violence in Aristophanes' dialogue is ever staged: that Peisetairos touches Iris, or the combat of the semi-choruses in *Lysistrata* was more than a symbolic dance. The tragedy convention, in which violence took place offstage, applied almost equally to comedy, which moreover left most manifestations of sexuality to the imagination.

ATTITUDE, GESTURE

Body-attitude begins with the feet. Sculptors achieved the lifelike attitude of a classical *kouros* by placing most of the apparent weight on one foot, which swings the pelvis, shoulders and head in alternate directions, on both vertical and lateral axes. This graceful asymmetry is static, but implies imminent action, when the subject should shift his weight to the other foot. A comic actor in a male role often distributes his weight evenly, standing flat-footed with legs far apart, or tightly together as if 'at attention'. Sometimes the broad stance can be functional, when he supports a drunk friend or behaves aggressively; otherwise, it seems lumpish or clumsy.[18] To move away from either posture, the actor would have to execute a reluctant little shuffle, shifting weight onto one foot in order to move the other. Moreover, an actor in comic costume standing at attention seems precariously overbalanced by his padded buttocks and belly. A Herakles who eats the offerings he has brought for Zeus, holding the dish behind his back with the other hand, seems ready to fall upon his fat bottom (Figure 34). Broad or narrow, the comic actor's stance is ungraceful, demonstrating his character's aesthetic deficiency. When a stage-naked actor strikes an heroic attitude, the graceless proportions of his undercostume seem to burlesque the nude hero of classical art (Figure 1).

Some comic characters may have been perceived by the audience as 'low' types, simply because they kept their bodies close to the ground. Actors cultivated this impression by adopting an angular, knee-bending walk, or by stooping and crouching. This practice originated in Old Comedy, and continued late. A dancer in the *Birds* scene crouches low, sharply bending his legs in the same manner as a child-actor in an Attic scene and, sixty years later, a slave in a portrait from Capua.[19] Actors stooping to peer upwards at a hoisted chest, or crouching to brandish a sword, show that their characters are low-down fellows, like the squatting Dionysos, and a stooping slave, in two Apulian scenes. We shall not be surprised to see similar attitudes in a 'chorus' of apes. Actors crouch to be beaten, turn a potter's wheel, or peer at a naked woman. With the recent publication of side views, we can see that three figurines from Syrakousai bend their knees at an angle of 40 degrees, stooping from the waist, enormous padded buttocks thrust out. An Athenian figure of a crone has the same S-shaped profile (Figure 35).[20]

Essential movements, standing, sitting, running and walking, express character and mood. As slaves, actors could run timidly or furtively, always absurdly. Culture-specific actions can also be performed well or ill, expressing character; but in a theatre, they must also illustrate the narrative. Consequently, actors usually 'played them straight'; they handled weapons, an *aulos* or *tympanon* realistically, or fed a stage-property baby in a perfectly serviceable way.[21] Because of this practice, comic figurines and vase scenes can yield glimpses of everyday gestural language. Vases illustrate, for example, how a citizen managed his walking-stick. In normal use, it was a status symbol, supporting only his dignity as he walked along, placing it erect before him with every step. To walk or gesture freely, a man might swing his staff across and under his left arm, the head pointed downwards. Standing still, young men on the reverse of vases hold it away from the body with the free right hand, while their elders, like the tragic *paidogogos*, wedge it between the body and the wrapped left hand. Any small deviation from conventional practice would be instantly recognized. Thus, when an actor props his stick against his stomach, ankles crossed and apparently risking a fall, he would be perceived as eccentric; to rely upon the staff for support is an undignified admission. Even a comic citizen rarely abandons *sophrosyne* so far as to use his staff as a tool or weapon.[22]

The Athenian elite lacked appreciation of the dignity of labour; physical work was regarded as degrading, and it deformed the body. Aristophanes scoffs at the stale humour of the slave who complained about his burden. A working citizen on a vase is portrayed as ridiculous, labouring at the harvest, directed by a younger overseer (Figure 36). Both actors are stage-naked. The old fellow bends until he faces the ground, a large sheaf clutched painfully to his back with both arms. One of the most widely distributed terracotta types is a citizen-farmer, who carries a large, cylindrical basket on his head. Filled with grain, it would weigh 12 to 15 kilograms; the actor hunches his shoulders and braces his legs to bear the simulated weight. Such a man, or a citizen whose *exomis* shows that he is prepared to work with his hands like a slave, exhibited a shameful disregard for *sophrosyne*. No doubt these characters were absurd and laughable in the eyes of privileged Athenians, but we do not know whether poor citizens shared their perspective, or how well this kind of humour went over with a Tarentine audience.[23] Men bearing a water jug (*hydria*), a shopping-basket, or a spit of baked goods were common sights in any city. Actors carrying these burdens do not seem downtrodden or comical, although the slaves have awkward gaits.[24] Their functional gestures are efficient. We recognize a traveller by the bedroll on his back, but a man who is further encumbered by a basket strapped to his chest may be a free pedlar, either a poor citizen *or* a metic; legs wide, head thrust forward, he leans heavily upon a walking-stick. Slave travellers stand erect, as though pleased with the temporary freedom of the road, but two terracotta cooks in Berlin seem to find their loads of kitchen gear irksome.[25]

Drama thrives on conflict, and burdens can become contentious. Scenes of domestic strife are rich in gestures. While we cannot always discern the subject of a dispute, we can easily recognize a squabble, and the character types of the participants. Apulian artists made two pictures of an encounter between a slave who carries a bedroll and a small chest (*kiste*), and his master, who carries the symbolically crooked walking-stick of an old citizen. In the first scene, the slave points at the old man with two fingers of the hand that holds his traveller's staff. The master turns his head to look at him. The second scene is more dramatic (Figure 37). Both men lean forward, one leg advanced. The slave's head is thrown back, chin out, his free hand raised before his master, who reaches towards the *kiste* with both upturned hands. Between them, the old man's staff balances upright.[26] These signs are easily read. Body-language shows that a dispute has broken out, and the old man's functional gesture indicates that the *kiste* is its subject: he reaches for it so urgently that he lets go of his stick. The slave does not respond with physical denial; we understand his vague gesture only with reference to his defiant chin, and because his hand is raised directly in his master's face. The first picture provides no clear context. The slave's bedroll and stick suggest he has brought the *kiste* from a distance, but he cannot be on the point of arrival because, like his master, he stands still. Therefore, the old man has turned, not because he has just caught sight of his messenger, but because he hears him speak, confirmed by a forward inclination of the slave's body. Does his right-hand gesture suggest what the slave says, or how he says it?

TYPES OF GESTURE

Emblems

When we seem to recognize a familiar gesture on a Greek pot, it is easily misinterpreted, but the slave's two-fingered sign is uncontaminated by contemporary western usage. Behaviourists would call it an 'emblem', a symbolic, culturally specific action that expresses an idea rather than an emotion. It can be decoded if the same sign is found in an intelligible context from the same culture and period. This is easy, so long as we discard the irrelevant staff, because the unencumbered gesture is found in many scenes (Figure 38a). In those related to tragedy, a *paidogogos* admonishes or rebukes a headstrong hero. The best-known example has Darius, king of Persia, enthroned and grasping his sword, while the *paidogogos* gestures a warning against his proposed invasion of Greece. Indeed, this 'admonitory' emblem is so characteristic of the wise old mentor that it is almost an attribute, like his ornate *kothornoi*. Ironically, one doomed hero turns it back upon the *paidogogos* who has been warning him against a tragic course of action. The same gesture is found in four scenes of comic argument; in similar contexts, our familiar single-finger admonishment is used instead, as when a steward points his finger straight upwards before a cringing old man.[27]

We can distinguish between similar hand gestures, provided parallel iconography is available. For instance, a flat hand, palm outwards, bent upwards at the wrist, signs 'stop' (Figure 38b). Apollo interposes it at arm's length between a Fury and Orestes, who clings to the Omphalos, and a priestess signs 'stop' towards Kassandra in a satirical 'rape of Ajax'. The comic 'stop' is a broad gesture, as when a slave raises his arm to warn Tyndareos against chopping Leda's egg open with an axe – Helen is hatching – and another tries to prevent his master from beating him. Recognition of this gesture modifies our understanding of a scene in which Apollo seeks refuge from Herakles on the roof of his own Delphic shrine: since the slave's sign warns the god against dropping his bow and laurel, he can scarcely be Iolaos, who would help his friend to rob Apollo of his attributes.[28] In a related gesture, the fingers are cupped. The meaning is near that of the 'stop' sign, but less authoritative: we might call this a 'warding' gesture (Figure 38c). This is the sign Orestes makes towards Iphigeneia in Tauris, who must kill Greek strangers, and an actor who wears the white mask of a snub-nosed young woman directs it at a middle-aged man, who seems to recoil from her gesture. Seeking sanctuary on an altar, a slave makes this sign towards his approaching master, and a comic Priam, towards Neoptolemos, who seems on the point of killing him; but this is comedy, and no doubt they will 'exit at the end as new friends, and no one dies at anyone's hands'.[29]

Most mythological scenes can be interpreted easily enough, because we know the story, but we can only guess what is happening in scenes of everyday life. Comic conflict is expressed by a variety of gestures, but we cannot always explain why one sign is used rather than another. In argument, a forefinger is hooked while the other fingers thrust downwards; perhaps a master who aims this gesture at his slave accuses him (Figure 38d). If this is correct, the actor who similarly points at an *auletris* must be rebuking her. We may guess that a slave explains or protests, when he bends his wrist like a question-mark, turning his open hand downwards, and that his master's spread fingers stabbing down signify rejection (Figure 38e). Without the visible context of a dispute, we cannot know what a running slave means when he makes a similar gesture behind him, or a woman raises her cupped hand, palm uppermost, to shoulder height (Figure 38f). And what are we to make of the familiar ring-gesture, which an old man makes while he watches pipers dancing? In 360 BC, this cannot be read as today's familiar emblem signifying 'OK'.[30]

Affective gestures

Greek actors probably believed in the universality of affective gestures. This means that the passions everyone feels produce identical gestures in everyone; and that, recognizing those signs, an audience will share the affects. This may have worked with Greeks, but if gestures were truly universal, hellenized barbarians two millennia later ought to be able to read them in scenes of Greek comedy.[31] Alas, we cannot. Emotional gestures in comedy are as difficult to decode as any other sort. Only 'surprise' can be read with any certainty, and again, scenes related to tragedy hold the key. An attendant in Asian costume throws up both hands at the sight of Sleep and Death in flight with the corpse of Sarpedon. Recognizing Theseus by his sword, Medea raises one hand, confirming her surprise by dropping a *hydria* from the other. When Hermes leads a *choreut* to meet Dionysos, he leaves the man only one free hand to fling up in surprise. In a comic scene, the citizen who discovers a foundling can raise only his right hand because the left is wrapped in his *himation*.[32] The gesture resembles warding, except that the fingers are straight, and usually, spread apart. One Sicilian scene has a subtle variant: gesturing two-handed surprise towards a young couple, an old transvestite spreads index and little fingers wide, holding the two fingers between tightly together (Figure 39). Signifying grace in female subjects, both human and divine, this posture of the hand has been handed down by actresses from the Renaissance to the present. Perhaps this ladylike version of surprise is an emblem of shifting significance, like the 'horizontal horns' which ward against the Evil Eye in some cultures; amongst schoolboys in the 1940s it signified 'Bull! You lie.'

Whereas female characters commonly express themselves by manipulating their clothing, males manipulate their own bodies: a slave holds his nose, a young man clings to his *phallos*. Most frequently, hands manipulate each other. The significance of clasped hands varies according to their position relative to the body. An old man's hands, folded on his stomach, seem to express contentment, but this is difficult to confirm. Regardless of its theatrical improbability, a mask with a beatific expression and closed eyes agrees with our instinctive reading of the wearer's gesture, his palms joyfully pressed together over his heart (Figure 40). A slave-figurine clasps his hands to his chest; without context, the gesture can be interpreted only by comparison with his counterpart on a vase, who wrings his hands in anxiety under his master's baleful glare. Beneath his chin, an old man clasps his hands on the head of his staff and leans towards centre stage; he watches something happening there, but the rest of the scene is lost. The tragic *paidogogos* adopts the same attitude when he watches events with a doubtful outcome: Alkestis dying, Europa riding the bull.[33] Other signs associated with tragic *katastrophe* attend the petty disasters of comedy. It is likely that a comic actor who raises a hand to his cheek expresses apprehension, because Iocasta makes the same gesture when the Messenger tells his story to Oidipous. Pondering its implications, the king touches his chin with his fingers.[34]

At the moment of tragic *katastrophe*, a *protagonist* or witness may either touch fingers to his forehead, gesturing 'alas', or clap a hand to the head as if it were about to explode. When employed by a comic actor, this tragic gesture has been misinterpreted as an 'old man spying' (Figure 4).[35] In comedy, it is principally used to burlesque tragedy or myth, as in the comic Perseus scene, and it would be entirely appropriate for Lamachos:

Attatai, attatai!
Hateful as hell these icy pains; wretched am I!
I am undone, by foeman's spear struck down.

                                          (*Ach.* 1190–2)

A comic Herakles signs 'alas' when a woman unveils herself; on this occasion the gesture may mean that he is astonished, like Dionysos reacting to an acrobatic stunt performed before his face by a naked woman, and again when Aigisthos is abruptly confronted by comic *choregoi*.[36]

When the *katastrophe* has passed, the tragic *protagonist*'s settled grief is expressed with the head tilted to one side, the cheek resting on a hand. This is Niobe's mute attitude on vases, in Aischylos' tragedy as Euripides describes it in *Frogs* (910–20) and of Andromeda's mother Kassiopeia. It is seldom found in comedy, perhaps because it stands for a sorrow that is profound and sustained. Comedy's happy ending will soon erase the melancholy of the slave who sits with his chin propped on his fist.[37]

One or more fingers touching the lower lip denote doubt or appre-hension. Approaching Alkmene on the pyre to which he has mistakenly condemned her, Amphitryon touches his lip. In a domestic scene, a young wife with a lamp fingers her lip as she hurries to open the door for her drunken husband. In a scene from a comedy, a young traveller offers a shoe to a madam who touches her lip; instead of a finger, an old woman with a tablet in her lap touches her stylus to her lip as she watches her steward browbeating an old citizen. Gnawing one finger in a corner of his wide mask-mouth, a terracotta Herakles appears both anxious and foolish.[38]

ACTING WOMEN

When an actor put on a woman's mask he changed his style of movement. His old citizens and slaves were *geloios*, laughable, their absurdity mani-fested in an awkward gait and clumsy gestures. Rarely a source of humour, women's roles were often little more than plot mechanisms, their func-tion determined by character type. Before they rebelled, Lysistrata and her friends were always being ordered to be silent (506–28): since few women in comedy had much dialogue, the actor used signs to show the audience what type of woman his character was. His principal tools were costumes, masks and body-language. Like his outer costume, which resembled women's everyday clothes, the gestures, movements and attitudes an actor used to identify women's types were easily understood because they were modelled upon the socially conditioned, daily behaviour of Athenian women. No doubt actors simplified and exaggerated, to make signs legible from the rear of the *theatron*. Masks divided women into three broad categories which broadly followed the archetypal triad of maiden, mature woman (in comedy, a wife) and crone. The older women could be safely stereotyped and caricatured, but the signs that distinguished between sub-types of young women were subtle. These could only be defined as they were in the *agora*.

The maiden

The young women in vase scenes and figurines express their characters entirely in relation to men, and they are typed according to modesty, real or assumed, or its absence. The male actor behind her mask took no pains to make a young woman funny; it was his job to communicate character type. Since comedy conventionally occurs out-of-doors, a female character behaved as though she were in public, with men present. We have only one comic vase scene in which men play no part.[39] Perhaps older women could express themselves more freely, but a young woman in comedy was an object of pursuit. Her availability was established by her type: was she the modest sort a citizen might marry, or was a relationship potentially commercial? The audience was alert to visual clues. Given the way female characters are defined, surprisingly few scenes express even muted sexuality. In a rare exception, a woman fondling an old man is easily identified as a *hetaira* by her mask type, costume, behaviour towards the man – and by the purse in his hand. Clothes can type a character quickly and clearly. A girl who wears a wreath must consort with men, at the *symposion* or brothel. When two men – perhaps father and son – fight over a homely woman, we might suppose her to be a burlesque Helen, were it not for the gold pattern on her *chiton*.[40] Often, however, the signs are subtler.

Two figurines offer a convenient comparison. Modelled near the end of the fifth century, probably in the same Athenian workshop, they represent young women who must be the 'romantic interest' in comedies, a *kore* and a *hetaira*, respectively modest and bold. In relation to an invisible male presence, each displays signs which define her type.[41] The *kore* (Figure 41b) distributes her weight equally upon both feet, which are parallel and slightly parted; no sway or twist is imparted to her body. The head is inclined slightly to the left, eyes apparently turned aside. Her *himation* is wrapped tightly about her upper body; the left arm clasps it to her side, while the swathed right veils her mask almost to the eyes. Her hair is neatly dressed in a roll over the forehead, with a fold of her cloak behind, like a hood (*kalymma*). The other woman (Figure 41a) wears a similar hairstyle, but the bun is higher and the hood farther back. These subtle differences are a fair measure of the signs that distinguish antithetical types. Neither mask is in the least grotesque, but a wide mouth and full chops give the *hetaira* a well-fed look. Her features are less significant than their deliberate display: like the *kore*, she has veiled her face until a moment ago, but now she draws her veil aside with the right hand, which rests, still wrapped, beside her cheek. At the same time, she cocks her left arm akimbo, a provocative sign which no respectable young woman would make; it frees the front of her *himation* to fall open. There is no averted glance or downcast eye; head erect, she gazes directly ahead. A short step forward bends her left knee, which shifts her balance, inclining body and head forward.[42]

Another 'city comedy' type is the *pseudo-kore* who poses as a maiden of the citizen class. She was a familiar character in many comedies between 350 and 325, when her figurines were widely distributed. She displays contradictory signs, some designed to snare a suitor, while others inadvertently betray her to the audience. The naturalistic mask may be expressionless or smiling, the hairstyle plain or elaborate. She unveils, lifting the *kalymma* high with a graceful, curved gesture of the right hand (Figure 41c). This may seem innocent, but she stands with an arm akimbo and advances a bent leg, either with an alluring sway or immodestly leaning towards an invisible man. Unveiling in the same way, an actor in a vase scene leaves us in no doubt about its significance. His character is a prostitute, soliciting trade outside a brothel; the raised arm lets the cloak fall away, exposing the false breasts of his undercostume.[43] Other fake virgins can be detected by an accident of surviving colour. We might be taken in by the restrained gestures and serious mask-features of one, or the way the other idly lifts a corner of fabric, an elegant gesture associated in art with respectable figures of tragedy and myth. But both have red hair, suggesting either dye or barbarian origin; a *kore* comes from the citizen class, and would never colour her hair. The same ladylike gesture is an affectation by an otherwise immodest *hetaira* in an Apulian vase scene.[44]

Significantly different is a woman who holds her *himation* diagonally across her lower face. The gesture is dynamic; she has snatched up the front of her cloak and ducks her head to hide in its folds. Somebody has offended her modesty, which is perfectly genuine. She displays no *pseudo-kore* body-language, and her hair is its natural black.[45] Another mask with black hair is worn by an actor as a young woman whose head droops upon her right shoulder in a conventional expression of melancholy confirmed by a universal gesture: she hugs her chest, the right hand lying flat against her left shoulder (Figure 41d). A Sicilian figurine of maiden type inclines a cheek against one hand, while supporting her elbow with the other. It is difficult to guess what place these dejected women took in a comic plot, but we can be quite sure that it was not a disreputable one.[46]

The wife

Dramatically, a wife was an obstacle, interfering with her husband's pleasures, and consequently regarded as a disagreeable character. Wives were not popular subjects for terracotta portraits, but because she was essential to many plots the wife is found in a dozen vase scenes.[47] Her body-language most frequently expresses exasperation or anger, awaiting her errant husband with both arms akimbo, or leaning with legs crossed; when he returns she hurries to ask 'Where have you been?' And once he is caught she advances one foot, throwing her weight back upon the other, while she gives him a piece of her mind. Her meaning is clear, particularly when she raises two fingers in an 'admonitory' gesture borrowed from the *paidogogos* of tragedy. Others wives offer good advice to a husband (and perhaps, a son) while he is engaged in business (Figure 42).[48] Only two married couples seem to be harmonious. Sharing a tray of sweetmeats with her old husband, Charis stands in the graceful attitude of Athene on a famous *stele*, the toes of one foot lightly touching the stage, but the pose and her name (Grace) are turned to irony by her mask, with its large mouth and ears, and the wart on her snub nose. Only in a rare terracotta is a wife shown in an unequivocally positive situation: an old couple stand side-by-side, their stocky bodies planted on symmetrical feet, ungraceful but together, her arm about his shoulder.[49]

The crone

When an actor played an old man or a slave, his funny walk or abject manner of running provoked laughter, but their images suggest that actors did not usually adopt a special, comical gait when playing older women, although the bent profiles of some figurines suggest pain (Figure 35). Even in rapid motion, pictures show the majority of women in much the same way as in myth, tragedy or daily life.[50] Age and class are not distinguished: a *hetaira* who hurries to help a drunken youth moves in the same way as the old woman who hastens towards her delinquent husband, and each moves in much the same manner as a real *auletris* in a scene in St Petersburg. A virgin and an old madam both seem awkward, only because each faces an approaching threat while simultaneously turning to retreat, but neither is laughable.[51] If audiences were expected to find these character types fundamentally amusing, we might expect to see some sign of it in their gait, but we do not; nevertheless, 'crones' are almost as popular as young women as subjects for Attic figurines. Outside the 'women's plays', the crone is an infrequent character in Aristophanes, and seldom participates in comic vase scenes. When she does, she is usually identifiable as a madam or an old wife, types who advance the plot. Exceptions are two women gossiping, and an outraged market-woman, like Myrtia in *Wasps* (1388–1412), who demands a malefactor's arrest.[52] In one scene only, we can glimpse humour (Figure 48). An old woman is arguing with a naked youth, when an old man enters. His crown and eagle-sceptre show that he is Zeus, and his familiarity, that she should be Hera. She stands, heavy and flat-footed, but her shawl blows in a graceful arc above her head, like the beautiful Aura's. We may suspect the intervention of a props man equipped with starch and wire. Masked with ironic ugliness, Iris in *Birds* might have looked something like this.[53]

Wearing the almost-neutral mask of a young woman, an actor supplied the subtle gestures that allowed the audience to read her character, but an old woman had no reason to dissemble. Significantly, while most cover their heads, none draws a *kalymma* across the mask, which often expressed character so forcefully that an actor needed only to find equivalent body-language. Crones are usually either aggressive or sad, depending upon how the actor's body-language supports his mask. She is not a decayed *kore*; the crone has been neither gently bred nor well used. Unlike the *phaulos* old man, her eyes do not bulge, but she has the snub nose and wide mouth of his base physiognomy, accentuated by thick lips. Her hair may be scanty, or, if it is abundant, her wrinkled forehead is low. Eyebrows are a heavy ridge, or crooked above lowered eyelids; the jaw is prognathous, bony and square.

The ghastly white mask looks aggressive when the actor holds his head erect or tilts it backwards, which thrusts the jaw forward and makes the eyes seem superciliously hooded. At the same time, he leans forward from the waist, one swathed elbow cocked high towards the object of the crone's wrath, the other akimbo (Figure 43). The hag Penia (Poverty) must have looked much like this, rebuking the old men for attempting to restore Wealth's sight. 'Maybe she's a Fury from tragedy', Blepsidemos exclaims, 'she does have a rather crazed and tragic look.' At the end of the scene, she is sad, defeated. 'This is terrible; what am I to do? . . . Where in the world shall I go?' To change his mood, the actor had only to look down, tucking the chin into his chest, arms crossed in a submissive, protective gesture. Now the eyes seem downcast, and without the thrusting elbow, the leaning body appears to stoop humbly (Figure 35).[54]

There are other old women, but only the madam is found frequently enough to be regarded as a type. The aggressive Athenian crone becomes a bawd in Sicily with the simple addition of a wreath. The same adornment combined with an enormous mouth and pointed eyebrows identify others, all gesturing freely, and interacting with men in vase scenes. No doubt they played an active part in plots. The Greek comic cliché, that women love wine, generated images of old women clutching huge drinking vessels.[55] Slave women are either scarce or we have failed to decipher signs of slavery. While we recognize several male slave-mask types, a slave woman is recognizable only when she carries a burden for others, like two old nurses with babies. A woman balancing a basket on her head and a pot on her arm may be either a slave or a poor farmer's wife. The stage 'props' would be light, but the actor braces his legs and hunches his shoulders to mime a heavy load.[56]

PROBLEMS OF INTERPRETATION

Despite our best efforts at deciphering them, many vase scenes still mystify us. A Tarentine artist we know as the McDaniel Painter has left us a picture of a distinctive theatrical moment. An actor as old man enters through a stage door carrying a spear. A younger man sits on a stool, stage-naked except for a round shield and a helmet.[57] The older man advances the spear, while the other raises his arm, hand flat, fingers spread. What is happening? The artist hoped potential buyers would recollect the scene, and buy his pot as a memento, but we can only guess at its meaning. Comparative iconography confirms that the soldier signs surprise, but why? The spear is not aimed at him. He looks up at the other's face, surprised at the old man's identity perhaps, or by something he says. We may never know what it was, because, unlike the painter and his customer, we missed the show.

Our reaction to a gesture and our consequent reading of a scene are naïve, remote in time, alien in culture. Our attempts to interpret body-language may occasionally hit the mark, but assumptions can lead to misinterpretation. If we study details, compare other scenes and figures, we may begin to understand the significance of a comic scene or figurine and avoid the error of supposing that we know enough. Three examples will illustrate my meaning.

Helping the sick

An Apulian scene shows a beardless youth bending forward, while a woman reaches towards him (Figure 44). In a flight of anachronism, a scholar once interpreted this as 'a wife forcing a man to drink from a milk bottle'. Her long stride and fluttering clothes show that she moves quickly, to catch him before he falls on his face. The 'bottle' is his thumb, which she pulls away from his mouth with one hand, holding his head with the other. An Athenian picture and a line of Aristophanes show what is happening. Inside a wine-cup, the Brygos Painter finds humanity and grace in a moment late in a *symposion*, when a youth vomits his wine while a *hetaira* holds his head. Help like this was appreciated. Disgusted at Lamachos' war-panoply, Dikaiopolis exclaims, 'Now take hold of my head so I can puke! I'm sickened by your crests!' The Apulian scene is comic in style. An actor plays a drunken youth, who has been trying to induce vomiting by sticking his thumb down his throat, when a second actor, playing a *hetaira* – not a wife – hastens to his aid (Figure 44).[58]

Mistaken identity

A correct interpretation of a Sicilian scene was unlikely so long as scholars knew it only from an inaccurate drawing and a murky photograph. With the reopening of the Museo Archeologico in Lentini, direct study has corrected significant errors (Figure 45).[59] At opposite ends of the stage, a slave and a crone watch the action at centre. Contributing nothing to the narrative, they might as well be bookends. Herakles is at centre, gesturing and moving strangely before a young woman who stands beside a shrine. It has been suggested that the comedy is a burlesque of Euripides' lost *Auge*, in which Aleos, king of Tegea, committed his daughter's virginity to the care of Athene until she was violated by a drunken Herakles, and became the mother of Telephos. Thus, the slave would be Aleos, and the crone, a nurse.[60] The marble statuette on the shrine should be Athene, whose attributes are helmet, spear and *aegis*; however, she has none of this warlike gear. Instead, she carries a wreath and a *phiale*, as if to pour a libation. Since these attributes identify no particular divinity, there is nothing to identify the *kore* as Auge. Whoever she may be, she is close to the anonymous deity; her body-attitude, and the positions of her arms and feet mirror those of the little statue beside her. Lacking any royal attributes, the slave is unlikely to be Aleos, or the old woman the girl's nurse: instead of hindering Herakles, she permits him to lean his club against her hip.[61]

The young woman's mask and costume are those worn in tragedy, as shown in two stage scenes by related painters. The mask is presented as her 'real' face, with the closed mouth of a mute character, and the richly patterned sleeves are almost identical to those in the tragic scenes. Yet

Herakles and the others are costumed and masked for comedy. Thus, the damsel must be a comic actor dressed as in tragedy, but what tragedy, or myth?[62] There is no evidence that it is *Auge*. Nevertheless, the iconography allows us to guess what happens next. Herakles' body-language is distinctive: tiptoeing away from the girl, he twists his head and upper body around to face her, reaching out until his fingers touch her cheek. By this time, we are familiar enough with the physical style of comedy to recognize that this contorted reversing movement violates the canons of serious art, but in a manner that is quite alien to the style in which comedy inverts them. Instead, it is characteristic of satyrs. Herakles is behaving like a satyr, and consequently, whoever she is, this *kore* is in trouble.[63]

Terracotta husbandmen

Terracotta figures can be difficult to interpret because their meaning often appears to be simple and straightforward. In the case of the 'old man spying', vase scenes supplied the context that disclosed the real meaning of his gesture (Figure 4).[64] However, figurines representing comic actors who carry domestic animals across their shoulders are not so easily interpreted (Figure 46). The earliest is Attic, three are Boiotian, and one Cypriot.[65] As with other figurines, we might suppose that the Athenian original was imitated by coroplasts elsewhere, with minor variations. In the Athenian example, the animal's head is on the actor's right, while in the Boiotian it is on the left in each case. The beast is variously described as a calf, kid, sheep or ram. The actor seems to play a simple herdsman. Despite the wreaths worn by all but the Cypriot, I confess to having agreed, until I saw the *moschophoros*. This life-sized archaic statue must have been familiar to every Athenian citizen, for it stood upon the Akropolis. Conceived in the idealized *kouros* tradition, the figure is nevertheless bearded and mature; he wears a wreath and carries a calf, its head to the right. Pausanias saw a similar statue in Tanagra, where it commemorated a miracle of Hermes, who saved the city from a plague by carrying a ram around the walls. The statue is lost, but its image is preserved on Tanagran coins, with the ram's head on the god's left, as in the Boiotian figurines.[66]

There can be little doubt that the figurines refer to comedies which parodied heroic art, as myth was often burlesqued. No matter that Hermes wore comic costume and a slave-mask: the audience knew him by his ram and wreath. The Athenian figurine was also wreathed, and bore a calf as the *moschophoros* did; but the Boiotian figurines carried the satire a step farther, substituting a billygoat for the god's sacred ram.[67] As for the actor from Cyprus, his animal is very large, but certainly a sheep; his mask is not that of a slave, and it wears no wreath. Parody of mainland art would not resonate in remote Cyprus; no doubt he plays the part of a simple herdsman.

How did these actors manage their business? Were their burdens really lightweight 'props'? The only stage sheep this writer has ever seen were ludicrous failures. Were Greek prop-shops more successful, or were ancient actors obliged to perform while striving to restrain a frightened animal? It is proverbial in the theatre that children and animals are irresistible upstagers.

CHAPTER 8

The masks of comedy

In the 1950s, two plaster masks hung above the screen in my local cinema, the corners of their gaping, stylized mouths sweeping downwards
for tragedy, and up for comedy. Every popcorn-eating kid at the Saturday
matinee understood that these were symbols of theatre and film. They still
are: a website dedicated to them offers 500 designs.[1] Today, we use 'mask'
as a verb, synonymous with 'hide' or 'conceal': cedar siding masks an ugly
concrete wall, a villain is unmasked. A Greek actor's *prosopeion* concealed
his face, but perhaps not his identity, which the judges must have been
able to recognize in order to award a prize. Each time he donned a fresh
mask, it instantly defined a dramatic character, showing the audience a
new face (*prosopon*), a separate being who was more than an actor pulling
faces. Recognizing its general characteristics, spectators could promptly
identify each mask by type: *hetaira* or *kore*, slave or old citizen. Within a
type, distinctions between Peisetairos and Euelpides, or the individuality
of Lysistrata and the Sausage-seller, emerged with further acquaintance.

WHAT MASKS WERE LIKE

No Greek masks have survived, but thousands of images in painting,
sculpture, terracotta models and bronze show that the actor's head was
entirely enclosed. Masks were composed of a rigid, moulded face, with
attached hair, in varying proportions according to type. Tragedy masks
usually had abundant hair, which the actor could simply lift in order to
enter from the rear. Since comedy masks were often bald on top, the crown
must have been moulded in one piece with the face; hair at the back and
sides completed the mask. The face surrounded the actor's head sufficiently
to carry the ears, which were often large; for satyr plays they were inhuman,
pointed and obviously artificial.[2] Masks of men were brown, those of young
women, white. The mouth of a mute 'extra' could be closed, but a speaking
character's mouth was necessarily open, and often very large, but without

166

visible teeth except in several Hellenistic replicas, where the actor's mouth may be seen inside.[3]

A tight mask induces claustrophobia. Fitted over the actor's head, Greek masks were large for the actor's body, a disproportion which audiences conventionally ignored, in exchange for features which were legible to everyone in the *theatron*. Old Comedy masks were strongly characterized, but my cinema masks were distorted, founded upon anachronism and misconception. Lucian describes a tragic actor as 'a repulsive and ... frightful spectacle' appealing only to an effete few, but his intention is satirical, and he refers to the second century CE. Pictures of distorted masks are widely published, and errors are regularly repeated. An ivory figurine of Lucian's time illustrates his description, but, presented as an image of classical tragedy, 'it has done incalculable harm to the conventional picture of the Greek stage'. Masks in 'ancient Greek tragedy' are often said to have incorporated megaphones, whereas 'The point is not that the mouth functions as a megaphone, but that the mask as a whole works as a resonator.'[4] In fact, images of the classical period consistently show that tragic masks were naturalistic.

The masks of Old Comedy must be understood in terms of tragic masks of the same period. Like classical sculpture, these represented an ideal of feature and bearing, which comic masks inverted, very much as comedies often burlesqued tragedy, making heroic actions ridiculous. A vase from Taras helps us to compare the genres.[5] A comic scene between three actors is interrupted by a handsome young man in tragic costume, who has entered from the *skene*. The painter faithfully shows how actors expressed their characters' reactions to the situation, by gesture and body-language. The tragic figure labelled 'Aigisthos' signs 'alas', the slave 'Pyrrhias' is frozen in a broad rhetorical gesture, the older 'Choregos' gestures surprise and, farther away, the younger tilts his head quizzically. Gestures are to be expected, because masks cannot directly signal emotional changes, although actors may sometimes have altered a mask's expression by altering its angle.

While some gestures and styles of movement are characteristic of either comedy or tragedy, the fundamental difference between comic and tragic masks lies in their relative state of being, which could be read in their physiognomy. In the conventions of classical art, an individual's *ethos* was reflected in facial features. The comic actors in the *choregoi* scene are clearly identified as such, by their transparently theatrical costumes and masks, but Aigisthos is not shown to be masked; he looks like a 'real' personage, according to the conventions of tragic vase painting. He has level eyebrows and the indispensable 'Grecian profile' common to serious figures in classical art: the straight bridge of his nose continues the slope of the forehead. He is *spoudaios* (significant); like all gods and heroes, he displays *sophrosyne* in his expressionless countenance. The comic masks are his antithesis, with bridgeless snub noses, bulging eyes and heavy brows, wide mouths and incipient baldness.[6] Theirs is the *geloios* (laughable) mask, 'ugly and twisted, but not painfully' because their nature is *phaulos*, the antithesis of *spoudaios*. In this instance, physiognomy may be ironic; the Aigisthos of legend is morally *kakos*, while the behaviour of comic heroes like Dikaiopolis, Lysistrata and Trygaios marks each of them as morally *agathos*, in spite of their masks (Figure 25).[7]

The expressionless tragic *prosopeion* was not unlike the 'neutral mask' used in modern acting schools, 'a perfectly balanced mask which produces a physical sensation of calm'. Comic masks can be compared to a good 'expressive mask', which Jacques Lecoq insists 'must be able to transform, to be sad, happy, excited, without ultimately becoming fixed in the expression of a single moment'. An actor wearing a good comic mask can express half a dozen of these 'aspects'.[8] While classical conventions lasted, it is unlikely that tragedy was able to employ speciality masks, such as the blind and sanguineous horror that is often proposed for the climax of *Oidipous Tyrannos*. As usual, comedy is different. Its expressive masks could convey a clear impression of character, and perhaps 'dominant emotional states', but strong emotions were avoided, perhaps because a visible response to immediate stimuli was difficult to contrive on stage. One terracotta actor, masked as a young woman, grieves ostentatiously, her gaping mouth, wrinkled nose and narrow eyes tilted upwards to show her grief to the heavens, and her right hand is clapped to her cheek to catch her tears. If this is a faithful picture, it could be our only classical speciality-mask; but if the eyes were level, and the hand removed from the cheek, her expression could be read as no more than a state of habitual indignation.[9]

SIGNIFICANCE OF THE MASK

Spiritual or practical?

Masks in some cultures are believed to have independent power. Balinese *Rangda* and *Barong* masks are kept in temples, and respected. The carving process is sacred, the carver must be purified before he can begin and a priest asks the spirit of the *pulé* tree for permission to use its wood. These masks, however, are primarily religious paraphernalia. *Topeng* dance-drama enacts secular stories from Balinese history, and many of the characters are comic;

some masks would not seem out of place in Old Comedy. Nevertheless, performers make offerings and pray before donning the mask, and while *Topeng* is intended to entertain a present audience, it is also danced for 'an absent other'. Japanese *Noh* mask-making involves no overt religious observance, although it is regulated by tradition, and masks of the Muromachi period (1392–1573 CE) that are still in use are treated with reverence. A new mask is completed when the eyes are drilled out, symbolically giving it life, and a short prayer is said.[10]

We do not know whether Greek actors ever believed that their masks had independent life or power, or whether tragic and comic masks were regarded in the same way. Still, the festivals at which plays were performed were Dionysian, with the god's image placed in the front row. It would be strange if actors failed to acknowledge this present and visible 'other'. Masks were directly associated with the god's cult, when Dionysos was acknowledged in the form of a mask set upon a column and clothed in something not unlike tragic costume.[11] In the fifth century, the masks used in a victorious production were dedicated to the god and hung in his temple near the theatre. Green believes that 'an underlying motive for the dedication of masks in the earliest days of the theatre was . . . to leave behind with the god in his sanctuary the "otherness" created in his honour'.[12] A frequent theme in fourth-century vase painting is the comic actor who attends the god as a member of his band of revellers (*thiasos*). In the same period, travelling actors claimed sacred immunity, and Greek states granted them safe passage. While the nominal service of Dionysos was a useful passport, and respect for the gods was sound policy, it is more likely that practical considerations of security and convenience played a greater part than religious enthusiasm in an actor's travel planning. By the later fourth century, the masks were probably demystified by familiarity, and a climate of rationalism.

To speak pragmatically rather than mystically, without the dramatic mask neither the *agon* nor the *choregia* could have played its competitive part in the development of Greek drama. The mask encouraged 'doubling', which permitted festival rules to restrict the number of actors, while encouraging creativity. There are more than twenty speaking parts in *Acharnians* and *Lysistrata*, requiring actors to 'double' several roles, which provided learning opportunities for the junior actor (*tritagonist*) and allowed a *protagonist* to display his versatility when a subordinate 'stood in' for him while he played a small but effective 'cameo'. Masks and outer costumes could be changed in the course of a few lines, allowing actors to appear in characters of different ages, genders and temperaments.[13] Comedies of mistaken identity were easily outfitted with look-alike masks, and it is possible (but by no means certain) that the pointed satire of Old Comedy was exploited with portrait-masks caricaturing well-known Athenians, such as Sokrates in *Clouds*, or Perikles in Kratinos' comedies. Most significantly, the mask was a stroke of genius, or luck, in the formation of the Hellenistic age. The nuclear acting troupes imposed by the *choregic* system turned out to be ideal for touring, broadcasting Attic theatre throughout the Greek world, where it became a unifying force equal to the gods and their temples.

Mask and metatheatre

It has been said that Old Comedy masks 'have no meaning except in relation to the body of the human animal to which they belong', and are 'associated with the other elements of the comic body: the belly, buttocks and *phallos*', in order to invert the classical ideal.[14] On the contrary, however, it could be said that the actor's mask was distanced from his undercostume, which was more intensely metatheatrical. Vase painters drew the viewer's attention to the costume's artificiality by invariably showing seams and wrinkled tights, but while the comic mask was sometimes acknowledged, its artificiality was never exposed. Aristophanes frequently draws attention to the *phallos*, as when Trygaios points to his 'oar', or Euripides' Kinsman shuttles his *peos* in a vain attempt to escape exposure as an infiltrator at the women's festival. Dialogue that calls attention to a character's feminine beauty may be ironic if the mask's features are ugly, but they are always described as belonging to the character, never acknowledging the mask as a *prosopeion*. Aristophanes' only direct reference to a mask is negative, because Kleon's portrait-mask was never made. It appears, then, that comic costume was linked to the actor, but the mask was capable of independently manifesting a personality. Even when disembodied, its eyes could glitter with mischievous intelligence.[15]

Actor and mask

Dionysos regards such a mask on an *oinochoe* from Paestum, as actors and poets do in several media. These are sometimes interpreted as theatre artists submerging themselves in a character, but according to Lecoq, 'There is no point in contemplating the mask for hours, with heaven knows what mystic concentration, before performing. It must be jolted into life.'[16] It is doubtful whether Greek actors either rehearsed with masks or had time to study them. Perhaps the mask was used as it is in some acting schools, with the object of transferring expression from the face to the whole body, or to 'cast off personal idiosyncrasies, and to rediscover how to use the body'. Masks also help to liberate the actor's emotional expression, and facilitate an escape from naturalism. Some artists believe the masked actor 'loses his ego and can only function as a character', while others see the mask as an 'alienating device' that distances the actor from the role. In the 1920s, Dadaists used masks in their 'search for primordial essences'. Today, performance researcher Michael Chase uses his masks to 'create sounds and movements that are so extreme' that they can express the 'archetypal fields of experience' he finds in Aischylos.[17]

Much of this applies most directly to tragedy. Perhaps masks set actors free of the 'surly bonds of earth' in Aristophanic fantasy, giving them permission to take their clowning 'over the top', but an actor who abandoned his ego to play the Sausage-seller (*Knights*) might not find the exchange profoundly fulfilling. An Athenian male would be unlikely to exchange his ego for any woman's, least of all Lysistrata's. If we recall that no Greek actor or poet is known to have practised both genres, at least before the Hellenistic period, we shall understand that they were regarded as separate arts. Perhaps a tragic actor could submerge his personality in a superior being (*spoudaios*), but the comic actor did something different: his mask stood for an inferior (*phaulos*). Rather than assume such a character, the actor presented it. From the beetle's back it is not the mask of Trygaios but the actor wearing it who calls upon the operator of the *mechane* to be careful (173–6). This alienation breaks no illusion, because in comedy there is none.[18] Tragedy was representational theatre, but Old Comedy was largely presentational and metatheatrical. The mythological burlesques of the fourth century probably offered little incentive for actors to change their methods, but as city comedy developed towards Menandrian psychology comic actors can scarcely have failed to begin internalizing their characterizations. This type of comedy evoked the lives and concerns of ordinary citizens.

Symbolism

To Greeks, masks were symbolic, more profoundly than they are to us today. They became cultural symbols in Hellenistic times, standing for the theatre which, with the Olympian gods, identified a person or community as Greek. In the Peiraeus museum there is a great bronze tragic mask. No doubt it once hung in the theatre there, perhaps with a comic counterpart, in order to convey much the same message as the plaster masks in the

cinema. Actors' monuments show them holding a mask as an attribute.
As Taplin says, 'the mask was fundamentally the sign of the act of impersonation. By putting on the mask the actor declared that he was not just
narrating the story but was *doing* the story.'[19] Masks became ubiquitous as a
decorative theme, in public and private. To decorate one's *symposion* room
with masks was to re-create the Sanctuary of Dionysos. Comic masks adorn
a tomb in the Catacomb of S. Sebastian in Rome, silver serving-bowls for
wine have feet in the form of masks and tiny masks join the delicate chains
of a gold hairnet from Alexandria. They suggest good times, or recall happy
days.[20]

HOW MASKS WERE MADE

Origins

It is uncertain what materials Greeks used in making theatrical masks,
and it would be naïve to suppose that materials and construction methods
remained the same for centuries. Most surviving masks are clay miniatures
a few centimetres high; a few are life-sized or larger, but they are too heavy
and fragile to be worn in the theatre. They are simply decorative, often
bored for a cord for hanging on a wall. All are dated to the fourth century
and later.[21]

There is little literary evidence. The *Souda's* description of masking
experiments by Thespis, combined with other accounts, may point in the
right direction. Thespis began by disguising his face with white lead; next
he hung purslane over his face and, finally, 'linen alone'. A mystifying
reference to *batracheion* says 'they' used to paint their faces this froggy-
green shade 'before masks were invented'. Horace refers to performances
of Thespis' tragedies by men with wine-lees (*faecibus*) smeared on their
faces. Another account has early comic performers smearing gypsum on
their faces when they visited Attic villages to sing comic verses. Aischylos
is said to have introduced masks painted with colours.[22] All of these brief
accounts refer to the sixth century, but the sources are much later. We
do not know how they came by the information, but different versions
of a common tradition may lie behind the face-painting stories. Nor is it
known whether these stories sprang from real events, or from Alexandrian
scholarly speculation; but we can try to assess their probability.

White lead is thoroughly toxic, but it has been used as a pigment since
early antiquity. As *cerussa*, carbonate of lead was used as a cosmetic by

Roman ladies, no doubt with calamitous consequences for their health. The first old woman who accosts the young man in *Ekklesiazousai* (928–9) knows it as *psimythion*, the same word used by the *Souda*. It is possible that Thespis used this familiar preparation as make-up, but it might also be the first cosmetic a mythographer could think of. Next, Thespis turned to purslane, which Pickard-Cambridge interprets as 'flowers';[23] and indeed common purslane has small flowers, but it also has fleshy leaves and thick stems. A man who wore it before his face would resemble a walking shrub. We may perhaps be excused for doubting the veracity of this version, at least for use beyond ritual. For his third attempt, the creator of tragedy wore a mask made of linen alone (*mone othone*), which has been explained as either unpainted or unstiffened. The former fits with the attribution of mask painting to Aischylos, but the latter misses an opportunity of making sense of the reference to gypsum. This must have been in the form we call plaster of Paris, which is made by heating and powdering naturally occurring gypsum. Mixed with water, it makes a stiff paste which could easily be smeared on the face with much the same initial effect as white lead (minus the poison); however, one of the plaster's notable properties is its rapid drying rate. It would have cracked and fallen off long before the last *attatai* was uttered.

Pseudo-Plutarch has probably misconstrued the use of gypsum, by applying it as make-up, in the same way as the *Souda*'s *psimythion* and *batracheion*, or Horace's wine-*faeces*. Perhaps make-up preceded masks in pre-dramatic rituals or performances, but it is unlikely to have evolved into a mask, which is an entirely different way of presenting a character. The purslane, bizarre as it seems, is nearer the idea of masking, if only of some folkloric Green Man from *The Golden Bough*. No doubt the compilers of the *Souda* simply assembled all of the accounts they found attached to the name of Thespis. The most promising version is linen because, unlike the herbs, it could represent a face.

Fabric and plaster

If 'linen alone' refers only to plain, loose fabric, perhaps with eye- and mouth-holes, it could function as no more than a 'mask' in the sense that it conceals the wearer's identity. Because a *prosopeion* stands for the *face* of a separate being, colour may be optional but shape is essential. That is where gypsum comes in. The procedure is simple. On a face-shaped mould of clay or carved wood, the grotesque features are built up, using the same material. Strips of fabric soaked in liquid plaster of Paris are laid over the lubricated mould, adding layers for thick lips or deep wrinkles. When the plaster has dried, the fabric shell is removed from the mould, eyes and mouth are cut out, and facial hair is added. The resulting whitish 'neutral mask' can be very expressive. Nevertheless, white skin in Greek art suggests a woman, because women's conventional place was indoors; men are distinguished by a darker colour, representing the tan that resulted from the outdoor life of a citizen. Brown or russet would be applied to male masks; types and individuals could be further distinguished by painting on features, as Aischylos may have done. A wig was added, turning the mask into a complete 'headpiece'.[24]

If this is how masks developed, they were well suited to theatrical conditions in Athens during the fifth century. The slight evidence for linen-gypsum masks is supported by circumstances which we know to be true. Every festival required a great many masks. A tragic/satyric tetralogy might require between twenty and forty individual masks and up to sixty for the chorus. Comedies needed twenty-four for each chorus and a variable number for speaking and silent characters: *Acharnians* has more than forty. A modest estimate for one Great Dionysia suggests 240 masks would be needed for the tetralogies and 170 for the comedies. All of these masks had to be completed a mere two months after the Lenaia, which must have imposed a considerable demand on the mask-makers. Only the linen-gypsum technique could meet requirements on this scale, because it dries quickly, facilitating mass-production: chorus masks could be rapidly duplicated using a single mould. Even the complex animal masks which we see on early chorus-vases and the *Birds* scene (414) could be easily built up from linen and plaster.

Athens must have supported busy workshops, where many mask-makers laboured to fill orders for the festival season in Gamelion (January/February) and Elaphebolion (March/April). Aristophanes refers to them only once, in *Knights* (230–2) when the First Slave says the mask-makers (*skeuopoioi*) were afraid to make a 'likeness' of Paphlagon/Kleon.[25] Perhaps to mention a mask risked misplacing it within the same metatheatrical context as the comic undercostume, but reticence is more probably attributable to literary distaste for manual labour, some of which may have been carried out by slaves. In contrast, Balinese carvers are highly respected, but their methods are inappropriate to mass-production. Working fast, a skilled man can make a *Topeng* mask in a week. At that rate, wooden masks for a single Great Dionysia would take more than 3,000 man-days to carve.

Wood

Linen-gypsum masks suited the Athenian domestic system of single performances at festivals, with mass-production for choruses. It is less likely
that they were suitable for the tours which began in a small way in the
last years of the fifth century, and developed extensively in the fourth. The
masks are quickly made and light to carry, but they are far from durable.
In modern practice, the plaster-impregnated fabric must be coated with
several coats of polyurethane; otherwise, an actor's breath softens the plaster, the mask loses its shape and ultimately disintegrates. As a consequence,
touring actors probably used masks carved from wood. One hint that this
may have been the case is found in the fourth-century proliferation of clay
masks. Some no doubt decorated *symposion* rooms, but others may have
been dedicated in temples in place of valuable wooden masks. It does not
do to cheat a god of his offerings, but substitution has a long history.

Noh masks are made of cypress, which is abundant in Greece and southern Italy. It is light and easily carved, like the cedar used for ceremonial
masks by First Nations carvers on the Pacific coast of North America. Wood
permits sharp details and a smooth surface; it is also more resonant than
linen. However, it lends itself neither to mass-production nor to the fanciful forms of animal-choruses, which are difficult to carve and expensive to
duplicate. Perhaps a touring *protagonist* might seek to avoid the expense and
aggravation of travelling with a large group of young men by reducing the
size of the chorus, or even eliminating it altogether. This would also have
reduced the cost and difficulty of commissioning and transporting masks
and costumes. We would be going too far to suggest that poets ceased to
write comedies with bird-choruses because they were too cumbersome to
travel, or that type-characterization was developed to permit efficient use
of a small touring stock of masks.[26] There is no doubt, however, that these
innovations made touring easier and more profitable. For New Comedy,
a company had only to carry one mask for each stock type – the father,
witty slave, *pseudo-kore*, parasite – which could be worn for every play in a
troupe's repertoire.

MASK TYPES

Words were the business of a rhetorician, and one chapter of an *Onomas-*
tikon (word book) composed by Iulius Pollux expounds the meanings of
many terms related to Hellenistic theatrical practice. Writing in the second
century CE, he sometimes draws upon sources of questionable value, but

his account of masks may be based upon a first-hand account, 400 years old in his time.[27] Many of Pollux' descriptions of forty-one New Comedy mask types correspond reasonably well with the evidence of terracotta mask models and figurines. Webster identified these with the descriptions, noting that some types were carried over from Old and Middle Comedy. Systematically organizing the types, he identified them by letters of the alphabet, which he used in catalogues of theatrical artifacts; this method was developed in subsequent editions compiled by his successors, and in Trendall's catalogue of the so-called *phlyax* vases.[28]

Webster's analysis of the *Onomastikon*'s comic types has long been the standard prosopography in any discussion of comedy masks. For his analysis of development in theatrical practices in the fourth century, Green has gathered Webster's types into broad classifications according to gender and age: old women, wives and young women, slaves, old or young men, and Herakles. His statistical analysis of masks in comic scenes and on figurines shows fluctuations in the popularity of different kinds of comedy. Old men are most frequent in early Middle Comedy (31 per cent). Slaves are almost as frequent at first (27 per cent), becoming more popular (35 per cent) as old men decline (19 per cent). Young women of any type are initially rather scarce, but by the third quarter of the century their masks represent 28 per cent of the total. These developments suggest that knockabout comedies, such as mythological burlesques and parodies of tragedy, dominated early Middle Comedy, gradually giving way to city comedies of sex-intrigue anticipating New Comedy.[29]

The archaeological evidence shows that many masks of late Middle Comedy anticipate New Comedy to a degree of which Pollux is unaware. Before the middle of the fourth century, comic masks were usually grotesque, 'ugly and twisted, but not painfully' as Aristotle says. Young men were infrequent, and like the younger Choregos, they are no better-looking than their elders and their slaves, with features that express their inferiority as clearly as their padded costume and exposed *phallos* (Figures 19, 37, 48). Unpalatable as it may seem, young women's masks were not much more attractive. Because *Lysistrata* is the favourite Greek comedy in our repertoire today, we may be reluctant to see the heroine staged as a comedy-wife, the least popular of the comic female triad, considered 'generally boring if not unpleasant'. Perhaps she was an exception.[30]

After the middle of the fourth century, young women's masks, like those of the young men who pursue them, become quite presentable. In fact, mask-makers seem to have adopted a new aesthetic for the young lovers, by which, Wiles says, 'Their primary purpose was not to idealize or caricature, but to express something of how people really are.'[31] Nevertheless, the old convention applied to other character types, and continued to do so in Roman comedy. Old men, whether good-natured or irascible, remained ugly and distorted. The nurse, leading slave, cook and parasite are also grotesquely masked, although in a style that differs somewhat from the ugliness of Middle Comedy.

After the middle of the fourth century, the fashion for comic vase scenes was coming to an end. In Paestum, where touring companies seldom visited, Asteas extracted the comic actor from his theatrical context and reassigned him, along with satyr and maenad, as a follower of Dionysos. Painters in Taras turned to portraits of actors in character, or pictures of a single mask hanging by a cord in a frame of Dionysian ivy or grapevine. These are mostly small, personal *symposion* vessels like the *oinochoe*, painted in the fashionable polychrome Gnathia style. Nine-tenths are naturalistic masks of young women, with the blonde, coiffed hair associated with *hetairai*. Masks were reminders of Dionysian good times, at the *symposion*, where wives never ventured but a *hetaira* was a good companion, and the theatre. Most are drawn in profile, but a full-face mask sometimes flashes the broad grin that symbolized comedy in my neighbourhood cinema long ago (Figure 47).

CHAPTER 9

Costumes of Old and Middle Comedy

Articles of clothing are amongst the most frequently named objects in extant comedies and fragments. Stage costume serves as a narrative device, and a visual signifier of character and status. Because garments worn by actors were in many respects the same as everyday dress, Greek audiences read their subtle codes with ease, but a modern audience or costume designer may be baffled by terminology. 'Where did you get that *thoimation*?' asks an Informer. 'Yesterday I saw you wearing a *tribonion*' (*Wealth* 881–2). The Informer's words are a verbal stage direction, prescribing what the Honest Man must wear in an earlier scene as well as in this one. Evidently he has changed his clothes, but what sort of change is implied? Have overalls replaced his Sunday suit? If a gloss explains that he has exchanged a homespun cloak for a woollen one, we may understand that his fortunes have improved, but we may not be able to visualize both garments. When we turn to images the Greeks made of comedies in action, we are inevitably puzzled. Much of our evidence for comedy in the classical age is visual, designed to communicate within a specific culture, time and place. If we are to understand comedy, we must attempt to decode its visual language.

Old and Middle Comedy flourished longer than modern Greece has been a nation. Beginning as an amateur choral event on the fringe of an Athenian festival, it was gradually transformed into a narrative performed by transnational celebrities. It would be strange if costume conventions failed to evolve. Fortunately, visual evidence is now abundant enough to permit us to glimpse some of the earliest comic costumes, and to follow developments during much of the classical period.[1]

CHORUSES

Archaic

For more than seventy years after their first appearance in the sixth century, comedy choruses attracted the interest of Athenian vase painters, no doubt for their imaginative and colourful visual presentation. The artist usually shows a piper leading as many as eight dancers, who may represent a larger group. Each chorus has a distinct identity. Heavily bearded men in hoplite helmets with tall, archaic crests hold patterned cloaks before their faces; some carry severed heads, others ride dolphins. Cloaked men with hunting spears are mounted on ostriches, and others in strange armour ride men costumed as horses. These pictures seek to capture the impact of a spectacular *eisodos*, the entrance of a costumed chorus. We can easily imagine the excitement when an apparently endless procession of giants 3 metres high swayed majestically up the *parodos* and into the *orchestra*, where they turned out to be twenty-four *choreutai* on stilts, wearing pointed hats designed to add to their height (Figure 15).[2] The hoplites excepted, choruses seldom wear the costume of ordinary Athenians. Headgear is either unique, like the pointed hats worn by the stilt-giants, or alien. The 'knights' wear exotic helmets, dancers in both long and short tunics have pointed caps with ear-flaps, or headbands, sometimes adorned with feathers or animal ears. While the dancers' dress is normally as consistent as their steps, several choruses display individual variety in decoration and colour.[3]

Most of these choruses are not obviously represented as masked, but men with flowing white hair and beards, who ran with torches and then stood on their heads, must have been young chorus-men in disguise. The horse-masks expose their wearers' black-figure faces; minotaurs or river gods wear bull-masks, and two men are clearly masked as cartoonish cocks. A pair of dancing bird-men do not seem to wear full head-masks: like some of the hoplites, their beards protrude below a half-mask with a pointed beak-nose, and a four-pointed cocks-comb.[4] Nothing anticipates the masks worn by comic actors after *c.*430, or their unique undercostume. Vast cloaks often hide inner costumes, but those we can see have neither padding nor an artificial *phallos*. The bull-men in one scene wear tufted tights with tails attached, and the bird-dancers have tights with small feathers, but there is neither padding nor an exaggerated *phallos*. The small actor-figure who faces ostrich-riders (Figure 24) wears a long mantle and a half-mask, rather than the indecently short cloak and grotesque head-mask of later comic actors.[5]

Later choruses

Shortly after an *agon* for comedies was established at the Great Dionysia *c.*486, vase painters turned to other subjects. We have no images of comedy in Attic vase painting between *c.*480 and *c.*430, when a few modest pieces begin to turn up, suggesting no more than a desultory interest. Most new subjects are actors, but two scenes show the first choruses in more than sixty years. A pair of bird-men (430) wear tights, patterned to represent plumage, with ithyphallic short-drawers like those worn by satyr chorus-men. Centaurs drawing Nike's chariot should be part of a chorus (410); their peculiar ears and ugly, identical faces show that they are masked, but the artist does not show us how the quadrupedal bodies were achieved (Figure 18). Several fourth-century pictures from Athens and Megale Hellas also seem to show members of a comic chorus. The discernable costume parts are depicted realistically, but they lack the fantasy of archaic choric dress; little distinguishes their costume from the actors'.[6]

THE ACTOR'S UNDERCOSTUME

Athenian painters overlooked comic actors until shortly after the first Lenaian *agon c.*432. The first pictures seem tentative, as though the artists were unsure of the appropriate convention for the representation of their costumes. Most of the pots are in poor condition, but it is clear that actors are usually shown without outer clothing, the better to display the remarkable basic costume which became established in all essentials by *c.*415. I have dubbed this unique garment 'undercostume' because it is unlikely that any Greek terms found in late sources apply to the costumes worn in comedy in the fifth or fourth centuries.[7] Ancient literature fails to commemorate its 'inventor', but the earliest fragmentary picture has been dated *c.*430. The undercostume was swiftly adopted by all comic actors, and remained in continuous use for more than a century.

We might call its main components the 'torso' and 'fleshings'. Unlike a tightly fitted 'leotard', which is designed to show off an athletic body, the comic torso was a body-modifier, intended to make the actor look fat and funny. As Aristotle might have said, when the torso achieved its true nature, it was richly padded at buttocks, stomach and, sometimes, breasts, and skin-coloured, with details like nipples and body hair painted on (Figure 1).[8] Like a one-piece bathing suit, supported by shoulder straps, it was entered from above and behind. 'Fleshings' is a term borrowed from the theatre of the nineteenth century: these were usually skin-coloured, tubular fabric sheaths that covered all four limbs, and were fastened to the torso, which was further adorned with an oversized leather *phallos*, either long and dangling or coiled like a chorizo sausage.

The complete undercostume stood for the skin of the actor's dramatic *persona*; wearing it without any covering costume, he was 'stage-naked'. Worn with the mask, it left only the bare neck, hands and feet to reveal the actor. More than the grotesque comic mask, the undercostume was self-referentially theatrical. Illusion was neither sought nor achieved.[9] The fabric must have been woven wool, only moderately close-fitting and, consequently, wrinkled. Vase painters and coroplasts faithfully reproduced wrinkles, hems at wrists and ankles, and sometimes the length-wise seams of legs and arms. Indeed, on a western Greek vase which seems to represent comedy, any male figure without visible hems or wrinkles is probably not a comic actor.

An actor wore the undercostume throughout his performance, regardless of the type or gender of the characters in which he was required to 'double'. Only male characters are shown stage-naked, because the undercostume represented a male body: there is no evidence of a version with 'female attributes'. Comic male costume was short enough to expose the *phallos*, which was hidden by a woman's long gown, but the padding could make her appear to be pregnant (Figure 41b).[10] The gender ambiguity of the convention led comedy along productive paths, as it did Shakespeare with his boys playing girls playing boys: Rosalind, Viola, Imogen. Aristophanes has two lively cross-dressing scenes, as well as the women's unmasking of Euripides' Kinsman in *Thesmophoriazousai*, which takes full advantage of the concealed *phallos*. In the same comedy, Agathon's sexual ambiguity exploits audience awareness of the *phallos* beneath the feminine dress. The Kinsman asks the effeminate poet, if he is a man, 'Where's your *peos*? Where's your *chlaina*?' (142) The absurdly exposed *phallos* and masculine cloak are equally important in anchoring gender.[11]

The undercostume's origins are not certainly known. Attempts to trace it from cult practices, which are believed to underlie the 'fat men' on archaic Corinthian and Attic vases, are difficult to maintain. The last Attic *komos* scenes were painted a century before our first picture of a comic actor; and while some of the dancers seem to wear padded costumes, most are simply bottom-heavy. In any case, as Seeberg points out, 'the comparison is between the actors of plays and the *chorus* of dancers'. It may be possible that the actor's grotesque physique and similar but apparently unrelated images like the 'fat men' developed independently, as inversions of the classical ideal, manifesting characteristics which Greeks found amusing and contemptible: a large mouth, snub nose, bulging eyes and a fat, unathletic body adorned with a large, flaccid *phallos*. Such men were *phaulos*, physically and morally inferior. Their untended bodies and public privates implied a lack of self-respect. No doubt their appearance could attract 'alienating laughter', because their grotesque appearance made the audience feel superior.[12]

OUTER COSTUME: EVIDENCE

Attic vases provide our scanty evidence of early comic undercostume, but pictures of the other garments worn in comedy must be sought elsewhere. Fortunately we have a great many. A thoroughly realistic convention for depicting comic performances was devised by vase painters in the western Greek fabrics of Metapontion and Taras by the end of the fifth century, leaving us almost 400 images of comic actors by mid-century. Meanwhile, Athenian workshops began to produce crisply detailed terracotta figurines of actors in character, including women's roles. Often brightly painted, these were turned out in large numbers. By 325 more than a hundred different types had been made in Athens, exported and imitated throughout the Greek world. New types continually appeared, many manufactured on the small island of Lipari, which generated almost as many as Athens. More than 250 costumed characters of Old and Middle Comedy have been identified, many in multiple copies.[13] Perhaps inevitably, these media tell somewhat different stories; indeed, until recently, most scholars believed that distinct *genres* were represented. The actors on vases and terracottas from western Greek cities were thought to be strolling players who 'wandered around' playing crude local *phlyax* farce on temporary stages. According to Bieber, 'Everything is more grotesque and realistic in this low-class Italian popular farce than Attic comedy.'[14] Since only the Athenian terracottas were regarded as relevant to Aristophanes, fourth-century figurines and vases from the Greek west were of serious interest to no one, except T. B. L. Webster.

The comic costume controversy

In 1948, Webster suggested that the costumes on the vases were the same as those on the terracottas, and that both represented Attic comedy. Pickard-Cambridge summarily rejected the idea, and when Webster expanded his arguments, Beare took up the cudgels. The subsequent controversy generated more heat than light, but through the din of battle we can infer that Beare was unable to accept the possibility that Aristophanes countenanced the *phallos*. Refusing to accept the vases as evidence, Beare took the *parabasis* of *Clouds* for his text: 'this new comedy of mine . . . hasn't come with any dangling leather stitched to her, red at the tip and thick, to make the children laugh' (534–9). The dispute could not be resolved because Webster believed in archaeological evidence and Beare in Aristophanic text, where most references to the *phallos* are ambiguous enough to pass over if one has the will.[15]

Evidence in two media

This controversy faded away long ago. As a result of new research and shifting attitudes towards visual evidence, it is now widely recognized that the *phlyax* vases of Apulia and Sicily, as well as many terracotta figurines, show scenes and characters from Attic comedy and, probably, local comedy composed on the Attic pattern. This acknowledged, we can seek new explanations for differences in the evidence of the two media. In part, they differ as a function of the inherent characteristics of each. Large vases give a painter space for a whole scene, but a single figurine must be a portrait of an individual actor in a role, rarely in a scene. The physical characteristics of the media govern how each displays the *phallos*. Vase painters were free to follow the theatrical *phallos*-maker's fancy and humour, but the fragility of terracotta deterred coroplasts from moulding small projections. Consequently, while two-thirds of the figurines have a 'looped' *phallos*, vases show two-thirds wearing the dangling leather creations which Aristophanes pretends to repudiate in *Clouds* (536–9).[16] His clay limited the coroplast's accuracy in other details. Free Athenians seldom went out without a long walking-stick (*bakteria*), which is carried by one-quarter of all males on vases, but no more than six clay figurines originally had them, and four of those have been broken. The form of both *phallos* and *bakteria* were useful clues to characterization, but the fragile clay dictated their sacrifice. Indeed, terracotta actors as women rarely carry anything at all. An exception is a fat woman whose *polos* (crown) shows that she is royal or divine. In her extended right hand, the coroplast placed a shaft, perhaps of a sceptre, composed of bronze or some other material that was stronger than clay. Examining it closely, one can see that the shaft has broken away, splitting the hand, arm and shoulder length-wise.[17]

WOMEN'S COSTUME

Tunics

When he dressed for a female role, an actor donned a costume that resembled the everyday dress of his wife or mistress. Outside her home, a respectable woman modestly covered her light indoor tunic with a mantle. In most situations, comic actors do the same.[18] Thus, figurines usually show only the lower skirts of an ankle-length tunic. Some vase painters, however, developed individual techniques for drapery, and apparently enjoyed practising them. Their pictures show details of tunics, which are draped in two basic styles, each using a simple rectangle of fabric. The differences lie in the size and orientation of the rectangle, and whether it passes over or under the wearer's arms. In the style known as 'Doric', the vertical dimension is normally greater than the horizontal, in a ratio of 2.5 or 3 by 1.5 metres. This is folded horizontally at the wearer's shoulder height and passed under one arm (usually the left); front and back are then pinned together at both shoulders. The fold hangs in an overfall, modestly covering the bosom in a second layer. A belt closes the open right side. In the 'Ionic' type, the horizontal dimension is two or three times greater than the vertical, which is only slightly higher than the wearer's shoulder. It is folded vertically on the left side and pinned at intervals along the top, leaving gaps for the wearer's head and left arm; another pin can be inserted beneath the right arm. When it is slipped over the head, the pinned sides resemble sleeves (Figure 20).[19]

Dialogue refers to two types of tunic, the *chitonion*, a diminutive of *chiton*, and the *krokotos* or *krokotidion*. Context shows that both are better than everyday wear, but the former is the finer garment; Lysistrata calls hers 'diaphanous' and 'transparent' (48, 150), which suggests a luxurious indoor gown no respectable woman would wear outside her home, whereas a *krokotos* could be worn in public on special occasions. An old coquette wears hers to claim a lover (*Ekk.* 879). Dye from the stigmata of the saffron crocus gave the *krokotos* its yellow hue, which was regarded as distinctively feminine, and hence irresistibly risible when worn by a male, as when Euripides' Kinsman borrows one from Agathon to attend the Thesmophoria (*Thes.* 253, 1220), or Dionysos descends to the Underworld (*Frogs* 46). Indeed, at these moments 'when men dress as women', donning the *krokotos* 'marks the essential change of identity'.[20] Nevertheless, both tunics were no more than variants of the generic *chiton*. Blepyros tells his neighbour that he could find nothing to wear but Praxagora's *krokotidion* (*Ekk.* 332), but Chremes calls the same garment a *chitonion* forty lines later (374). The distinction depended not upon the garment's form but the fabric of which it was made. A *krokotos* was made of fine linen, but a truly diaphanous *chitonion* must have been composed of rare, silk-like fabrics.[21]

The texts supply names for articles of clothing which we can try to apply to the costumes worn by actor-figurines, or in vase scenes, wherever their drapery takes a distinctive form. How should we proceed, however, when identification depends upon fabric quality? Red-figure vase painters were sparing in their use of applied colour, but terracotta could be painted. We cannot be certain that surviving colours accurately reflect costumes in the theatre, but the evidence of the *krokotos* suggests that they do; Gnathia portraits of elegant *auletrides* confirm that a yellow *chiton* was special, and that therefore yellow gowns ought to be uncommon, and so they are. The exposed skirts of nineteen figurines retain traces of paint, but only two are yellow, one worn by a modest young woman and the other by a crone, like the old coquette in *Ekklesiazousai*. Others are blue (10), white (3), red (2) and pink (2), which suggests that in comedy, if not in the city, plain white tunics were by no means the rule. In fact, it is not unlikely that by the later fourth century the colour of an actor's costume conventionally defined his character.[22]

Vase painters used decoration to signify fabric quality; the richer a garment's borders and pattern, the finer the viewer should understand the fabric to be. This equivalency may have been based upon practice in the theatre, where the audience sat too far from the actors to assess fabrics. It is likely that tragic actors wore intricately patterned costumes to signify the 'dignified garb' appropriate for heroes. Such splendour was not for the world of comedy (except perhaps in parody), but borders and patterns of varying complexity distinguish the finer garments of both men and women. On comic vases, women's tunics of either type may have borders or a decorative panel embroidered on the front of an Ionic type.[23]

Very fine fabrics seldom work well on the stage. Sheer textiles were available, but Lysistrata can merely talk about her *diaphani chitonia*, because its transparency would reveal the actor's undercostume with its *phallos*. This might be suitable for Euripides' Kinsman on the Telephos burlesque vase, but the painter represents his simple Doric tunic as opaque. A strapping *hetaira* in a Sicilian scene wears a transparent gown, but the unmistakably feminine physiology underneath must be attributed to the artist's imagination (Figure 8). More convincing are a *hetaira* who opens her cloak to show that she wears no tunic underneath, coyly flaunting the false breasts of the undercostume, and an absent-minded old woman who has forgotten to wear her *chiton*. A fabric with a pattern, however, could stand for a *hetaira's* alluring 'little *chiton*'; on one vase, it is apparently embroidered in gold.[24]

Outerwear: cloaks, headgear

Comic scenes take place outdoors, where women would normally wear a cloak called an *enkuklon* ('encircler') or *himation*, a word which is also used generically to signify 'clothes'. Anchored by the left arm, this woollen rectangle passes round the back, under the right arm and across the front to the left arm again (Figures 41b, 42). It can cross below the stomach, or be gathered under the chin with the right hand inside; the left can be wrapped as well. A fold can serve as a hood or veil, known as a *kalymma*, held demurely before the face by a true *kore*, or coquettishly away by a false one.[25]

Most female headgear is designed to maintain the *krobulos*, the hair dressed in a roll like a crest above the forehead: the bandana-like net *kekryphalos*, a metallic diadem (*stephane*) and a snood (*mitra*).[26] These have all been taken to identify the wearers as *hetairai*, a slur that is unjustly applied even to modestly veiled young women, whether their hair is dressed in a *krobulos* or simply parted in the middle, as though the mere possession of a hairbrush were enough to convict the owner of moral turpitude. Apply the same criterion to sculpture, and many a goddess would have cause for indignation. It is more prudent to call no woman a whore unless her deportment is immodest by Athenian standards: wearing a patterned gown and fondling an old man, unveiling with an arm akimbo, or wearing a *symposion* wreath.[27]

Shoes

The women's footwear named by Aristophanes are *persikai* and *kothornoi*. The former are Persian slippers, suitable only for indoor wear, but when Praxagora appropriates her husband's boots (*embas*) to attend the Assembly in male disguise, he must slip on her *persikai* to go outside. They also serve as 'bootees' for the 'baby' in *Thesmophoriazousai* (734) and for a peculiar experiment at the Thinkery. *Kothornoi* are associated with Dionysos, who wears them in *Frogs* (557); an ornate variant is worn by tragic messengers, and an actor who holds a hero-mask.[28] Women wore them out of doors, like the old women's semi-chorus in *Lysistrata* (667). *Kothornoi* are not seen on comic figurines or vases, but *persikai* are shown in added white in several scenes, and they are probably the shoes drawn uncoloured in others. They seem to have been simple slippers of soft leather. On vases, most female figures with visible feet are barefoot, but coroplasts often choose the easy way, showing only rounded slipper-toes peeping from beneath a skirt.[29]

MEN'S COSTUME

Tunics

When they played men, comic actors wore the tunics and cloaks of contemporary Athenians, with one notable difference: both garments were so short that the *phallos* was ludicrously exposed. The *chiton* was a rectangle of fabric pinned at both shoulders. Fastened only at the left in order to leave the right arm free for labour, it was known as an *exomis* (Figure 26). This form is most frequently worn with a slave-mask, but quite often with that of a free citizen, usually an old man. By the middle of the fourth century the *exomis* is to be seen less frequently amongst slave or free, partly because cloaks are now more widespread. In the earlier part of the fourth century, no more than half of the male characters in vase scenes and terracottas wear cloaks; after mid-century two-thirds wear cloaks. At the same time, there is a significant shift in the wearers' character types. Now slave-masks are more numerous, and more slaves wear cloaks. Jokes and stage business in comedies show that these garments were expensive. Trygaios looks forward to the return of peace, when *chlaniskidia* will again be available for his slaves. In later fourth-century comedy, those days seem to have returned.[30]

Cloaks

We can easily distinguish the types of men's tunic, because they are pinned differently, but untangling the cloaks worn in comedy is a challenge. Dialogue names a bewildering variety, as modern literature refers to trench coats, blazers, windcheaters and mackinaws. The most common are *chlaina*, *chlanis* and *tribon*, but Aristophanes also names *sisura*, *spolas*, *kaunakes*, *sagma* and *xustis*. A light, summer cloak may be called *theristron* or *lidos*. Today we casually speak of almost any outer garment as a 'coat', and Greeks applied the terms *himation* (or *thoimation*) in much the same way.[31] In one speech, Euelpides refers to the same cloak as both a *himation* and a *chlaina* (*Birds* 493–8). *Himation* seems to refer to any cloak that was wrapped about the body, but probably not to exotic garments (*kaunakes*, *sagma*), countrymen's skin jerkins (*diphthera*, *spolas*), the hairy *sisura*, the fitted *xustis* worn by the *auletes* in the theatre (Figure 21) or the *chlamys*.

Unlike the *himation* genus, a *chlamys* is defined by the way it is worn. It is not wrapped about the body, but worn like a cape, fastened at the neck with a knot or brooch. It may be light and fine, flying behind the wearer, usually decorated with a border or a pattern (Figure 23). It is worn by the young and active, like the horsemen of the Parthenon frieze, and by travellers: when Moschion in Menander's *Samia* (659) pretends he will travel, he calls for a *chlamys*. Orestes, Perseus and Bellerophon wear it in tragedy scenes, but it is also a determinant of the *paidogogos*, the old family retainer who witnesses and reports *katastrophe*.[32] The only *chlamys* named in Aristophanes belongs to the Spartan Herald in *Lysistrata* (987), but it is found on nine figurine types and eleven vase figures. Several of these, which seem to be hairy, might represent the rustic *sisura*. Soldiers wore a red or purple *phoinikis*, which was probably a thicker *chlamys*. Perhaps the terracotta slave who sits on an altar, wearing a *chlamys* with traces of red paint, has stolen a soldier's *phoinikis*.[33]

The primary distinction amongst gowns of the *himation* type rests with the quality of the fabric. The poorest is the homespun *tribon*, which is worn by the chorus of *Acharnians* (342); in *Wealth* the slave Kario's *tribon* is full of holes (714). Improvement of a man's fortunes can be marked by the exchange of his *tribon* for a *chlaina*, which is a superior *himation*, warm and sometimes used as a metaphor for good quality. The *lidos* is a lighter, summer version, but the Poet's thin *lidarion* signals his poverty, prompting Peisetairos to give him a warm *spolas* (*Birds* 915–34). The *chlanis* is luxurious, made of the finest white wool. It may be an exaggeration to claim that a *chlanis* is big enough to supply fabric for three ordinary cloaks, but no doubt it was a large cloak.[34]

As with female costume, a Greek audience cannot have assessed fabric accurately, and conventional equivalents evolved for stage. In the theatre, fabric seems to have been classified by size, borders and patterns. Regardless of quality, any *himation* was a simple rectangle of woven cloth, and size determined how it was draped. In comic costume, the smallest (style α) is the most common (Figure 33). The fabric is gripped beneath the left arm, drawn tightly across the chest, usually in a roll, passes under the right arm, across the back and hangs over the left shoulder, often wrapping the left arm. Style β is a variant of α, in which the fabric is unrolled to cross the chest diagonally from the left shoulder before passing under the right arm. Style γ loosely envelops the entire upper body, often with swags below the throat; both arms are swathed (Figure 40). Because this style seems to have required the largest rectangle, a cloak draped in this fashion may be a *chlaina*.[35]

No *himation* was easy to maintain, as several comic scenes demonstrate. In order to use both arms, one had to tuck it up at the waist, like the old fellow who helps a friend upstairs. A man had to maintain his *sophrosyne*, lest it become disarranged. A momentary distraction by surprise or curiosity allowed it to slip off a shoulder (Figure 27), and to run or strike a slave without removing it could be disastrous. A miser struggling with thieves loses his *himation* altogether (Figure 10).[36] Styles α or β leave the right arm free, hampering action without utterly prohibiting it, as style γ must; it is worn to show that one has no need to work. Daos asks wealthy Sostratos whether he plans to stand about in his fancy *chlanis* and watch others toil (*Dyskolos* 364–5). This is the festive gown, the 'Sunday best' which Peisetairos wears to wed Basileia at the *exodos* of *Birds* (1693).

Styles α and β cannot be identified with the *tribon* and *chlaina*. A poor man had no reason to drape his homespun differently from the style his prosperous neighbour used for his woollen cloak. The only convention a coroplast could apply, in order to distinguish the *chlaina*, was its greater size, but on vases the finer fabric is signified by a border, pattern or fringe. More than half of styles α and β combined are decorated, and their masks identify the wearers as the sort of men we would expect to wear a *chlaina*. Almost all are citizens, and six are shown by their attributes to be gods or kings, burlesqued of course, but nevertheless unlikely to wear a *tribon*. The plain *himation* of either style would represent the homespun *tribon* worn by slaves and poor citizens – or stingy old men like Philokleon in *Wasps*.[37]

Shoes

Athenian men normally wore shoes outdoors. Aristophanes scoffs at barefoot eccentrics, but if the terracottas and vases are to be believed, few actors wore shoes in male characters, particularly early in the fourth century. Footwear become more common later, though most slaves are still barefoot. Nevertheless, shoes were sometimes used to make a point. Praxagora's verbal stage directions require the chorus to put on masculine *lakonikas*, leaving their dainty *persikai* for their husbands. Agathon's lack of *lakonikas* is significant too; no doubt he wears feminine slippers. Rough *embas* were characteristic of the sort of men who also wore the *tribon*, but nothing of the kind has been identified in figurines or comic scenes; perhaps actors avoided them because they would clatter on a wooden stage. Aristophanes devises excuses for their omission: the Honest Man has removed his, Strepsiades' have been lost and when Demos is given a pair at last, he has gone without for 900 lines.[38]

Most vase painters show little interest in shoes, but two dominant types can be identified. The finer must be *persikai*, thin-soled slippers, scooped low at the ankle, rising again at the heel. Frequently rendered in added white, they may have been laced: Dionysos often wears a version with

white dots which may represent golden studs for laces. More common is a
sturdy sandal (*sandalon*), worn by both citizens and slaves; it encloses the
heel but is open at the toe and strapped or laced across the foot. These are
painted with care in Apulian Gnathia portraits of actors (Figures 3, 33).[39]

Headgear

Comic costume makes little use of hats for characterization and identification. The round *polos* can identify a king when he also carries a sceptre
(Zeus, Figures 34, 48), a priestess if she is adding incense to a *thymiaterion*,
or a deity, but only when appropriate attributes are present. Combined
with his *kerukeion* (herald's staff), the broad-brimmed *petasos* identifies
Hermes. Asians are recognized by the 'Phrygian' cap. Travellers wear the
conical felt *pilos*, often with the *chlamys*, but so too do countrymen and
other types.[40]

DEVELOPMENT AND TRANSITION

The *pilos* is a useful indicator of change in comedy, almost disappearing
after the middle of the fourth century. Similarly, old citizens who wear
a fold of their cloaks as a hood are fairly common before 350, but rare
afterwards. Because the garments worn as outer costume differed little
from those of Greeks in the street, aside from the indecent length of the
male *chiton* and *himation*, changes like these may be attributable to shifts
in fashion and social conditions.

The undercostume defined the comic actor. When we first see it on a
fragment of an Attic cup dated *c*.430, the fleshings and torso are clearly
delineated, but the stomach is not padded; indeed, only two scenes painted
before 410 show the padding which had become ubiquitous when the first
comic figurines were made, about a decade later. Thereafter, the undercostume was unchanged until the middle of the fourth century, when some
actors began to wear a dark torso that contrasted with skin-coloured fleshings. Asteas paints the torso in added red, usually with breasts of a lighter
shade, while other artists working in Sicily and Apulia show a black or red
torso.[41]

This innovation may reflect a new practice by one or more travelling
troupes. The costume convention was old and no doubt the humour of the
dangling *phallos* was stale. Why not resuscitate it by taking metatheatricality
as far as it could go? Other actors soon saw that the opposite direction was
available and moved towards greater illusion, as practised in tragedy. New

poets wrote comedies in which young women appeared frequently and prominently; for them and their young admirers, *phaulos* masks would have been incongruous or inappropriately ironic. Now masks were divided into two classes, grotesques (slaves, older people) and naturalistic young folk. For the young men, the padded torso was abandoned and, with it, the exposed *phallos*: their *chitonia* and cloaks were now much like those of everyday life (Figures 8, 39). While slaves and old men still wore short clothes that exposed the *phallos*, it shrank to normal human proportions, as though from embarrassment. There are no more scenes of stage nudity.[42] By 325, New Comedy was but one small step away.

47 *Hetaira* mask, full-face. Photo: A. Hughes.

48 Comic divinities: Hera and Zeus with a young, stage-naked man who also appears in the 'Goose Play' scenes. Gift of Barbara and Lawrence Fleischman, The J. Paul Getty Museum, Villa Collection, Malibu, California.

49 An acrobat who shoots arrows with her feet is representative of many performing women. Antikensammlung. Staatliche Museen zu Berlin – Preussischer Kultur.

50 A comic actor and a woman acrobat perform together. Ashmolean Museum,
University of Oxford.

51 This Hellenistic figurine of a comic slave shows that comic actors could wear padding after the padded undercostume ceased to be ubiquitous. Soprintendenza per i Beni Archeologici dell'Etruria Meridionale.

52 Street scene, showing costumes, masks and hairstyles of New Comedy. Soprintendenza Speciale per i Beni Archeologici di Napoli e Pompei.

53 Menander and three New Comedy masks. Photo: Musei Vaticani.

54 Actors as street musicians in a mosaic derived from an original painting contemporary with Menander. Soprintendenza Speciale per i Beni Archeologici di Napoli e Pompei.

55 Actors as women gossip at table in a mosaic derived from an original painting contemporary with Menander. Soprintendenza Speciale per i Beni Archeologici di Napoli e Pompei.

CHAPTER 10

Comedy and women

Klytemnestra, Elektra, Alkestis: Phrynichos and Aischylos made tragedies from the sad and terrible legends of Bronze Age princesses like these, and composed their choruses of Phoenician, Theban and suppliant women, but women seem to have been entirely absent from archaic Attic comedy. We do not know when the first comic actor put on a woman's mask, but it may not have been in Athens. In Sicily, Epicharmos and Phormis were writing mythological comedies before Magnes' first known victory, and they do not seem to have confined their parodies to all-male myths. Attributed titles include *Muses*, *Prometheus and Pyrrha*, *Bacchai* and *Atalanta*, which suggests women as leading characters, and perhaps in choruses as well.[1]

As far as we know, Kratinos (active from *c.*453) was the first Athenian comic poet to dress his choruses as women. His *Thrattai* (*Women of Thrace*) satirized an alien cult, and *Kleoboulinai* refers to a poetess known for riddles. Women as individual dramatic characters were infrequent in early comedy. There are no women's roles in *Knights* or *Clouds*. Helen may have appeared in Kratinos' *Dionysalexandros*, a travesty of the Paris story, and fictional *hetairai* were the title roles in Pherekrates' comedies, *Coriander* and *Leaf*, but that does not guarantee they were given a great deal to do, or even that they spoke at all.[2] It would be helpful if we could date his *Cheiron*, in which a personification of Music vilified the New Musicians who had been her lovers, or learn whether *Tyrannis* preceded *Lysistrata* (411). Aristophanes is credited with the first comic heroine who is inescapably a *protagonist*'s role, an innovation of great consequence in the development of comedy. We do not know whether Music or the female Tyrant was a harbinger or merely a participant in the developments that followed. Women's names turned up more frequently in titles attributed to poets transitional to Middle Comedy, such as Nikochares, Theopompos and, of course, Aristophanes: about

20 per cent of the speaking parts in his extant comedies are women, but in *Ekklesiazousai* women make up the majority of speakers.[3]

The actors' prizes at the Lenaia (*c*.432) acknowledged the growing significance of dramatic character, and the wider variety of types. Towards the end of the fifth century, interest in actors and their characters stimulated a market for terracotta actor-figurines in Athens. Concurrently, a modest revival in comic vase painting was transmitted to the Greek cities in the west, where touring troupes created a market. The proportion of women portrayed in these two media roughly corresponds to their numbers in Aristophanes' *dramatis personae*: about 15 per cent of characters on the vases, and 20 per cent of figurines made in Attica before 350 are female. At first, older women predominate, but later, young women – mostly *hetairai* – are the more popular subjects.[4] After the middle of the fourth century, women are represented by one-third of the figurines from sites in Megale Hellas and Sicily, of which Lipari was the most important. At the same time, suspended masks of young women became a favourite decoration on small polychrome wine-jugs (Figure 47).

Comic masks defined most women as either old or young, crone or nymph. In comedy, as in Athenian society, there were two kinds of young women: naughty, for fun, or protected, for marriage and the breeding of citizens. Old women past child-bearing were free to go where they chose without imperilling any man's honour: our only scene of women alone has two crones disputing, out-of-doors like men.[5] Their masks are hideous. Audience reaction to any character is partially directed by appearance. While a Greek audience may have been inured to 'the beauty of the ugly' in comic mask and costume, the frightfulness of a few masks exceeded conventional bounds, no doubt deliberately provoking revulsion. Thus, the first spectators of *Ekklesiazousai* recoiled with young Epigenes when his sexual favours were commandeered by three hags, each uglier than the last, like three women in the New York group of terracottas. There was worse to come: the features of some later masks are downright bestial.[6]

Young women's masks are not idealized, but rarely grotesque. A bottle-nosed bride and a large-mouthed woman over whom a father and son fight are exceptions, but ridicule is directed at their admirers, rather than the women. A bridgeless or turned-up nose is associated with comic *hetairai* until the end of the period, but it is also seen on the masks of respectable young women. A wide mouth is frequently combined with 'forward' body-language, such as unveiling or standing with an arm akimbo, to show that a young woman is immodest.[7] Around the middle of the fourth century, however, their appearance becomes more naturalistic. A large head may be the only hint at a mask (Figure 45). Perhaps in some cases the padded undercostume was omitted, although there can be no visual evidence that it ever was. This would have been practicable only when a comic heroine was on stage in almost every scene, so that the actor was not required to double in other parts: this is the type of role a *protagonist* would prefer to play.[8]

Protagonist *roles: Lysistrata, Praxagora*

A *protagonist*'s role, for a slim, attractive heroine: this describes the Lysistrata or Praxagora of our imagination, and most modern productions. We will not take Lysistrata seriously if she is pot-bellied and masked as the unloved wife, the least popular of the comic feminine triad. Did audiences in 411 and 392 take Aristophanes' heroines seriously? If Lysistrata was truly an innovation, predicting public response cannot have been easy: she was unconventional, neither the passive object of sexual pursuit and rivalry nor a submissive wife, but the instigator of a plot against the male citizens, against the audience itself. This was also the case with Praxagora, but after twenty years the innovation may have been less shocking.

Like most of Aristophanes' surviving comedies, the 'women's plays' are fantasies. Athenians were not expected to accept as probable the propositions that women might end the war with Sparta, or take over the management of the *polis*: nor were they obliged to believe that anyone could fly to heaven on a dung-beetle. Probability was not the point. Aristophanes wanted his audience to agree that it was desirable to end the war, or to reform the way the state was governed. These propositions were driven home by the comic incongruity between their fantastic solutions and their source: young wives. Praxagora's name, meaning 'woman effective at speaking in public', would be perceived as an oxymoron; respectable women were scarcely seen in public. Moreover, she is young: in her disguise, Chremes takes her for a young man. Athenian husbands were normally older than their wives, but Blepyros is old for a husband; he fears that the new sexual demands will exceed his ability to perform.[9] Lysistrata ('disbander of armies') may be a little older, but her account of how 'we' will drive the men wild with sexual frustration suggests that she is still young and attractive. She recounts a conversation with her husband, which can be dated 419–418. If she married at 14 or 15, she would be 23 to 25 in 411. She describes her unnamed husband's repressive behaviour, but we never meet him. Perhaps she is a widow: when the other women complain of their husbands' absence at war, Lysistrata says nothing about hers.[10] She goes abroad modestly veiled in a *kalymma*, but she overawes the *proboulos* by sheer strength of will. She takes command confidently, and presides serenely over the peacemaking.

How might these comic heroines have been presented in the theatre? The achievements of Trygaios or Peisetairos were not diminished by their absurd masks, wrinkled tights and *phallos*, but an Athenian woman's dignity was more fragile. The texts say little about appearance. Chremes describes Praxagora as pale and good-looking, but this may be qualified by the perceived tastes of the speaker.[11] Aristophanes deflects the sexual terms of the peace negotiations from Lysistrata to Diallage ('Reconciliation'), carefully preserving his heroine's modesty, but avoiding our question: what does she look like? Comic mask and costume normally invert the Greek ideals of physical beauty, implying that the behaviour of a comic personage must be *phaulos* rather than *spoudaios*. Lysistrata inverts custom and propriety by abandoning the woman's realm (*oikos*) for the man's (*polis*); did this merit a parallel inversion in appearance? The comedy-wife is an ugly spoilsport; can Lysistrata's incongruous behaviour cancel visual typing?[12]

Archaeology provides our best evidence. Lysistrata may have evaded the wife-stereotype because she preceded it. The earliest examples that have been found so far are Charis and the mother of the wineskin-baby in two scenes by Apulian artists, which cannot be dated before 390. Nearer Lysistrata's home and time, two Athenian figurines show us women of the right age, but neither is a wife. The *hetaira* has a wide mouth and rather heavy features, but the mask is not grotesque (Figure 41a). The modest *kore* allows us to see little of her mask, because, like Lysistrata, she is veiled; however, the actor's padded belly makes her appear either corpulent or pregnant (Figure 41b). The only intact Attic scene with an actor in a female role was painted close to the date of the performance (Figure 18).[13] Nike is presented as a capable young divinity, who drives a chariot drawn by centaurs, with Herakles as her passenger. Aristotle might have considered her mask *geloios* (laughable), although certainly not *aischros* (painful) to behold because her turned-up nose falls short of the classical ideal, but she is no ugly wife. Moreover, Nike is slim: the actor wears no padding.[14]

Lysistrata was a radical innovation, a *protagonist*'s part and a woman. She could be presented without regard to precedent. The spoilsport wife's mask would not be created for at least twenty years; therefore, the *protagonist* could choose amongst a narrow range of young women's types, or an entirely new speciality-mask could be created for Lysistrata. The comic actor's undercostume was still developing; in 411 padding was probably optional. Because Lysistrata is almost continuously 'on', the *protagonist* was not required to double in any other character; and consequently, there was no practical reason to wear pads or a *phallos*. We do not know the *protagonist*'s name, or what he decided; but the Lysistrata of our imagination cannot be entirely ruled out as an anachronism.

When Praxagora made her entrance twenty years later, conventions had solidified. Ugly wife-masks were in use, and there is no evidence that any actor 'went on' without his padded undercostume and *phallos*. Moreover, while Praxagora is a *protagonist* role, her last exit comes 450 lines before the end. All hands were needed for the *paignion* of Epigenes and his four admirers (877–1111), which offers the *protagonist* opportunities to demonstrate his versatility; moreover, he probably doubled as Chremes earlier in the play.[15] It is likely that Praxagora was presented as fat and funny-looking, which might have made her Platonic utopia ridiculous in the eyes of the audience.

Deities

Nike is allegorical, a personified abstraction like Peace, Wealth or Iris (the rainbow), whose brutal humiliation by Peisetairos is treated as a joke. Herakles is the most popular figure in comedy, usually characterized as an oafish glutton. His foil in *Frogs* is a cowardly Dionysos, who is frequently mocked at his own festival. Neither is a first-class Olympian, like Poseidon or Hermes, who are satirized gently in *Birds* and *Peace*, but vase scenes show that neither Apollo nor Zeus himself was immune to comic burlesque. In view of this irreverence, it is surprising to find that the Olympian goddesses escaped virtually unscathed, both in Aristophanes and the material evidence.[16]

There cannot have been any law or taboo against impersonating them in a theatre. Athene is a benevolent character in five extant tragedies, but Euripides characterizes Aphrodite as malicious, destroying Hippolytos, to the chagrin of Artemis. In a fragment of Platon's *Phaon*, Aphrodite seems to be portrayed as the stereotypical drunken woman of comedy, but Hera is the only Olympian goddess who appears on a comedy vase (Figure 48). She plays a scene with Zeus and a naked, arrogant-looking young man who was a leading character in the 'Goose Play'. Masked and costumed as an ordinary old couple of comedy, only their divine attributes showed that Zeus and Hera were gods. In another scene, a young Hera is enthroned, sceptre in hand, with '*HPA*' painted above her crown. She watches a combat of comic actors. Nothing identifies the figure as an actor with a

mask. The artist has drawn her face and hair exactly as he renders those
of a mortal woman, but quite unlike his only female comic mask. This
is the goddess herself, perhaps only present in spirit, to supervise a comic
fight in a mythological burlesque: the actors are labelled Daidalos and
Enyalios.[17]

REAL WOMEN

'Drama, like all public poetry in the classical period, was written, produced and performed only by men.'[18] That is accepted history. Henderson
reminds us of an axiom, something we think we know, so obvious it need
scarcely be mentioned and, consequently, seldom is. Indeed, in the ancient
literature that has come down to us, it is never said at all, perhaps because it
was self-evident. Or is it possible that there other reasons? A wise historian
once said, 'in using accepted history we must make sure that it deserves
to be accepted. It is a gift horse that cannot be looked too often in the
mouth.'[19]

Looked in the mouth, Henderson's assertion is broad and unqualified.
'Public poetry' should refer to *genres* sanctioned by a *polis*, and presented at a
public event, such as a festival. Little is known about festivals in cities other
than Athens, but that cannot justify the wholesale application of what we
know or assume about Athenian festivals to other *poleis*. Like Coriolanus,
we must protest, 'There is a world elsewhere.' The dithyrambs and hymns
of Praxilla of Sikyon and Korinna of Tanagra were public poetry, classical
in date, written by poets who were no less Greek for being neither Athenian
nor men.[20] Can we be certain that no women practised dramatic poetry?
The troupes that toured throughout the Greek world in the fourth century
did not all originate in Athens. Syrakousai and Taras generated their own
performances, in a variety of *genres*. In accepted history, the term 'drama'
has been applied only to tragedy, comedy and satyr play, to scripts that
have passed into literature: but they were written to be performed in the
theatre, and the Greek art of the theatre includes the miscellaneous forms
we call 'mime'.[21] We have fragments by Sophron of Syrakousai, whose
fifth-century prose mimes Plato allegedly enjoyed; his successor Xenarchos
wrote at the court of Dionysios I, and was known to Aristotle. Like early
dithyrambs and comedies, mimes could be composed rather than written.
We know neither the names nor the gender of their composers, but there is
evidence that many of their performers were women.[22] Indeed, women may
sometimes have taken part in Aristophanic comedy, even in fifth-century
Athens.

Women in the audience

Could women attend the theatre? This debate has run longer than *The Mousetrap*. In the nineteenth century, some scholars believed that Athenians, anxious for the moral welfare of women and boys, excluded them from the theatre, or at least from comedy. Noting the practical difficulty of ejecting part of the audience before the comedy began, Haigh combed ancient literature for evidence which showed, he argued, that 'Men, women, boys and slaves were all allowed to be present.' In a vigorous riposte, Rogers, translator and bowdlerizer of Aristophanes, used the same evidence to argue that 'no women were present at any of these comedies', although 'An Athenian maid or matron, walking through the streets . . . could not choose but witness on every side, and indeed at every door, signs and symbols of (to Christian minds) "unspeakable pollution".' Fifty years later the same evidence prompted Lucas to assert that 'women were admitted to tragedy, and probably even to comedy'. Dover added with equal conviction that women could take a seat only after male citizens were accommodated. Today, little has changed. Podlecki has assembled the *testimonia*, which impartially support both Henderson's persuasive argument that women must have been admitted to the theatre, and much of Goldhill's equally well-argued case for the opposite view.[23]

The literary evidence is scanty, ambiguous and consequently open to contradictory interpretations: that is why Webster called it 'treacherous'.[24] A new approach is needed, but on this subject archaeology has (so far) nothing to offer. Aristophanes addresses his audience as 'gentlemen', but Henderson brings a fresh perspective to the dispute by arguing that this homogeneous masculinity was merely 'notional'. Women were present in the Theatre of Dionysos, but Athenian 'protocols of silence' drew about them a curtain of 'conventional invisibility'. Moreover, a pragmatic poet knew that the judges were male citizens: their peers in the audience might be persuaded to influence their votes, but an appeal to women could recoil upon the poet.[25] Approaching the dispute through Athenian religious observances, Sourvinou-Inwood argues that since the basket-bearer (*kanephoros*) and the Priestess of Athena Polias participated in the rituals, other respectable women could hardly have been excluded from the performances.[26] To these arguments, I must offer an observation from a lifetime in the theatre. The composition of theatrical audiences, and of any acting class, show that any attempt to exclude women from the theatre would be futile. 'The feminine', says Zeitlin, 'is the mistress of *mimesis*, the heart and soul of the theater.'[27] Despite customary repression of women,

Athens neither enacted laws to exclude them from the theatre nor possessed powers of coercion capable of keeping them away. In Dorian cities
like Syrakousai and Taras, where women were less confined by custom,
they must have formed a substantial proportion of audiences.

Almost everything we know of repression is derived from Athenian
literature, which may express the male citizen's ideal more accurately than
it describes reality. Men thought it was ladylike to stay at home, but in
the hard times that prevailed for much of Aristophanes' career, few could
afford to keep their wives and daughters in strict *purdah*, or to enforce it
while they were away on campaign. Poor citizen-farmers like Dikaiopolis
needed their women's help. Many widows must have fended for themselves,
and it is likely that women enjoyed more freedom as they grew older. By
'women', we frequently mean the citizen minority, outnumbered by metics
and slaves who were nevertheless women. *Hetairai*, *auletrides*, dancers and
prostitutes made careers of going where respectable citizen-class women
could not. For that matter, so did poor fishmongers and market-women.
None of these had anything to lose by attending the theatre.

Poets

The southern slope of the Athenian Akropolis has yielded fragmentary but
extensive inscriptions which we call *Fasti*, 'victor lists' and '*didaskaliai*'.
They name a great many poets whose plays were performed at the Great
Dionysia and the Lenaia throughout the classical period, and on into the
second century.[28] More poets are named in ancient literature, by authors
as serious as Aristotle or frivolous as Athenaios of Naukratis, who claims
to have read 800 Middle Comedies. The names are relentlessly male. This
is taken to mean that only men wrote comedies (or tragedies), and indeed
there is no evidence to the contrary. Nevertheless, some women were quite
capable of writing plays; we have a few names and poetic fragments, and
while none are Athenian, highly literate women must have lived in the
city and attended the theatre.[29] Such a woman would be aware of the
inevitable outcome, were she to ask the *archon* for a chorus in her own
name, but another avenue was open. An educated, witty woman, such as
a superior *hetaira*, would be intimately acquainted with members of the
literary elite, men who could plausibly submit a comedy. We know that an
experienced *didaskalos* and poet sometimes presented a beginner's comedy
as his own: Kallistratos 'fronted' the first three comedies of Aristophanes,
who subsequently provided his son Araros with a comedy or two.[30] Thus, it
was not impossible for a woman to write a comedy and to see it produced,

but her authorship would remain hidden unless someone tattled. Why not? If we knew George Eliot only as a name on an inscription, we never would have heard of Mary Ann Evans.

Design and production

Comic costumes could be fanciful – dogs in *Wasps*, War in *Peace*, choruses of birds or clouds – but there is no record of whose fancy conceived them. Only a skilled professional could have built the centaur-costumes for Nike's chariot-team, or the animated eel in *Acharnians* (881–94). Today, costume design for an entire production is co-ordinated by a specialist, but it has not always been so. As late as the 1880s, a leading lady's personal designer created her costumes, while the rest of a large cast were dressed by a contractor. Perhaps a *protagonist* arranged for his own costumes, and the *choregos* handed over the chorus to a workshop, where many hands would be employed to produce two dozen costumes. It is improbable that the cutting and sewing was all done by men. The same conditions apply to mask-making, and the skilled leather-workers who built those extravagantly artificial *phalloi*. Running crew would certainly have included dressers, indispensable for the quick changes that were essential to doubling, and some version of our stage managers, who keep their heads when actors are losing theirs. Backstage staff, cottage-workers, factory hands, slave or free: it is impossible that all were male.

WOMEN PERFORMING

Musicians

In tragedy and satyr play, dithyramb and comedy, the chorus was always accompanied by the *aulos*. In vase scenes of early comic choruses, the piper is often conspicuous in his handsome *xustis*, sometimes drawn larger than the dancers, emphasizing his importance. In the later fifth century, the most illustrious *auletai* composed their New Music for dithyrambs, leaving the simpler music of comedy to musicians of less consequence. Exceptionally, a *choregos* might engage a specialist for a scene requiring more difficult music, like the Tereus solo or Prokne's 'song' in *Birds*.[31]

Women played the *aulos* at private *symposia*, but there is no evidence that they played in public before the fourth century. In Athens, *auletrides* may have been prohibited from playing at the Great Dionysia. Around 350, painters in Taras found a market for *symposion* vessels decorated with portraits of popular entertainers, actors in character and glamorous *auletrides*.[32] Painters in western workshops show them as official pipers in comedies. In an Apulian scene, two actors carrying food on a spit follow an *auletris* across a stage. Scenes from Campania show *auletrides* performing with comic actors, one of whom speaks and gestures from the stage towards the woman who plays her pipes in the *orchestra* below. Like the male pipers in Attic scenes of satyr plays, she wears a patterned, long-sleeved *xustis*. Two scraps of fourth-century evidence imply that an *auletris* could sometimes accompany a comic chorus in Athens, perhaps at the Lenaia. Vase fragments in the Benaki Museum show a chorus of old men who dance to the accompaniment of an *aulos* played by a pair of white hands; white is a vase painters' convention for women's skin. And part of a figure leading a comic chorus on a marble relief has been interpreted as an *auletris*, because small feet in Persian slippers peek from beneath the long *chiton*.[33]

Women on stage

The series of portraits from Taras includes a lively picture of an *orchestris*, a dancer. In the background, double doors, half-open, seem to signify a *skene*, and that she dances upon a stage, although not necessarily in a theatre. It is abundantly clear that she is a real woman, because she is almost naked. Like the *auletrides* she is fair, probably bleached. Physically she is remote from the classical ideal: her voluptuous figure and awkward gait suggest that she is a comic dancer, probably in a mime show rather than comedy. She is uniquely significant as the first woman performer whom we know by name: it is painted above her head, 'Konnakis'. Similar evidence links other women who performed as dancers, jugglers and acrobats as performers of mime with comedy, and with Dionysos.[34]

Attic scenes apparently illustrate schools of mime, where musicians accompany women who rehearse a variety of dances and acrobatic feats. Several of their performances correspond with Xenophon's description in *Symposion*, our only classical account of a mime performance. A small troupe from Syrakousai performs at a private dinner. As in the school scenes, an *auletris* plays accompaniment. A youth dances and acts Dionysos to the Ariadne of an *orchestris*, who is also an accomplished acrobat. She juggles twelve hoops, bends backward so that her body resembles a hoop, turns somersaults in and out of a circle of upright swords. Moreover, she is ready to begin some sort of performance on a potter's wheel, when she is forestalled by Sokrates.[35] Pictures from Megale Hellas supplement the school scenes, with women tumbling and hand-standing amongst swords and *kottabos*-stands, or upon potter's wheels. Often upside down, women juggle hoops, balls and a spinning top; most remarkable is the Greek Annie Oakley who rests on her forearms to shoot an arrow with a bow held in her feet (Figure 49).³⁶

Comparison of these scenes, Athenian, Apulian, Campanian and Sicilian, supplemented by figurines in bronze and terracotta, clarifies several issues. While the sword-dance and the 'Pyrrhic' dances of armed girls might sometimes have cult significance, they were also performed as entertainment. A graceful dancer, modestly cloaked and veiled, could strip down to a brief *chitonion*, or to nothing all, and execute a sprightly dance with castanets (*krotala*). And all of them, together with grotesque dancers like Konnakis, acrobats, satyrs, maenads and comic actors, were perceived as belonging to the *thiasos* of Dionysos, his band of revelling companions. They dance together, in the Greek imagination, and around the rim of an Apulian oil-jug.³⁷ Two scenes by Asteas, the Sicilian emigrant who founded the Paestan fabric, link the acrobat-mime directly with comedy. In one, a woman balances on her hands upon a potter's wheel, which is turned by an actor (Figure 50). The other shows a white-skinned acrobat hand-standing on a low stool in front of Dionysos, who gestures astonishment. It is clear that her act is part of a comedy, because she is performing upon a stage, two actors watch her and two others masked as women are framed in *skene* windows above.³⁸

There is no doubt that women were employed in mime during the classical period. Acrobats, musicians and dancers performed at private functions, and when these engagements failed they must have played in *agora* and street while a colleague passed the *pilos*. It is not easy to determine how mimes and comic actors worked together. Fragments of Middle Comedies do not refer to them, nor is any dialogue attributable to mimes. Perhaps they seldom spoke: they are mute in Xenophon, even in the little play of Ariadne and Dionysos. Greek scripts contain no explicit stage directions, but Aristophanes embeds verbal and implicit stage directions in his dialogue, showing that eight of his extant comedies call for thirteen mute adult females.³⁹

Mutes

Most of Aristophanes' mutes are allegorical, representing 'social, political or quasi-religious abstractions', and sometimes serving as sexual mechanisms for the rejuvenation of *protagonists*.⁴⁰ At first sight of the female Peace

Treaties, Demos asks, 'Is it OK if I lay them down and ratify them?' Most
are passive, like the attendants on Peace who serve to gratify the *boule*
and marry Trygaios, much as Basileia exists merely to confirm Peisetairos'
victory by becoming his consort. In *Lysistrata*, Diallage is no more than a
symbol of the renewed fertility which Reconciliation will bring.

    Peace is a statue, but the other mutes must be acted. An early editor
thought naked slave-prostitutes were used, and a second suggested men
with female masks and tights with painted female genitalia.[41] No controversy developed, but scholars subsequently adopted one position or the
other. Opinions were evenly divided until Stone's *Costume in Aristophanic
comedy* pronounced in favour of men in 'leotards'; since then, advocates
of nudity have been scarce.[42] Both hypotheses were devised to accommodate assumptions whose purity is unsullied by evidence. Since no Athenian
woman of the citizen class would consent to appear naked in public, one
party assumed that a *hetaira* could be paid or compelled to perform sat-
isfactorily at the Lenaia, at a date when the average mean temperature in
Athens today is about 10 degrees Celsius. The contrary position is founded
upon a similar chain of assumptions: men played all parts, therefore men
played the mute women, but since these characters are naked females, the
men wore 'leotards'. Comic actors' tights bore scant resemblance to the
physique-flattering innovation of Jules Léotard, the original 'daring young
man on the flying trapeze'. Some sixty-five vase pictures of stage-naked
actors, clad only in the comic undercostume, show us exactly what it
looked like. It is inconceivable that any of them could have been intended
to represent a woman.[43]

    Both parties imagine that the mute women must be naked because male
characters comment upon their anatomy; therefore 'spectators in the last
rows should be able to see something of the described particulars'. Because
Lysistrata's Athenian allies admire her breasts, Lampito was 'demonstrably'
played by a man in tights 'with breasts and pubic hair'.[44] In the theatre, the
reverse is demonstrable: some things are better described than displayed.
A fundamental convention links Noh with Theatre Sports, Aischylos with
Pinter. Dialogue describes precisely those things which spectators *cannot*
see: 'Be your tears wet? Yes, faith,' says Lear. Only his words tell the gallery
that Cordelia is weeping. Audiences readily embrace the 'willing suspension
of disbelief . . . that constitutes poetic faith'.

> Think, when we talk of horses, that you see them
> Printing their proud hoofs in the receiving earth.[45]

If the hypotheses of real or artificial nudity are set aside, how can the mute women have been presented? We can discern amongst them several types, and no doubt Aristophanes' audience recognized others, both in the comedies we possess and in those that are lost. Only the chance survival of an ancient commentary permits us to distinguish between the statue Eirene (Peace) and the merely passive Opora and Theoria. Perhaps the latter, and the allegorical Basileia, were costumed as veiled brides. We can only guess how any of the passive figures was played, because we have no evidence. Some roles would require 'speciality performers', such as children, musicians, dancers and the singer of Hoopoe's monody.[46]

A specialist of a different stamp may have appeared as the *auletris* abducted by Philokleon in *Wasps*. Some editors give her a final exit before the bread-woman's entrance (1388), but we should consider why Aristophanes specified that the woman the old reveller brings home should be a musician. In *Acharnians*, Dikaiopolis also returns drunk from a party, accompanied by two girls who establish his rejuvenation in sexual terms remarkably like those in *Wasps*;[47] but the text does not specify what sort of women they are – *hetairai*, dancers or even acrobats – and, coincidentally, they have little to do.

Philokleon's rejuvenation is unique, because it is expressed in dance. After the short *parabasis*, Xanthias tells us that the old man was so delighted by the *aulos* at the *symposion* that he is still dancing, inside his house (1474–81). We have seen him bring the *auletris* inside the *skene*: now we must hear her music. In a moment Philokleon enters through the double doors, dancing extravagantly. Next, he dismisses the three dancer-sons of Karkinos, each in a few words, because words are of small importance here. This scene is a dance *agon*, which would play longer than the dialogue implies: each son dances his challenge, only to be discountenanced by Philokleon. In a thoroughly practical way it demonstrates the superiority of good old 'Thespis dances' to the crabbed modern dance associated with the New Music which Aristophanes satirizes at every opportunity.

A man could not dress as the *auletris* because it was impracticable to wear a mask and play the *aulos* simultaneously.[48] More probably, the specialist was presented from her first entrance as a respectable *auletris*, dressed in the *xustis* of her profession. The guest-list suggests that the *symposion* from which she was snatched was not the sort where a tawdry flute-girl was expected to confer favours later in the evening: it was an elegant affair, until Philokleon disrupted it.[49] Moreover, Bdelekleon recognizes the woman at first sight, calling her by name, Dardanis (1371). It is likely that she was a well-known personality, like the *auletrides* in the Tarentine portraits, and that the actor's job was to let the audience know it.[50]

The case of Elaphion may have been similar. Whenever Aristophanes brings Euripides upon the stage as a character, he satirizes the poet's music in the new style, which 'wi-i-i-i-nds' a single vowel through many notes. Near the end of *Thesmophoriazousai*, Euripides rescues his Kinsman with the aid of a dancer and an *auletes* he calls 'Teredon'.[51] Again, a specialist was recruited to perform the New Music, but this time Aristophanes gives him an ironic name which suggests the 'shipworm' that bores winding holes through a ship's planking. Euripides calls the dancer 'Elaphion' ('Fawn'), probably a stage name.[52] In order to distract the Scythian policeman, she prepares to dance by taking off her shoes and '*thoimation*' (1181, 1189); this recalls the muffled dancers in the school scenes, who have set aside their cloaks to dance in a brief *chitonion*. If this was Elaphion's working costume, the role could not be danced by a man, either in his own skin or the actor's grotesque and phallic undercostume.

The scene makes little sense unless Elaphion is a real woman. She might be young and nimble as her name implies and the Scythian observes (1180); or perhaps 'Fawn' was ironic, and she was a comic dancer like Konnakis, whose ample endowments and graceless dance would delight the barbarian and burlesque the Euripidean music. The Scythian's enthusiasm would certainly be funnier.[53] Either way, there is reason to suppose that she and Dardanis were in fact the women they appeared to be.

CHAPTER II

New Comedy

Anecdotes in which Philemon dies laughing are difficult to believe; he was a poet of New Comedy, which was no great laughing matter. If Old Comedy can be described as 'men dressed up being funny', a century later the new type had evolved into something like Euripides-and-water. If we are disappointed to find that Menander is lacking in hilarity, perhaps we have been misled by his successors, from Molière to Alan Ayckbourn. Humour was not his first priority.

John Fletcher might have been referring to New Comedy when he said, 'A tragi-comedy is not so called in respect of mirth and killing, but in respect it wants deaths, which is enough to make it no tragedy, yet brings some near it, which is enough to make it no comedy, which must be a representation of familiar people, with such kind of trouble as no life be questioned.' In Menander's *Aspis* (*The Shield*), the bloated corpse which Daos mistakes for his master's, and the covetous gloating of Smikrines, the young man's uncle, set a sombre mood from which the play does not easily break free. Circumstances in *Samia* are similar to those which lead to the *katastrophe* in *Hippolytos*, and Demeas uses Euripidean language to express his emotion.[1] The people of New Comedy may meet with real harm and genuine distress, for its themes play upon avarice, misanthropy and loneliness, love, loss, jealousy and, of course, the rapes of maidens. 'As Tragedy was becoming more deliberately artificial, less natural in appearance, Comedy was moving towards taking over the ground of creating situations, through so-called "situation-comedy" that the ordinary man-in-the-audience could relate to from his own experience. This too must have been seen as startlingly new.'[2]

Frequently, some obstacle or misunderstanding stands between a young man and the woman he wants – her desires are not considered. Menander takes care to give his audience the advantage of his characters, constructing ironic situations in which this privileged knowledge assures us that all will be well in the end, when the obstacle is removed, either by chance or stratagem. In *Samia*, the prologue tells us that Demeas' suspicions shall be groundless. Shakespeare uses a similar device in *Twelfth Night*, when the audience is shown that Viola's grief at the supposed loss of her brother will eventually dissolve in a joyful reunion.

Aristophanic fantasy is replaced by commonplace urban settings in which human actions never transcend probability (although frequent coincidences strain credibility). Comic heroes like Trygaios or Peisetairos, who fly to Olympos or challenge the gods, have yielded to new types, soldiers, or sons of affluent citizens. Now an old farmer like Knemon in *Dyskolos* (*The Peevish Fellow*) becomes the 'blocking agent' between young Sostratos and the girl he desires, rather than an innovative thinker like Dikaiopolis, who contrives a Peace. Expectations of individual success supplant dreams of peace and prosperity for the *polis*. As Handley aptly says, 'In Menandrian comedy it is not so much what happens, as how.'[3]

If Anaxandrides constructed plots about 'love affairs and the rapes of maidens', city comedy preceded Menander by half a century, but it was only one amongst a variety of Middle Comedy types.[4] Tragic parody and mythological travesty, in which heroic characters and stories were translated into low life, were popular still; but political and personal satire had declined. Defeated by Sparta in 404, Athenians may have lost some of their zest for politics, and their sense of their city's importance, but we must not oversimplify. Democracy was promptly restored, Athens recovered her imperial ambitions, and embarked upon those triangular rivalries – Athens and Thebes against Sparta, Sparta and Athens against Thebes – that make fourth-century history exasperating. Politics and warfare continued as usual, leaders arose, were assassinated (Thrasyboulos, 389), exiled (Kallistratos, 382) and reviled each other (Demosthenes and Aeschines), but none of this left its mark on comedy, where the audience came to prefer characters and plots that reflected their own lives. A significant change in taste had taken place, and was sustained for the entire Hellenistic era.[5]

In a manifesto of another revolution in literary taste, Wordsworth promised 'to adopt the very language of men'. Aristotle refers to a similar change: 'In comedy . . . the poets construct the plot on the basis of probability, and only then supply arbitrary names; they do not, like iambic poets, write about a particular person.'[6] He prefers probability, and believable, fictional characters, rather than fantasy, or the invective which was characteristic of the anapaestic *parabasis*. Aristotle's observations apply to the state of comedy between the middle of the fourth century and 335, when, on the brink of the Hellenistic age, he established his school. New Comedy was the dominant drama of Alexander's blend of Greek and Asian cultures, in which the Greek component was manifested almost equally by its gods and temples, Athenian drama and theatre buildings. When Aristotle called for realism, city comedy was becoming dominant, and mythological burlesques were becoming rare.[7] As early as the 350s, the young poet Alexis began to practise elements of the emerging style. Some of his titles are *hetaira*-names like *Agonis*; others suggest a foreign-born woman, such as *Olynthia and Milesia*, foreshadowing comedies like Menander's *Samia*. Forms of versification common in New Comedy, and character types like the cook and parasite, are found in fragments of Alexis, who also foreshadowed the formula Menander used to introduce his chorus.[8]

CANONICAL POETS

Perhaps because much of his long career belongs chronologically to Middle Comedy, posterity excluded Alexis from the canonical triad of New Comedy poets. Diphilos first competed *c*.335, and Philemon won his first victory at the Lenaia in 327. Menander was the youngest, and the last to compete. He was an immediate success, victorious with either his first comedy, the lost *Orge* (*Anger*), or *Dyskolos*, between 317 and 315.[9] Perhaps the judges rewarded a young poet's fresh wit and lively characterization, but Menander enjoyed few subsequent victories, probably no more than eight. Nevertheless, posterity made him the most popular author after Homer and Euripides. His surviving comedies cannot be measured against those of his rivals, which are all lost, but they were performed and read for centuries. The secret of Menander's posthumous success may be discerned amidst posterity's hyperbole. 'O Menander and life', Aristophanes of Byzantion gushes, 'which of you copied the other?' Quintilian praises his accurate representation of human types, temperaments and moods. His diction, says Plutarch, 'comports with every nature, disposition, age', giving 'to a king his dignity, to an orator his eloquence, to a woman her artlessness, to an ordinary man his prosaic speech, to a market lounger his vulgarity'. His characters are believable, as Aristotle prescribed: 'he held up a mirror to life and enshrined the image in his works'.[10]

The output of these New Comedy poets was prodigious. About 100 comedies are attributed to each of Menander, Diphilos and Philemon, and Alexis is alleged to have written almost 250.[11] Anecdotes attribute extraordinary longevity to Alexis and Philemon, but Menander had a career of no more than thirty years, averaging more than three plays a year, three times the rate of the Old Comedy poets. Aristophanes produced only forty plays in his career of forty-one years; Eupolis and Kratinos, respectively, staged seventeen comedies in eighteen years, and twenty-seven in twenty-five or thirty years.[12] How can we explain this difference in the practice of comic poets? Were Aristophanes and his rivals less industrious than their counterparts in tragedy, who composed annual tetralogies in order to be eligible for competition? Conceivably, custom discouraged a poet from entering comedies in both the Lenaia and the City Dionysia in one year, at least in his own name; but no such limitation can have applied in Menander's time.[13] A great deal had changed in the theatre.

FAME AND FORTUNE

In the fifth century, writing plays, and acting in them, had been avocations; now they were professions, and potentially lucrative. Alexis was said to have come from Thurii in Italy, Diphilos from Sinope on the southern Black Sea, Philemon from either Syrakousai or Soli, 1,200 kilometres away in the north-eastern Mediterranean. Correct or not, these accounts acknowledge that Athens remained the unquestioned theatrical metropolis, where success generated fame, which for actors led to profitable tours and invitations. Satyros performed for Philip at Olynthos; Lykon, Phormion and Ariston at Alexander's wedding in Susa. When Lykon inserted a line in a comedy, asking for 10 talents, Alexander gave them. To rebuild Apollo's temple at Delphi the tragic actor Theodoros gave 70 drachmas; no other individual offered more than 15.[14]

It is unclear how a poet converted fame into fortune. No doubt the tyrant Hieron made it worth Aischylos' while to visit Syrakousai, and Archelaos surely rewarded Agathon for joining the Macedonian court, but we hear of no comic poets in Alexander's entourage. Nevertheless, more than one-third of Menander's premières must have taken place beyond Athens, where there were still no more than two annual opportunities to present a comedy. We have little direct evidence of touring, but it must have been common. Perhaps a *protagonist* would commission a new comedy for his tour. No doubt some cities offered prizes for comedies, with wealthy citizens serving as *choregoi*, as an inscription shows Delos to have done in 282.[15]

Another significant change in Athenian theatre was its gradual accommodation of repertoire. In the fifth century, the Great Dionysia and the Lenaia remained festivals of new plays, written and performed (once only) by amateurs. Shortly after the death of Aischylos, performances of some of his tragedies were presented as 'modern classics', perhaps outside the *agon* for new tragedies at the Dionysia. *Frogs* was so successful that it was revived, probably in 404. As the renown of Athenian tragedy and comedy spread, first the Attic demes and then distant cities revived plays for themselves, and welcomed touring companies which performed a repertoire of classics. In Athens itself, professionalism inevitably led to revivals: audiences wanted to compare Thettalos with Polos as Orestes, as Londoners compared Olivier with Gielgud as Hamlet. 'Old' tragedies were revived at the Great Dionysia in 386, and had become a regular part of the festival by 341; comedy followed, irregularly in 339, officially in 311. These performances were ineligible for the poet's prize, but they were vehicles for actors. The date of the first *agon* for comic *protagonists* at the Great Dionysia is uncertain, but the actor's growing importance was recognized when the victor's name became a matter of public record between 329 and 312.[16]

Significant changes were made in the relationship between the *polis* and its dramatic festivals. The *choregia* was probably established by Peisistratos in the sixth century. It was conceived as a 'liturgy', a form of tax which obliged a wealthy citizen to equip a warship or to outfit a chorus for competition at the Great Dionysia. While some welcomed this opportunity to display their wealth and to court public favour, others resented the liturgy, both for the administrative exertions required of a *choregos*, and as a financial disaster equivalent to losing a lawsuit; when a man is chosen as *choregos*, complains a speaker in a comedy of Antiphanes, 'furnishing golden robes for the chorus he himself wears rags, or hangs himself as *trierarch*'.[17] After Alexander's death, his regent Antipater defeated an Athenian revolt and established an oligarchy, composed of the elite. At some point between 317 and 307, the Macedonian-appointed governor, Demetrios of Phaleron, abolished the *choregia*. It was replaced by a single administrator (*agonothetes*), who was elected annually. This does not appear to have been a bad system. It survived the restoration of democracy in 307 and subsequent political upheavals. It was imitated abroad, as the *choregia* had once been.[18]

NEW THEATRES

Theatre buildings are normally constructed, and subsequently modified, to meet the requirements of contemporary performances. Therefore, the reconstruction of the Theatre of Dionysos, completed under the financial administration of Lykourgos (338–326), was designed to accommodate performances of dithyramb, tragedy and late Middle Comedy. We would expect such a building to be a compromise. Moreover, the site imposed restrictions of its own, hemmed in as it was by the *temenos* of Dionysos Eleutherios, the wall of the Akropolis and the Odeion.[19] Nevertheless, the reconfigured building has much in common with theatres elsewhere, some of which were built on unencumbered sites. These include Epidauros, where the *orchestra* and seating are well preserved, and Priene, where the lower storey of a Hellenistic stage building still stands. For our purposes here, the form and uses of these structures are more important than their relative priority.[20]

The configuration of earlier *orchestras* had evolved as roughly rectangular or trapezoidal. These new theatres were the first to be furnished with a circular *orchestra*, clearly defined by stone benches which surrounded more than half of its circumference. Vase scenes show that earlier stages were no more than 1.5 metres high, and frequently lower, connected to the *orchestra* by steps (Figures 8, 39, 45). Some scholars have contended that the altered Theatre of Dionysos had no *logeion* at all, but the consensus holds that it was furnished with the characteristic Hellenistic *logeion*, isolated from the *orchestra* by its height: at Priene, stage level was more than 2.5 metres above ground level.[21] What contemporary performances were these new arrangements designed to accommodate?

Orchestra

An *orchestra* had always been a place for dancing. It belonged to the choruses which, as an expression of the *polis*, retained their essential role in the Dionysia. Actors in comedy and tragedy might become celebrities, but they were neither numerous nor fully integrated as members of one of the ten tribes established by Kleisthenes. The tribes were directly represented by the men and boys of the dithyramb choruses, a thousand strong, who competed for a prize.[22] No doubt some spectators attended in order to see renowned actors playing new comedies and revived classics; but many more were personally engaged with a son, brother, nephew, pupil or client in a chorus. The permanent stone benches of the reconstructed *theatron* could accommodate a bigger crowd than the old wooden ones, perhaps twice as many spectators.[23]

The architectural relationship between seating, stage and *orchestra* shows unequivocally where the centre of interest was expected to be. Sightlines from the encircling benches on the slope of the *koilon* focussed upon the circular floor, where friends and relatives danced and sang, as spectators in a modern theatrical balcony enjoy the best view of a corps de ballet. The view of the *logeion* was less advantageous. Front-row-centre seats were farther from the stage than the distance between the back wall of the 'first circle' and the proscenium arch in a large Victorian theatre.[24] Seats at the outside ends of each row were closer, but spectators would have to turn sideways to see the stage.

Our traditional circus ring, which is designed to accommodate equestrian acts, is 13 metres in diameter, but the new *orchestra* measured more than 20.[25] Too large for a tragic chorus of fifteen, or even twenty-four comic *choreutai*, it can only have been intended to accommodate a dithyrambic chorus of fifty, giving each man some 6 square metres of space in which to manoeuvre. And whereas the quadrilateral *orchestra* of the old Theatre of Dionysos was not inconvenient for comic choruses, whether they danced in rectangular formation as Pollux claims, or in less formal groupings, a round dancing-place was best for dithyrambs, which were known as 'circular dances'.[26]

Logeion

It is likely that the front of the new *logeion* was supported by timber posts; adapting this Athenian prototype, later Hellenistic theatres substituted stone pilasters. Grooves and sockets at Priene, Aphrodisias and Oropos show that the spaces between pilasters could be filled with changeable units, such as doors, or *pinakes* not dissimilar to our theatrical 'flats' (Figure 12). This allowed for a variably decorated background and adjustable entrances at ground level, which could be useful for revivals of old tragedies in which actors and chorus interacted.[27] Again, dithyramb may have been the chief beneficiary, because this façade could complement the spectacle of a chorus decked out in rich costumes, and provided 'upstage' entrances. Choruses traditionally entered through the *parodoi*, but in 348 Demosthenes complained that a rival *choregos* barricaded the *paraskenia* in order to obstruct the entrance of his dithyrambic chorus. At this time, if these doors opened onto a low stage, short flights of steps must have been provided to facilitate their descent into the *orchestra*. This option was no longer possible in the Lykourgan theatre, where the *paraskenia* gave access only to a high *logeion* without any direct access to the *orchestra* more than 2 metres below. However, entrances between the pilasters of the supporting colonnade would permit a chorus to enter the *orchestra* directly, as an alterative or supplement to the *parodoi* on either side.[28]

The headroom required for practicable doors at *orchestra* level helps to account for the height of the new *logeion*. As far as we know, this lofty platform was used primarily by the three actors in new plays, tragic or comic. It was isolated from a chorus in the *orchestra* below, a situation which Hellenistic tragedy turned to advantage, emphasizing the heroic stature of its legendary personages. New masks with 'contorted expressions' expressed their enormous passions, and a 'tower of hair' above the forehead added physical stature: by the second century, thick-soled boots made the actor taller still. Tragic heroes were perceived as superior to common mortals like the chorus, who consequently drew closer to the audience.[29] In performances of all types, the high stage compensated spectators in the upper tiers for their distance from the stage, and the packed earth of the *orchestra* reflected an actor's voice upwards in circular waves. Greek actors and audiences set a high value on speech and voice.[30]

While considerations like these account for the *logeion*'s height, its size is more difficult to explain. Hellenistic stages were shallow, varying between 2 and 3.2 metres from brink to *skene*, but they made it up in breadth: in the Theatre of Dionysos, the new *logeion* was more than 20 metres wide. This must have been rather awkward for comedy or tragedy, but certainly not because it was 'a cramped area for a play with as much lively action as *Dyskolos*'.[31] The stages of our largest modern theatres are very much deeper, but none is so broad: compare the Metropolitan Opera House, New York, the Bolshoi, Moscow and the Four Seasons Centre, Toronto, respectively 16.6 metres, 17 metres and 18.4 metres at the proscenium arch. At a mere 12 metres, the stage in London's Royal Opera House, Covent Garden, comfortably accommodates the Royal Ballet, whose performances can be a good deal livelier than *Dyskolos*, and employ a larger cast. By any standard, the Athenian stage was vast; with no more than three actors, New Comedy must have been overwhelmed by vacancy.[32] What, then, was the thinking behind such a large stage? Perhaps the architect wanted to unify his design by using *skene* and *logeion* as an imposing visual link between the arms of the *theatron*: Moretti concludes that the *proskenion* is more significant architecturally than for dramatic 'spectacle'.[33] If the architect persuaded a committee that his building would revive the glory of imperial Athens, this was not the last stage to be designed without consulting its destined users.

Besides offering a convenient venue for touring performances, a theatre could serve a variety of purposes, like a 'community centre' today. In a democracy, it was a suitable meeting place for the Assembly and for a large jury on the Athenian model. Theatres accommodated the *agones* of rhapsodes, choruses and musicians that were inseparable from any Greek festival; we may speculate that theatres in various regions of the Greek world harboured popular entertainers of many kinds, such as itinerant mime troupes and acrobats (*kybistai*); perhaps some of them discovered that the round *orchestra* was suitable for equestrian acts.[34]

THE DETACHED CHORUS

It has been suggested that dramatic choruses could perform on the high stage with the actors, but Sifakis shows that the *orchestra* was their exclusive territory.[35] The *logeion* belonged to the actors. Like a speaker in a fragment of Alexis, Menander's characters describe the chorus as drunken *komastai* or 'muggers', groups to be avoided by exiting into the *skene* and shutting the door.[36] It is believable that Daos or Chairestratos would avoid drunks or footpads approaching along the street, but they had nothing to fear from anyone in the *orchestra*. Two and a half metres below, the chorus had no direct access to the stage; indeed, the *orchestra* was a separate imaginative dimension, representing no believable urban space.

Menander's chorus was detached from the dramatic narrative. Neither its leader nor the chorus as a whole engaged actors in dialogue, as they often did in Aristophanes. With the stage direction 'ΧΟΡΟΥ' (*chorou*), our texts mark the point where a choral ode is to be performed, but its verses are omitted. It is uncertain how this came about. Menander may have composed subtly appropriate odes, which were subsequently deleted for performance where no chorus was available; or perhaps indolent copyists skipped the odes, because they seemed to be irrelevant. However, since the plays suffer no apparent loss of coherence from their absence, perhaps neither Menander nor his rivals provided odes in the first place. The chorus performed *embolima*, interludes without direct relevance to the dramatic context, which could have been selected from a catalogue of 'Comedy odes for all occasions'. Aristotle deprecated them, because he believed 'The chorus should be treated as one of the actors . . . as in Sophokles. With the other poets, the songs are no more integral to the plot than to another tragedy.'[37] This influential opinion has generated a widespread belief in a 'decline of the chorus'.

The chorus must have been accompanied by the traditional *aulos*, and therefore the *auletes* too was distant from the actors, at least during *embolima*. In Menander, Handley says, 'the use of music, and with it the demand for actors to sing and dance, is almost at a vanishing point', but there are exceptions. Between choral odes, the piper was free to accompany action on the *logeion*, as a conventionally invisible source. Since pipers in two New Comedy scenes wear masks, and consequently could not really play an *aulos*, we must suppose that the official *auletai* either played at *orchestra* level or mounted internal stairs to play within the *skene* (Figures 22, 54).[38]

No doubt comic choruses changed in the course of the fourth century. Birds and beasts disappeared, along with fantastic plots. Aristophanes reduced the participation of his chorus in the plot of *Ekklesiazousai*, and it has almost dropped out of our text of *Wealth*, but its alienation from plot and actors appears to have been discontinuous and incomplete. Even in the later Middle and New Comedy periods, some titles apparently refer to a distinctive chorus that engaged with the actors. Euboulos' *Wreath-sellers* would have been women, no doubt haggling with actors about the price of a garland for the *symposion*. It is easy to imagine the antics of Alexis' *Poietai* (*Poets*), or of Antiphanes' *Scythians*, who might have been Athenian slave-police, like the oaf in *Thesmophoriazousai*. Did they sing a broken-Greek equivalent of 'tarantara tarantara'?[39] One of our latest pictures of a chorus is a relief from the Athenian *agora*, with *choreutai* who wear masks with bulging eyes and pointed, archaic beards. If they are correctly identified as comic soldiers, they would be a suitable chorus for a late Middle Comedy titled *Stratiotai*.[40] The realism of 'city comedy' required a chorus that could be identified as a group who might be encountered in the streets of a Greek city. Drunken *komastai* were a familiar sight, singing and dancing, but a crowd of them could not plausibly utter social criticism. Menander transferred his commentary to a character like Knemon in *Dyskolos*, retaining the metre and *aulos* accompaniment that had been inseparable from the old *parabasis*.[41]

None of these changes signified unqualified decline. There is no reason to suppose that comic choruses in the late fourth century were inferior to their predecessors; indeed, their professional *didaskaloi* may have improved their discipline. Fifth-century actors cannot have differed much from *choreutai*; they too were amateurs with no more than two opportunities a year to perform in Athens, perhaps supplemented by occasional appearances in a deme theatre. A century later, actors had become polished professionals. Playing opposite an ordinary citizen-chorus, they would have made the inexperienced amateurs seem inadequate. Moreover, the skills which New Comedy required of actor and *choreut* differed to such an extent that, performing together, they would have appeared to inhabit different worlds. Dance and song do not mimic exterior reality, they interpret its essence. While actors on the *logeion* walked and talked like secular men, the chorus in the *orchestra* below followed the Dionysian music of the *aulos*.[42]

Actors turned professional in response to demand abroad. A *protagonist* who had made a reputation as a victor in Athens could extend his potential audience by following his fame throughout the Greek lands. Fortuitously, the rules of the Dionysia limited casts to a *protagonist* and two assistants.

They could travel together easily and inexpensively, like the Victorian 'star', who toured with only a leading lady and an old actor 'who got the worst of all the stage fights except the final fatal thrust under the arm'.[43] Sometimes a local chorus might be pressed into service to perform any *embolima* they happened to know; if none were available, the *protagonist* and his assistants could play Menander without. It was impracticable to tour with a chorus; aside from the expense, and the challenge of maintaining discipline amongst two dozen young men, their *polis* could not be expected to exempt them from military service for several months.[44]

HELLENISTIC THEATRES

Communities with a shared culture have often sought to duplicate the configuration of a theatre in their dramatic metropolis. Roman theatres in St Alban's and Ba'albek resemble the Theatre of Marcellus in Rome, and Greeks everywhere came to believe that no proper *polis* should lack a theatre. Before the end of the fourth century, the examples of Athens and Epidauros had generated a pan-Hellenic movement to build new theatres, and to remodel old ones in stone, on the new pattern with circular *orchestra* and high *logeion*.[45] When Philip of Macedon rebuilt a captured Thracian town and named it Philippi (357–356), he ordered the construction of a theatre. Demetrios the Besieger did likewise when he refounded Pagasai in Magnesia as Demetrias. Corinth and Delos reconstructed their theatres, and the new configuration was adopted in Tegea, Delphi and Sikyon on the Greek mainland; Vergina in Macedon; Aphrodisias, Miletus, Erythrai and Troy in Asia; Rhodes, Mytilene and Delos in the islands; Monte Iato, Heloros and Tyndaris in Sicily; Rhegion in Italy; and Nea Paphos in Cyprus. Thebes at last succumbed to the Athenian passion for theatre, but Sparta held out until after the Roman conquest.[46]

COSTUMES, MASKS

The everyday character types of New Comedy, and its familiar urban setting, sustained a measure of dramatic illusion which might have been imperilled by a spectacular chorus. Physically distanced from the dramatic action, and frequently characterized as young revellers, tradition may have required the young men to wear masks. We have no material evidence to show whether they did, or if their *choregoi*, like Demosthenes, commissioned rich cloaks and golden crowns.[47]

We are better provided with evidence of the actors' appearance. Costumes and masks began to change 'in the direction of greater naturalism' after the middle of the fourth century, but less thoroughly than Menander's characterization might lead us to expect. Playing women, actors in New Comedy continued to wear everyday clothing; a modest young woman's *chiton* seems less voluminous than in Middle Comedy, but the fashion of draping the *himation* is unchanged.[48] Developments in male costume were more pronounced. While some companies exaggerated the artificiality of the undercostume by dying the torso in contrasting colours (Figures 10, 23), others dressed young lovers in long *chitonia*, hiding the artificial *phallos*. As young women, some actors seem to have discarded the traditional padding of stomach and buttocks, although it was retained for breasts (Figures 39, 45).[49] This naturalistic look became standard in New Comedy.

It is assumed that actors no longer wore the *phallos*, but we cannot be certain because we have no pictures of New Comedy actors stripped to their undercostumes, which were still being worn. Figurines and detailed scenes continued to show tights on arms and legs ('fleshings'), which must have been anchored to something. This might have been an inconspicuous adaptation of the old torso, without permanent padding. Some characters were still presented as corpulent. The 'fat old woman' was a standard character, a braggart soldier or a parasite could be fat, and pot-bellied slaves continued to be seen on the comic stage for five more centuries. Changing for these parts, actors must have put on the padding with the rest of the costume (Figure 51).[50]

Costumes identified a character's place in society, but it was the mask which expressed character as Greeks were beginning to interpret it. Until the middle of the fourth century, masks retained the grotesque features derived from Old Comedy. Most were ugly, but laughable rather than painfully repulsive, showing the audience that the comic character was inferior. Costumes and masks identified broad types, such as old and young citizens or slaves, and distinguished the female triad, but individual character was conveyed by action, body-attitude and gesture.[51]

Green's study of a great many surviving replicas of New Comedy masks confirms the development of a systematic 'standardisation of a sophisticated series of comic masks that were linked to current readings of physiognomy'. Wiles identifies a fundamental 'tetrad' of New Comedy mask types, old men, slaves, and young men and women. The grotesque 'old style' continued in use, primarily for the first two, who remained the most popular characters; these were modified to accommodate current fashions and notions of physiognomy.[52] As in Middle Comedy, features are *phaulos*, with protuberant eyes beneath pronounced eyebrows which are often asymmetrical, and drawn down in the middle, emphasizing the flattened, bridgeless nose. The slave's beard was now stylized as the characteristic New Comedy 'trumpet', a spade-shaped funnel surrounding a wide mouth which sometimes gapes to reveal the actor's lips, and even his teeth.[53] Men's hairstyles may have linked members of a family, father, son and slave; a smooth roll of hair often frames the forehead and is swept smoothly back over the head. The hair became longer after *c*.250, making a triangle of the mask by thrusting outwards at the back as though artificially stiffened. Most old men wore long beards, often dressed in stiff, corkscrew curls. Like the tragic *onkos*, this style suggested the archaic, implying the conservative attitudes of a strict father (Figure 52).[54]

Concurrently with these modified grotesques, masks in a 'new style' emerged, so stylistically consistent as to give 'every appearance of being invented by a single individual'.[55] Representing young men and the women towards whom their amorous attentions are directed, these masks are frequently characterized as naturalistic. Wiles explains, 'In Aristotelian terms, New Comedy was to represent men as neither worse than they really are (like Aristophanes) nor better than they really are (like Sophocles), but as they are – like Euripides. Their primary purpose was not to idealize or caricature, but to express something of how people really are.'[56] Pictures and replicas of masks bear this out; masks in the new style rarely embody the Hellenistic ideal, but they could be worn in the streets without frightening the horses. Moreover, mask-makers may have made the new masks 'thin-walled and snugly fitting', so that these characters no longer appeared to have disproportionately large heads. Some youths and young women have regular features, and the lack of expression that betokens *sophrosyne*. Other youths have bulbous eyes or heavy brows like comic slaves.[57] Jacques Lecoq showed how movement of his 'neutral masks' could express varied emotions and moods, but the expressions of some New Comedy masks are too disagreeable to be overcome by movement. Padded costumes confirm an impression that some masks were intended to represent overweight, unattractive young men.[58]

Variations within the generalized types imply that character can be recognized in the features, 'the face can be interpreted in isolation'. This belief permits New Comedy to 'demonstrate universal truth – which is to say, what a certain type of person would necessarily do in a given situation'.[59] The significance of mask physiognomy underlies descriptions in the *Onomastikon* of Iulius Pollux, which was compiled, like the *Souda*, from sources of variable reliability. His account of New Comedy masks seems to be reasonably sound.[60]

Identifying mask types

No original masks survive, but Webster catalogued representations in a variety of media, seeking to match them with descriptions in the *Onomastikon*. This endeavour was inevitably inconclusive, but a sample will serve to show how Pollux, several monuments and one of Menander's comedies can be brought together to illuminate each other. In four well-known pictures, Webster identifies many of the forty-four masks described by Pollux. Wherever possible, identifications are referred to characters in Menander's *Epitrepontes* (*Men at arbitration*).

(a) Marble relief in Naples with a scene from an unknown comedy. An old citizen restrains another from confronting a drunken youth, who is supported by a slave (Figure 52).

(b) Marble relief in the Vatican, with Menander and three comic masks (Figure 53).

(c) Mosaic in Naples by Dioskourides of Samos with a scene in *Theophoroumene* (*The girl possessed by the goddess*). Before a stage door representing the girl's house, two young men play small cymbals and a *tympanon*, accompanied by a third actor as an *auletris* (Figure 54).

(d) Mosaic in Naples by Dioskourides of Samos with a scene in *Synaristosai* (*Women at breakfast*). Three women are seated at a table in an apparent room approached by steps (Figure 55).[61]

Old men

Mask 3: leading old man (a) at left, restraining another old man, mask 4.

Mask 4: old man with wavy beard or hair (a) second from left, (b) mask on table at right.

Mask 7: the 'Lykomedean', *Smikrines*.

Young men

Mask 10: excellent youth (c) at right with *tympanon*, perhaps (b) in Menander's hand.

Mask 11: dark youth, perhaps (b) in Menander's hand, *Charisios*.
Mask 12: curly-haired youth, perhaps (b) in Menander's hand.
Mask 13: delicate youth (c) centre, with cymbals.
Mask 16: second wavy-haired youth (a), drunken youth third from left, *Chairestratos*.

Slaves

Mask 22: leading slave, *Onesimos*.
Mask 23: slave with low, or straight, hair, *Daos*.
Masks 25, 26: cooks (bald), 'Maison' and 'Tettix', *Karion*.
Mask 27: wavy-haired leading slave (a) supports his drunken master, *Syros*.

Old women

Mask 29: fat woman (d) at right.
Mask 30: little housekeeper, *Sophrone*.

Young women

Mask 34: first false maiden (b) centre on table, perhaps *Habrotonon*
Mask 35: second false maiden (d) at centre facing front.
Mask 39: voluptuous *hetaira* (c), *auletris* at left (d).

EPILOGUE

While the ancient world endured, comedy retained a place in it. Inscriptions show that the comic *agon* at the Athenian Dionysia continued into the second century BCE. There is evidence of performances at Tanagra and Argos in the first century, comic actors participated in a great festival at Delphi in 105, and plays by Menander were performed in 196 and 168.[62] By the second century BCE, the epicentre of Greek theatre had shifted from Athens to the great new city of Alexandria, and emergent Rome was appropriating New Comedy to itself. With the fall of Taras (Tarentum) in 272, Rome seized control of the theatrical metropolis of Megale Hellas. Public festivals had long accustomed Romans to music, dance and related entertainments. In 240 a Tarentine Greek calling himself Livius Andronicus presented a Latin version of a Greek comedy at the Ludi Romani.[63]

This seems to have established a pattern followed by subsequent writers of the Republican period. We have twenty-one comedies by Titus Maccius Plautus (career *c.*205–184) and six by Publius Terentius Afer (166–160). Known as *fabula palliata*, all were Greek in setting and costume: the Latin *pallium* refers to the Greek *himation*. These comedies were adaptations of Greek originals, rather than translations; Plautus turned to Diphilos and Philemon as frequently as Menander, but Terence preferred Menander, adapting four plays with their Greek titles, and two by Apollodoros of Karystos.[64] Comedies were performed in temporary theatres erected for the *ludi*; Rome possessed no permanent theatre before 55 BCE. Subsequently, Roman theatres spread throughout the empire, frequently in modified Greek structures.

Neither the *palliata* nor the home-grown *fabula togata* (comedy in Roman dress, the *toga*) spread with the theatres. Under the empire, Romans with literary tastes preferred private readings to public performance. Amongst those who read Greek, Menander was widely admired: Ovid thought the poet's fame was safe forever, sculptors turned out imaginary likenesses, and mosaics of scenes from his comedies decorated houses in Pompeii and Mytilene as late as the fourth century CE.[65] It was Aristophanes, however, whose pure, classical Attic led to the survival of the Old Comedies we have today. They were copied for use in school exercises, but Menander's vernacular Greek, adapted to a wider market, led to his neglect in the Byzantine libraries and schools that carried Hellenic culture forward into the Middle Ages.[66] Egyptian papyrus copies survived, to be discovered in the twentieth century, sometimes in the 'cartonnage' of mummy cases. Until then, Menander was known only by reputation and random quotations of various authenticity: 'Whom the gods love, die young.'

When the Renaissance brought a revival of interest in antiquity, Roman plays were the models. Comedies from a manuscript of Plautus were performed in Rome in the fifteenth century, and Italian translations of Plautus and Terence were staged in Ferrara. When printed texts made the plays accessible, writers adapted and imitated. In England, Nicholas Udall's *Ralph Roister Doister* (*c.*1553) drew upon the *Miles Gloriosus* of Plautus. Early in Shakespeare's career, experiments with classicism led to his Senecan tragedy *Titus Andronicus*, and *The Comedy of Errors*, from Plautus' *Menaechmi*. From there, the poet moved on to romantic comedy, but Molière established classicism in French comedy, and, after the Restoration (1660), it migrated to the English mainstream until Romanticism took possession of the stage in the early nineteenth century. Classical dramatic structure, and preoccupation with families and their private lives have returned, of course: by way of French 'well-made plays', to Noël Coward, A. R. Gurney, Alan Ayckbourn and a myriad others who carry their neo-classicism jauntily or unconsciously.

Catalogue of objects discussed

Each object is identified by the name of a city, and inventory number in its major archaeological collection, except where otherwise indicated. Thus 'Amsterdam' refers to the Allard Piersen Museum, and 'Athens Kanellopoulos' refers to the Museum of Paul and Alexandra Kanellopoulos.

Dates are BCE, *and approximate unless otherwise indicated. Figure numbers in bold type refer to figures in this book.*

VASES

Red-figured unless otherwise indicated. BF – black-figured.

Adolphseck 179, Apulian bell *krater*, Adolphseck Ptr, 370–360, *RVAp* 4/51, BArch 1003416, *RVSIS* pl. 110.

Amsterdam 2579, Apulian *kalyx krater* fragment, Ptr of the Birth of Dionysos, 400–385, *RVAp* 02/010 pl. 9,2.

Amsterdam 3356, Attic BF cup, Heidelberg Ptr, 560, BArch 300600, *ABV* 66.57, *IGD* I.8, *GVGetty* no. 1 figs. 4a–b.

Apollonia 325, Sicilian emigrant *kalyx krater*, unattrib., 360–350, Eggebrecht 1988 no. 204.

Athens 13027, Attic *lebes*, Ptr of the Athens Dinos, 420, *MTS*² AV23, *ARV*² 1180.2, BArch 215628, Brommer 1959 abb. 2. **Figure 21**.

Athens 15499, Attic black figure *dinos*, Sophilos, 580–570, BArch 305075, Froning 2002 35 abb. 27.

Athens 17752, Attic *oinochoe*, unattrib., 400, *PhV*² no. 5, BArch 15483, Hoorn 1951 no. 117 fig. 148.

Athens BΣ518 (once Vlasto coll.), Attic *oinochoe*, Gp of Perseus Dance, 420, *ARV*² 1215.1, *PhV*² no. 1, BArch 216566, Hughes 2006b figs. 1, 2.

Athens CC1927 (1391), Corinthian bell *krater*, unattrib., 375–350, *PhV*² no. 14, *BH*² fig. 203.

Athens Agora Museum P23856, Attic polychrome *oinochoe* fragment, 415–410, *PhV*² no. 10, Webster 1960 B2 pl. 65.

Athens Agora Museum P23900, Attic polychrome *oinochoe*, unattrib., 415–410, *PhV*² no. 11, Crosby 1955 pl. 35a.

Athens Agora Museum P23907, Attic polychrome *oinochoe* fragments, unattrib., 415–410, *PhV*² no. 12, *IGD* IV.6, Crosby 1955 pl. 35b, 36a.

Athens Agora Museum P23985, Attic polychrome *oinochoe*, unattrib., 415–410, *PhV*² no. 13, Crosby 1955 pl. 34c.

Athens Agora Museum Z1259 (P10798), Attic cup fragment, Ptr of Heidelberg 211, 430, *ARV*² 945.28, *PhV*² no. 8, BArch 212760, M. Moore, *The Athenian Agora* vol. xxx. *Attic red-figured and white-ground pottery* (Princeton, NJ: American School of Classical Studies at Athens 1997) no. 1449, 136.

Athens Benaki Museum 30890, Attic *oinochoe* fragments unattrib., 375–350, BArch 44577, Hughes 2008 fig. 1 and cover (colour).

Athens Kerameikos Museum 5671, Attic BF *lekythos*, Theseus Ptr, 490–480, BArch 330667, *ABV* 518.2, *GVGetty* no. 13 fig. 16.

Atlanta L1989.2.2 loan from priv. coll., Apulian bell *krater*, Berkeley Gp, 375–350, *RVAp* supp. ii 10/60c pl. XI,1, *Comic angels* pl. 13.10.

Atlanta 2008.4.1, Attic *pelike*, unattrib., 450, E-newsletter, Michael C. Carlos Museum, Emory University, fall 2008, 6; Csapo 2010 figs. 1.5, 10.

Bari 2795, Apulian *kalyx krater*, Ptr of Bari 1523, 375–350, *RVAp* 6/199, *PhV*² no. 74, *BH*² fig. 519, Green 2001 fig. 16.

Bari 2970, Apulian bell *krater*, unattrib., 375–350, *PhV*² no. 17, *IGD* IV.20, *BH*² fig. 483.

Bari 3899, Apulian bell *krater*, Dijon Ptr, 380–370, *RVAp* 6/96, *PhV*² no. 18, *IGD* IV.26.

Bari 4073, Apulian bell *krater*, unattrib., 350, *PhV*² no. 19, *BH*² fig. 498.

Bari 8014, Apulian bell *krater*, Cotugno Ptr, 375–350, *RVAp* 10/45, *PhV*² no. 37, *IGD* IV.27.

Bari priv. coll., Apulian *oinochoe*, unattrib., 350, *PhV*² no. 107 pl. VIIa.

Basle S21, Apulian *Loutrophoros*, nr Laodamia Ptr. 350–340, *RVAp* 18/16, Green 1999 pl. 3.

Basle S34, Apulian *kalyx krater*, Darius Ptr, 330, *RVAp* 18/64, Green 1995b pl. 6a,b.

Basle 1921.384, Campanian stemless cup, nr Danaid Ptr, 350–325, *LCS* II.3/551, *PhV*² no. 139 pl. XIa.

Basle priv. coll. HC849, Attic BF cup fragment, unattrib., 490–480, BArch 14650, *GVGetty* no. 15 fig. 18.

Benevento from Montesarchio T.1625, Paestan bell *krater*, Asteas, 340, Hughes 2003, 291–301, fig. 4.

Berlin 1969.7, Apulian Gnathia stemless cup, unattrib., 330–320, Griefenhagen 1975, abb. 1.

Berlin 1983.4, Apulian *oinochoe*, unattrib., 360, Hughes 2006a fig. 11.

Berlin 1984.41, Apulian volute *krater*, Darius Ptr, 330, *RVAp* supp. iii 18/41b pl. XXXV.4, Green 1999 pl. 25.

Berlin F1697, Attic BF amphora, Ptr of Berlin 1686, 540–530, BArch 320396, *ABV* 297.17, *GVGetty* no. 3 fig. 6.

Berlin F1830, Attic BF amphora, unattrib., 480, BArch 2698, *GVGetty* no. 11 fig. 14.

Berlin F2301, Attic cup, Brygos Ptr, 500–450, *ARV*² 378.125, BArch 204027, Boardman 1975 pl. 250.

Berlin F3043, Lucanian *kalyx krater*, Amykos Ptr, late. fifth cent., *LCS* I.212 pl. 16.5–6, *PhV*² no. 75, *IGD* IV.15.

Berlin F3044, Sicilian/Paestan *kalyx krater*, Asteas, 360–350, *RVP* 2/175 pl. 44, *IGD* IV.14. **Figure 10**.

Berlin F3045, Apulian bell *krater*, nr Eton-Nika Gp, 400–375, *RVAp* 4/92, *PhV*² no. 21, *BH*² fig. 493.

Berlin F3047, Apulian bell *krater*, Felton Ptr, 350, *RVAp* 7/67, *PhV*² no. 23, *BH*² fig. 510.

Berlin F3444, Apulian Gnathia *pelike*, unattrib., 350–340, *BH*² fig. 579b. **Figure 49**.

Bonn 1216.183–5, Attic bell *krater* fragments, unattrib., 420, *MTS*² AV24, *ARV*² 1180.3, BArch 215629, *TAGS* fig. 2.20.

Boston 00.349b, Apulian stamnos, Ariadne Ptr, 400–390, *RVAp* 1/104, *IGD* III.3.45.

Boston 00.363, Apulian Gnathia *kalyx krater*, Konnakis Gp, 350, *PhV*² no. 177, *BH*² fig. 502b, Hughes 2006a fig. 8.

Boston 01.8036, Campanian *oinochoe*, unattrib., 350–325, Padgett, Redmond 1993 no. 81.

Boston 03.804, Apulian volute *krater*, nr Varrese Ptr, 350–340, *RVAp* 17/075, *IGD* III.4.2.

Boston 03.831, Campanian *hydria*, unattrib., 350–325, *PHV*² no. 132, *BH*² fig. 516.

Boston 13.93, Apulian *oinochoe* (type 5), Ptr of Toronto 972.182.1, 350, *PhV*² no. 129, *BH*² fig. 526.

Boston 20.18, Gift of the heirs of Henry Adams, Attic BF *skyphos*, Heron Gp 490–480, BArch 4090, *ABV* 617, *IGD* I.11, *GVGetty* no. 17 figs. 20a–b. **Figure 24**.

Boston 69.951, Apulian bell *krater*, McDaniel Ptr, 380–370, *RVAp* 4/250, *Comic angels* pl. 11.3.

Boston 97.371, Attic phiale, Phiale Ptr (name vase), 475–425, *ARV*² 1023.146, BArch 214328, M. Robertson 1992 fig. 221.

British Columbia priv. coll, Apulian Gnathia *oinochoe*, unattrib., 330–320. **Figure 47**.

Brooklyn 09.35, Attic BF amphora, unattrib., 490, *GVGetty* no. 9 figs. 12a–b.

Caltanissetta 1751, Sicilian *kalyx krater*, Gibil Gabib Gp, 330, *LCS* III/98 pl. 235.2–3; Taplin 2007 no. 105 p. 261 (colour).

Caltanissetta G258, Sicilian *kalyx krater*, Gibil Gabib Gp, 330, *LCS* III/95 pl. 235.1.

Cambridge GR4.1943, Attic pyxis, Curtius Ptr, 475–425, *ARV*² 935.75, BArch 212591.

Cambridge MA Sackler Museum TL15601.2, Apulian Gnathia *krater* fragment, 350, Mayo, Hamma 1982 no. 122.

Cambridge MA Sackler Museum TL331.86, Apulian bell *krater*, McDaniel Ptr (name vase), 400–375, *RVAp* 4/244, *PhV*² no. 024, *IGD* IV.16.

Catania Museo Civico Castello Ursino MB4232 (Biscari 735), unattrib., 380–370, *PhV*² no. 25, Libertini 1930 pl. 83.

Christchurch University of Canterbury 41–57, Attic BF amphora, Swing Ptr, 500–475, BArch 340567, *IGD* I.10, *GVGetty* no. 4 fig. 7. **Figure 15**.

Copenhagen 15032, Apulian bell *krater*, Jason Ptr, 350, *RVAp* 5/295, Braemme 1976 no. 26, fig. 2. **Figure 27**.

Crotone from Cantieri Messinetti, Sicilian/Paestan bell *krater* fragment, Asteas, 360–350, Hughes 2006a fig. 9.

Dresden ZV2891, Campanian fragment, Caivano Ptr, 350–325, *LCS* II.2/565, *MTS*² PV6, *BH*² fig. 105.

Edinburgh 1978.492, Apulian *oinochoe*, Gp of Lecce Ptr, 350, Trendall 1995 pl. 41, 3–4.

Ferrara 29307, Attic plate, Ptr of Ferrara T101, 425–400, *ARV*² 1306.8, *MMC*³ AV1, BArch 216846, Rusten forthcoming 2011.

Firenze 3773, Attic BF amphora, Castellani Ptr, 575–525, *ABV* 95.8, 683, BArch 310008, Froning 2002, 35 abb. 28 (colour).

Frankfurt B602, Campanian bell *krater*, Libation Ptr, 350–325, *LCS* II.3/337, *PhV*² no. 15, Schaal 1923 pl. 55b.

Gela 36056, Sicilian *krater* fragment, Asteas, 360–350, Hughes 2003, 286, fig. 2.

Gela 36057, Sicilian fragment, unattrib., 360–350.

Gela 643, Sicilian skyphoid *krater*, Manfria Gp, 340–330, *PhV*² no. 98, *LCS* III/9 pl. 231.2.

Gela 750, Sicilian fragment, Manfria Gp, 340–330, *PhV*² no. 99 pl. IXd.

Gela 8255–6, Sicilian/Paestan *kalyx krater* fragments, Asteas, 360–350, *RVP* I/102, Pugliese Carratelli *et al.* 1983 pl. 630 (colour), Hughes 2003 figs. 1, 6.

Geneva priv. coll., Apulian bell *krater*, Chevron Gp, 350–340, Cambitoglou *et al.* 1986, 200.

Geneva coll. G. Ortiz, Apulian *oinochoe*, nr Felton Ptr, 380–360. **Figure 36**.

Genoa 1142, Apulian *kalyx krater*, Rohan Ptr, 375–350, *RVAp* 5/244, BArch 9004269, Zscheitzmann 1960, 183.

Göttingen Hu582a, Apulian *oinochoe*, unattrib., 350–325, *PhV*² no. 109, BArch 1006120, *CVA* Deutschland 2851 pl. 18.1–3. **Figure 44**.

Heidelberg B134, Attic bell *krater*, unattrib., 400–375, *PhV*² no. 7, *BH*² fig. 208.

Heidelberg U6, Apulian bell *krater*, Ptr of Heidelberg U6 (name vase), 375–350, *RVAp* 10/35, *PhV*² no. 29, *BH*² fig. 520, Green 2001 fig. 11.

Heidelberg U8, Apulian *krater* fragment, unattrib., 380–370, *PhV*² no. 30, BArch 1004107, *BH*² fig. 518.

Kiev from Olbia, Museum of the Academy of Science, Attic bell-*krater* fragment, unattrib., 430–420, Froning 2002 abb. 88.

Lentini 2B, Sicilian *kalyx krater*, Manfria Gp, 340–330, *PhV*² no. 79, *LCS* III/74 pl. 231, 3–4, *BH*² fig. 488a. **Figure 45**.

Lipari 11171, Campanian bell *krater*, Mad-Man Ptr, 375–350, *LCS* supp. iii II.3/1a, BBTL fig. 114.

Lipari 2241, Sicilian *kalyx krater*, nr Maron Gp, 360–350, *PhV*² no. xviii, *LCS* supp. iii III.46j, Arias 1962 pl. XLIX (colour).

Lipari 927, Sicilian *kalyx krater*, Asteas, 360–350, *RVP* 1/99 pl. 12f, Charbonneau *et al.* 1969 pl. 371.

Lipari 9604, Sicilian/Paestan *kalyx krater*, Asteas, 360–350, *RVP* 1/91 pl. 11a.

London 1772.3–20.33 (F269), Apulian *kalyx krater*, Varrese Ptr, 350, *RVAp* 13/11, *PhV²* no. 81, *IGD* IV.21.

London 1772.3–20.881 (F188), Paestan bell *krater*, Asteas, 350–340, *RVP* 2/26 pl. 22c.

London 1814.7–4.1224 (F289), Campanian bell *krater*, nr NYN Gp, 350, *LCS* II.3/14, *PhV²* no. 40, Romagnoli 1923 fig. 4.

London 1842.7–28.787 (B509), Attic BF *oinochoe*, Gela Ptr, 500–490, BArch 330555, *ABV* 473, *IGD* I.12, *GVGetty* no. 8 figs. 11a–c.

London 1842.7–28.979 (B658), Attic BF *lekythos*, Beldam Ptr, 525–475, BArch 331227, *ABV* 586.67, *GVGetty* no. 18 fig. 21. **Figure 16**.

London 1849.6–20.13 (F151), Apulian bell *krater*, McDaniel Ptr, 380–370, *RVAp* 4/25a, *PhV²* no. 37, *IGD* IV.35.

London 1865.1–3.27 (F150), Paestan bell *krater*, Asteas, 350–340, *RVP* 2/45, *BH²* fig. 501.

London 1865.1–3.29 (F233), Campanian *oinochoe*, Spotted Rock Gp, 350–325, *LCS* 2/94, *PhV²* no. 111, *BH²* fig. 539, *Comic angels* pl. 16.15.

London 1867.5–8.941 (F591), BF plate, Psiax, 530–520, BArch 320366, *ABV* 294.20, Richter 1987 fig. 450.

London 1873.8–20.347 (F189), Paestan bell *krater*, Python, 350–325, *RVP* 2/280 pl. 103a.

London 1875.8–18.9 (F557), Apulian Gnathia *pelike*, Naples Harp Gp, 330, Forti 1965 tav. xviia.

London 1898.2–27.1, Attic polychrome *oinochoe*, unattrib., 415–410, *PhV²* no. 9, *IGD* IV.5, Crosby 1955 pl. 37.

London 1927.4–11.8, Campanian bell *krater*, Majewski Ptr, 300, *LCS* 2/933.

London 1946.9–25.3 (F157), Lucanian *kalyx krater*, Dolon Ptr, 400–375, *LCS* 1/533 pl. 52.3.

London B308, Attic BF *hydria*, unattrib., 550–500, BArch 9996, *GVGetty* no. 5 fig. 8.

London E270, Attic amphora, Kleophrades Ptr, 500–450, BArch 201668, West 1994 pl. 25.

London market 1996 whereabouts unk., Apulian *oinochoe*, unattrib., 350–325, Ede 1996 no. 12. **Figure 32**.

London market 2002 whereabouts unk., Apulian squat *lekythos*, unattrib., 350, Ede 2002 no. 10.

London Victoria and Albert Museum 1776–1919, Apulian bell *krater*, Iris Ptr, 380–360, *RVAp* 5/259, *PhV²* no. 41, *IGD* IV.25.

Los Angeles priv. coll., Attic BF cup, Leafless Gp, 490–480, Hamma 1989 no. 22.

Madrid 11026 (L388), Sicilian *kalyx krater*, Dirce Ptr, 380–360, *RVP* 1/6, *PhV²* no. 96, Trendall 1952 no. 5 pl. 1.

Madrid 11094, Paestan *kalyx krater*, Asteas, 350–340, *RVP* 2/124, *BH²* fig. 479b.

Madrid 11129, Attic *hydria*, Ptr of Tarquinia 707, 440, *ARV²* 1112.2, BArch 214707, Hughes 2008 fig. 5.

Madrid 1999/99/122, Apulian bell *krater*, Cotugno Ptr, 375–350, Hughes 2006a fig. 2.

Malibu 85.AE.102, Apulian volute *krater*, nr Sisyphus Ptr, 420–400, *RVAp* supp. ii 1/90a, BArch 1002035, *RVSIS* pl. 44.

Malibu 86.AE.412, Sicilian *kalyx krater* fragment, unattrib., 375–350, Hughes 2003 fig. 6.

Malibu 96.AE.112, Apulian bell *krater*, Rainone Ptr, 370–360, *RVAp* 4/224a, Getty Museum 1994 no. 57.

Malibu 96.AE.113, Apulian bell *krater*, Cotugno Ptr, 370–360, *RVAp* supp. ii 10/46a (postscript), Green 2001 pl. 8. **Figure 48**.

Malibu 96.AE.114, Apulian *askos*, Meer Gp, 360–350, *RVAp* supp. ii 11/133b pl. XII,5–6.

Malibu 96.AE.118, Apulian *situla*, Konnakis Group, 360–350, Getty Museum 1994 no. 63. **Figure 33**.

Malibu 96.AE.238, Apulian bell *krater*, Adolphsek Ptr, 360, *RVAp* supp. ii 4/61c pl. II,2. **Figure 37**.

Matera 9579, Lucanian bell *krater*, Ptr of the Phlyax Helen, 370–350, *LCS* supp. iii I.C145, *IGD* IV.28, *PhV²* no. 44 pl. IIIc.

Matera 164507, Apulian bell *krater*, Graz Ptr, 350, *RVAp* supp. ii 6/213a, Schauenburg 1988, 644, pl. 11.

Melbourne D14/1973, Campanian bell *krater*, Libation Ptr, 350–324, *LCS* supp. iii II.3/337a, *Comic angels* pl. 15.13.

Melbourne D17/1972, Apulian Gnathia squat *lekythos*, Konnakis Gp, 350, Hughes 2008 fig. 2.

Melbourne D391/1980, Paestan bell *krater*, Asteas, 350, *PhV²* no. 56, *RVP* 2/24 pl. 21c.

Melbourne University MUV77, Ian Potter coll., Campanian [?] Pagenstecher *lekythos*, late fourth cent.

Messina 11039, Sicilian *kalyx krater*, Manfria Gp or Adrastus Ptr, 350–325, Bacci, Tigano 2001 fig. 23. **Figure 39**.

Metaponto 29062, Lucanian *skyphos* fragments, Dolon Ptr, 400–375, *LCS* supp. iii D63, Adamestianu *et al.* 1975 no. 163, fig. 52. **Figure 1**.

Metaponto 29340, Lucanian *skyphos* fragments, Dolon Ptr, 400–375, *LCS* supp. iii D64, Adamesteanu *et al.* 1975 no. 163, fig. 52.

Metaponto 297053, Apulian bell *krater*, nr McDaniel Ptr, 350, Green 2001 pl. 9.

Milan Civico Museo Archeologico A.0.9.2841, Apulian bell *krater*, Choregos Ptr, 400–380, *RVAp* supp. ii 1/123, *PhV²* no. 45, *IGD* IV.18.

Milan Civico Museo Archeologico A1872 (ST6873), Apulian *kalyx krater*, Lycurgus Ptr, 350–325, *RVAp* 16/6, *IGD* III.4, Green 1999 no. 24.

Milan priv. coll. formerly HA coll. 239, Apulian volute *krater*, Ilioupersis Ptr, 375–350, *RVAp* 8/4 pl. 60,3.

Milan Scala 668, Sicilian *oinochoe*, unattrib., 375–350, *PhV²* no. 112 pl. VIIb.

Milan Scala 749, Sicilian *skyphos*, Manfria Gp, 340–330, *PhV²* no. 95, *LCS* III/68 pl. 231.1.

München 8729, Attic black-figure cup, Exekias, 575–525, BArch 310403, *ABV* 146.21, *BH²* fig. 59.

Naples 81372 (3370), Apulian bell *krater*, nr Eton-Nika Ptr, 375–350, *RVAp* 4/95, *PhV²* no. 49 pl. IVb.

Naples 81398 (H3232), Attic *hydria*, Polygnotos, 450–425, *ARV²* 1032.61, BArch 213444, Matheson 1995 pl. 14a–d.

Naples 81673 (H3240), Attic volute *krater*, Pronomos Ptr, late fifth cent., BArch 217500, *TAGS* fig. 2.19.

Naples 81674 (H2419), Attic *stamnos*, Dinos Ptr, 430, BArch 215254, *CAD* pl. 20B.

Naples 81947 (3253), Apulian volute *Krater*, Darius Ptr (name vase), 340, *RVAp* 18/38, Taplin 2007 no. 92, 235.

Naples 81952, Apulian amphora, Darius Ptr, 340–325, *RVAp* 18/46, Green 1999 no. 30, fig. 13.

Naples 82113 (3223), Apulian volute *krater*, Iliupersis Ptr, 375–350, *RVAp* 8/3, *BH²* fig. 116, Taplin 2007, 151, no. 47.

Naples 82266, Apulian loutrophoros, Darius Ptr, 350–325, RVAp 18/58, *IGD* III.3.11.

Naples 82270 (3249), Apulian volute *krater*, Black Fury Ptr, 380–370, *RVAp* 7/13, Charbonneau *et al.* 1969 pl. 363.

Naples 118333, Apulian *kalyx krater*, Varrese Ptr, 350, *RVAp* 13/12, *PhV²* no. 83, Green 2001 fig. 2 (colour). **Figure 8**.

Naples 127971, Campanian *krater* with lugs, NYN Ptr, 360–340, *PhV²* no. 92, *LCS* II.3/12 pl. 138.6.

New York 16.1407, Apulian bell *krater*, Sarpedon Ptr, 400–380, *RVAp* 7/1, *IGD* III.1.17.

New York 24.97.104, Apulian *kalyx krater*, Tarporley Ptr 400, *RVAp* 3/7, *IGD* IV.13.

New York 37.11.19, Attic *chous*, unattrib., 450–400, *ARV²* 183.15632, BArch 539, Hoorn 1951 no. 761, pl. 117.

New York 51.11.2, Apulian Gnathia *kalyx krater*, Compiègne Ptr, 350, *PhV²* no. 180, *BH²* fig. 525, Mayo, Hamma 1982 no. 118.

New York 1988.11.3, Attic BF *hydria*, manner of Lydos, 550, BArch 12278, *IGD* I.20, *GVGetty* no. 2 fig. 5.

New York 1989.281.69, Attic BF *psykter*, Oltos, 510, BArch 275024, *ARV²* 1622.7, *GVGetty* no. 6 fig. 9.

North Germany priv. coll., Paestan *situla* fragment, Asteas, 350, *PhV²* no. 77, *RVP* 1/104 pl. 13d.

Once Altomonte, whereabouts unk., Apulian *krater* fragment, unattrib., 375–350, *PhV²* no. 103, Festa 1912 fig. 1.

Once Berlin F3046, whereabouts unk., Apulian bell *krater*, unattrib., 375–350, *BH²* fig. 487.

Once Deepdene Hope coll. 224, whereabouts unk., Apulian *skyphos*, unattrib., early fourth cent., Tillyard 1923 pl. 31,6.

Once Malibu 82.AE.83, whereabouts unk., Attic *kalyx krater*, nr Ptr of Munich 2335, 440–430, BArch 13689, *GVGetty* no. 1 figs. 1–3.

Once Malibu 96.AE.29, whereabouts unk., Apulian bell *krater*, Choregos Ptr, 400–380, *RVAp* supp. ii 1/124, *Comic angels* pl. 9.1.

Once Melbourne priv. coll., whereabouts unk., Apulian *oinochoe*, nr Felton Ptr, 380–360.

Once Taranto coll., Baisi 166, whereabouts unk., Apulian fragment, Varrese Ptr, 360–340, *RVAp* appendix 7/34d, Schauenburg 1988, 639, pl. 7.

Once Zurich Ruesch coll., whereabouts unk., Campanian *kalyx krater*, Sikon Ptr (name vase), 370–360, *LCS* I/72, *PhV²* no. 91, Green 1995b pl. 11e.

Oxford AN1945.43, Paestan *kotyle*, Asteas, 350–335, *PhV²* no. 96, *RVP* 2/33 pl. 24f. **Figure 50**.

Oxford 1971.866, Attic *oinochoe*, Phiale Ptr, 450–425, BArch 4692 (colour), M. Robertson 1989 pl. 34, 1–2.

Oxford 1971.903, Attic BF cup, nr Wraith Ptr, 510–500, BArch 2593, *GVGetty* no. 7 figs. 10a–b.

Paestum 104378, Paestan *oinochoe*, nr Asteas, 350–340, Hughes 2003 fig. 5, Cipriani *et al.* 1996, 187 (colour).

Paestum 20198, Paestan bell *krater*, Asteas, 340, *RVP* 2/173 pl. 72a,b.

Paestum 48431, Paestan *lebes gamikos*, Asteas workshop, 350–330, *RVP* 2/148, Matt, Zanotti-Bianco 1962 fig. 73.

Palermo CAT2816, Attic BF *lekythos*, Athena Ptr, 490–480, BArch 4638, *IGD* I.14, *GVGetty* no. 14 fig. 17.

Palermo Mormino Museum 742, Apulian *pelike*, Berkeley Gp, 350–340, *RVAp* 10/68.

Paris CA1924, Attic BF cup, nr Theseus Ptr, 490–480, BArch 351585, Beazley 1971 no. 259, *GVGetty* no. 16 figs. 19a–c.

Paris CA2938, Attic *oinochoe*, unattrib., 420–410, *PhV²* no. 2, BArch 2721, Webster 1970 pl. 2a.

Paris CA7249, Sicilian *kalyx krater*, Lentini-Manfria Gp, 350–325.

Paris E742, Attic BF cup, *Komast* Gp, 600–550, BArch 300356. **Figure 14**.

Paris G574, Attic *oinochoe*, Phiale Ptr, 475–425, *ARV²* 1020.98, BArch 214278, J.D. Beazley, 'Narthex' *AJA* 37 (1933) 402, fig. 6.

Paris K18, Apulian bell *krater*, Hoppin Ptr, 375–350, *RVAp* 5/59, *PhV²* no. 52, *BH²* fig. 515.

Paris K240, Sicilian bell *krater*, Asteas (his name vase as Ptr of Louvre K240), 360–350, *PhV²* no. xii, *RVP* 1/94 pl.11e,f.

Paris K404, Campanian bell *krater*, nr Ptr of British Museum F63, 330–320, *LCS* II.2/702, *MTS²* NVI, *BH²* fig. 253.

Paris K523, Campanian *kalyx krater*, NYN Ptr, 350, *LCS* II.3/13, *PhV²* no. 85, *BH²* fig. 495, Hughes 2006a fig. 6.

Paris N3408 (M9), Attic *oinochoe*, Nikias Ptr, 410, *ARV²* 1335.34, *PhV²* no. 3, BArch 217495, *IGD* IV.2. **Figure 18**.

Paris Cabinet des Médailles 243, BF Panathenaic amphora from Rhodes, unattrib., 550–500, BArch 1047, Shapiro 1989 pl. 12C–D.

Paris Cabinet des Médailles 1046, Campanian squat *lekythos*, Foundling Ptr (name vase), 350–325, *LCS* II.3/115, *IGD* IV.12.

Policoro from Aliano, Apulian fragment, unattrib., 360–350, Green 2001 fig. 1.

Policoro 35296, Lucanian *hydria*, Policoro Ptr, 400, *RVSIS* pl. 28.

Prague Charles University 60.31, Attic *hydria* nr Nekyia Ptr, 475–425, *CVA* Prague 1, 46 pl. 36.2, 37.4, BArch 1459, Seeberg 2002–3 fig. 13.

Princeton 50–64, Campanian bell *krater*, Libation Ptr, 350–325, *LCS* II.3/336, *PhV*² no. 55, *BH*² fig. 531.

Pulsano priv. coll. 48, Attic BF *skyphos*, Athena Ptr, 500–475, BArch 15467, Fedele *et al.* 1984 no. 14, pl. 43.

Reggio Calabria 3303, Apulian plate, unattrib., 350–325, *PhV*² no. 142, Putorti 1938 pl. V,2.

Reggio Calabria 6999, Apulian plate, unattrib., 350–325, *PhV*² no. 143, Catteruccia 1951 pl. 11.

Rio de Janeiro 20940–1040 (1500), Campanian bell *krater*, CA Ptr, 350–325, *LCS* II.4/334 pl. 187.6, *PhV*² no. 56 pl. IVc, *Comic angels* pl. 15.14.

Rome priv. coll. 52, Apulian *kalyx krater*, Suckling-Salting Gp, 360–350, *RVAp* 15/28 pl. 140. **Figure 22**.

Rome Villa Giulia 50279, Paestan *kalyx krater* fragment, Asteas, 350–340, *RVP* 2/130, *PhV*² no. 86, *IGD* IV.30.

Rome Villa Giulia 64224, Attic *kylix*, nr Euergides Ptr, 520–510, BArch 352430, Riccioni, Amorelli 1968 no. 24 pl. Ib.

Ruvo 901, Apulian bell *krater*, Reckoning Ptr, 375–350, *RVAp* 4/46, *PhV*² no. 57, Palo 1987, 144, Hughes 2006a fig. 4.

Ruvo 1402, Apulian *askos*, Felton Ptr, 380–360, *RVAp* 7/68, *IGD* IV.12.

S. Agata dei Goti priv. coll. 1, Apulian bell *krater*, Rainone Ptr, 380–370, *RVAp* 4/224, *PhV*² no. 59, pl. IVa, Hughes 2006a fig. 13.

Salerno Pc1812, Paestan bell *krater*, Asteas, 350, *IGD* IV.31, *RVP* 2/19 pl. 20c. **Figure 23**.

Sèvres 80, Apulian *oinochoe*, unattrib., 350–325, *PhV*² no. 116, *CVA* France 13 pl. 40,19.

Siracusa 29966, Sicilian/Paestan *rhyton* fragment, Asteas, 360–350, *RVP* 1/103, *PhV*² no. 134, Trendall 1952 no. 60, pl. 5a.

Siracusa 66557, Sicilian *kalyx krater* fragment, Capodarso Ptr, 340–330, *LCS* supp. iii III/98a, *Comic angels* pl. 6.112.

Siracusa from Grammichele, Sicilian *krater* fragment, Manfria Gp, 340–320, *PhV*² no. 88, *LCS* III/75 pl. 231.5.

St Petersburg Б201 (St.1538), Attic *hydria* Pan Ptr, 490–480, BArch 206338, *TAGS* fig. 3.22.

St Petersburg Б299 (St.1775), Apulian bell *krater*, Iris Ptr, 370–360, *RVAp* 5/260, *PhV*² no. 31, *IGD* IV.22, *BH*² fig. 482. **Figure 34**.

St Petersburg Б1660 (St.1777; W1155), Sicilian/Paestan bell *krater*, Asteas, 360–350, *RVP* 1/105 pl. 13e, *PhV*² no. 32.

St Petersburg Б1661 (St.1779; W1120), Apulian bell *krater*, Reckoning Ptr (name vase), 380–370, *RVAp* 4/45, *PhV*² no. 33, *BH*² fig. 514. **Figure 6**.

St Petersburg Б2074, Apulian bell *krater*, Dijon Ptr, 375–350, *RVAp* 6/97, *PhV*² no. 34, *Comic angels* pl. 14.12.

St Petersburg Б2079 (W1065), Sicilian *olpe*, Adrano Gp, 330, *LCS* III/104 pl. 237.

St Petersburg ФА1869.47, Attic *oinochoe*, nr Meidias Ptr, 400, *PhV*² no. 6, BArch 10930, *IGD* IV.3, *BH*² fig. 184.

Switzerland priv. coll., loan to Geneva Musée d'art d'histoire, Apulian Gnathia *kalyx krater*, Compiègne Ptr, 350–325, Cambitoglou *et al.* 1986, 27 (colour). **Figure 3**.

Switzerland priv. coll., Apulian Gnathia *olpos*, unattrib., 375–350, J. Dorig, *Art antique: collections privées de Suisse romande* (Geneva 1975) 276.

Sydney NM47.05, Apulian bell *krater*, Tarporley Ptr, 400–390, *RVAp* 3/15, *PhV*² xxxii, *RVSIS* pl. 104.

Sydney NM53.10, Apulian fragment, nr Lykourgos Ptr, 360–350, Green *et al.* 2003, 62, no. 26.

Sydney NM53.30, Lucanian *skyphos*, Schwerin Gp, 430–400, *LCS* I/352 pl. 33.1.

Sydney NM75.2, Apulian *oinochoe*, Truro Ptr, 350, *RVAp* 5/141 pl. 3, Green *et al.* 2003 no. 19 (colour). **Figure 42**.

Sydney NM88.02, Apulian bell *krater*, Lecce Ptr, 350, *RVAp* supp. ii 5/200b, Green *et al.* 2003 no. 17 (colour).

Sydney NM95.16, Apulian *skyphos*, Woman-Eros Ptr, 330–320, Green *et al.* 2003 no. 43 (colour).

Sydney NM97.172, Apulian fragment, Palermo Ptr, 400, Green *et al.* 2003 no. 11 (colour).

Syracuse, New York [reported], Lucerne market. Fischer sale catalogue 1941, Apulian *oinochoe*, unattrib., 375–350, *PhV*² no. 118 pl. VIId, Hoorn 1951 no. 920, fig. 411. **Figure 19**.

Tampa 2.95.1 loan from priv. coll., Apulian black-glazed *guttus*, 330–320, *TAGS* fig. 3.8.

Tampa 7.94.4 loan from priv. coll., Apulian black-glazed *guttus*, 330–320, Zewadski 1995, Black Glaze 43.

Tampa 7.94.8 loan from priv. coll., Apulian Gnathia *kalyx krater*, Konnakis Gp, 350, *TAGS* frontispiece.

Tampa 86106, Apulian *situla*, V and A Gp, 350, *RVAp* 15/51 pl. 143,4–6.

Taranto 4600, Apulian *kalyx krater*, unattrib., 400–375, *RVAp* 2/11, De Juliis, Loiacono 1985 no. 288.

Taranto 4658, Apulian *oinochoe*, unattrib., 375–350, *PhV*² no. 119, De Juliis, Loiacono 1985 no. 311.

Taranto 8263, Lucanian volute *krater*, Karneia Ptr, 410–400, *LCS* I/280 pl. 24, D'Amicis, Dell'Aglio 1991 no. 14, 131–7. **Figure 20**.

Taranto 8264, Apulian volute *krater*, Ptr of the Birth of Dionysos (name vase), 400–375, *RVAp* 02/6, BArch 9005337, Pugliese Carratelli 1996 no. 197 (colour).

Taranto 8935 Apulian amphora, Varrese Ptr, 360–340, *RVAp* 13/4 pl. 109,1.

Taranto 9120–9121, Apulian *kalyx krater*, unattrib., 340–330, *PhV*² no. 89, Charbonneau *et al.* 1969 pl. 367.

Taranto 114090, Attic *oinochoe*, Schlaepfer Ptr, 350, *RVAp* 9/175, Hughes 2008 fig. 12.

Taranto 121613, Apulian bell *krater* fragment, Iris Ptr [?], 400–375, *PhV*² no. 61, Hughes 2006a fig. 10.

Taranto 122627 *bis*, Apulian bell *krater* fragments, nr McDaniel Ptr, 380–370, *PhV*² no. 62 pl. Vd.

Taranto 29031, Apulian *oinochoe*, Felton Ptr, 370–360, *RVAp* supp. ii (1991) 7/V5, D'Amicis, Dell' Aglio 1991 no. 6.4, 67, Hughes 2008 fig. 11.

Taranto 54724, Apulian black-glazed *oinochoe*, unattrib., 375–350, *PhV*² no. 121, D'Amicis *et al.* 2004, 36 (colour).

Taranto 56048, Apulian *oinochoe*, unattrib., 375–350, *PhV*² no. 122 pl. VIIIa, *IGD* IV.23.

Taranto IG4638, Apulian Gnathia bell *krater*, Konnakis Ptr (name vase), 350, Hughes 1997 pl. 1.6.

Taranto priv. coll. 6, Apulian black-glazed *olpos*, unattrib., 350, *PhV*² no. 128 pl. VIIId.

Taranto priv. coll. 106, Apulian fragment, unattrib., 375–350, *PhV*² no. 148 pl. IXi.

Taranto priv. coll. 123, Apulian *oinochoe*, Schlaepfer Gp, 350, *RVAp* 9/174, pl. 80.

Thebes BE64.342, Attic BF *skyphos*, unattrib., 480, BArch 4635, *IGD* I.13, *GVGetty* no. 12 fig. 15a–b.

Toronto 972.182.1, Apulian *oinochoe* (type 8), Ptr of Boston 13.93, 350, *PhV*² no. 127, Csapo 1993 pl. 10,1. **Figure 26**.

Vatican 6283, Attic column *krater*, Pan Ptr, 500–450, *ARV*² 551.8, BArch 206283, Beazley 1974 no. 6, pl. 26.2.

Vatican U19 (17106), Paestan bell *krater*, Asteas, 350–340, *RVP* 2/176, *PhV*² no. 65, *IGD* IV.19, *BH*² fig. 484.

Vienna 466 (10.36), Apulian bell *krater*, Ptr of Heidelberg U6, 375–350, *PhV*² no. 66, *RVAp* 10/036 pl. 88,1–2.

Würzburg H4600 (832), Apulian Gnathia fragment, Konnakis Gp, 350, BArch 1007014, *MTS*² GV3, *BH*² fig. 306a, Charbonneaux *et al.* 1969 pl. 368 (colour).

Würzburg H4689 (959), Apulian bell *krater*, McDaniel Ptr, 380–370, *RVAp* 4/245, *PhV*² no. 67 pl. IIId.

Würzburg H4696, H4701, Apulian Gnathia fragments, Konnakis Gp, 350–340, BArch 1007015, Charbonneaux *et al.* 1969 pl. 360 (colour). **Figure 9**.

Würzburg H5697, Apulian bell *krater*, Schiller Ptr, 380–370, RVAp 4/4a, *Comic angels* pl. 11.4.

Würzburg H5846, Apulian *oinochoe*, unattrib., 375–350, BArch 1006985, *CVA* Würzburg pl. 22, 5–7.

Würzburg K479, Attic cup, Brygos Ptr, 490–480, BArch 203930, *ARV*² 372.32, Boardman 1975 fig. 254.

Würzburg L344, Attic BF *oinochoe*, Ptr of Villa Giulia M.482, 490, BArch 320445, *ABV* 434.57, *GVGetty* no. 10 fig. 13.

Würzburg L823a, Apulian *krater* fragment, unattrib., 380–370, *PhV*² no. 151, *BH*² fig. 522.

Zurich University 4007, Apulian *hydria*, Ganymede Ptr, 350–340, *RVAp* supp. i 18/11a, pl. IX.1.

TERRACOTTAS

Figurines, unless otherwise stated.

Amsterdam 261, Attic, 350–325, *MMC*³ AT113g, pl. XIIIb.

Amsterdam 881, Attic, 400–375, *MMC*³ AT5a, Ghiron-Bistagne 1976 fig. 57. **Figure 4**.

Athens 4794, Attic, 325–250, *MNC*³ 1AT4, Pickard-Cambridge 1953 fig. 134.

Athens 6074 (P398), Attic, 375–350, *MMC*³ AT70b pl. IVc–d.

Athens 12507, from Greece [?], 350–325, *MMC*³ UT8.

Athens 13015 (1422), Attic, 375–350, *MMC*³ AT73a, *BH*² fig. 162.

Athens Agora Museum T1683, Attic, 400–375, *MMC*³ AT5a, Thompson 1952 no. 44 pl. 38.

Athens Agora Museum T1684, Attic, 350–325, *MMC*³ AT110b pl. 11c.

Athens Kanellopoulos Museum 1460, Attic, 350–325, Hughes 2006a fig. 7.

Basle market 1958, whereabouts unk., Corinthian, before 400, *MMC*³ CT1, *Münzen und Medeillen* 1958, 29.xi.

Berlin TC6823, Attic, 375–350, *MMC*³ AT37, *BH*² fig. 133.

Berlin TC6876, Attic, 375–350, *MMC*³ AT67a, Bieber 1920 no. 89 taf. 73.

Berlin TC6907, Attic, 375–350, *MMC*³ AT79 (incorrect inv. no.), Bieber 1920 no. 158 taf. 101.

Berlin TC7086, Attic, 375–350, *MMC*³ AT40.

Berlin TC7089, Attic, 375–350, *MMC*³ AT69a, *BH*² fig. 163, Rohde 1968 fig. 26b.

Berlin TC7603, Attic, 375–350, *MMC*³ AT62, *BH*² fig. 157.

Berlin TC7604, Attic, 375–350, *MMC*³ AT61, *BH*² fig. 158.

Berlin TC8265, Boiotian from Thespiai, 375–350, *MMC*³ BT14a, Rohde 1968 fig. 26a.

Berlin TC8405, Attic, 375–350, *MMC*³ AT84, *BH*² fig. 134. **Figure 30**.

Berlin TC8838, Attic, 375–350, *MMC*³ AT26c, Bieber 1920 no. 73 taf. 73.

Boston 01.7679, Aegean after an Athenian model, 150–50, *MNC*³ 3DT28a, *BH*² fig. 297, Csapo 1993 pl. 5.

Boston 01.7838, Attic, 375–350, *MMC*³ AT46a, F. Jones 1951 pl. 10.

Boston 13.99, Boiotian, 375–350, *MMC*³ BT2, F. Jones 1951 pl. 8.

British Columbia priv. coll., once London coll. Embirikos, Attic, 350–325, *MMC*³ AT115a. **Figure 41d**.

Brussels A302, Attic mask, 325–250, *MNC*³ 1AT41a, *TAGS* figs. 4.10a–b.

Bucharest coll. Sloboziuanu, east Greek from Kallatis, 325–250, *MNC*³ 1DT1, Canarache 1969 fig. 251.

Cambridge GR85b.1937, Attic, 325–250, *MNC*³ 1AT16 pl. 3a.

Catania 2347, Sicilian, 350–325, *MMC*³ ST78, BBTL fig. 349, Libertini 1930 no. 1171 pl. CXVI.

Christchurch University of Canterbury 65–62, Egyptian, 350–325, *MMC*³ XT15 pl. IIc.

Copenhagen 759, Attic, 375–350, *MMC*³ AT85f, Breitenstein 1941 no. 325 pl. 39.

Copenhagen 1067, Boiotian, 325–300, *MMC*³ BT22, Breitenstein 1941 no. 330 pl. 39.

Copenhagen 1068, Attic, 400–375, *MMC*³ AT14b, Breitenstein 1941 no. 329 pl. 39.

Copenhagen 1947, Boiotian [?] from Thespiai, 350, Breitenstein 1941 no. 297 pl. 34.

Copenhagen 4715 from Thebes, Boiotian, 375–350, *MMC*³ AT26p, Breitenstein 1941 no. 326 pl. 39.

Copenhagen 4738, Boiotian, 375–350, *MMC*³ BT7, Breitenstein 1941 no. 328 pl. 39. **Figure 40.**

Copenhagen 7367, Attic mask, 325–250, *MNC*³ 1AT51a, *TAGS* fig. 4.8.

Corinth MF1608, Corinthian, 350–325, *MMC*³ CT8, *MMC*² pl. IIIb.

Dresden ZV732, Attic, 325–250, *MNC*³ 1AT3, *BICS* 27 (1980) 127, no. 36a pl. 8b.

Glasgow 03–70dp, Sicilian from Lipari, 350–325, *MMC*³ AT9h, *Scottish Art Review* 12 (1969) 6–7, fig. 9.

Heidelberg TK46, Attic, 375–350, *MMC*³ AT28b, Bieber 1920 no. 94 taf. 75.

Heidelberg TK47, Attic, 400–375, *MMC*³ AT16, Catteruccia 1965 tav. II. **Figure 41a.**

Heidelberg TK48, Attic, 375–350, *MMC*³ AT48, Pickard-Cambridge 1953 fig. 83.

Kassel T559, Attic, 350–325, *MMC*³ AT112, Sinn 1977 no. 78 pl. 2.

Kavalla 240 (E489), Boiotian plaque with six masks, 325–250, *MNC*³ 1BT5, *TAGS* fig. 5.6.

Larnaka Pierides Foundation Museum 5242, Cypriot, 375–350, *MMC*³ KT1 pl. XIIb, www.cobb.msstate.edu/dig/pierides/ no. 5242.

Larnaka Pierides Foundation Museum 5245, Cypriot, 350–325, *MMC*³ KT9 pl. XIIId, www.cobb.msstate.edu/dig/pierides/ no. 5245.

Leiden KvB204, Attic, 375–350, *MMC*³ AT58b, Leyenaar-Plaisier 1979 no. 179, pl. 30.

Lipari 356i, Sicilian, 350–325, *MMC*³ ST13, BBTL E54a fig. 125.

Lipari 722, Sicilian, 350–325, *MMC*³ ST9a, BBTL E98 fig. 96.

Lipari 2356c, Sicilian, 350–325, *MMC*³ ST47a, BBTL E76 tav. XVI.2 (colour).

Lipari 3243, Sicilian, 350–325, *MMC*³ ST45a, BBTL E65a fig. 140.

Lipari 3252, Sicilian, 350–325, BBTL E75 fig. 148.

Lipari 3266, Sicilian, 350–325, *MMC*³ ST50a, BBTL E81 fig. 155.

Lipari 3426, Sicilian, 325–250, *MNC*³ 1ST2, Bernabò Brea, Cavalier 1965 C101 pl. CXCVII.1.

Lipari 6913, Sicilian, 350–325, BBTL E96 fig. 165.

Lipari 6941, Sicilian, 350–325, BBTL E24 fig. 93.

Lipari 9725, Sicilian, 350–325, BBTL E5 fig. 76.

Lipari 9727, Sicilian, 335–250, *MNC*³ 1ST3, BBTL fig. 237.

Lipari 9814, Sicilian, 325–250, *MNC*³ 1ST4, BBTL E14 fig. 85.

Lipari 10782, Sicilian, 325–325, BBTL E59a tav. XV.4 (colour).

Lipari 11962, Sicilian, 350–325, BBTL E61a fig. 135.

Lipari 12982, Sicilian, 350–325, *MMC*³ ST21, BBTL E10a fig. 80.

London 1842.7–28.750, terracotta mask, from Melos, 325–250, *MNC*³ 1DT20, *DFA*² fig. 127, Burn, Higgins 2001 pl. 47.

London 1842.7–28.752, Attic, from Melos, 375–350, *MMC*³ AT24b, Burn, Higgins 2001 pl. 47, Green, Handley 1995, 60, pl. 34. **Figure 29**.

London 1856.12–26.255 (D325), Attic, 325–350, *MNC*³ 1AT9.

London 1865.7–20.43, Attic, 350–325, *MMC*³ AT114, Higgins 1954 no. 746 pl. 98.

London 1867.2–5.22, Corinthian, 375–350, *MMC*³ CT2a, Higgins 1954 no. 963 pl. 36d. **Figure 31**.

London 1875.3–9.10, Attic, 375–350, *MMC*³ AT59a, Higgins 1954 no. 740 pl. 97.

London 1879.3–6.5, Attic, 350–325, Higgins 1954 no. 743 pl. 98. **Figure 28**.

London 1887.7–25.7, Attic, 325–250, *MNC*³ 1AT24, *BH*² fig.354, Green, Handley 1995 fig. 46.

London 1907.5–20.79b, Attic, 350–325, *MMC*³ AT115a, Higgins 1954 no. 745 pl. 99.

London 1907.12–19.1, Attic, 375–350, *MMC*³ AT25a Higgins 1954 no. 724 pl. 94.

Madrid 3370, Campanian mask, 325–250, *MMC*³ 1NT6b, Laumonier 1921 no. 856.

Madrid 4016, Attic, 350–325, *MMC*³ AT16c, Laumonier 1921 no. 703 pl. LXXVIII,3.

Madrid 4045, Campanian mask, 325–350, *MNC*³ 1NT15, Laumonier 1921 no. 855.

Milan Scala 37, Tarentine, 325–250, *MNC*³ 1TT4, Roberti 1976 no. 107 fig. 83.

Montpelier 99, from Myrina, east Greek, 325–300, *MMC*³ MT1 pl. XIIIc.

München 5389, Attic, 375–350, *MMC*³ AT39, *BH*² fig. 147.

München 5394, Attic, 375–350, *MMC*³ AT65, *BH*² fig. 178.

München 6931, Attic, 375–350, *MMC*³ AT66a, *BH*² fig. 173.

München SL199, Attic, 325–350, *MNC*³ 1AT11a, Sieveking 1916 pl. 79.

New York 13.225.13, Attic, 400, *MMC*³ AT12a, *BH*² fig. 188.

    13.225.14, Attic, 400, *MMC*³ AT14a, *BH*² fig. 190.

    13.225.16, Attic, 400, *MMC*³ AT21a, *BH*² fig. 197.

    13.225.17, Attic, 400, *MMC*³ AT23a, *BH*² fig. 164.

    13.225.18, Attic, 400, *MMC*³ AT20a, *BH*² fig. 196.

    13.225.19, Attic, 400, *MMC*³ AT22a, *BH*² fig. 198.

    13.225.20, Attic, 400, *MMC*³ AT15a, *BH*² fig. 191.

    13.225.21, Attic, 400, *MMC*³ AT16a, *BH*² fig. 192.

    13.225.22, Attic, 400, *MMC*³ AT13a, *BH*² fig. 189.

    13.225.23, Attic, 400, *MMC*³ AT10a, *BH*² fig. 186.

    13.225.24, Attic, 400, *MMC*³ AT19a, *BH*² fig. 195.

    13.225.25, Attic, 400, *MMC*³ AT17a, *BH*² fig. 193.

    13.225.26, Attic, 400, *MMC*³ AT9a, *BH*² fig. 185.

    13.225.27, Attic, 400, *MMC*³ AT11a, *BH*² fig. 187.

    13.225.28, Attic, 400, *MMC*³ AT18a, *BH*² fig. 194.

New York priv. coll. A1992.20, Attic or Boiotian, fourth cent., Rothwell 2007 pl. VII.

Nikosia 1934.vii–12.3, Cypriot, 325–250, *MNC*³ 1KT1 pl. XIIb.

Once Cyprus Cesnola coll., whereabouts unk., Cypriot, 375–350, *MMC*³ KT3, Cesnola 1882 fig. 211.

Oxford 1922.207, Attic, 375–350, *MMC*³ AT74b pl. XIIIa, Green 2001 fig. 14.

Paris AM34, Cypriot, 325–250, *MNC*³ 1KT3, *BH*² fig. 407.

Paris AM36, Cypriot, 350–325, *MMC³* KT11.

Paris AM39, Cypriot, 375–350, *MMC³* KT8, *BH²* fig. 167.

Paris CA20, Attic, 375–350, *MMC³* AT46a, *BH²* fig. 140, Besques 1971 C635 pl. 2a.

Paris CA239, Boiotian, 375–350, *MMC³* BT14b, Besques 1971 C641 pl. 95e. **Figure 46**.

Paris CA479 (297), Attic, 375–350, *MMC³* AT63, *BH²* fig. 179, Besques 1971 C642 pl. 96a.

Paris CA806 from Thebes, Boiotian, 500, Besques 1963 pl. VII.

Paris CA1510, Attic 350–325, *MMC³* AT98, *BH²* fig. 409, Besques 1971 D443 pl. 96e.

Paris CA1816, Attic, 400–375, *MMC³* AT24a pl. XIb, Besques 1971 C645 pl. 96d.

Paris CA4234, Tarentine, 375–350, *MMC³* TT20, Besques 1986 D3707 pl. 66c.

Paris Cp.4951, Campanian, 350–325, Besques 1986 D3709 pl. 67b.

Paris ED2070, Tarentine, 250–150, *MNC³* 2TT3b, Besques 1986 D3717 pl. 68a.

Paris MNB2720 Attic, 325–250, *MNC³* 1AT2b, Besques 1986 D3715 pl. 68e.

Paris N4878 (MN638), Attic, 375–350, *MMC³* AT70a, Besques 1992 C647a pl. 40b. **Figure 43**.

Princeton 48–50, Boiotian, 325–300, *MMC³* BT20, *BH²* fig. 144.

Reggio Calabria 156, Sicilian, 350–325, Costabile 1991, 173.

Rostock University, from Megale Hellas [?], 350–325, *MMC³* UT7, *BH²* fig. 165.

Rostock University 485, Sicilian from Megara Hyblaia, 375–350, *MMC³* ST2, *BH²* fig. 136.

Siracusa 1522, Sicilian, 350–325, *MMC³* ST62, Westcoat 1989 pl. 23.

Siracusa 1523, Sicilian, 350–325, *MMC³* ST61, Westcoat 1989 pl. 24.

Siracusa 1524, Sicilian, 350–325, *MMC³* ST63, Westcoat 1989 pl. 25.

Siracusa 1527, Sicilian, 350–325, Bernabò Brea, Cavalier 2002 fig. 20.

Siracusa 18971, Sicilian, 350–300, Bernabò Brea, Cavalier 2002 fig. 68, Hughes 2008 fig. 10.

Siracusa 23001, Sicilian from Camarina, 450–440, *MMC³* ST1, Orsi 1904, 802, fig. 21. **Figure 2**.

Siracusa 68133, Sicilian, 350–300, Bernabò Brea, Cavalier 2002 fig. 18.

Siracusa inv. unk., Sicilian, 350–325, *MMC³* ST66.

St Petersburg ББ92, Attic, 375–350, *MMC³* AT74a, *MMStP* no. 60.

St Petersburg ББ160, Attic, 350–325, *MMC³* AT91, Peredolskaja 1964 pl. 8.2–3.

St Petersburg ББ165, Attic, 350–325, *MMC³* AT89a, *MMStP* no. 58, Peredolskaja 1964 pl. 4,3.

St Petersburg ББ166, Attic, 400–375, *MMC³* AT10h, Green 2001 fig. 13, Peredolskaja 1964 pl. 4,1. **Figure 41b**.

St Petersburg Г701 (Б1888) Corinthian 375–350, *MMStP* no. 74.

St Petersburg Г1167, Attic, 375–350, *MMC³* AT60b, *SovArch* new series 4 (1960), 258, figs. 1, 2.

St Petersburg Г1432, Attic, 350–325, *MMC³* AT90, *MMStP* no. 76. **Figure 35**.

St Petersburg П1841.75, Attic, 375–350, *MMStP* no. 69, Hughes 2006a fig. 1 and cover (colour).

St Petersburg П1874.34, Attic, 350–325, *MMC*³ AT116a, *MMStP* no. 68. **Figure 41c.**

Tampa 88.34.10, loan from priv. coll., first cent. [?], Ede 1985 no. 18.

Tarquinia RC1346, *MNC*³ 1AT19, 325–250, Stefani 1984 no. 120 pl. 35c.

Tarquinia RC1764, *MNC*³ 1AT14, 325–250, Stefani 1984 no. 119 pl. 35b. **Figure 51.**

Thebes from Thebes Kolonaki, Boiotian, 375–350, *MMC*³ BT6 pl. IIIa, *ArchDelt* 22 (1961) pl. 162.

Vienna V1567, from Myrina [?], 150–50, *MMC*³ 3DT25a, *BH*² fig. 299, Csapo 1993 pl. 7.

OTHER MEDIA

Athens Agora Museum S1025, 1586, marble relief fragments, 350–325, *MMC*³ AS3 pl. IX, *BH*² fig. 181.

Athens Akropolis Museum 623, marble statue attrib. to Phaidimos, 575–550, Richter 1987 pl. 70.

Istanbul 1768, stone statuette, Roman period, *BH*² fig. 582, www.pbase.com/dosseman/archaeological_museum_istanbul&page=2photos(colour).

London 1975.5–198-I, Boiotian coin, fourth cent., Tanner 2006 fig. 2.8d.

Malibu 92.AM.8.1, Alexandrian gold hairnet, second cent., Pfrommer 2001 pl. 3a.b.c.

Malibu 96.AB.155, Attic bronze figurine, second cent., Getty 1994 218–19, no. 108.

Naples 6687, marble relief, 50–25, *MNC*³ 4XS1, *GTP*² C49 pl. 24a, *BH*² fig. 324, Green 1985 pl. 52 fig. 1. **Figure 52.**

Naples 9985 from Pompeii, mosaic, Dioskourides of Samos, late second cent., *MNC*³ 3DM2, *BH*² fig. 346, *TAGS* fig. 5.5. **Figure 54.**

Naples 9987 from Pompeii, mosaic, Dioskourides of Samos, late second cent., *MNC*³ 3DM1, *BH*² fig. 347, Green, Handley 1995 fig. 50 (colour). **Figure 55.**

New York 1972.118.95, bronze figurine, third–second cent., Richter 1987 fig. 291.

New York 1981.11.18, 1981.11.12, silver bowls, Hellenistic, P.G. Guzzo, 'A group of Hellenistic objects in the Metropolitan Museum', *Metropolitan Museum Journal* 38 (2003) 66–8, no. 14, figs. 49–52, no. 15, figs. 55–8.

Paris Petit Palais DUT192 from Riete, ivory figurine, second to third cent. CE, *MTS*² 93, II, 1, *TAGS* fig. 6.10.

Pompeii Casa di Casca Longo, wall painting, first cent. CE, *BH*² fig. 395, Hughes 1991, 13, pl. 5.

Stockport Lyme Hall, marble relief, 350–325, *MMC*³ AS1, *BH*² fig. 201, *TAGS* pl. 3.20.

Toronto 953.171, Attic bronze figurine, fourth cent., *MMC*³ AB1f pl. VIa, Mitten, Doeringer 1967 no. 118.

Vatican 9985 (once Lateran Museum 487), marble relief, 150–50, *MNC*³ 3AS5a, *GTP*² C49 pl. 24b, *BH*² fig. 317. **Figure 53.**

Notes

1 COMEDY IN ART, ATHENS AND ABROAD

1 Aischylos, *Persians* is dated 472; the death of Sophokles, 406/5.

2 *Birds* was performed 414, London 1842.7–28.787 is dated 500–490; *Knights* was performed 424, Berlin F1697 is dated 540–530: see Chapter 4, 85–8.

3 The 'Perseus Dance' vase, once Vlasto/Serpieri coll., now Athens BΣ518, was known to scholars only through old photographs and a questionable reconstruction, Hughes 2006b.

4 Webster 1948; reaction, Pickard-Cambridge 1949. Traditional view, *BH*² 45 on the figurines, 129–46 on *phlyakes*, which Bieber discusses after New Comedy in order to link them to early Roman comedy.

5 Csapo 1986; Taplin 1987; and *Comic angels*.

6 Abel 1963, 59–60; *TAGS* 26–7. Green 1997, 132 refers to 'further reality *of the myth*', not of the tragedy, as implied by Small 2003, 68–71.

7 London 1946.9–25.3; Metaponto 29340, 29062 (Figure 1), fragments from a kiln.

8 Painters seldom signed their names. A.D. Trendall named them for the subject of a vase (Amykos, Choregos), the inventory number of a 'name vase', or a collection that contains it (Louvre K240, Adolphseck).

9 The attractive Gnathia portraits date *c*.350, and include a picture of Konnakis, the first woman performer whose name we know, Taranto IG4638. Two of the scenes are linked by geese on stage, and all three by a stage-naked character with a distinctive, beardless mask and a slim, straight walking-stick; see below p. 14, and Figure 48.

10 Taplin 2007 looks for 'signals' that a vase scene may be 'enriched and informed' by tragedy, such as tragic costume or a *paidogogos* figure.

11 Poseidonia was remote from Megale Hellas, and controlled by Oscan-speaking Lucanians; the extensive theatre-building of the third century passed it by: Poseidonia and Asteas, Hughes 2003, 281–3. Albania, Apollonia 325; in Campania, only the Libation Ptr accurately reflects comedy. Late Sicilian scenes, Messina 11039 (Figure 39), Lentini 2B (Figure 45), Paris CA7249; four actors are on stage in Berlin F3044 (Figure 10) and Lipari 927.

12 New York 13.225.13–28, *TAGS* 34–5; Paris CA1816 and London 1842.7–28.752 (Figure 29, a Herakles, known in eighteen copies) belong stylistically with the New York Group. A fine Hellenistic example from Athens, Boston 01.7679.

13 More than 150 vases and nearly 200 figurines have been studied in 70 museums and 4 private collections; others were collected as photographs. Only demonstrably theatrical scenes are accepted as evidence; excluded are those known only from drawings or engravings.

14 Green 1999; Csapo 2001, 17; *TAGS* 56–7. Taplin 2007, 37–41 finds eight dramatic 'signals' which may indicate tragic connections.

15 Paris N3408.

16 Athens BΣ518; perspective, Hughes 2006b, 421–3.

17 See Small 2003, 53. Construction of steps in the *choregoi* scene, once Malibu 96.AE.29, is traditional practice for a ship's companionway; also see Varrese Ptr, Naples 118333 (Figure 8); Libation Ptr, Melbourne D14/1973; Manfria Ptr, Lentini 2B (Figure 45).

18 Schiller Ptr, Würzburg H5697, Csapo 1986, Taplin 1987, *Comic angels* 36–40, *TAGS* 65. Small 2003, 68 is uncertain whether the painter saw a performance or read the text.

19 New York 24.97.104, Boston 69.951, Malibu 96.AE.113 (Figure 48). The comedy must have been played several times in Taras, because the scenes were painted at least thirty years apart.

20 See Chapter 9, 180–2.

21 Only Berlin F3044, from St Agata dei Goti, has a provenance anywhere near Paestum.

22 Sousarion, prototypes, see Chapter 4, 82–7.

23 Dearden 1990, 156–9.

24 Plato, *Laws* 770c–701a condemns the readiness of audiences to judge for themselves. N. Slater 1999 examines Aristophanes' manipulation of his audience; and see Revermann 2006, 20, and 159–75.

25 Shapiro 1992 is a well-illustrated account of the Panathenaia. Celebrated in February/March, it began with an enactment of the god's return from Asia; in the fourth century it may have included a comic *agon*, *DFA*[2] 15–16. Dionysos in his ship, with dolphins, München 8729; his Asian associations, Euripides, *Bacchai* 13–20.

26 Chapter 4, 81–2. Csapo, Miller 2007, 8 distinguish dithyramb as cultic song with Dionysian content from 'theatrical' circular choruses.

27 *CAD* 107. Other *choregoi* were responsible for tragic trilogies and dithyrambs. Before the choral festival began, poets publicly presented their actors in a *proagon*; it is unknown whether comedies participated. Officially, the original competition was amongst *choregoi* and *didaskaloi* (chorus directors) who might not be the poets. Competitions for poets, actors and 'old' plays were added later.

28 *CAD* 108, 141.

29 The previous location of the Lenaia is disputed, Chapter 3, n. 19. Because sea travel was hazardous in winter, few foreign visitors were present, *Ach.* 503,

DFA^2 41, 359. Direct evidence of five competing comedies refers only to 284 BCE, *CAD* 123–4. Tragic *protagonist*'s prize, Great Dionysia 449; N. Slater 1988, 53–7 makes a case for a comic actors' prize by 421; the first secure date is 329–312.

30 *CAD* III.71,135; fragment of a commentary, frag. 590 trans. J. Henderson, Aristophanes V, 2007; Eratosthenes on Old Comedy says the comedy was *Rabdouchoi* (*Theatre Police* or *Mace Bearers*); perhaps in the following year's *parabasis* the poet claimed he was 'shunted back to the Lenaian competition', Biles 1999.

31 Csapo 2004, 54–76; Plato, *Republic* 475d trans. P. Shorey 1943. Aelian, *Historical Miscellany* 2.13; Aeschines, *Against Timarchos*, 157; Aristotle, *Rhetoric* 1404b. N.F. Jones 2004, 124–7 argues that since epigraphic evidence refers to these festivals only as *ta Dionysia*, 'agrarian' might be more appropriate than 'rural'; Kollytos and Peiraeus were within the city walls. The 'Perseus Dance' vase may show part of the theatre at Thorikos, Hughes 2006b, 428.

32 Eupolis and Kratinos averaged one play a year. When Aristophanes participated in both festivals, one comedy was presented under another man's name: Philonides (*Proagon* 422, *Amphiaraos* 414) or Kallistratos (*Birds* 414, *Lys.* 411). If this was a rule, either it was relaxed in the fourth century or poets wrote for performance elsewhere.

33 *Poleis* is Plato's word at *Republic* 475d; his 'villages' are not *demoi* but *komas*, a term Aristotle identifies as Doric, *Poetics* 1448a.

34 Dearden 1999, 225.

35 Hieron, tyrant of Syrakousai, expelled the population of Katana, repopulated and renamed it Aitna. Dates are uncertain; for Aischylos in Sicily, see Dearden 1999, 230–1, and his *Life, CAD* I.23A–B,14. Lefkowitz 1981 challenges the authenticity of ancient poets' *Lives*. Phrynichos and the Lenaia, Harvey 2000, 114–15; Dover *et al.* 2000, 521; *CAD* III.76D,137.

36 Thasos, Hippokrates, *Epidemics* I,12; Aristotle, *Poetics* 1448a refers to Hegemon of Thasos, whom the *Souda*, eta 52 calls a poet of Old Comedy; Grandjean, Salvat 2000, 105.

37 Chares, *Histories of Alexander* 10, *CAD* IV.31D,237; Plutarch, *Alexander* 72.1, 29; Demosthenes, *On the false embassy* 192f, *CAD* IV.29,232; *On the peace* 6, *CAD* IV.32,237.

38 P. Wilson 2007, 360–4, 355; Hezychios, s.v. *pente kritai*, *CAD* III.120B,162. Plato, *Laws* 657a–c trans. R.G. Bury 1961. Plato travelled to Syrakousai in 367 and 362; the context is an *agon* in *mousike*, which could include drama: Dearden 1999, 232. The Athenian *choregia* was abolished between 317 and 307 by Demetrios of Phaleron. Orchomenos in Boiotia employed a *choregia*, Fossey 1990, 247.

39 Sifakis 1995, 16–17; this question, together with several proposed solutions, is discussed in Chapter 6, 113.

40 *Tritagonist*: a junior actor, perhaps the *protagonist*'s kin; an *aulos*-player might be his mistress. Dearden 1999, 229 adds a mask-maker and either a single chorus-man or a nuclear chorus.

41 *BH*² 146. Dearden 1999, 226 takes Plato's response to actors who ask permission to 'set up their stage in the *agora*' of his ideal *polis* (*Laws* 817a c, trans. R.G. Bury, 1961) as evidence that he regarded 'wandering troupes of actors as a normal part of Athenian life'.

42 On the stages shown in the vases, see Billig 1980, Hughes 1996, here Chapter 3, 66–73.

43 Walking-sticks, Zewadski 1995, and Chapter 9, 183. Baskets, *Danaids* frag. 259, trans. J. Henderson, Aristophanes V, 2007 from Pollux 9. 'Props' include chairs, kitchen utensils, hand mirrors, chests and small trees.

44 Sicilian, Siracusa 23001; Basle market 1958: both masks have the large, open mouth and protuberant eyes and ears; neither has the exposed *phallos*. Several Corinthian figures have similar masks, London 1867.2–5.22 (Figure 31), St Petersburg Γ701, but the stylized *chiton* displays the *phallos*. Gesture, compare Corinth MF1608. Rostock University 485, from Megara Hyblaia, perhaps our second-oldest Sicilian figure, derives from an Attic model, London 1907.12–19.1. Cypriot figurines have wide-mouthed masks, Larnaka 5242; a bow-legged stance suggests a comic walk found nowhere else, Paris AM36. Deinolochos, *Souda*, delta 338, born in the seventy-third Olympiad, would have been in his early 40s in 440.

45 Tragedy, Dearden 1999, 235–8. *Thes.*, Würzburg H5697. The *choregoi* scene, once Malibu 96.AE.29, may burlesque Euripides' *Elektra*. 'Goose Play', New York 24.97.104, Boston 69.951, Malibu 96.AE.113; possible interpretations, *Comic angels* 30–2, Marshall 2001.

46 Menander I, trans. W.G. Arnott 1997, xxiii–xxiv.

47 Comic actors by the Dolon Ptr, Metaponto 29340 and 29062 (Figure 1), and the Dionysian Karneia vase, with *auletris* and theatre-influenced satyrs, Taranto 8263 (Figure 20). Besides vases with tragedy-related scenes, Ruvo has yielded Naples 81673 ('Pronomos', satyr play), comic scenes on Ruvo 901 and St Petersburg Б299, Б1661.

48 Between 375 and 350, of theatrical material with known provenances the islands and Asia Minor have yielded about 27 per cent as much as Magna Graecia; between 325 and 250, 21 per cent, *TAGS* 134, 68, 108.

49 Olynthos, destroyed by Philip II in 348; comic figurines have been excavated; Satyros was victor in a comic *agon* there, Demosthenes, *On the false embassy* 192f, *CAD* IV.29,232.

50 *CAD* 239–42. The earliest record of the *technitai* in Athens dates 279/8, Dearden 1999, 229.

2 POETS OF OLD AND MIDDLE COMEDY

1 If five comedies were performed at the Great Dionysia 486–404, and at the Lenaia 442–404, the total is 610. With only three comedies at each festival during twenty-eight war years, the total is reduced to 498. From the fourth century we have two by Aristophanes, one by Menander, almost complete, and more than half the texts of four more.

2 *Poetics* 1449a–b. From a tenth-century MS, Janko 1984 reconstructs parts of Aristotle's lost work on comedy, but has not won wide acceptance. Athenaios of Naukratis (died *c.*230 CE) quarries comedy for references to food and drink. Useful data is found in the *Souda*.

3 The scenes are discussed in Chapter 4, 85–7, and illustrated in *GVGetty*.

4 Sousarion's date is calculated from its position on the 'Parian marble', see Chapter 4, 82–3. Scenes: Amsterdam 3356, cup, 560; New York 1988.11.3, *hydria* (water jug), 550.

5 Birds, London 1842.7–28.787. The origins and early development of comedy are disputed: see further discussion below, Chapter 4, 82–7.

6 *Poetics* 1449b calls the performers 'volunteers'. First tragedy *agon c.*528.

7 *Souda*, chi 318, alpha 280. Athenaios 137e, 638d doubts the authenticity of *Beggars*. Instructing a chorus, Plutarch, *Moralia* 46b. *Protagonist*s and supporting actors, Chapter 6, 113.

8 Boston 20.18, discussed Chapter 6, 109–10.

9 Dover *et al.* 2000, 517–18 who emend as *Titakides*, which was a *polis*. *Souda*, mu 20, where some titles may be inferences from *Knights* 520–5, but the date of Magnes' victory is secure. *Poetics* 1451b,1448b; Athenaios 367f, 646e refers to two versions of *Dionysos*.

10 Kratinos, Rusten 2011, 173–4. Krates as actor, scholion to *Knights* 537, *CAD* IV.5,225. *Poetics* 1449b, 1448b trans. S. Halliwell 1999. Conceivably, Aristotle's text should read '*not* much earlier'.

11 Rusten 2011, 59–60, 194–7.

12 Handley 1985, 117 argues that Epicharmos had a chorus; Dearden 1990, 158 discusses evidence. *Souda*, phi 609 spells 'Phormos', names mythological titles, *Admetos*, *Sack of Troy*, and calls him tutor to the children of Gelon, Hieron's predecessor. Pausanias, 5.27.1–7 says he came from Arcadia. *Souda*, delta 338, Deinolochos, born 488–485, was son or student of Epicharmos, and wrote fourteen plays. Sophron is difficult to date, Hordern 2004, 1–4; Xenarchos, *Poetics* 1447b, *CAD* 370.

13 Rusten 2011, 173–4, 189–90, 199.

14 Thucydides II, 21–2. Egg, Bari 3899; *kiste*, Malibu 96.AE.112. Revermann 2006, 301 rejects the *Nemesis* identification because the *hypothesis* places Helen in the basket, but we need not believe everything written on papyrus. Perhaps Helen stood for Aspasia, who was implicated in the Megarian Decree according to Dikaiopolis, *Ach.* 520ff.

15 Rusten 2011, Kratinos frag. 203, 206. Attempted identification of the cartoon Berlin F3047 with *Pytine* has been refuted, Green 2008, 195. Ruffell 2002, 138 interprets *Knights* 526ff as part of an intertextual *agon* between the poets.

16 Aristotle, *Poetics* 1449b; Dover *et al.* 2000, 513; Athenaios 267e–268a.

17 Sidwell 2000, 247 says the two forms we call Old and New Comedy 'were already distinct and distinguished from each other by the last quarter of the fifth century'.

18 *Thes.* II, frag. 347, trans. J. Henderson, Aristophanes V, 2007; *Knights* 537–9, trans. J. Henderson, Aristophanes I, 1998; Edmonds 1957, I, 995 dates *Samioi* 441, probably by connecting it with the revolt.

19 *CAD* IV.6,225; *Agrioi*, Lenaia 320; Dover *et al.* 2000, 519; Plato, *Protagoras* 327d; Rusten 2011, Pherekrates frag. 6, 150; fragment, Plutarch, *Moralia* 1141d–f.

20 Konstantakos 2002, 152, and see Henderson 2000. *Cheiron*, London 1849.6–20.13; *Korianno*, Ruvo 901.

21 Csapo 2010, 28–9 identifies a scene on a polychrome fragment, Athens Agora P23985, as Phormion teaching Dionysos to row. 'Pyronides', implying a fiery character, is fictional. A vase scene where he seizes the famous kitharodist Phrynis, see Figure 23, Storey 2003, 174, 78–9; disputed, Green 2008, 212–13.

22 Rusten 2011, 244, Eupolis frag. 58, 226; Storey 2003, 39; Xenophon, *Symposion* is a fictional account of the same event. Kallias and his father Hipponikos are mentioned at *Birds* 283 and *Frogs* 429.

23 Dover *et al.* 2000, 515. See Anon. *De comoedia* and Platonios *Distinctions* in Dover *et al.* 2000, 516; or 'insulting and obnoxious', 'charming' and 'sublime' Rusten 2011, test. 2A, 34, 222–3.

24 Storey 2003, 59. On the alleged drowning, see Nesselrath 2000, 233–46.

25 *Equites* were citizens who could afford a horse; known comedies and dates, trans. J. Henderson, Aristophanes I, 1998, 3–6. Alexis was said to have written 245 plays, Menander 100, Chapter II, 217–18.

26 Trans. J. Henderson, Aristophanes I, 1998, 16.

27 Rusten 2011, 197, 244; Kratinos frag. 167, 198; Ameipsias frag. 9, 357; Eupolis frag. 157, 245; Thucydides III, 36–50.

28 No consensus has been reached on the issue of free speech, whether it was limited by legislation, or whether comic poets enjoyed 'implicitly recognized legal immunity': see a concise summary and bibliography of the dispute, Green 2008, 192–3. (A Lamia is a bogey that eats children.)

29 In *Clouds* 554–7, Aristophanes claims Eupolis 'hacked over' *Knights* in *Marikas*.

30 Extant comedies average nearly 1,400 lines. Shakespeare's comedies (excluding *The Tempest*) average 2,500. *Birds* is longest, at 1,765; Shakespeare's shortest, *Comedy of Errors*, 1,782, is based on Plautus, *Menaechmi*, itself adapted from New Comedy.

31 Hall 2006, 179–80.

32 *Birds* 1353–7. A fragment refers to this theme, 'You don't give your father enough to clothe himself', frag. 445, trans. J. Henderson, Aristophanes V, 2007.

33 Webster 1953, 17; Sikon portrait, once Zurich Ruesch coll.; *Life* of Aristophanes in trans. J. Henderson, Aristophanes V, 2007, 9. Platonios says there was no chorus, but Henderson suggests semi-choruses of sisters and brothers, *ibid.* III–13.

34 *BH*² 48; Sidwell 2000; Norwood 1931, 38; Haigh 1896, 421; Csapo 2000, 124.

35 Csapo 2000, 115–20 describes the accidents which resulted in the 'dogma' of the periods of comedy and the canonization of poets.

36 *Poetics* 1449a–b.

37 Arnott 1996, 14; Leskey 1966, 633; Athenaios 336d.

38 Nesselrath 1997, 277.

39 Cicero, *Letters to Atticus* 6.1.8, says Hesychios refuted the tale about Alkibiades and Eupolis. *Choregoi* were not elected; the *choregia* was not abolished before 317. We know nothing of Platonios except that he is late, and frequently wrong.

40 Three were required, because there were three canonical tragic poets. Most of Aristophanes' surviving plays may have been preserved precisely because they were his most political, and best illustrated the evolutionary view.

41 *De comoedia*, ed. Koster 1975, III, 7–10.

42 Webster 1952, 13–26, and 1953, 37–97; *TAGS* 63; Nesselrath 1990, 204–41; Sommerstein 2000, 444–5.

43 Csapo 2000, 126.

44 Storey 2003, 230.

45 Arnott 1996, 15–18.

46 *Souda*, alpha 2735, epsilon 3386, alpha 1138, 1982. Antiphanes, Rusten 2011, 87; Alexis, Menander I, trans. W.G. Arnott 1996, 10; Euboulos, Hunter 1985, 22. Supposed origins are not all to be taken seriously: the *Souda* describes Aristophanes as 'a Rhodian or Lydian, though some said an Egyptian, some a Kameirean; but an Athenian by adoption', alpha 3932. No doubt Alexis came from Thurii, but Menander was not his nephew.

47 Arnott 1972, 72–3.

48 If Catania MB4232 is dated correctly (380–370), it may be too early to illustrate Euboulos, but it certainly illustrates a *Kerkopes* comedy.

49 Athenaios 223a trans. S.D. Olson 2008; from the lost comedy *Poesy*. Chremes is a comedy name, found in Aristophanes, Menander and in three of six comedies by Terence.

50 Handley 1985, 411; *Poetics* 1451b.

51 Nesselrath 1997, 278; Webster 1953, 76–8; Sommerstein 1980; Konstantakos 2002.

52 Arnott 1972, 76; Anaxandrides, *Souda*, alpha 1982; victory, Parian marble; revival, Rusten 2011, Anaxandrides test. 7, 462.

53 Athenaios 473e, 562c–d, 572a trans. C.B. Gulick 1943.

54 Webster 1953, 53–5, 44–6; Nesselrath 1997, 273–6.

55 Handley 1985, 411.

56 Vienna 466; Reggio Calabria 6999; Metaponto 297053.

57 Most are from Megale Hellas. A few must be omitted because damage resists interpretation, or they refer to comedy only indirectly, see Chapter 1, 5–7.

58 Webster 1953, 17; Zeus, Vatican U19; Priam, Berlin F3045; Aristotle, *Poetics* 1453a. Green 2002, 114–15 and Handley 1997, 194 argue that the slave is dressed as a bride.

59 Apparent tragic parodies are parenthesized, because positive identification is difficult. Of fifty-seven titles ascribed to Euboulos, half are mythological and eleven are shared with Euripides, Arnott 1972, 73.

60 Portraits, Chapter 7, 150; Konnakis, Chapter 10, 210. Figure 3, Switzerland priv. coll. loan to Geneva Musée d'art et d'histoire.

61 Thirty-eight total, eight Gnathia. Herakles in red-figure, Taranto priv. coll. 6; black-glaze ware, Tampa 7 94 4; Hermes, Rome priv. coll.; Telephos seems to hold a coal-scuttle on Tampa 2.95.1; *Birds*, Sèvres 80. Slaves outnumber old men twenty-seven to eight.

62 Exceptions are an old man who seems to threaten an enemy, Berlin TC6823; a pair of drunken friends, Berlin TC8405 (Figure 30); an elderly couple, Paris AM39; two slaves fighting, Paris Cp.4951.

63 *TAGS* 72–4. Green's census includes multiple copies of figurines, from widespread sites. For example, *MMC*³ lists nineteen copies of a young woman running (AT28) and thirteen of a slave carrying a *kiste* on his head; one copy was made in Kertsch in the Crimea (AT46i). This points to broad popularity, but the four copies of a slave sitting on an altar (AT110a–d) found in a coroplast's dump suggest the opposite. Therefore I have carried out a census of figurine types, summarized here.

	Old men	Slaves	Young men	Old women	Young women	Total
Before 350	53	34	8	12	12	119
%	44.5	28.6	6.7	10.1	10.1	
After 350	44	49	8	16	25	142
%	31.0	34.5	5.6	11.3	17.6	
Late fifth century to 325	97	83	16	28	37	261
%	37.2	31.8	6.1	10.7	14.2	

The table confirms Green's conclusions, except that young women are not so frequent after mid-century as his numbers show.

64 The 'yellow set' of the New York group are also unified by their unusual activity; Herakles, New York 13.225.27; yellow set, 13, 14, 20, 22, 23, 27. 'Alas' Athens Agora T1683; the gesture is clearer on AT5f, Amsterdam 881 (Figure 4) and a Cypriot version, Larnaka 5242; Niobe, Lipari 3266; Kadmos, Reggio Calabria 156; Hephaistos, Copenhagen 759; men with babies, London 1875.3–9.10, St Petersburg Γ1167; Telephos, München 5394.

65 Alexis, Antiphanes, Anaxandrides, Philemon, *Souda*, alpha 1138, alpha 2735, alpha 1982, phi 327; Aristodemos, Neoptolemos, Satyros, O'Connor 1966, no. 62, 82, no. 359, 119–20, no. 428, 131. Taplin 2007, 10 suggests that a tragic actor in an Apulian vase portrait could be Aristodemos, Würzburg H4600.

66 No theatre has been excavated at Sinope, but trade made the city prosperous enough to afford one, and nearby Amisos has yielded theatrical figurines. Diodoros of Sinope competed with a comedy at Delos in 284, and his brother, a younger Diphilos, at the Lenaia in 280. *GTP*² 160, O'Connor 1966, no. 141, 91.

67 Cartoons, Rome Villa Giulia 50279; Berlin F3047. Provincial, London 1927.4–
   11.8.
68 London 1865.1–3.29, *Comic angels* 40–1; St Petersburg Б2079; Caltanissetta
   G258.
69 Cypriot, Paris AM36; Siracusa 1522, 1523, 1524; Rhinthon, epigram attributed
   to Nossis of Lokri, *Comic angels* 49–50; *Souda*, rho 171.

3 THEATRES

1 *Koilon* signifies a hollow place and *theatron* a place for seeing; neither term necessarily implies benches (*ikria*). *Agamemnon* 138, 176 in R. Lattimore, *Aeschylus* I
   (University of Chicago Press, 1953). There is a fine photograph of such a
   threshing-floor in Roloff Beny, *A time of gods: a photographer in the wake of
   Odysseus* (Toronto: Longmans 1962) 96.
2 Moretti 1999–2000, 378.
3 East, N. Robertson 1998, 255–83; Plaka, S.G. Miller 2005, 201–2, 218–19, with
   bibliography of the controversy. Both with maps.
4 *Apology* 26e, *Laws* 817c; and see Thompson, Wycherley 1972, 126-9. There is
   no direct archaeological evidence, Hammond 1972, 401–2, with map.
5 Early illustrations of *ikria*: Athens 15499, Firenze 3773, Paris Cabinet des
   Médailles 243. *Ikria*: *Souda*, iota 275, wooden benches or bleachers; also Photius,
   Lexikon Synagoge, 2.323. Hesychios, who names Eratosthenes as his source,
   describes *ikria* as planks, attached like steps to upright timbers, Hammond
   1972, 391.
6 Pratinas, *Souda*, pi 2230; N. Slater 1986, 263–4; Plato, *Apology* 26e; Rehm 2002,
   43; Kourouniotes, Thompson 1932, 107–9. Scullion 1994, 52–62 suggests that
   ikria in Aristophanes and Eupolis means 'auditorium', and *theatron* refers to
   stone benches built in the later fourth century.
7 Csapo 1999–2000, 395; dates, Moretti 1999–2000, 394. The larger sections of
   wall are designated, respectively, D/SM3 and R/SW1: Dörpfeld, Reisch 1896,
   plan; Fiechter 1936; Dinsmoor 1950. Both wall sections are polygonal masonry
   in Akropolis limestone; the cutting seems to be a drain: Scullion 1994, 18–
   26, Moretti 1999–2000, 395. Wiles 1997, 46–52 defends Dörpfeld's circular
   orchestra.
8 See Ashby 1988, Gebhard 1974, Polacco, Anti 1981, Moretti 1999–2000, 381–9,
   Green 2008, 71. Rectilinear forms persisted into the fourth century.
9 Csapo 2007, 87–98.
10 Moretti 1992, 80–3. In the *Oresteia* (458), Aischylos uses the *skene* with practised
   skill.
11 Sourvinou-Inwood 2003, 143, 160–2: near a hearth-altar, ritual dining in the
   skene was perhaps a part of the Dionysia. Single door, see Taplin 1977, 438–40;
   it is usually assumed that there was only a central door. Polacco, Anti 1969, 158
   suggest that subsequent construction either obliterated the Aischylean theatre
   or that it was located elsewhere; Ley 1989, 36 argues that Athenians employed
   the new technology of marine slipways for an *ekkyklema*, discussed below, 76–7.

12 *Skene* of this type, Moretti 1999–2000, 396–7; Peiraeus contract, Csapo 2007, 90 2. Taplin 1977, 452 9 argues that the first *skene* should be dated near 458.

13 Kratinos (*c.*453) favoured mythological burlesque; Krates (*c.*450) was known for narrative plots: see Chapter 2, 20.

14 *GTP²* 6, *CAD* 80,105, and III.4–8,109–10; Scullion 1994, 11. Green 1995a, 49 notes that some scholars identify this building as the *Prytaneion*. Kratinos compared its pointed roof to the peculiar shape of Perikles' head, Plutarch, *Perikles* 13. Rusten 2006a argues persuasively for this revision of the traditional date.

15 Moretti 1999–2000, 382–4 gives exact dimensions of bench segments, from which I have reconstructed a centre row of segments *c.*1.45 metres long, and the wings of 1.75-metre segments (Figure 5).

16 Marble, Goette 2007, 116. *Thes.* 395 and scholiast, Kratinos fragment 349 trans. Rusten 2011, 217; Moretti 1999–2000, 386–9. The dates of reconstruction are discussed below, 74, n. 55.

17 Metics were resident aliens. Most scholars now believe capacity was 6–7,000: *TDA* 141; *CAD* 286–7; Csapo 2007, 97.

18 The state paid jurors 2 *obols* a day. Roselli 2009 argues that a similar subsidy was occasionally paid as early as the 460s, but a *theoric* fund was not established until the middle of the fourth century. It was abolished by the oligarchy between 322 and 317, *CAD* 287–8. Competition, *CAD* 286; foreigners, *Ach.* 501–8, Aelian, *Historical Miscellany* I 2.13.

19 *DFA²* 40 locates the Lenaion in the *agora*; a date near 440 is supported by the Victor Lists, *CAD* 133–4. According to Hesychios, the Lenaion sanctuary was in the city, *CAD* III.62,113; N. Slater 1986, 255–64 locates it in 'Limnais' (marshes), and argues that the Lenaia was relocated only after the Lykourgan reconstruction. Travlos 1971, 557 believes both dramatic competitions were transferred at the same time.

20 Polacco 1987, 268, referring to the Theatre of Dionysos.

21 Athens BΣ518 was found in Anagyros, near Thorikos, where the deme theatre has early stone benches, see Hughes 2006b. Hourmouziades 1965, 58–74 presents evidence for a low wooden stage in the fifth century. Moretti 1992, 80–2 believes a substantial wooden *skene* might have left traces at Thorikos or Athens, but a booth would leave none.

22 Ginouvès 1972, 65; Csapo 2004, 67; Csapo 2010, 102; Gebhard 1973, 24–6 and 1974, 438–9, 478; *TDA* 120. Aristotle, *Poetics* 1448a refers to Hegemon of Thasos, a poet of Old Comedy according to the *Souda*, eta 52; also, Hippokrates, *Epidemics* I.12, and see Grandjean, Salvat 2000, 105; Velia, Green 2008, 67.

23 The tragedians probably presented performances at Aigai, the old capital, Sourvinou-Inwood 2003, 41. The theatre at Pella, the new capital where Philip was killed, is fourth century: Diodorus Siculus, *Biblioteca Historia* XVI 92–4 describes the assassination and a private performance by the Athenian tragedian Neoptolemos the night before.

24 Cyrene, Ceccarelli, Milanezi 2007, 197, and Bonacasa, Ensoli 2000, 123. Megalopolis, *Description of Greece* 8.32.1. Aegean, from Csapo 2010, 102.

25 See *CAD* 44–52.

26 Sophron, fragment 123 (K128), Kassel, Austin 2001, i, 239; he wrote prose mimes in Syrakousai, fourth century.

27 Anti 1947; Polacco, Anti 1981; Bieber 1949, 61; Pickard-Cambridge 1948, 126. Anti's date is challenged by Bernabò Brea 1967 and Mertens 2004. A reconstruction of the 'theatre of Demokopos' was published by a colleague, Welles 1947, 297.

28 Siracusa 1522–4, *c*.350–325. An early scene by Asteas, inv. 29966, from Epipolai, supports the conjecture that his career began here.

29 Rhinthon is associated with Taras; in an epitaph, Nossis says he came from Syrakousai. He wrote 'comedy-tragedies' or *phlyakes*, long after the last comic pot was painted, *Comic angels* 48–50.

30 Cassius Dio, *Roman history* ix, 39.5.

31 The Pisticci Ptr, an Athenian immigrant, set up shop in Metapontion *c*.430; fragments by his colleague the Dolon Ptr were found in a kiln, *RVSIS* 18. Earliest comic scene, Berlin F3043; also Metaponto 29340 and 29062 (Figure 1), and the Dionysian Karneia vase, with *auletris* and theatre-influenced satyrs, Taranto 8263 (Figure 20).

32 The *ekklesiaterion* is 62 metres in diameter. De Juliis 2001, 160–3; Mertens 2001, 61–2, *RVSIS* 17.

33 Asteas, Lipari 927 shows details of a stage and *skene*. On the terracottas, see Ghiron-Bistagne 1976. Lipari was the setting of Euripides' *Aiolos* and Aristophanes' burlesque *Aiolosikon*, see Chapter 2, 34.

34 *BH*² 146; Beare 1964, 338.

35 Chares, *Histories of Alexander* 10, *CAD* IV.31D, 237. Fourth-century 'stars', see Chapter 11, 218.

36 Perseus, Athens BΣ518. No scholar was permitted to see the pot before 2004, after it passed from private ownership to the National Museum, see Hughes 2006b. Comic and tragic: Apulian 35, Lucanian 1, Campanian 2, Paestan 4, Sicilian 12. Omitting the stage but showing elements of a *skene*: Apulian 10, Campanian 1, Paestan 1, Sicilian 4. Excluded are three reported Sicilian fragments I have not seen, and several others of doubtful value.

37 Bari 2970, London 1849.6–20.13.

38 Structural detail, Milan Civico Museo A.0.9.2841; awkward perspective, Bari 2970. Apulian scenes with tragic subjects sometimes used synecdochic perspective, showing a cut-away temple, e.g. Naples 82113, Milan priv. coll., Amsterdam 2579.

39 London 1849.6–20.13, Bari 2970, New York 24.97.104; all seem to be between 115 and 130 centimetres deep.

40 Green 1995a, 34; square, Bari 2795; Doric, Copenhagen 15032 (Figure 27); Ionic, Bari 4073.

41 Fluting, compare Bari 2970 with 4073 and Matera 164507; on Copenhagen 15032, Doric fluting is omitted. I have examined thirty-two Apulian vases with useful scenes of theatre structures, omitting a lost scene with Herakles beating at a door behind a heavy column (perhaps *Frogs* 464), once Berlin F3046, and a scene with a stage apparently made of logs or masonry, London Victoria and

Albert 1776–1919, which recalls pictures that interpret masks as severed heads, see Green 1989, 76–7.

42 Perspective in another Apulian scene, Ruvo 901, is discussed in Hughes 2006a, 98–9.

43 The Perseus Dance scene, Athens BΣ518, introduces a similar crude perspective, but views the stage from one end, see Hughes 2006b, 421–2. The boards run across the narrow axis of the stage, but in Apulian scenes they parallel the long axis, as in Figures 6 and 7.

44 Ionic columns, Bari 2970; Rome priv. coll. 52 (Figure 22). Plain columns, Naples 118333 (Figure 8), London 1772.3–20.33 may have been painted shortly before the reconstruction; Matera 164507 belongs to this period. A vase of this date with wide posts, Edinburgh 1978.492; if it is a little earlier than dated, it belongs with the wide-post perspective group.

45 Matera 164507; column, Würzburg L823a; pilaster, Metaponto 297053, where an actor as *hetaira* leans against it. Double doors in West Greek iconography normally signify either a temple or the theatre, Hughes 1997, 244–6.

46 The earliest and latest comic scenes show a roof and columns, New York 24.97.104, Naples 118333. Plain buttress and roof, London 1849.6–20.14, and in scenes from remote towns which may have lacked theatres, Capua, Melbourne D14/1973; in a tragic scene from Paestum, Madrid 11094; two in a scene by a Sicilain *émigré*, Apollonia 325.

47 Würzburg H4696/4701. A Campanian *Iphigeneia in Tauris* of the same period has similar entrances, Paris K404. *Paraskenia*, see *TDA* 169–72. Neither scene shows central doors, which leads Webster to doubt their evidence, *GTP*² 105. Ashby 1999, 65–80 argues that there was no such entrance.

48 Costumes, see Chapter 9, 190. Mass-production: Paestum 20198 and Benevento from Montesarchio T.1625 are virtually identical, but mirror-images. Python's only picture of a stage is probably indebted entirely to his master's teaching, Salerno Pc1812 (Figure 23).

49 Berlin F3044, Lipari 927, Gela 8255–6. The maeanders show that the circles must also be decorations, not the ends of beams as Trendall suggests, *RVP* 47, *IGD* IV.14: 'beams' would be no larger than 5 centimetres in diameter.

50 Apollonia 325 shows entrances at each side of a stage, but none in the middle. Double doors on an Asteas fragment, Gela 36057.

51 London 1865.1–3.27, Vatican U19.

52 Milan Scala 668, a Sicilian scene which may precede Asteas, shows comic actors on a plain platform of boards supported by two posts, like the earlier Apulian stage, and in Madrid 11094, Asteas illustrates *skene* doors with a roof. Since violence was never staged, the door with its buttressed roof and unique gallery may not show a specific *skene*; no stage platform is indicated.

53 Syrakousai 66557, Caltanissetta 1751. Other scenes by related artists may refer to stage performances of unknown type. Caltanissetta G258 shows a drunken dancer; in St Petersburg Б2079 an old person pours wine on a prone Herakles from behind double doors. The figures may be masked, but they are not seen to wear comic costume.

54 Doric columns with florals, Gela 643; Gela 750; Milan Scala 749. Lentini 2B (Figure 45) is the most careful, but columns are Ionic; the incense-burners (*thymiateria*) are appropriate to the scene onstage, which takes place in a shrine. This might be a kind of scene painting, or an artist's comment.

55 The notion of a Periklean theatre is attributable to Fiechter 1936, and dates of different parts vary from the early century to the Peace of Nikias (421–415), *BH*² 60, Dinsmoor 1950, 208–9, *TDA* 21. A decree of 343–342 may signal the start of the new project, *TDA* 136; the foundations were constructed of *breccia*, which was not used before the fourth century, N. Slater 1986, 255, Travlos 1971, 537, Moretti 1999–2000, 381, Gebhard 1974, 434; but K. Kübler in Fiechter 1936, 44–9, Scullion 1994, 31.

56 Mikalson 1998, 29.

57 This official is named in an Athenian inscription of 337/6, and was looking after sanctuaries by 346, Csapo 2007, 109–11. He replaced the *theatrones*.

58 Capacity, *TDA* 141, Csapo 2007, 97. *Kerkides*, Pollux, *CAD* 396; *prohedria*, 'front seats', carved in the form of a *klismos*, the ubiquitous Greek chair, Richter 1966, 33–7.

59 Sifakis 1967, 130; sightlines, and *orchestra* dimensions, Chapter 11, 220–1, Csapo, Miller, 2007, 8 distinguish dithyramb, as a cultic song with Dionysian content, from a 'theatrical' circular chorus.

60 Fiechter designated the wall 'HH', and the sockets S1 to 10: they are 0.4 metres square. The *stoa* was not part of the theatre. Travlos 1971, 537, Scullion 1994, 7, N. Slater 1986, 255, Moretti 1999–2000, 381.

61 Townsend 1986, 424 confirms the colonnade. Porches on either side of the stage are conventionally known as *paraskenia*, but there is 'no certain authority' for this usage, *TDA* 169. The stout foundations led Pickard-Cambridge to believe the *paraskenia* were 'massive', *TDA* 172; early interpreters reconstructed ponderous stone structures, *BH*² 60, figs. 239–42; lighter construction is advocated by Moretti 1999–2000, 396–7, who believes in an 'invariable' central double door, and Ashby 1999, 62–80, who favours *paraskenia* doors alone. Representations in scenes related to tragedy: Würzburg H4696/4701, Paris K404, Madrid 11094, Dresden ZV2891. A fragment has a figure in tragic dress falling through the double doors, and a comic actor's bare feet, Sydney NM53.10. Hourmouziades 1965, 58–74 offers mainly literary evidence for a low wooden stage.

62 Old tragedies were revived irregularly from 386, annually from 341.

63 The platform is designated 'T', Kübler in Fiechter 1936, 48. *TDA* 21–4, N. Slater 1986, 255.

64 The platform, Scullion 1994, 7–8. Pollux, second century CE, trans. *TDA* 397. Seeberg 2002–3, 64–6 suggests that a vase scene refers to the *ekkyklema*, Prague 60.31. Testimonia and sceptical commentary, *TDA* 111–22. *Agamemnon* 1371, *Ajax* 346, *Herakles* 1029. Agathon is rolled out, *oukkykloumenos*, and in again, *eiskyklisato*, *Thes.* 96, 265. Euripides is rolled out in similar terms, *Ach.* 408.

65 *Medea* 1296–7, 1321; dragons, Policoro 35296; Aristotle, *Poetics* 1454b; Plato, *Kratylos* 425d, *CAD* 77F, 269.

66 Mastonarde 1990, 288. None of the six allegorical or divine speakers admits to aviation.
67 Antiphanes, *Poetry*, in Athenaios 223a trans. S.D. Olson 2008; Aristophanes' lost *Daidalos*, frag. 192 trans. J. Henderson, Aristophanes V, 2007; Theodoros, Plutarch, *Moralia* 674b. The sound of a *mechane* may have been the rattle of a pawl on the ratchet, which would have acted as a brake on a laden drum.
68 Pollux, *CAD* 397, and scholiast on Lucian, *ibid.* 771, 270. The *mechane* was no doubt adapted from constuction machinery and naval practice. Mastonarde 1990, 272ff and Moretti 1999–2000, 396 describe this type of crane; Ashby 1999, 81–7 wisely adds the double purchase, to inhibit load spin, but it is unlikely that Athenians had spars equal to Ashby's lodgepole pine.
69 Bieber places an unworkable *mechane* inside the *skene*, BH^2 76, and Moretti 1999–2000, 398 locates his behind the *skene*.
70 Six 1920, 186–9; Eteokles and the Chorus refer to the towers at 549 and 822–4.
71 *Namque primum Agatharchus Athenis Aeschylo docente tragoediam scaenam fecit et de ea commentarium reliquit, De architectura 77*; Pollitt 1990, 146. Aischylos died in 456; according to Plutarch, Agatharchos was a rival of Zeuxis, contemporary with Alkibiades and, thus, active no earlier than 430, *Perikles* 13, *Alkibiades* 16. Rumpf 1947, 13 suggests he may have painted an Aischylos revival.
72 *Poetics* 1449a, see A.L. Brown 1984, 1–8, who suggests that it refers to a 'permanent set'.
73 Ley 1989, 35 prefers the Victorian model for Aristophanic 'visual illustration'. Moretti 2004, 180 believes that 'illusionist' scenery was used in Athens before the stone *skene* was built.
74 Relief, Naples 6687 (Figure 52); mosaics, Naples 9985 (Figure 54), *Theophoroumene* (*The girl possessed by the goddess*), and 9987 (Figure 55), *Synaristosai* (*Women at breakfast*). The sculptor who carved the relief in the first century BCE may have updated details of the door, see Chapter 11, 227–9.
75 Revermann 2006, 113.

4 THE COMIC CHORUS

1 Ruffell 2008, 50. Comic metatheatre expresses 'solidarity, rather than an act of alienation'.
2 Csapo, Miller 2007, 1–38 summarize the history of ritualism, its principal arguments and scholarly reception.
3 Jacoby 1904 transcribes the text. The Ashmolean Museum maintains a website with photographs, Greek transliteration and translation: www.ashmolean.org/ash/faqs/q004/
4 Archaeological, epigraphic or anecdotal evidence points to theatres in as many as fourteen, according to Whitehead 1986, 219–20; N. Jones 2004, 127, 140 counts nineteen; see list, Csapo 2010, 102. Most of the evidence is relatively late. Ikarion and Sousarion: later sources embroider. Sousarion was first to use iambic trimeter; his parents are named, and he acquires Megarian origins,

perhaps to agree with Aristotle, *Poetics* 1448a. A verse is attributed to him, Gerber 1999, 511; related testimonia, West 1972, II, 147–8 and Kassel, Austin 1989, VII, 661–3. Much of this is repeated as fact in handbooks and references, from W. Smith's dictionary (1844–9) to *Wikipedia*. Breitholtz 1960, 74 doubts Sousarion's existence; Kerkhof 2001, 38–50 questions Megara and Ikaria. Rusten 2006b gives a balanced assessment, addressing the problem of his unique name, Sus (lily) and Arion ('inventor' of dithyramb).

5 The *Souda* is available as a 'lookup facility' at www.stoa.org/sol/

6 Sifakis 1971a, 20; P. Wilson 2000, 83. Euripides taught a chorus to sing odes, Plutarch, *Moralia*, 46b. Chionides is historical; *Souda*, chi 318 names four of his comedies, two of which, *Heroes* and *Beggars*, were extant in Hellenistic times, Dover *et al.* 2000, 512.

7 *Poetics* 1449a–b; plots are *mythoi*. The first Sicilian comic plots to reach Athens may have been mythological burlesques by Epicharmos, which were adopted by Kratinos; Krates probably went a step further with fictional plots, anticipating those of Aristophanes, see Rusten 2001.

8 *CAD* 103. Dates are based upon interpretation of the Parian marble inscriptions; the same source has dithyramb introduced *c.*509–507. The *Fasti* are inscriptions commemorating Dionysian victors; the first record is dated just before 500, immediately after the democratic reforms. The date of the introduction of tragedy is disputed: the traditional reading of the Parian marble suggests 534, but a more recent scholarly consensus points to 502–501, Rehm 1992, 15. Connor 1990 proposes 508–507; Burnett 2003 argues for 528; West 1989 agrees.

9 Csapo, Miller 2007, 8–10; Csapo 2010, 8–12; *Poetics* 1449a–b; *Ach.* 241–79, where phallic song is presented as rural Dionysian ritual.

10 An entire volume is devoted to the subject, Csapo, Miller 2007; Csapo 2010, 11. Rothwell 2007, 22 believes that 'padded dancers' may be the 'ancestors' of comic actors. See Paris E742 (Figure 14).

11 Seeberg 1995, 5–6 argues that this distinction rules out any link; Green 2007, 96–7 warns that transfer of evidence from Corinth to Athens overlooks cultural diversity.

12 Smith 2007, 51–2. For a brief account of the evidence, see *CAD* 90; and of the debate, Seeburg 1995. Webster sees the white female figures, which sometimes accompany the male dancers, as men in costume, *GTP²* 32–3, but Smith 2002 argues that they are women. The first picture of an actor wearing the undercostume is dated 430, Athens Agora Z1259; padding is not seen until 420–410, Paris CA2938, London 1898.2–27.1.

13 The same aesthetic accounts for the pot-bellied and phallic figures in Kabeiric scenes from Thebes, 400–375, see Wolters, Bruns 1940.

14 *TAGS* 28.

15 Sifakis 1971a, 3. Rothwell 2007, 36–57 regards some of the earliest scenes as pre-comic *symposion* entertainments, or *komoi*. See also Csapo 2003, 86–90 and Csapo, Miller 2007, 8, who distinguish between dithyramb and circular chorus. Rusten 2006b, 52–4 proposes a sixth-century 'comic perversion' of dithryamb. A Parian marble entry says that 'choruses of men' first competed –

presumably at the Great Dionysia – in *c*.510–508; this does not make any of the choruses 'pre-dithyrambic'.

16 Earliest, New York 1988.11.3, Amsterdam 3356. Stilts, Christchurch 41–57 (Figure 15); knights, Berlin F1697. On alien elements, see *TAGS* 28–9.

17 Dolphins, New York 1989.281.69, see Sifakis 1967, 36–7; birds, London 1842.7–28.787; bulls, Oxford 1971.903, London B308. Rothwell 2007, 51–2 suggests that the bull-men represent rivers of Greek colonies in Sicily and Megale Hellas.

18 Long beards, Brooklyn 09.35, Würzburg L344, Pulsano priv. coll.; heads, London 1842.7–28.979 (Figure 16)

19 Dolphin-riders, Athens Kerameikos 5671, Palermo CAT2816, Basle priv. coll. HC849, Attic BF, Los Angeles priv. coll., Paris CA1924, Boston 20.18. (Figure 24).

20 Shipwrecked on their way from Sparta to found a colony in Italy, Phalanthos and his companions were rescued by dolphins, Rothwell 2007, 66–7. The *psykter* is dated *c*.510.

21 Sifakis 1971a, 86. Old men, Thebes BE64.342; the second scene may refer to the story of Hippokleides, who 'danced his wife away', Herodotus 6, 126–31.

22 Cocks, ostriches, Berlin F1830, Boston 20.18 (Figure 24).

23 *CAD* 53.

24 The audition described in Plato, *Laws* 817d is more ideal than real. Henderson 1990, 287 suggests that a victor was accepted more easily. See *CAD* 105 on weak performance.

25 Demosthenes accuses an exempt *choreut* of shirking service, *Against Boiotos* 1.16; also *Against Meidias* 15, and P. Wilson 2000, 78. It would be difficult to rehearse a chorus if its members were liable for service at short notice.

26 Euelpides has about 160 lines to the leader's 215, Lamachos, 65 to 145.

27 Winkler 1990, 20–62 thinks they were *epheboi*, aged 18–20. *CAD* 352 disputes this, acknowledging that 'choreuts were normally enlisted from the young', because choral work was strenuous. Athenaios 20f, 21e, 22a; *Life of Sophokles*, *CAD* IV.3A,225; professionals, *CAD* 352. Rehearsal, Revermann 2006, 93, after the lexicographer Phrynichos of Bithynia. Aristotle, *Politics* 1276b.

28 Boston 20.18 (Figure 24). This personage has been variously interpreted, see Chapter 6, 109–10. Actor portrait, Athens Agora Z1259.

29 *DTC*² 78–9. Testimonia, *CAD* IV.7–9,225–6. The first extant tragedy requiring three actors is *Seven against Thebes* (467); Sophokles first competed in 468.

30 Animal titles, Sifakis 1971a, 76–7, supplemented in Rothwell 2007, 104. The significance of plural titles, A. Wilson 1977, 278–83. Lost comedies, Dover *et al.* 2000, 510–16.

31 Except perhaps two terracotta bird-men with removable masks, Tampa 88.34.10, New York priv. coll. A1992.20.

32 *Krater*, once Malibu 82.AE.83; Green 1985a; A. Wilson 1977; Revermann 2006, 217–19; Froning 2009, 115–24. The 'new' *pelike*, Atlanta 2008.4.1, see Csapo 2010, 9–10. The bird-men are ithyphallic, with short-drawers like those worn by satyr choruses, which are always composed of satyrs.

33 London 1898.2–27.1; Webster, *GTP*² 57 suggests this might represent the chorus of Archippos' *Fishes*.

34 Paris N3408, which Csapo 2010, 27–8 interprets as an artist's parody of a hypothetical heroic painting.

35 Heidelberg B134; *himation*, see Chapter 9, 186.

36 *Nicomachean Ethics* 4.2.20; Sifakis 1971b argues that this was pretentious, because cloaks would be discarded after the *parodos*.

37 *Clouds* 537–40. See Lawler 1964, 69–88; the *kordax* is connected with comedy in the *Souda*, kappa 2071; Athenaios 20e; Lucian, *The Dance* 26; Pollux, *CAD* 394; Theophrastos, *Characters* 6.3. Webster says it was danced by maidens for Artemis, *GTP*² 131. *Thes.* 983, *Wealth* 290–321. Dance, see Chapter 5, 103–5.

38 Tzetzes (twelfth century CE), *CAD* IV.308,361; Pollux, *Onomastikon* (second century CE) *CAD* 394.

39 *TAGS* 34.

40 A Sicilian chorus is known to have been travelling from Messana for a performance in Rhegion when they were lost at sea, P. Wilson 2007, 358–9.

41 See Csapo 2000, 124–5 on 'contact' *vs* 'apathy theory' as explanation for the changing role of the comic chorus.

42 Würzburg H5697. Epicharmos' *Choreutai* certainly needed a chorus, P. Wilson 2007, 362–3.

43 Once Malibu 96.AE.29, see *Comic angels* 55–60; Rome priv. coll.; Revermann 2006, 157 suggests that two 'nymphs' in a *cartouche* on London 1849.6–20.13 denote a chorus.

44 Once Altomonte; Syracuse, New York [reported].

45 Melbourne D14/1973; Princeton 50–64. In a badly damaged scene, the CA Ptr, Rio de Janeiro 20940–1040, seems to follow the Libation Ptr's practice.

46 *Poetics* 1456a.

47 See Chapters 5 and 11.

5 MUSIC IN COMEDY

1 West 1994, 54–8; Landels 1999, 61.

2 Shapiro 1992, 54–7.

3 West 1994, 81–7; Landels 1999, 16, 24–46. The *aulos* was still played early in the twentieth century, in Calabria as *fiscarol* and in Sicily as *fischietto a pariglia*, N. Douglas, *Old Calabria* (London: Martin Secker 1930), 240.

4 Berlin F1697 (540–530); once Malibu 82.AE.83 (440–430).

5 W. Slater 2007, 21.

6 Plutarch, *Moralia* 1141d–f, Demosthenes, *Against Meidias* 13; Melanippos, *Souda*, mu 454, flourished *c*.440–415; P. Wilson 2000, 61; West 1994, 357–8.

7 The 'Pronomos Vase', Naples 81673. Pausanias saw a statue of Pronomos in his native Thebes, *Description of Greece* 9.12.5–6. P. Wilson 2002, 54. On the status and origins of pipers, see Scheithauer 1997, 107–27. Lyric poets, see Chapter 6, 106.

8 On *auletrides*, see Chapter 10, 209–10, and *Comic angels* 105–10; vases, London 1875.8–18.9; Melbourne D17/1972. Würzburg H5697, painted in Taras 380–370, has a scene in *Thes.* (688ff) which cannot have been performed without a chorus.

9 Landels 1999, 31–2, 154–7; Mathieson 1999, 221; *auletes* with *phorbeia*, London E270; without, Taranto 8263 (Figure 20).

10 Stone 1981, 183. Plutarch, *Alkibiades* 32 refers to an *auletes* playing, dressed in the *xustis* of his profession; he takes the anecdote from Douris of Samos, but casts doubt upon its authenticity. To be a 'basket-bearer', or *kanephoros*, was such an honour that the tyrannicides Harmodias and Aristogeiton assassinated the Peisistratid Hipparchos in vengeance for his rejection of the former's sister as a *kanephoros*. Families adorned their daughters with a *xustis* for the occasion.

11 See Chapter 9 and Glossary for these terms. Tree, Rome priv. coll. 52. Other scenes in which masked actors seem to play the *aulos* omit the real source of the music. It was impossible to play while wearing a mask; Syracuse, New York [reported]; Madrid 11026.

12 *Aulos* and early choruses, Chapter 4, 85–7. Leading *choreutai*, Berlin F1830; facing the chorus, Berlin F1697. The piper on Sydney NM97.172 may follow a chorus, now lost.

13 Athenaios 617b trans. *CAD* IV.268,338. See *DFA*² 270, West 1994, 39.

14 Melbourne D14/1973; Storey 2003, 320; Dardanis, see Chapter 10, 213–14.

15 Chairis was a real *auletes*, ridiculed in *Ach.* 16, 866 and *Peace* 951–5. See *Comic angels* 5–6. It cannot be determined whether he was the official piper in *Birds*.

16 Or perhaps he played from the *skene* roof. Because Tereus' monody seems too difficult for an ordinary *tritagonist*, the *choregos* may have been obliged to hire a specialized singer to 'stand in' as Tereus. The staging is controversial, see Dearden 1976, 162–4; Hall 2002, 30–1; Craik 1990, 81–4.

17 451–9, 539–46, 629–33.

18 Text trans. J. Henderson, Aristophanes III, 2000, with my literal interpolations.

19 Taplin is uncertain whether Prokne is required to play or to sing, *Comic angels* 106–7. Plausible alternatives for staging are proposed by Romer 1983 and Barker 2004, and stage directions in Henderson 2000 and other editors.

20 Aristotle, *Poetics* 1449a; discussed, Sifakis 2002.

21 *Hamlet* 1.5.189–90. Shakespeare sets up cross-rhythms between iambics and the natural emphasis of the words: To *be* or *not* to be; *that* is the *quest*ion' (3.1.56).

22 Landels 1999, 113.

23 Discussion, *CAD* 331–2, Landels 1999, 116–19.

24 Respectively 627, 504, 684: also *Peace* 735 in slightly different terms. Pollux, *CAD* 395.

25 West 1994, 40 translates as 'parallel recital'; Aylen 1985, 104–5 compares it to Gregorian chant and opera; Hall 1999, 107 questions these as facile equivalents.

26 West 1994, 355; Hall 2002, 31. The young lovers and old woman in *Ekk.* 877–1111 sing popular songs; Davidson 2000, 41–55 argues that this scene is an interpolated *paignion*, an erotic mime.

27 West 1994, 44–5; see Chapter 6, 116 on Hegelochos' notorious slip.
28 P. Wilson 2002, 45; *DFA*² 270; West 1994, 205; Landels 1999, 16–17.
29 Athens Agora Z1259; proposed earlier dates seem unlikely, if the prize date is secure, Green 2008, 199.
30 Music's speech is quoted in Plutarch, *Moralia* 1141d–f. Phrynis, Salerno Pc1812: relevance to Eupolis is disputed, Green 2008, 212–22.
31 Craik 1990, 81–4, Dearden 1976, 162–4.
32 P. Wilson 2000, 357; *CAD* 333, and Dionysios of Halikarnassos, *On the arrangement of words*, *CAD* IV.278,340–1.
33 *Frogs* 1314, 1349 trans. J. Henderson, Aristophanes IV, 2002: appropriately, the verb means 'wind' or 'turn round and round'. Mathieson 1999, 110–24 shows that two fragments of Euripidean music alter textual rhythm and duplicate syllables.
34 *Clouds* 1370–2 trans. J. Henderson, Aristophanes II, 1998; *Aiolos*, later satirized by Aristophanes in *Aiolosikon*, see Chapter 2, 34.
35 *CAD* 351,155; Athenaios 628c–f trans. C.B. Gulick 1943.
36 *Moralia* 732f trans. F.C. Babbitt 2004; Athenaios *The learned banqueters* 22a trans. S.D. Olson 2006.
37 The *deuteragonist* and *protagonist* are already present, as Euripides and his Kinsman.
38 Hall 2002, 30–1.
39 *Wealth* 290–321.
40 Trans. J. Henderson, Aristophanes II, 1998, who has Karkinos enter near the end; a year later, *Peace* 781–96 ridicules the father and warns against dancing with the sons.

6 ACTING, FROM LYRIC TO DUAL CONSCIOUSNESS

1 *Histories* 1.23. Arion, Alkman and Stesichoros are all dated to the seventh century.
2 *CAD* II.I,95. By the late sixth century, literacy was 'virtually universal among the men who made up the political and social elite', W.V. Harris, *Ancient literacy* (Cambridge MA: Harvard University Press, 1989), 29–30. On the *exarchos*, see Csapo 2008.
3 Wise 1998 attributes the displacement of epic and lyric poetry by comedy and tragedy to literacy, whose rapid growth amongst the Athenian elite in the sixth century seems to have coincided with the growth of the new choral forms.
4 *Poetics* 1449a–b; *Rhetoric* 1403b trans. J.H. Freese 1947.
5 Aischylos' first victory was in 484, Parian marble; Aristotle attributes the second actor to him, *Poetics* 1449a.
6 Inventors, *Souda*: Kadmos kappa 21, Alkman alpha 1289, Anacharsis alpha 258; Athenaios 11; Parian marble, Chapter 4, 82–3. Later sources embroider: Sousarion was the first to use iambic trimeter; he acquires named parents, and Megarian origins, to agree with Aristotle, *Poetics* 1448a. A verse is attributed to him, Gerber 1999, 511; related testimonia, West 1972, II, 147–8; Kassel, Austin

1989, VII, 661–3. As noted in Chapter 4, much of this is repeated as fact in handbooks and references, from W. Smith's dictionary (1844–9) to *Wikipedia* Breitholtz 1960, 74 doubts Sousarion's existence; Kerkhof 2001, 38–50 questions Megara and Ikaria, but believes that while the tradition is inconsistent, there is no reason to doubt his existence. Rusten 2006b gives a balanced assessment, addressing the problem of the name Sus (lily) Arion ('inventor' of dithyramb).

7 See Chapter 4, 85–7; alien men, New York 1988.11.3, Amsterdam 3356; stilts, Christchurch 41–57; knights, Berlin F1697. On alien elements, see *TAGS* 28–9.

8 See Chapter 4, 83; Aristotle, *Poetics* 1449b.

9 See Sifakis 1971a, 68. It is probable that the archaic *exarchos* was also the poet; his function devolved upon the classical *koryphaios*, who speaks in the first person as though he were the poet, *Clouds* 518ff.

10 But see Aristotle *Poetics* 1449a on satyric origins, a contentious topic beyond the scope of the present discussion. Else 1972, 59 suggests *hypokrites* refers to a second or third actor. N. Slater 2002, 23, 'acting begins on the margins of choral performance'. Thespis, *Souda*, theta 282, and phi 762 on Phrynichos. The Parian inscription, now illegible, is transcribed as saying that he acted; supported by a fictitious anecdote in Plutarch, *Solon* 29. On poets and dance, see Chapter 5, 103–5. Perhaps the earliest extant dialogue is a fragment of Bacchylides, dithyramb 18, a strophic exchange between a chorus and their king (Aigeos) about Theseus, probably influenced by early tragedy, trans. R. Fagles 1961, 57–60.

11 *Poetics* 1449a; date, Parian marble.

12 A.L. Brown 1984, 1–5 argues that the sentence in *Poetics* 1449a, attributing the third actor to Sophokles, is spurious. Aischylos, *Oresteia* (458) is the earliest datable use of three actors.

13 Boston 20.18 (Figure 24), dated 490–480. *TAGS* 29. Actor, Sifakis 1971a, 93; *exarchos*, Csapo 2008, 60–4; according to Csapo 2010, 11 he *leads* the chorus, but in fact he *confronts* them. *BH²* 37 sees him as a dancing dwarf, like the sons of Karkinos in *Wasps*; he is Pan, according to *IGD* I.ii. For Csapo, Miller 2007, 23: 'he is costumed and clearly masked as a satyr', but the idealized features are the reverse of those of satyr-masks, and he has neither horse-ears nor a tail. His ears and skinny legs are identical, respectively, with those of the piper and the ostrich-riders. The half-mask is not unique in the period: *choreutai* wear half-masks above their own beards in another early scene, London 1842.7–28.787, dated 500–490.

14 *Poetics* 1449b.

15 Dearden 1990, Rusten 2001.

16 Lenaia date, Rusten 2006a. Dates vary according to interpretation of fragmentary inscriptional evidence. *DFA²* 93–4 gives 442 for comic actors and 442–440 for comic poets, 440–430 for tragic poets and actors; N. Slater 2002, 28 has 442 for comic actors; *CAD* 406 has 432 for all Lenaia actors. N. Slater 1988, 53–7 argues that there is evidence for a contest for comic actors at the Great Dionysia in 421.

17 The *Life of Sophokles* says he 'did away with the custom of poets acting', *CAD* IV.3A,225; scholion to *Clouds* 1267, *CAD* IV.10A,226. N. Slater 2002, 29 refers to an inscription dated 418, but there may have been earlier instances.

18 *TAGS* 12–13.

19 *CAD* IV.9,226; O'Connor 1966, 117–18.

20 *TAGS* 36.

21 Athens BΣ518, Agora P23907, P23900. London 1898.2–27.1, Paris N3408, St Petersburg ΦΑ1869.47.

22 *Phallos*, Paris CA2938; the slave in Paris N3408, Athens 17752, St Petersburg ΦΑ1869.47. Unpadded torsos, Athens Agora P23907, P23900, latest Paris N3408 (Figure 18); padded, London 1898.2–27.1. Aquiline, mask at left, St Petersburg ΦΑ1869.47, Ferrara 29307; on the strength of his nose, Caputo 1935, 274 took the Perseus dancer for an Italian.

23 The *Fasti* end in 329; the earliest reference in the *didaskaliai* to comic actors at the City Dionysia is dated 311/12. Scholia to *Clouds* 541 identify Hermon, O'Connor 1966, no. 183, 95; Aristophanes names four tragic actors, notably Hegelochos (below, 116), N. Slater 2002, 35.

24 Aristodemos and Neoptolemos were Athenian ambassadors to Philip, *CAD* IV.30A,233.

25 Plato knows of no such law or regulation of the festivals, *Republic* 395a, *Symposion* 223d, O'Connor 1966, 39–44. Possible exceptions, Sutton 1987, 9–26. Aristotle, *Politics* 1276b implies that *choreutai* could cross genre lines. Apollogenes, a third-century *tragodos*, was also a successful pugilist (*palaistes*), O'Connor 1966, no. 40, 80; Stephanis 1988, no. 239, 63.

26 Sutton 1987, 24–5; Kallippos and family, O'Connor 1966, nos. 278, 269, 275.

27 *Poetics* 1449a, 'nature' (*physis*). Peisetairos meets ten minor characters, plus messengers, in *Birds* 863–1466. *CAD* 222 assigns three actors to *Knights* and *Wealth*, five to *Clouds* and *Acharnians*, and four to the rest of Aristophanes. Revermann 2006, 13–14 makes a case for a fourth actor in *Clouds*. Sifakis 1979 shows that apprenticeship could begin in childhood.

28 *Protagonist*, Sifakis 1995, 16–17, *DFA*² 95, Csapo 2002, 136, Henderson 2007, 25 *testimonia* no. 22. Dearden 1976, 86–94 believes comedy was unlikely to have been allowed more actors than tragedy, suggesting that 'extras' could be given short speeches. MacDowell 1994 argues for four actors, and Marshall 1997 favours three augmented by mutes and 'ventriloquism'.

29 Sifakis 1971a, 19–20; Lada-Richards 2002, 410; *physis*, *Life of Sophokles* 6.

30 On illusion, Sifakis 1971a, 7–14, N. Slater 2002, Silk 2000, 90–1. Bibliography of comic illusion, *TAGS* 27, and n. 22.

31 Plutarch, *Demosthenes* 7 trans. B. Perrin 1967. Probably fictional, the story must have been plausible. Actors were useful ambassadors because they successfully claimed 'sacred immunity and free passage, justified by drama's connection with religious ritual', *CAD* 223.

32 *Rhetoric* 1404b; Sifakis 2002, 155; O'Connor 1966, no. 230, 100; Csapo 2002, 127–47; Rehm 1992, 50.

33 *DFA²* 156–7; Hall 1999, 96–122, particularly 99, 107–8. *Parakataloge*, Chapter 5, 98; applied to comedy, this term is inferred from tragedy, 98, *DFA²* 163–4. Mimicry, Plutarch, *Moralia* 18c, 674b.

34 *Ach.* 627, *Knights* 504, *Frogs* 303, fragments of Strattis and Sannyrion, *CAD* IV.75B,C,D, 268. Pollux 9, trans. *CAD*, see O'Connor 1966, no. 183, 95.

35 Bremmer 1991, 15–35; Green 1997, 132–3; Aristotle, *Poetics* 1449a. Stage behaviour was derived from accepted 'social norms of proper or improper physical behaviour', Green 2001, 40.

36 *Iphigeneia in Aulis*, 900–1, ed. C.R. Walker (University of Chicago Press 1958); *Oedipus the King*, 1074–5, ed. D. Grene (University of Chicago Press 1954).

37 Exceptions are Siracusa 66557, Caltanissetta 1751, scenes from *Oidipous Tyrannos* and another tragedy, both on a stage; faces have the expressionless classic 'Grecian' profile of tragic masks.

38 Achilles in Boston 03.804; a woman shows elegance by holding a fold of her garment away from her shoulder with thumb and third finger, Taranto 8264.

39 Henry Irving, *The drama: addresses* (London: Heinemann 1893) 57.

40 *BH²* 82; see Chapter 8, 170–1. Poet (Menander) Vatican 9985 (Figure 53); Dionysos, Paestum 104378.

41 Aulus Gellius, *Attic Nights* 6.5.35–6 trans. J.C. Rolfe 1948.

42 Plato, *Ion* 535c–e; Theodoros, Aelian, *Historical Miscellany* 14.40; Plutarch, *Moralia* 545f; Kallipides, Xenophon, *Symposion* 3.11; Parmeno, Aristotle, *Problems* 948a.

43 See Lada-Richards 2002, 395–418, and Hughes 1987, for more extensive discussions of the actor's process.

44 *Talma on the Actor's Art* (London, 1883).

7 TECHNIQUE AND STYLE OF ACTING COMEDY

1 Green 2006, 143–5; Foley 2000, 298.

2 Large gestures, Siracusa 23001 (Figure 2), Würzburg H4689; cooks, Athens CC1927; capering, Paris N3408 (Figure 18), Ruvo 1402; dance, once Altomonte, London 1772.3–20.881. Revermann 2006, 49–50 rejects the notion that the text told Greek actors all they needed to know about 'significant action'; action may be most significant when it cannot be expressed in verbal stage directions.

3 Bremmer 1991, 18–20; Green 2001, 42.

4 Csapo 1993, 41–58 shows that running slaves in Greek comedy anticipate a common type in Roman comedy; he cites two Apulian vases, Toronto 972.182.1 (Figure 26) and Boston 13.93, both with slaves who run *away* from an unseen fear. So do slaves on Taranto 114090, London 1814.7–4.1224 (who pauses in his flight). Running *towards*, Reggio Calabria 3303, New York 51.11.2, and once Deepdene Hope coll. 224.

5 Beating, Berlin F3043. Pseudo-Xenophon, *Constitution of the Athenians* 10, written *c.*425.

6 *Himation*, Boston 00.363, Copenhagen 15032; also Chapter 9, 187–9. Pursuit, Malibu 96.AE.114; on Sydney NM88.02 a slave pursues Herakles with his own club, a frequent comic licence of undignified behaviour.

7 Vase scenes with slaves on altars, Gela 643, Taranto 9120–9121. Two fragments have men on altars, but neither is a slave, Malibu 86.AE.412, Gela 8255. New York Group, old citizens on altars, 13.225.16, 13.225.18; slaves on stools 13.225.19, 13.225.20, adapted in Copenhagen 1067, Paris CA1510; Lipari 722 adapts New York 13.225.18, with hand to ear: also Athens Agora T1684; London 1879.3–6.5 (Figure 28). A New Comedy example, holding his ear, hugs himself and crosses his ankles, Cambridge GR85b.1937. With sack, Paris AM34; kneeling, Siracusa 68133; with baby, Berlin TC6876.

8 Zeus, St Petersburg Б299 (Figure 34); Priam, Berlin F3045. Crossed ankles, Christchurch 65–62, and Athens 4794, a New Comedy figure. Dionysos, Lipari 927; Hera, London 1772.3–20.33, shown as 'real' deities; compare gods on the Parthenon frieze, Richter 1987 pl. 145. Zeus Ammon, Bari 2970; squatting Dionysos, lyre player, Taranto 121613, 122627, Rio de Janeiro 20940–1040.

9 The cross-legged Herakles terracotta is known in eighteen copies, such as Berlin TC8838, Copenhagen 4715 from Thebes; imitated in three known variants, and known in seven other Herakles-types. On vases he is usually in action, although in two scenes he stands to attention, in one, submitting to a scolding, St Petersburg Б299, Taranto 56048. He crosses his legs even while lying down to feast, London, Victoria and Albert 1776–1919.

10 *Komastai*, Berlin TC8405; fight, Paris Cp.4951; Telephos, München 5394; angry man, Berlin TC6823; rhetorical, Corinth MF1608, London 1867.2–5.22.

11 Our earliest fragment with an actor seems to be a portrait, Athens Agora Museum Z1259; most portraits are Apulian red-figure, like Sèvres 80, or Gnathia from the Konnakis Ptr's shop, like Tampa 7.94.8. Donkey, Basle 1921.384.

12 Reggio Calabria 3303; Switzerland priv. coll; London market 1996.

13 Philopotes, Berlin 1969.7, Derkylos, Tampa 7.94.8. The gesture in Malibu 96.AE.118 resembles 'stop', but it is aimed at no second person (as in Figure 38b), and the arm is introverted. The portrait of the dancer Konnakis belongs with this series, see Chapter 10, 210.

14 According to the scholiast, his *lazzo* was an old man beating someone with his stick, N. Slater 1999, 358–9.

15 Green 2001, 38, Policoro from Aliano; *Birds* 1253ff, *Clouds* 1493ff the naked figure in Gela 36056 may be a young woman.

16 Violence, Berlin F3044, Ruvo 901, Salerno Pc1812, London 1873.8–20.347, S. Agata dei Goti priv. coll. 1. Four of these were found in remote locations; Asteas remembered comedy from his native Sicily, but may have improved it for a naïve audience, and his pupil Python, as naïve as his customers, merely imitated his master, Hughes 2003. Friendly, London 1849.6–20.13; Göttingen Hu582a; ram, Malibu 96.AE.112, Kratinos, *Dionysalexandros*, see Chapter 2, 22–3.

17 Boxing, Boston 03.831; spears, London 1772.3–20.33; beating, Berlin F3043, once Melbourne priv. coll. Lover, London 1865.1–3.27; thief, New York 24.97.104.

18 Berlin TC8405 (Figure 30), TC6823.
19 Once Malibu 82.AE.83, Athens 17752, Naples 127971.
20 Copenhagen 15032 (Figure 27), Paris CA2938, Taranto 121613, apes, Rome Villa Giulia 64224, Berlin F3043, Oxford AN1945.43, Lipari 927; three slaves, Siracusa 1522; crone, St Petersburg Γ1432.
21 Weapons, London 1772.3–20.33; *aulos*, Bari priv. coll.; *tympanon*, Paris CA479; baby, London 1875.3–9.10.
22 Walking, Athens 17752; under arm, Tampa 7.94.8; leaning, once Malibu 96.AE.29; *paidogogos*, Berlin 1984.41; crossed ankles, Siracusa 29966; Zeus walking, supported, Madrid 11026. Violent knocking, New York 37.11.19; *paidogogos* swats a swan, Tampa 86106; striking a slave, once Melbourne priv. coll.
23 Old man, Geneva coll. G. Ortiz. *Frogs* 1–35, the cook, *Dyskolos* 393–402. Basket, Paris CA20; variant, legs braced, Boston 01.7838; a smaller basket, Larnaka 5245.
24 *Hydria*, Copenhagen 1068; basket, New York 13.225.22; spit, Athens Agora P23907; harvest, St Petersburg Б2074.
25 Terracotta pedlars have lost their sticks, München 5389, Berlin TC7086, Boston 13.99, Thebes from Thebes Kolonaki. Slave, once Cyprus Cesnola coll.; cooks, Berlin TC7603–4.
26 Bari 2795, Malibu 96.AE.238.
27 Morris *et al.* 1979, 98–118; Green 1999, admonitory pl. 1, 2, 25; Darius, Naples 81947; with staff, Cambridge MA TL15601.2; Milan Civico Museo A1872; Milan Scala 668; back-handed, Sydney NM75.2 (Figure 42); Würzburg H5846; steward, St Petersburg Б1661 (Figure 6).
28 Naples 82270; Rome Villa Giulia 50279; Bari 3899; once Melbourne priv. coll.; St Petersburg Б1660, interpreted *BH*² 131.
29 Warding, tragic scene, Paris K404; young woman, Bari 8014; slave, Taranto 9120–9121; Priam, Berlin F3045, Aristotle, *Poetics* 1453a trans. S. Haliwell 1999. The Bari scene has been interpreted as Helen rejecting Menelaos in Kratinos, *Dionysalexandros*, see *IGD* IV.27.
30 Matera 164507; Melbourne D14/1973; Taranto 4658; upward, Paris K18; open hands, Heidelberg U8; running, Taranto priv. coll. 123; ring, Rome priv. coll. 52.
31 Hughes 1987, 128–9. The theory of affects is found in Aristotle, *De anima* 403a, *Rhetoric* 1404a, 1407a and subsequently in Cicero and Quintilian. Modern behavioural research does not support their view, except for facial expressions, which are not directly relevant to acting in a masked theatre.
32 New York 16.1407; Adolphseck 179; St Petersburg Б201; Paris, Cabinet des Médailles 1046.
33 Stomach, Montpelier 99; joy, Copenhagen 4738; slaves, Lipari 6941; Gela 643. This was the attitude of both *choregoi*, once Malibu 96.AE.29, until the elder began to saw the air towards Aigisthos. Europa, Naples 81952; both myths have happy conclusions.
34 Oidipous, Siracusa 66557; a figure in the east pediment at Olympia uses the same gesture for apprehension, see Dover 1982, 60 and pl. 13. Comic figures, Kassel T559, and New York 13.225.28.

35 *MMC*[3] on Athens Agora T1683, in many copies and Sicilian adaptations, e.g. Amsterdam 881 (Figure 4), Lipari 9725 and Siracusa 1527, on which Bernabò Brea, Cavalier 2002, 54, fig. 20 are nearer the mark with 'disappunto'.

36 Perseus, Athens BΣ518; Herakles, Milan Scala 749; Dionysos, Lipari 927; Aigisthos, once Malibu 96.AE.29.

37 Niobe, Taranto 8935; with *paidogogos* signing 'alas', Zurich University 4007; Kassiopeia, Naples 82266. Comic terracottas, Heidelberg TK48, Lipari 3266; chin on fist, New York 13.225.19, München 6931.

38 Taranto 4600, New York 37.11.19; madam, Metaponto 297053; Herakles, New York 13.225.13.

39 Heidelberg U6, two women conversing.

40 Policoro, from Aliano. A wreathed young woman clutches a bottle, another clue, Athens Kanellopoulos 1460; a wreathed old woman is a madam, Lipari 356i; fight, Ruvo 901.

41 *Hetaira*, Heidelberg TK47; modest girl, St Petersburg ББ166. Both survive in several copies, and variants: Madrid 4016 is an adaptation of the *hetaira*, veiled to the eyes.

42 Green 2002, 119. This subtle leg-bend of 3 or 4 degrees is undetectable in published photographs. *MMC*[3] 47 seems to classify the *kore* as Mask V (*hetaira*) by hairstyle alone. By this criterion, many a goddess would stand condemned. Green 2002, 116–20 astutely compares six similar young women, but leaves little room for modesty.

43 St Petersburg П1874.34; Amsterdam 261 is from the same mould. Brothel scene, Metaponto 297053. Elegant gesture, Copenhagen 1947; Sthenoboia in Departure of Bellerophon, Boston 00.349b; Hera in Judgement of Paris, Paestum 48431.

44 St Petersburg П1841.75; true elegance, Aura, Sydney NM53.30; false, Naples 118333 (Figure 8), where Green 2001, 55 notes signs of boldness.

45 St Petersburg ББ92, with traces of black hair. The interpretation in Green 2001, 56 is based on Oxford 1922.207, which differs in significant details. The large mouth need not imply vulgarity: it was a practical necessity – in St Petersburg ББ92 the actor's mouth is visible within the mask.

46 Green 1997 sees these figures as *hetairai*. I believe this is mistaken; two copies retain traces of black hair, London 1907.5–20.79b, and British Columbia priv. coll. Variants wearing a huge *stephane*, London 1865.7–20.43, and an exaggerated *symposion* wreath, Lipari 2356c, must be *hetairai*: nice girls did not attend.

47 Most wives are middle-aged or old; in terracottas, as with a head on a fragment, Taranto priv. coll. 106, older women *may* be wives, but lack a context to support the identification.

48 Akimbo, Lipari 3252. Meeting, Cambridge MA TL331.86, Paris K523. Scolding, Taranto 54724; admonitory, Würzburg H5846, Sydney NM75.2; one-fingered, Vienna 466; advice, Bari 3899, Berlin 1983.4, Madrid 1999/99/122.

49 Milan Civico Museo A.0.9.2841, Charis' attitude resembles the Mourning Athene, Athens Akropolis Museum, Richter 1987 pl. 129; Paris AM39.

50 See Klytemnestra, Berlin F2301. Female types on Theban Kabeiric vases (400–375) are also grotesque, but move normally, except for the monstrous Empousa, who is handicapped by one leg of bronze and the other of dung: *Frogs* 294–5, Levi 1964, 155 pl. 5–6.

51 Young, Göttingen Hu582a (Figure 44); old, Cambridge MA, TL331.86; *auletris*, St Petersburg Б2074. Windblown skirts signify speed, Atlanta L1989.2.2, Heidelberg TK46. Threat to the virgin is left to our imagination, but the madam faces a client who rises from a stool, grasping his *phallos*.

52 We have twelve crone-types and thirteen nymphs, but there are more known copies of the latter (sixteen of AT10, thirteen of AT16) than of the former (eight of AT9, four of AT17, nine of AT23). In Sicilian terracottas, young women outnumber old by more than three to one. Crones are the only females in scenes without a male, Heidelberg U6; market-woman, New York 24.97.104. On their rarity on comic vases, Green 2001, 37–64.

53 Malibu 96.AE.113; Aura (Breeze), Sydney NM53.30.

54 *Wealth* 423–4, 603–5, trans. J. Henderson, Aristophanes IV, 2002. Much of this is not apparent in frontal photographs; figurines are best studied from three sides, as a Greek audience would have seen an actor. Compare Berlin TC7089, Paris N4878, St Petersburg ББ165 and Г1432.

55 Wreathed, Lipari 356i, Paris CA4234. A woman talking with a young man in a doorway, Metaponto 297053, wears no wreath, but she is certainly a bawd. Wine, Lipari 10782, 3243.

56 New York 13.225.26, Sicilian variant, Glasgow 03–70dp, Rostock University from Megale Hellas. Basket, Athens 12507, compare farmer with baskets, Paris CA20.

57 Würzburg H4689.

58 Göttingen Hu582a, 'bottle', *BH²* 139. Brygos scene, Würzburg K479. *Ach.* 585–6, trans. J. Henderson, Aristophanes I, 1998.

59 Lentini 2B, from Lentini.

60 *BH²* 134, *IGD* IV.24.

61 Added white on face and arms shows that the statue is marble. A *phiale* is a broad, flat bowl used for libations; a comic slave carries the same paraphernalia in Reggio Calabria 6999. For a god, 'pouring a libation is primarily not a rite directed at somebody else, but a self-sufficient act in which sanctity is revealed...'; it 'has the qualities of an epiphany', Himmelman 1993, 125–8. Kings or gods in comedy may have slave-masks, but they are identified by attributes.

62 The stage, the woman's mask and costume, and her patterned sleeves resemble the treatment of tragic scenes, the 'Capodarso Oidipous', Siracusa 66557, and a scene from Castronuovo, Caltanissetta 1751. Painters depicted the masks of tragic actors as though they were the character's 'real' face: compare Aigisthos in the *choregoi* scene, once Malibu 96.AE.29. Green 2001, 55 notes patterned sleeves on a young woman in a comic scene, Naples 118333.

63 A satyr in the same attitude, Vatican 6283.

64 See above, 156.

65 Attic, Leiden KvB204; Boiotian, Paris CA239, Berlin TC8265 and Princeton 48–50; Cypriot, Paris AM36.

66 *Moschophoros*, Athens Akropolis 623; *Description of Greece* 9.22.1; coin, London 1975.5–198-I, see Tanner 2006, 44 pl. 2.8d; Paris CA806, miniature terracotta copy.

67 Of the Boiotian figures, only Berlin TC8265 has a provenance, Thespiai, near Tanagra; the only readily identifiable beast is Paris CA239, with goat-horns and beard.

8 THE MASKS OF COMEDY

1 www.angelfire.com/art/masks/

2 Naples 81673 and Sydney NM47.05 show details of tragic and satyric masks; actors London 1849.6–20.13 wear bald comedy masks with large ears. On a fragment in Kiev from Olbia, two *choreutai* as women wear white face-masks.

3 Words are painted beside a mask in New York 24.97.104; actor's mouth, Istanbul 1768.

4 Lucian, *The Dance*, 27–9 trans. A.M. Harmon 1955. Ivory statuette, Paris, Petit Palais DUT192; *DFA*² 204, n. 2; Wiles 2000, 151 paraphrases director Thanos Vavolis.

5 Once Malibu 96.AE.29.

6 Compare satyrs and burlesque figures on black-figured 'Kabeirion' vases, Wolters, Bruns 1940. Early Attic comic masks may have an aquiline or hooked nose and a bulging forehead, Athens BΣ518, Ferrara 29307.

7 *TAGS* 46; *Poetics* 1449a trans. S. Halliwell 1999. I am indebted to G.M. Sifakis for clarification of Aristotle's epithets here and in 1448a, where *beltion* and *cheiron* mean superior and inferior. *Agathos* and *spoudaios* are synonymous.

8 Lecoq 2000, 36, 56; see Williams 2004 on experimental archaeology with New Comedy masks from Lipari.

9 Athens 13015; confirmed by a duplicate in the Kanellopoulos Musuem, Athens.

10 J. Slattum, *Balinese masks: spirits of an ancient drama* (Singapore: Periplus 2003) 23–4; M. Coldiron, *Trance and transformation of the actor in Japanese Noh and Balinese masked dance-drama* (Lewiston: E. Mellen Press 2004) 8–84, 144–9, 175–6.

11 Naples 81674.

12 Masks could also be regarded as frightening, *TAGS* 78–81.

13 Doubling, see Sifakis 1995, and Chapter 6, 113–14.

14 Wiles 1991, 80, and 2006, 380–1.

15 *Peace* 142, *Thes.* 643ff. In *Birds* 1720ff, Basileia's youth and beauty may have been belied by a grotesque Old Comedy mask. Eyes, Basle S34, Melbourne D391/1980.

16 Lecoq 2000, 55. Paestum 104378; tragic actor, Würzburg H4600; Webster sees this as an actor taking his 'call', *GTP*² 118. Stockport, Lyme Hall is probably a poet; Vatican 9985 (Figure 53) is Menander with masks.

17 Vervain, Wiles 2001, 254–9; see also Wiles 2004.

18 Sifakis 1971a, 11.
19 O.Taplin, speaking at Oxford, May 2001.
20 Green 2008, 235–6. Bowls, New York 1981.11.12, 1981.11.18; hairnet, Malibu 92.AM.8.1.
21 Masks are catalogued in *MMC³*. Masks of clay, and other imperishable materials, such as bronze, could not be worn.
22 *Souda* on Thespis, theta 282; on Magnes, mu 20; Horace, *Ars Poetica* 276–7; Pseudo-Plutarch in *DTC²* 74; Aischylos' *Life* in Lefkowitz 1981, 157–60. Aristotle, *Poetics* 1449b does not know who introduced the mask to comedy.
23 *DFA²* 197; *BH²* 19 transforms it into cinnabar, a red or vermillion mineral. Webster rearranges the herbs as a wreath, *GTP²* 36.
24 Sommerstein 1996, 41; Marshall 1999, 188. *DFA²* 191 suggests that early masks were linen, 'perhaps artificially stiffened'; 'glued rags' according to Wiles 2000, 147; *MMC³* 3 offers the evidence of the scholion to *Frogs* 406 and a seventh-century CE encyclopaedist in support of 'stuccoed linen'. Hall 2006, 102–3 has deduced the process.
25 The title of Platon's lost *Skeuai* might be translated as *Theatrical costumes*, or *equipment*.
26 The reduced role of the chorus in *Wealth* and *Ekk.* may be explained as cuts, facilitating touring by reduced companies; and the chorus in extant New Comedy is conveniently detachable.
27 Aristophanes of Byzantium, *On Masks*, is lost to us. *CAD* 393–402; *TAGS* 153–4, 188 n. 52.
28 See Chapter 11, 228–9. On Old and Middle Comedy masks, see *GTP²* 55–73, New Comedy, 73–96; also *MMC³*, *MNC³*.
29 *TAGS* 69–76. Women's masks and the archetypal triad of maiden, mother and crone, Chapter 7, 157–62. In Green's analysis, young women include the *kore*, *pseudo-kore* and *hetaira*.
30 *Poetics* 1449a trans. S. Halliwell 1999; *TAGS* 72. Young slaves, see Figures 18, 19. First performance of *Lys.*, Chapter 10, 203–5. In Peter Hall's 1993 production, half-masks were grotesque but pleasant, and bodies were padded, *Plays and Players* 472 (July 1993) 23.
31 Wiles 1991, 68.

9 COSTUMES OF OLD AND MIDDLE COMEDY

The substance of this chapter was first published as Hughes 2006a.

1 Evidence still comes to light. Through the labour and perseverance of T.B.L. Webster, A.D. Trendall, J.R. Green, A. Cambitoglou and A. Seeberg, much has been catalogued in *MMC³*, *PhV²* and *MNC³*. I am indebted to Professor Green, who provided me with a draft of his forthcoming *PhV³*.
2 Archaic choruses, Chapter 4, 85–7. Hoplites, Brooklyn 09.35, Amsterdam 3356; with heads, London 1842.7–28.979 (Figure 16); on dolphins, New York 1989.281.69, Athens Kerameikos 5671, Palermo CAT2816, Basle priv. coll.

HC849, Los Angeles priv. coll., Paris CA1924. Ostriches, Boston 20.18; horses, Berlin F1697; stilts, Christchurch 41–57. Dancers with castanets (*krotala*) and helmets may be 'Pyrrhic' dancers rather than a comic chorus, Pulsano priv. coll.

3 A Scythian wears a similar pointed hat on a plate of this period, London 1867.5–8.941; *IGD* I.10 suggests the stilt-walkers may represent Titans. Feathers and ears, Amsterdam 3356, New York 1988.11.3, with variety, also Christchurch 41–57, and the shield-devices on the earliest dolphin-riders, New York 1989.281.69. See *GVGetty* 95–113, and *TAGS* 30–3.

4 Old men, Thebes BE64.342; minotaurs, London B308, Oxford 1971.903; cocks, Berlin F1830; bird-men, London 1842.7–28.787.

5 This figure is discussed in Chapter 6, 109–10.

6 Once Malibu 82.AE.83; compare satyrs, Sydney NM47.05; centaurs, Paris N3408, Chapter 4, 90–1.

7 Earliest, Athens Agora Z1259. Best are Athens BΣ518 and Paris N3408; faded, Athens Agora P23985; fragmentary, Athens Agora P23856. *Somation* is mentioned by Pollux 2.235, and Lucian, *Zeus Tragoidos* 41, amongst padded garments worn by tragic actors, and in the eighth century CE, Photius connects it with Plato *comicus*.

8 Early pictures do not always show a padded torso, which may have developed between *c.*430 and 410.

9 Sifakis 1971a, 11.

10 Female appearance, Chapter 10, 204–5. On Madrid 11026 an actor masked as a young woman wears male costume and a *phallos*, perhaps a metatheatrical joke.

11 Ambiguity in visual evidence, terracottas and figures in vase scenes, masked as men but costumed as women: St Petersburg ББ160; S. Agata dei Goti priv. coll. 1, Würzburg H5697, Messina 11039 (Figure 39). The complexities of gender are analysed in Taaffe 1993.

12 Seeberg 1995, 5–6; *CAD* 90–2; N. Slater 1999, 358. Origins and 'fat men', Chapter 4, 84–5. Recent discussion is reviewed by Foley 2000, 276–8. Similar types are found in Kabeiric black-figured scenes from Thebes, dated 400–375, see Wolters, Bruns 1940.

13 Chapter 1, 4–7 reviews this material evidence in more detail.

14 *BH²* 143.

15 Webster 1948, 21; Pickard-Cambridge 1949; Beare 1954. For bibliography of the controversy, Hughes 2006a, 45 n. 26.

16 Beare 1957, 184 calls this 'tied-up', but since there is no evidence that it was actually tied, 'looped' is preferred. The comedy *phallos* is rarely erect. Apart from the Getty Birds, once Malibu 82.AE.83, there are two examples: a small figure in a beast-mask, Malibu 96.AE.112, and an old man who seems to hold his *phallos* erect, Atlanta L1989.2.2.

17 Lost staffs, München 5389, Berlin TC7086, perhaps Boston 13.99, Thebes from Thebes Kolonaki. Unbroken staffs are moulded in relief, Paris AM39, Siracusa inv. unk. Fat woman, Catania 2347. Zewadski 1995 shows how painters use the *bakteria* for characterization.

18 Exceptions, Cambridge MA TL331.86, an older woman who is too agitated to heed propriety, and Naples 118333, a young one who is too shameless.

19 Copenhagen 15032, Ruvo 901. Sleeves, London 1849.6–20.13. Fabric sometimes hangs in a 'V' at the neck, St Petersburg П1874.34 (Figure 41c).

20 Storey 2003, 96.

21 Wild silk, called *tarantina* (Menander, *Epitrepontes* 489) or *amorgis* (*Lys.* 150); fine fabric was woven from the fibre of the *pinna nobilis*, a fan mussel, Hughes 2006a, 48–9 n. 42.

22 Green 2002, 103. *Auletrides*, London 1875.8–18.9, Melbourne D17/1972; yellow terracottas, Paris N4878, St Petersburg ББ166 (Figure 41b). Colourists of nineteenth-century theatrical portraits ('tuppence coloured') followed their fancy rather than theatrical observation, but Athenian figurines were less mass-produced, and perhaps the colours were more authentic. According to Pollux, *CAD* 395–6, only old women and whores wore colours in New Comedy, but that does not apply here.

23 *Wealth* 940, trans. J. Henderson, Aristophanes IV, 2002. Panels, *auletrides*, n. 22 above; on comic vases, it can be mistaken for an opening, but other pictures show it on a garment that opens at the side: Atlanta L1989.2.2, Malibu 85.AE.102, an Andromeda.

24 Telephos, Würzburg H5697; transparent, Naples 118333; breasts, Metaponto 297053, St Petersburg Б1661, perhaps Paris K523. The transparent Doric *chiton* worn by an old man as 'Antigone' may be a painter's narrative device, S. Agata dei Goti priv. coll. 1.

25 *Enkuklon*, *Lys.* 113; at *Thes.* 261 Agathon wears one. *Himation* as 'clothes', *Thes.* 250, expensive *Wealth* 530, rags 540, dignified 940. *Kalymma*, *Lys.* 530.

26 *Kekryphalos*, Copenhagen 15032; *stephane* also means 'wreath', London market 2002, whereabouts unk.; *mitra*, Ruvo 901.

27 Wreaths, Lipari 11962; Athens Kanellopoulos 1460; an old bawd, Lipari 356i.

28 *Persikai*, *Lys.* 229, *Ekk.* 319, *Clouds* 151; *kothornoi*, *Ekk.* 346, Green 1996 pl. 5–13; Würzburg H4600.

29 *Persikai*, Milan Scala 749, and the 'baby' in the *Thesmophoria* scene, Würzburg H5697. Twelve are barefoot, like Milan Civico Museo A.0.9.2841.

30 *Peace* 1002; his diminutive of *chlanis* may be peculiar to Trygaios. Statistics, Hughes 2006a, n. 58–61. The classical period in Athens was remarkable for the uniformity of citizens' clothing, Geddes 1987, 307–31. Class distinctions in clothes, Green 2001, 42–3.

31 *Thoimation* is a variant of *himation*; it refers to the same type of garment.

32 The *paidogogos*, Green 1999, 37–63. The *chlamys*, often associated with youth, was worn by a new *ephebe*.

33 *Chlamys*, Hermes, Vatican U19; *sisura*, *Clouds* 10, New York 13.225.16; *phoinikis*, from *phoinix*, Tyrian purple, *Peace* 303, 1173; slave, Copenhagen 1067. A soldier's slave-batman might legitimately wear a red cloak, but a slave sitting on an altar seeks to evade punishment.

34 Exchanges, *Wasps* 1131–2, *Wealth* 842ff; *chlaina*, *Lys.* 586, *Frogs* 1458–9; *chlanis*, *Wasps* 677, *Ekk.* 848; *Anagyros* frag. 58, trans. J. Henderson, Aristophanes V, 2007, 138, from *Souda*, alpha 3227, refers to three *hapligedas*.

35 In the combined media, style α is worn by half of both citizens and slaves with wrapped cloaks; before mid-fourth century style β is half as popular, followed by style γ; later, β is found less frequently, while γ is worn by more than one-third of relevant figures.

36 *Sophrosyne*, and its absence in comic characterization, Chapter 6, 116. Stairs, London 1849.6–20.13; surprise, Malibu 96.AE.112; curiosity, Copenhagen 15032; running, Boston 00.363; striking, whereabouts unk., once Melbourne priv. coll; miser, Berlin F3044.

37 Thirty-one of α plus β have borders, several patterned as in London 1873.8–20.347, and the headless figure on the Crotone fragment. Others are unusually long or fringed: Siracusa 29966 and, in terracotta, New York 13.225.14; Lipari 12982 has a long *himation* and Larnaka 5242 is fringed, a rare luxury, M. Miller 1997, 160–1. Old men: Policoro from Aliano, Naples 118333; slaves, St Petersburg Б1661, Taranto 54724.

38 Eccentrics, *Clouds* 103. Before 375, 92 per cent are barefoot; after 350, 49 per cent, but 64 per cent of slaves. *Embas*: *Ekk.* 269, 319, *Thes.* 142, *Wealth* 847, *Clouds* 719, 856, *Knights* 870–5.

39 White *lakonikas*, London 1865.1–3.27 (a lover climbing a ladder); Dionysos, Lipari 9604; sandals, Gela 643.

40 Zeus wears his *polos* in Figures 34 and 48; Aigisthos wears a *pilos* in the *choregoi* scene, once Malibu 96.AE.29; Phrygian, Priam on Berlin F3045.

41 Cup, Athens Agora Z1259; padding, Paris CA2938, London 1898.2–27.1. Torsos, Hughes 2003, 293–4 n. 20. Colour is rare on terracottas of this period, but a woman-figurine shows black fleshings, London 1907.5–20.79b, and women have red fleshings on some Sicilian vases, Messina 11039 (Figure 39).

42 Green 2006, 141–62. Nudity is found only in the work of provincial artists, Melbourne University MUV77, Lipari 11171, Boston 01.8036.

10 COMEDY AND WOMEN

Portions of the substance of this chapter were first published as Hughes 2008, the 2006–7 T.B.L. Webster Lecture, Institute of Classical Studies, London.

1 Phrynichos' first known tragedy is *The Capture of Miletos c.*492. The *Souda*, phi 767, credits him with an *Alkestis*, *Women of Pleuron*, *Daughters of Danai* and the first woman's mask. Epicharmos and Phormis, *Souda*, epsilon 2766 and phi 609, Athenaios 652a, Dearden 1990, 156–8. Epicharmos was in Syrakousai by 483; he and Phormis were active in the time of Hieron, 478–467/6. Magnes' victory, 472.

2 Early vases show only male choruses. Magnes, *Poastria* (*Grass-cutters*) may have had a chorus of market-women. Reasonably reliable dates from internal evidence are *Thrattai* (444/3) and *Dionysalexandros* (43/29), Dover *et al.* 2000, 513. On *Kleoboulinai*, Hall 2000, 413.

3 *Cheiron* fragment, Plutarch, *Moralia* 1141d–f. The extent of Pherekrates' contribution is uncertain; see Henderson 2000, but cf. Millis 2001.

4 Green 2001, 46 says women are rare on early vase scenes (before 380), referring to Milan Civico Museo A.0.9.2841, New York 24.97.104 and Würzburg H5697. Before 380 we can add four more women, two Attic and two Apulian: Nike, Paris N3408; Tyro, Athens Agora P23856; St Petersburg Б1661; Taranto 122627. Omitting choruses and masks, in the early period we have six females to twenty-nine males, seven to thirty-six in 380–360. Terracottas tell a different story: almost 30 per cent of Attic types dated earlier than 350 are female.

5 Heidelberg U6. A shrub locates them outdoors.

6 New York 13.225.17, 13.225.25, 13.225.26. Later masks, Athens 6074, Lipari 356i, 10782.

7 Fight, Matera 9579, Ruvo 901. Praxagora equates a pug nose (*simos*) with ugliness, *Ekk.* 705. *Hetairai*, Policoro from Aliano, Lipari 927, Gela 36057; hanging masks, Paris K240, Lipari 2241. Respectable women with turned-up noses, Würzburg H5846, Bari 8014, Heidelberg TK46, Athens 13015. Bold behaviour compared with modest, Chapter 7, 158–60. Figures 40, 41, 42.

8 Messina 11039, Lentini 2B, Bari 4073; an early example in terracotta is Berlin TC6907; see also Lipari 6913, British Columbia priv. coll. Green 2001, 51 sees the slim figure as an aesthetic choice. Costume changes would be longer if padding were removed and replaced.

9 Trans. J. Henderson, Aristophanes IV, 2002, 238. *Ekk.* 427–8, 465–71, 323.

10 *Lys.* 148–54, 512–15 (referring to amendments to the Peace of Nikias proposed 419/18), absent husbands, 99–110.

11 *Lys.* 1148–79, *Ekk.* 427–8. The *protagonist* doubled as Chremes and Praxagora.

12 Foley 1981 explores this subject.

13 Charis, mother, Milan Civico Museo A.0.9.2841, Würzburg H5697. Figurines, New York 13.225.21, 13.225.23. Nike, Paris N3408, *c.*410.

14 *Poetics* 1449a.

15 Davidson 2000, 50–8 argues that this scene is like a private mime performance, in which women might perform. Perhaps the girl's song (952ff) was mimed by a masked actor at a window, and sung by a woman, unseen within the *skene*.

16 *Birds* 1199–261; Herakles figurines, Chapter 7, n. 9. Apollo, Naples 81372, St Petersburg Б1660. Zeus, Vatican U19, Bari 2970, Malibu 96.AE.113, St Petersburg Б299, Taranto 121613, Madrid 11026.

17 Athene, *Eumenides, Ajax, Suppliants, Ion* and the spurious *Rhesos*; on Rome Villa Giulia 50279, Ajax clings to her image, the Palladion, in a cartoon by Asteas. Aphrodite, Platon frag. 188, Kassel, Austin 1989, VII trans. Rusten 2011, Platon 185 350, see L.R. Farnell, *CQ* 14 (1920), 139–46. Hera, Malibu 96.AE.113 (Figure 48), London 1772.3–20.33. Hermes associates Enyalios with Ares, *Peace* 457.

18 Henderson 1991, 134.

19 Renier 1950, 92.

20 Eusebius ranks Praxilla with renowned poets, and Hephaistion refers to her dithyrambs, Campbell 1992, 371, 377. If Korinna 'defeated' Pindar, it must have been in a public *agon*, Pausanias 9.12.3.

21 Hunter 1985, 196.

22 Dearden 1999, 228. The *Souda*, sigma 893, says Sophron wrote about women; Athenaios 110c–d called his *Mother-in-law* a comedy. See *Poetics* 1447c, and Hordern 2004, 1–4.

23 Haigh 1889, 297–301; Rogers 1902, xxix–xxxii; Lucas 1954, 11; Dover 1972, 17; Podlecki 1990, 27–43; Henderson 1991, 133–4; Goldhill 1994, 347–69.

24 *GTP*² xiii.

25 Henderson 1991, 146–7. See also Schaps 1977, 323–30; Sommerstein 1980, 393–418.

26 Sourvinou-Inwood 2003, 177–84.

27 Zeitlin 1985, 80.

28 Inscriptions, see *CAD* 39–43.

29 Before Praxilla and Korinna we have Sappho; later fragments survive from Erinna of Telos, Anyte of Tegea and Nossis of Lokri.

30 *Banqueters* (427), *Babylonians* (426), *Ach.* (425). Kallistratos served as *didaskalos*. Araros probably presented his father's *Kokalos* (387) and, later, the second *Aiolosikon*. It is uncertain how much of this was an open secret.

31 *Tereus* 667–74, see Craik 1990, 162–4. 'New Music', Chapter 5, 101–3.

32 Xenophon, *Hellenica* 2.2.23 says *auletrides* were forced to play at the demo-lition of the Long Walls; Athenaios 605 says Bromias was prevented from playing at the Pythia (*c.*350); Melbourne D17/1972; on London 1875.8–18.9 the *auletris* plays before a *thymiaterion*, suggesting participation in a religious ceremony.

33 Satyr play, Athens 13027 (Figure 21), Bonn 1216.183–5. Apulian, St Petersburg Б2074; Campanian, Rio de Janeiro 20940–040, Frankfurt B602, Melbourne D14/1973, with *xustis*, Princeton 50–64. Hands, Athens Benaki 30890. Relief, Athens Agora S1025,1586, and *BH*² 43; Webster thinks the figure may be Dionysos, *GTP*² 56.

34 Taranto IG4638, Hughes 1997, Dearden 1995. A *krater* inscribed with her name suggests she was still 'a person of some standing' twenty-five years later, Green 2008, 210.

35 Naples 81398, Madrid 11129, Boston 97.371, Cambridge GR4.1943. *Symposion* 11, 1–2, 8, 11, ix, 2–7. Xenophon's word for somersaults is *kybistan* (2.11), a term used by Homer, *Iliad* XVIII, 590. Acrobats and dancers, Hughes 2008.

36 Sword-dance, Geneva priv. coll.; *kottabos*, Genoa 1142; contortionist on a wheel, Sydney NM95.16; jugglers, with ball and hoops, Palermo Mormino 742; Annie, Berlin F3444.

37 Sword-dance as cult, Cambitoglou *et al.* 1986, 199. Male Pyrrhic dancers com-peted at the Panathenaia, Ceccarelli 1998. The *thiasos*, Ruvo 1402; the same painter has a muffled woman dancing with a comic actor on Taranto 29031. Compare the graceful bronze 'Baker dancer', New York 1972.118.95, with the provocative terracotta, Siracusa 18971; a muffled woman dances with a dwarf under a phallos-bird on Oxford 1971.866; all four school scenes have castanet dancers; also Paris G574, where she has discarded her *enkuklon*, Hughes 2008, 8–17.

38 Oxford AN1945.43 has no provenance, but Lipari 927 was found on Lipari, an island where intense interest in comedy is demonstrated by thousands of locally manufactured terracottas. It is unlikely that this market would have accepted a misrepresentation of comedy.

39 Two girls, *Ach.* 1198; Spondai, *Knights* 1390; *auletris* (Dardanis), *Wasps* 1326; Eirene, Opora, Theoria, *Peace* 520; Prokne, Basileia, *Birds* 667, 1717; Diallage, *Lys.* 1112; dancer (Elaphion), *Thes.* 1160; the 'muse of Euripides', *Frogs* 1306.

40 Hall 2000, 408.

41 Wilamowitz-Moellendorff 1927, 187. Vaio 1973, 379 reports that A. Willems (1919) came to the same conclusion independently, but that K. Holziger (1928) disagreed. Vaio calls the supposed tights a *somation*, after a term found in Lucian by Stone 1981, 137. Barker 2004, 199 anachronistically refers to the Muse of Euripides as 'a naked, dancing houri'.

42 Stone 1981, 148–9, 424.

43 Undercostume, Chapter 9, 180–2. Stone overlooked most of the visual evidence because she believed that *phlyakes* were irrelevant to Attic comedy.

44 Vaio 1973, 379; *Lys.* 87–8; Henderson 1987, 195–6 on Reconciliation (1106–27). See also *DFA*² 152–3.

45 *King Lear* 4.7.71–2; S.T. Coleridge, *Biographia literaria* 14; *Henry V* Prol. 26–7.

46 Dearden 1995, 84, and 1976, 88–9. On Hoopoe, Russo 1994, 55–8. Children, the Megarian 'piggies', *Ach.* 729ff. The sons of Karkinos (*Wasps*) may have played themselves.

47 Compare the stage business with the *phallos* at *Ach.* 1216–17 and *Wasps* 1342–3.

48 On Rome priv. coll. 52 (Figure 22), two masked chorus-men dance upon a stage and pretend to play *auloi*, while the real piper plays behind a property tree. Thus the *auletris* addressed in a fragment of Eupolis' *Baptai* might be either a masked actor pretending to play or a real woman: 'You, girl, play some start-up to a dithyramb on your pipe', Storey 2003, 320. Pipers played *in propria persona*. It would be feasible for an actor dressed as a girl to pretend while a specialist played within the *skene*, but the sound would be muffled.

49 *Wasps* 1301–15: they include Lykon, the wealthy host of both Xenophon's *Symposion* and the victory banquet in Eupolis' *Autolykos*. Literary sources imply that women who played at the *symposion* were invariably disreputable, but Bundrick 2005, 92–102 shows that even a respectable Athenian woman of the citizen class could enjoy a musical education.

50 Taplin 2007, 105 independently reaches a similar conclusion. Philokleon speaks as though Dardanis were a slave-prostitute (1353), but he also pretends she is a torch. Her name suggests that she comes from the Troad.

51 *Frogs* 1314, 1349. Stephanis 1988, no. 2396 understands Teredon as an *auletris*.

52 According to scholia, a pseudonym adopted by prostitutes; it refers to deer, with connotations of lightness. Sandbach 1977, 28 suggests that 'Fawn' was played by a (naked) slave woman.

53 Dearden 1995, 84.

11 NEW COMEDY

1 Handley 2002, 177–8.

2 Fletcher, 'To the reader', *The faithful shepherdess* (*c.*1609); Handley 1969, 24; Green 2008, 105.

3 Handley 1969, 25. Sandbach 1977, 69 suggests that after Demetrios of Phaleron (in power 317–307) abolished the *theorikon* subsidy for poor citizens, the audience was more refined; challenged by Rosivach 2000.

4 *Souda*, alpha 1982.

5 Handley 1997, 185 notes that New Comedy is not merely 'the last . . . of the forms of drama developed in Athens', but that its poets were the 'poets of the Hellenistic age'.

6 Wordsworth, 'Preface', *Lyrical ballads* (1800); *Poetics* 1451b trans. S. Halliwell 1999.

7 Webster 1952, 23 gives totals for mythology; the models for Plautus' *Menaechmi* and *Amphitruo* may have been Middle Comedies; the twins with the same name in Menander's *Dis exapaton* were a late survival.

8 On Pherekrates' *hetaira*-titles and 'city comedy', Chapter 2, 24. Alexis may have named the *parasitos* type, Arnott 1996, 20–3. Dates of Alexis' plays are often obscure, *ibid.* 10, n. 4.

9 Accounts conflict on all points, including his age at the time of victory, Menander 1, trans. W.G. Arnott 1997, xv. Canonical poets were selected by the same Alexandrian scholars who established the Old Comedy triad, Kratinos, Aristophanes and Eupolis.

10 Menander 1, trans. W. G. Arnott 1997, xxi–iii, n. 10; Quintilian 10.1.69; Plutarch, *Moralia* 853f, d trans. F.C. Babbitt 1936; Manilius, *Astronomica* 5.475–6 trans. G.P. Goold 1977.

11 We have 132 authentic titles of Alexis; he may have written as many as 220 comedies, Arnott 1996, 14.

12 Menander, perhaps 322/1–292/1, Green 2008, 112; Aristophanes, 427 to *c.*386; Eupolis, 429 to *c.*412; Kratinos, *c.*450 to 426, Dover *et al.* 2000, 507–25.

13 Comedies by Aristophanes were sometimes performed at both festivals, but, so far as is known, at least one was presented under another name, usually Kallistratos or Philonides, see above, 12–13, 34.

14 Demosthenes, *On the false embassy* 192ff; Plutarch, *Alexander* 29; Chares, *CAD* IV.32,237; O'Connor 1966, no. 13, 74 and no. 319, 114. Ten talents (60,000 drachmas) were almost enough to keep a war-trireme at sea for a year.

15 *CAD* I.107,44–5: the inscription does not necessarily refer to a new practice.

16 These 'old' comedies were revivals: *Fasti* inscription, *CAD* I.22B,14. Evidence of an 'actors' theatre' is Lykourgos' attempt to stabilize the texts of Aischylos, Sophokles and Euripides, preventing actors from enhancing their parts, *CAD* I.14,10. This can have had no effect upon touring actors. N. Slater 1988, 53–7 argues that a contest for comic actors at the Great Dionysia was held as early as 421.

17 Antiphanes, *Soldier*, *CAD* III.91,148.

18 Mikalson 1998, 55–7. The dates are established by inscriptions that must precede and follow abolition, *CAD* III.110,156.

19 The *stoa* behind the *skene* required the site of the sixth-century temple, which was replaced by a new temple in the fourth century, Moretti 1999–2000, 377–98.

20 The priority of either Athens or Epidauros is disputed. *TDA* 209 and Moretti 1997, 16 reject arguments that Athens was earlier; Winter 1983, and Wiles 1991, 38–9 disagree. Pausanias 2.27.5 attributes both the theatre and the *tholos* in the Epidauros sanctuary to the Argive sculptor-architect Polykleitos, but he is too early, and there is no evidence for a son by the same name. A. von Gerkan dated it to the late fourth or early third century; later discoveries suggest a start *c.*330–320, see Tomlinson 1983, 87.

21 *Logeion*, 'speaking place', is the stage, supported by the *proskenion*, the structure 'in front of the *skene*'; at Priene it is 2.7 metres high. Others were as high as 3.5 metres, Moretti 1997, 13. Scenes dated 350–325 show the same stage and steps: comic, Messina 11039 and Paris CA7249, tragic, Caltanissetta 1751, Chapter 3, 71–3. Moretti 1997, 37–8 argues that there was no *logeion* at this period, and that actors habitually performed in the *orchestra*, 'without rupture' from the time of Aischylos to the Roman imperial period; Townsend 1986 explores archaeological evidence for this view.

22 Many actors were foreign-born, often naturalized as citizens. Each tribe entered a dithyrambic chorus of fifty, either of men or boys.

23 Perhaps 15,000 instead of 7,000, Chapter 3, 63–4.

24 The Lyceum, London, measured 17 metres: 1881 plans, Public Record Office ref. LC 7/66.

25 Dörpfeld calculated the *orchestra* at Athens as 24 metres; Epidauros today is 21.5 metres.

26 See Csapo 2003, and Chapter 4, 85–7. Aeschines, *Against Timarchos* 10 says 'The dithyrambs are called circular choruses' (*choron ton kuklon*), trans. C.D. Adams 1948; Csapo, Miller 2007 define dithyramb as cultic and Dionysian, and 'circular *choroi*' as 'theatrical'. A victorious dithyrambic poet received a bull for sacrifice, and the *choregos* was awarded a bronze tripod, which he often dedicated as a monument beside the Street of Tripods; the winning comic and tragic poets received an ivy crown, *CAD* 106–8.

27 Priene, *BH*[2] figs. 422a–b; Aphrodisias, Oropos, Ashby 1999, figs. 38, 39 and 62–80 on the primacy of dithyramb. Moretti 1997 (reconstruction fig. 1) believes that at Athens a colonnade with three entrances served only to enhance the façade of the *skene*, and that performances took place at *orchestra* level; he argues that panels were decorative rather than scenic.

28 *Against Meidias* 14–16; sumptuous production and a larger chorus made dithyramb more expensive than tragedy for the *choregos*, *CAD* 140–1. Some theatres were equipped with stairs as long as scaling ladders, but their utility must have been limited, Sifakis 1967, 131–2.

29 *GTP*[2] 43–4, Sifakis 1967, 33–4, *TAGS* 104.

30 Wiles 1991, 38–9. Speech and voice, Chapter 6, 115–16.

31 P. Brown 2001, xviii compounds his error by stating that since Menander cannot have written for such a tiny stage, it must have been built later. Dimensions, Moretti 1997.

32 Webster 1974, 80; Gomme, Sandbach 1973, 17–18 argue that the 'rule of three actors' applied in New Comedy; also *MMC*³ 2.

33 Moretti 1997, 38.

34 For example, dithyrambic competitions on Delos in 282, *CAD* I.107, 44–5; and P. Wilson 2007, 358–9. *Kybistai*, Xenophon, *Symposion* 2.1, *Iliad* XVIII, 590.

35 Sifakis 1967, 126–30. W. Körte suggested that the chorus sometimes remained on the stage between odes, but he subsequently retracted, Dover 1968, 143–4; Webster, *GTP*² 21–2 thought they used a much lower stage, entering through *paraskenia*.

36 Drunks in Menander, *Dyskolos, Aspis, Epitrepontes, Perikeiromene*; as *lopodutas*, lit. clothes-thieves, 'muggers' in *Misoumenos* 247, Menander II, trans. W.G. Arnott, 1997, 247. Alexis, *Kouris*, Arnott 1996, 21 and Dover 1968, 145.

37 *Poetics* 1456a trans. S. Halliwell 1999.

38 Handley 2002, 173–4; the official *auletes* would play for the stage-*auletris* at *Dyskolos* 433, but at 880 and 910 Getas addresses a piper who might be in the *orchestra*, ready to lead a choral *exodos*. Internal stairs, Chapter 3, 70–7.

39 The policemen's song in *Pirates of Penzance*. Euboulos flourished *c*.360–340; *Skythai* is dated 320–310; Alexis' titles are dated 345–320 and 345–305 respectively. *Kouris* is not dated.

40 Athens Agora S1025, 1586, interpreted as soldiers, *MMC*³ 118.

41 Arnott 1972, 79 refers to his 'great speech of self-justification' in trochaic tetrameters (708ff); *aulos*, Handley 1969. City comedy is described in Chapter 2, 34–5.

42 It is doubtful that actors normally sang in early New Comedy, but some evidence suggests that comedies could be set to music at a later date, Hall 2002, 34–5.

43 G.B. Shaw, 'Preface' in C. St. John ed. *Ellen Terry and Bernard Shaw: a correspondence* (London: Reinhardt, Evans, 1931) xxiii. Perhaps a chorus-leader, a piper, or both, accompanied some tours.

44 Sifakis 1967, 72–4 shows that companies consisting of three actors, a *didaskalos* and a piper played the Delphic Soteria festival in several consecutive years, sharing a small chorus, possibly of professionals. On exemption for amateur *choreutai*, Demosthenes, *Against Boiotos* 1.16, *Against Meidias* 15; Delphic Soteria, 256 BCE, *CAD* III.165A,200–1.

45 Eretria may have had an early high *logeion*, P. Wilson 2007, 353–7, Moretti 1992, 87–8; there are similar colonnades of third-century date at Dodona and Oiniadai in the north-west.

46 The 'theatre' mentioned in Herodotus 6, 67 may be the Athenian author's term for an arena for athletics and military training.

47 Testimony of Pammenes, goldsmith, in Demosthenes, *Against Meidias* ed. D.M. MacDowell (Oxford: Clarendon Press 1990) 103.

48 Green 2006, 103. Compare old women, London 1887.7–25.7 with New York 13.225.25; the younger women in the *Synaristosai* mosaic, Naples 9987 (Figure 55), wear the Doric type, leaving arms bare; the Ionian style, pinned to form sleeves, is common in Apulian vase scenes.

49 Transitional and New Comedy costume, Chapter 9, 190–1.

50 An exception with a small *phallos* is Dresden ZV732; this may be an 'iconographic rather than a stage survival', as in figures on a series of black-glazed vessels of New Comedy date, such as Herakles, Tampa 7.94.4, and bronze actor-figurines manufactured as late as the second century BCE, Green 2006, 156–60. We have seventeen bronze slaves, such as Toronto 953.171. Malibu 96.AB.155 is distinct from the series, with a long *phallos*, dated second century BCE. Corpulent soldier, Paris MNB2720; wreathed youth, London 1856.12–26.255; slaves, Milan Scala 37; Paris ED2070; Pompeii Casa di Casca Longo; Tarquinia RC1346, 1764 (Figure 51).

51 Aristotle, *Poetics* 1449a 29–36. Female triad, Chapter 7, 157–62.

52 Green 2006, 103. Wiles 1991, 102. Popularity is estimated from the distribution and frequency of replicas in various forms, *TAGS* 108–17.

53 *Phaulos*, Paris AM34; London 1842.7–28.750; exaggerated trumpet, one of the popular Loeb Group of figurines, München SL199. Actor's teeth are visible in the slave-mask, Kavalla 240. Late Hellenistic trumpets were stylized as a huge mouth, as in Boston 01.7679.

54 *TAGS* 114, father, son and slave on a plaque, Kavalla 240, with swept-back hair; also Brussels A302. Triangular, Boston 01.7679; Vienna V1567; Naples 6687 (Figure 52), old man, second from left. Full, Lipari 9727; Bucharest coll., Slobozianu. Curled, Naples 6687, old man, first at left; Vatican 9985 (Figure 53), mask on table; Lipari 3426. An ironic variant is a *pornoboskos* with beard tied in pointed tails, Nikosia 1934.vii–12.3.

55 *TAGS* 100. Webster, *GTP*² 74, *MMC*³ 8 suggests that some might have been introduced by Menander himself, particularly those which link members of families by their hairstyles.

56 Wiles 1991, 68.

57 Madrid 4045; drunken youth, Naples 6687; Copenhagen 7367; brows, Paris MNB2720; Madrid 3370.

58 *MMC*³ 3. Unattractive masks, Brussels A302; London 1856.12–26.255; Paris MNB2720; Lipari 9814.

59 Wiles 1991, 80, 85.

60 Pollux wrote in the second century CE, Aristophanes in the second BCE, *TAGS* 153–4, 393 and *MMC*³ 6.

61 All are late copies of large-scale public paintings of Menander and scenes from his comedies, painted close to the end of the poet's career (300–275). a) Naples 6687; Handley 1997, 191 suggests this may be a scene from Menander's lost *Methe* (*Drunkenness*); b) Vatican 9985; c) Naples 9985; d) Naples 9987. Webster's analysis, *GTP*² 73–96. Pollux on New Comedy masks is translated in *CAD* 400–2; illustrations and discussion of each mask, *MMC*³ 6ff.

62 Sifakis 1967, 89–94; Menander 1, trans. W.G. Arnott 1997, xx.

63 Hunter 1985, 14; Beare 1964, 26–7.
64 Hunter 1985, 3; Handley 1985, 417, 424.
65 Pompeian mosaics, Naples 9985, 9987, dated second century BCE; Mytilene, fourth century CE, Charitonides *et al.* 1970, Csapo 1997 and Handley 1997, 190–1.
66 Menander I, trans. W.G. Arnott 1997, xxiii–xxiv.

Glossary

agathos   good, righteous, the reverse of *kakos*

agon, pl. *agones*   contest

agonothetes   administrator of the competition, festival

agora   market-place, often the location of government buildings

aischros   ugly, deformed, shameful

amphora   large container for transporting and storing wine, with carrying handles either side of the neck

architekton   theatre manager, in Athens elected by 337/6

archon eponymous   chief magistrate, responsible for the Great Dionysia; the second *archon* (*basileus)* administered the Lenaia

auletes, pl. *auletai*   piper, male

auletris, pl. *auletrides*   piper, female

aulos, pl. *auloi*   double pipes

beltion   better, compared against *cheironos*

boule, bouleterion   governing council, council's meeting place

cheironos   worse, compared against *beltion*

chiton, dim. *chitonion*, pl. *chitonia* tunic,   a basic garment worn by men and women

chlaina   woollen himation, good quality

chlamys   young man's or traveller's short cape, fastened at the neck

chlanis   large cloak of fine wool, best quality

choregia   Athenian institution whereby a citizen was responsible for financing and organizing a chorus

choregos, pl. *choregoi*   citizen charged with organizing and financing a chorus

choreut, pl. *choreutai*   chorus-man

chorodidaskalos   instructor of a chorus

chous   small, fat *oinochoe*

deme, properly *demos*   country district, township; there were 139 *demoi* in Attika, including Acharnia, Ikarion, Peiraeus, Thorikos

deuteragonist   second actor, assistant to *protagonist*

didaskaliai   fragmentary inscriptions, recording results of *agones* in the Great Dionysia and Lenaia

didaskalos, pl. *didaskaloi*   lit. teacher; stage director, trainer

eisodos   entrance

ekklesiaterion meeting place of assembly

ekkyklema rolling or rotating platform used to reveal a tableau from the interior of the *skene*

embas rough working shoes made of felt

embolima choral interludes, as in New Comedy

enkuklon woman's large cloak, 'encircler'

ephebos, pl. *epheboi* Athenian male 18 years old, ready for military service

eromenos loved one, usually a young male (from Eros)

exarchos, pl. *exarchontes* 'leader-off' of an archaic chorus, he may also be the poet, who improvised satirical verse while the chorus sang the refrain

exodos exit ode of a chorus; its exit from the *orchestra*

exomis man's *chiton* fastened at left shoulder, leaving the right bare

fabula palliata Latin, lit. stories dressed in the 'pallium', the *himation*; comedy with Greek characters and setting, adapted from New Comedy

Fasti modern name of fragmentary inscription recording victorious *choregoi* and *didaskaloi* in Great Dionysia, 473–328 BCE

fleshings Victorian theatrical term for flesh-coloured tights covering arms and legs

geloios laughable, grotesque

Gnathia polychrome vase-painting technique which became popular in Taras near the middle of the fourth century: Figures 3, 9, 33

hetaira, pl. *hetairai* lit. companion; courtesan, prostitute

himation, var. *thoimation* man's or woman's cloak; synonym for 'clothes'

hydria water jug with three handles

hypokrites lit. answerer; actor

hypothesis brief plot summary in manuscript of a play

ikria benches for spectators, in a *theatron* or other watching place

kakos bad, wicked, the reverse of *agathos*

kalymma fold of a cloak worn over the head, as a hood and/or veil

katastrophe lit. overturning; conclusion, unravelling of plot; in tragedy, reversal of fortune

katharsis cleansing, purging; in tragedy, of emotions of pity and terror

kekryphalos hair-net like a bandana, to keep the *krobulos* in place

kerkis, pl. *kerkides* wedge-shaped section of theatre seats, divided by stairways; term derived from a tapered rod used in weaving

kiste chest, box

koilon from *koilos* a hollow, a slope hollowed to make a *theatron*

komodos, pl. *komodoi* actor, actors of comedy

komos, komast, komastai revel or band of revellers, often drunken, with torches and song

kore maiden

koryphaios, pl. *koryphaioi* leader of the chorus in comedy of the classical period; he may speak for the poet in the *parabasis*

kothornoi high-cut boots associated with Dionysos, worn out-of-doors by women, and by tragic messengers *kottabos*   a drinking game in which wine lees were thrown at a target

kouros   youth

krater, bell   large bowl for mixing wine with water, with two small handles: Figures 23, 34, 37

krater, *kalyx*   mixing bowl with large, low-set handles: Figures 8, 10, 22

krater, volute   large, ornamental bowl with ornately coiled handles beneath lip, often decorated with mythic scenes

krobulos   roll of hair worn on crown of a woman's head

krokotos, dim. *krokotidion*   woman's fine tunic, saffron-coloured

krotala   castanets

kylix   shallow two-handled cup for drinking wine, often very large

lakonikas   men's shoes, a Laconian (Spartan) type

lazzo   a term from *commedia dell'arte*, comic business regularly practised by an actor in one character

lidos   lightweight summer cloak

logeion   lit. speaking place; stage platform above the *proskenion*

maenad   ecstatic female follower of Dionysos

mechane   lit. machine; crane and tackle for flying gods, and comic parodies

Megale Hellas   Latin Magna Graecia, the coast of southern Italy colonized by Greeks

metatheatre   a term coined by Lionel Abel; in Old Comedy it refers to the dramatic characters' pervasive awareness of their own theatricality, which they share self-referentially with the audience

metic   foreign Greek resident in Athens

mime   modern term for ancient performances other than classical comedy, tragedy and satyr play; also for a performer in any of these kinds

mimesis   lit. imitation, representation, impersonation; as acting, music, visual art imitate nature

mythos, *mythoi*   plot, myth

obol   a silver coin, worth one-sixth of a drachma

oinochoe   small jug for serving wine, usually with pinched lip, still manufactured in southern Italy: Figures 47, 26

onkos   stylized high frontal hair of later tragic masks

orchestra   lit. dancing place; ground-level performance space in front of *skene*

orchestris   dancer, female

parabasis   lit. stepping forward; comedy scene in which chorus and leader directly address the audience

parakataloge   manner of speaking or chanting choral anapaests, 'parallel recital' sometimes compared to 'recitative' in opera

paraskenion, pl. *paraskenia*   lit. (thing(s)) beside the *skene*; usually architectural projections with entrance doors

Parian marble (*marmor Parium*)   inscription, a chronological list of significant Athenian events, ending 254–253. Greek transliteration, and translation: www.ashmolean.org/ash/faqs/q004/

parodos, pl. *parodoi* entrance to *orchestra*, between *skene* and a wing of the *theatron*; song of the chorus at its first entrance

pelike smaller, low-slung amphora: Figure 49

persikai soft Persian slippers

petasos broad-brimmed hat

phalloi pl. form of *phallos*

phaulos inferior, insignificant, the opposite of *spoudaios*

phiale broad, flat bowl, used for libations: Herakles holds a *situla* in Figure 34

phlyax, pl. *phlyakes* performer(s) of southern Italian farce, formerly thought to be represented in comic vase scenes

phoinikis short red military cape

phorbeia head-strap securing the mouthpieces of the *auloi* in place

physis natural powers, best abilities

pilos conical felt hat

pinax, pl. *pinakes* painted panel(s), 'flats'

polis, pl. *poleis* city-state(s), collective body of (male) citizens

polos lit. pivot, the vault of heaven; a cylindrical hat worn as a crown

proboulos (in *Lysistrata*) magistrate, official of the *boule* (council)

prohedria front seats, reserved for dignitaries, sometimes carved in the shape of a chair

proskenion lit. the place in front of the *skene*; the structure beneath the *logeion*

prosopeion theatrical mask

protagonist leading actor, said to 'act the play' with *deuteragonist* and *tritagonist* as assistants

psykter wine-cooler, small enough to be set inside a *krater*

schemata dance steps and gestures: the *kordax* was associated with comedy, the *diple* with tragedy

situla cylindrical vessel with two upright handles for carrying like a bucket: Figure 33

skene lit. tent, booth; stage building

skyphos two-handled drinking vessel with a deeper bowl than a *kylix*

sophrosyne a citizen's ideal mental and physical state of emotional control and dignified deportment; in acting, see Chapter 6, 116ff

Souda Byzantine Greek historical encyclopaedia of tenth century CE

spoudaios significant, dignified, the reverse of *phaulos*

stasimon lit. standing: choral song in tragedy, other than the *parodos* and *exodos*

stephane, from *stephanos* crown, wreath; with women usually a diadem worn by a *hetaira*

stoa colonnade

symposion drinking party, all-male, often with entertainment, singing, debate and discussion

theatron lit. watching place, auditorium

theologeion lit. god's speaking place; acting space on the roof of the *skene*

thymiaterion pl. *thymiateria* incense-burner

torso   padded body of comic undercostume, to which fleshings and an artificial
   phallos were attached

tragodos   actor of tragedy

tribon, dim. *tribonion*   homespun cloak of a poor man

tritagonist   third actor, junior assistant to the *protagonist*

tympanon   drum; in comic scenes, it resembles a large tambourine: see Figure 54

undercostume   body-modifying, knitted suit representing a comic character's
   unclothed skin, always worn under the comic actor's stage costume

xustis   long soft robe of ornately decorated purple fabric, worn by both *aulos*
   players of both genders

Bibliography

ABBREVIATIONS

AA	*Archaeoligischer Anzeiger*
ABV	J.D. Beazley, *Attic black-figure vase-painters* (Oxford: Clarendon Press 1956)
AJA	*American Journal of Archaeology*
AJP	*American Journal of Philology*
AncW	*The Ancient World*
AntK	*Antike Künst*
ArchDelt	*Arkaiologikon Deltion*
ARV²	J.D. Beazley, *Attic red-figure vase-painters*, 2nd edn (Oxford: Clarendon Press 1963)
BArch	Beazley archive, www.beazley.ox.ac.uk/databases/pottery.htm
BBTL	L. Bernabò Brea, *Menandro e il teatro Greco nelle terracotte Liparesi* (Genoa: Sagep 1981)
BH²	M. Bieber, *The history of the Greek and Roman theater*, 2nd edn (Princeton NJ: University Press 1961)
BICS	*Bulletin of the Institute of Classical Studies*
BMCR	*Bryn Mawr Classical Review*, http://bmcr.brynmawr.edu/archive.html
CAD	E. Csapo, W. Slater, *The context of ancient drama* (Ann Arbor: University of Michigan Press 1995)
Comic angels	O. Taplin, *Comic angels and other approaches to Greek drama through vase-painting* (Oxford: Clarendon Press 1993)
CQ	*Classical Quarterly*
DFA²	A.W. Pickard-Cambridge, *The dramatic festivals of Athens*, 2nd edn, revised J. Gould, D. M. Lewis (Oxford: Clarendon Press 1968)
DTC²	A.W. Pickard-Cambridge, *Dithyramb, tragedy and comedy*, 2nd edn, revised T.B.L. Webster (Oxford: Clarendon Press 1962)
EchCl	*Echos du monde classique: Classical Views*
G&R	*Greece and Rome*
GRBS	*Greek, Roman and Byzantine Studies*
GTP²	T.B.L. Webster, *Greek theatre production*, 2nd edn (London: Methuen 1970)

GVGetty	J.R. Green, 'A representation of the *Birds* of Aristophanes' in *Greek vases in the J. Paul Getty Museum*, vol. II (Malibu: J. Paul Getty Museum 1985) 95–118
IGD	A.D. Trendall, T.B.L. Webster, *Illustrations of Greek drama* (London: Phaidon 1971)
Jdl	*Jahrbuch des Deutschen Archäologischen Instituts*
JHS	*Journal of Hellenic Studies*
LCS	A.D. Trendall, *The red-figured vases of Lucania, Campania and Sicily* (Oxford: Clarendon Press 1967)
MeditArch	*Mediterranean Archaeology. Australian and New Zealand Journal for the Archaeology of the Mediterranean World*
MMC³	T.B.L. Webster, J.R. Green, *Monuments illustrating Old and Middle Comedy*, 3rd edn, *BICS* supp. 39, 1978
MMStP	State Hermitage Museum, *Muses and masks: theatre and music in antiquity. The antique world on the St Petersburg stage* (St Petersburg: ARS 2005)
MNC³	J.R. Green, A. Seeberg, revised T.B.L. Webster, *Monuments illustrating New Comedy*, 3rd edn, *BICS* supp. 50, 1995
MTS²	T.B.L. Webster, *Monuments illustrating tragedy and satyr-play*, 2nd edn (London 1967)
OJA	*Oxford Journal of Archaeology*
PBSR	*Papers of the British School at Rome*
PhV²	A.D. Trendall, *Phlyax vases*, 2nd edn, *BICS* supp. 19, 1967
RVAp	A.D. Trendall, A. Cambitoglou, *The red-figured vases of Apulia* (Oxford: Clarendon Press 1978–82)
RVP	A.D. Trendall, *The red-figured vases of Paestum* (London: British School at Rome 1987)
RVSIS	A.D. Trendall, *Red-figured vases of south Italy and Sicily* (London: Thames and Hudson 1989)
SovArch	*Sovetskaja Archeologija*
TAGS	J.R. Green, *Theatre in ancient Greek society* (London, New York: Routledge 1994)
TDA	A.W. Pickard-Cambridge, *The Theatre of Dionysos in Athens* (Oxford University Press, 1946)
ZPE	*Zeitschrift für Papyrologie und Epigraphik*

TRANSLATIONS OF ANCIENT TEXTS

Aristophanes
 I *Knights, Acharnians* trans. J. Henderson (Cambridge MA, London: Harvard University Press, 1998).
 II *Clouds, Wasps, Peace* trans. J. Henderson (Cambridge MA, London: Harvard University Press, 1998).
 III *Birds, Lysistrata, Women at the Thesmophoria* trans. J. Henderson (Cambridge MA, London: Harvard University Press, 2000).

IV *Frogs, Assemblywomen, Wealth* trans. J. Henderson (Cambridge MA, London: Harvard University Press, 2002).
V *Fragments* trans. J. Henderson (Cambridge MA, London: Harvard University Press, 2007).

Aeschines, *Against Timarchos, The speeches of Aeschines* trans. C.D. Adams (Cambridge MA, London: Harvard University Press, Heinemann 1948).
Aristotle, *Poetics* trans. S. Halliwell (Cambridge MA, London: Harvard University Press 1999).
  Rhetoric trans. J.H. Freese (Cambridge MA, London: Harvard University Press 1947).
Athenaios, *The Deipnosophists* v–vii trans. C.B. Gulick (Cambridge MA, London: Harvard University Press, Heinemann 1943–51).
  The Learned Banqueters (*Deipnosophistai*) i–iv trans. S.D. Olson (Cambridge MA, London: Harvard University Press 2006–8).
Aulus Gellius, *Attic Nights* trans. J. C. Rolfe (Cambridge MA, London: Harvard University Press 1948).
Aulus Gellius, *Bacchylides, complete poems* trans. R. Fagles (New Haven: Yale University Press 1961).
Demosthenes, *'Against Boiotos', Private Orations* trans. A.T. Murray (Cambridge MA, London: Harvard University Press 1984).
Lucian, *The Dance* trans. A.M. Harmon (Cambridge MA, London: Harvard University Press 1955).
Manilius, *Astronomica* trans. G.P. Goold (Cambridge MA, London: Harvard University Press 1977).
Menander, i trans. W.G. Arnott (Cambridge MA, London: Harvard University Press 1997).
Menander ii trans. W.G. Arnott (Cambridge MA, London: Harvard University Press 1997).
Pausanias, *Description of Greece* vol. iv trans. W.H.S. Jones (Cambridge MA, London: Harvard University Press 1965).
Plato, *Laws* trans. R.G. Bury (Cambridge MA, London: Harvard University Press 1961).
  Republic trans. P. Shorey (London, New York: Heinemann, Putnam 1943).
Platonios, *On the Distinctions among Comedies*, W.J.W. Koster, *Scholia in Aristophanem*, i, fasc. ia, 3–6 (Groningen: Bouma's Boekhuis 1975). Also the Anonymous Περι κθμωδιας δια 7–10.
Plutarch, *Lives* vol. vii trans. B. Perrin (Cambridge MA, London: Harvard University Press 1967).
  Moralia trans. F.C. Babbitt (Cambridge MA, London: Harvard University Press 2004).
Pseudo-Xenophon (the 'Old Oligarch'), *Constitution of the Athenians* 10, trans. W. Bowersock (Cambridge MA, London: Harvard University Press 1968).
Xenophon, *Symposion* trans. O.J. Todd in *Xenophon* iv (Cambridge, MA, London Harvard University Press 2002).

MODERN COMMENTARY

Abel L. 1963. *Metatheatre: a new view of dramatic form* (New York: Hill and Wang).

Adamesteanu D. 1956. 'Monte Saraceno ed il problema della penetrazione radio-cretese nelle Sicilia meriodionale', *Archeologia Classica* 8, 121–46.

Adamesteanu D., Mertens D., D'Andria F. 1975. *Metaponto I, Notizie degli scavi, sopplemento al vol.* XXIX, no. 163, fig. 52.

Anti C. 1947. *Teatri greci arcaici da Minosse a Pericle* (Padua: Le Tre Venezie).

Arias P.E. 1962. *A history of Greek vase painting* trans. B.B. Shefton (London: Thames and Hudson).

Arnott W.G. 1972. 'From Aristophanes to Menander', *Greece and Rome* 19, 65–80.

1996. *Alexis: the Fragments* (Cambridge University Press).

Ashby Clifford 1988. 'The case for the rectangular/trapezoidal Orchestra', *Theatre Research International* 13, 1–20.

1999. *Classical Greek theatre: new views on an old subject* (Iowa City: University of Iowa Press).

Aylen L. 1985. *The Greek theater* (Rutherford NJ: Associated University Presses).

Bacci G.M., Tigano G. ed. 2001. *Da Zancle a Messina: un percorso archeologico attraverso gli scavi*, vol. II (Palermo: Assessorato dei beni culturali e ambientali e della pubblica istruzione).

Barker A. 2004. 'Transforming the nightingale: aspects of Athenian musical discourse in the late fifth century' in P. Murray, P. Wilson eds., *Music and the Muses* (Oxford University Press).

Beare W. 1954. 'The costume of the actors in Aristophanic comedy', *CQ* NS 4, 64–75.

1957. 'Aristophanic costume again', *CQ* NS 7, 184–5.

1964. *The Roman stage*, 3rd edn (London: Methuen).

Beazley J.D. 1971. *Paralipomena: additions to Attic black-figure vase painters and to Attic red-figure vase painters*, 2nd edn (Oxford: Clarendon Press) no. 259.

1974. *The Pan Painter* (Mainz am Rhein: P. von Zabern).

1967. 'Studi sul teatro greco di Siracusa', *Palladio* 17, 97–154.

Bernabò Brca L., Cavalier M. 1965. *Meligunìs–Lipára* II, *La necropoli greca e romana nella Contrada Diana* (Palermo: S.F. Flaccovio).

2002. *Terracotte teatrali e buffonesche della Sicilia orientale e centrale* (Palermo: M. Crispo).

Besques S. 1963. *Les terres cuites grecques* (Paris: Presses Universitaires de France).

1971. *Catalogue raisonné des figurines et reliefs en terre-cuite grecs, étrusques et romains. Époques préhellénique, géométrique, archaïque et classique;* III.II *Grèce et Asie Mineure* (Paris: Éditions des Musées Nationaux).

1986. IV.I *Italie méridionale, Sicilie, Sardaigne* (Paris: Éditions des Musées Nationaux).

1992. IV.II *Cyrénaique, Égypte ptolémaique et romaine, Afrique du nord et proche-orient* (Paris: Éditions des Musées Nationaux).

Bieber M. 1920. *Die Denkmäler zum Theaterwesen im Altertum* (Berlin: W. de Gruyter).

1949. Review of Anti 1947, *Art Bulletin* 31, 61–3.

Biles Z. 1999. 'Eratosthenes on Plato Comicus: *didaskaliai* or *parabasis?*' *ZPE* 127, 182–8.

Billig E. 1980. 'Die Bühne mit austauschbaren Kulissen: eine verkannte Bühne des Frühhellenismus?' *Opuscula Athenensia* 13, 35–83.

Blázquez J.M. 1975. *Castulo: excavaciones arqueologicas en España* 1 (Madrid: Comisaría General del Patrimonio Artístico).

Boardman J. 1975. *Athenian red-figured vases: the archaic period* (London: Thames and Hudson).

Bonacasa N., Ensoli S. 2000. *Cirene* (Milan: Electa).

Braemme E. 1976. *Katalog over teatervidenskabelige kilder i Nationalmuseets Antiksamling. Med en analyse af den såkaldte Phlyaker-vase* (University of Copenhagen Press).

Breitenstein N. 1941. *Catalogue of terracottas, Cypriote, Greek, Etrusco-Italian and Roman*. Nationalmuseet (Denmark) Antiksamlingen (Copenhagen: E. Munksgaard).

Breitholtz L. 1960. *Die dorische Farce im griechischen Mutterland vor dem 5. Jahrhundert: Hypothese oder Realität?* (Stockholm: Almquist, Wiksell).

Bremmer J. 1991. 'Walking, standing, and sitting in ancient Greek culture' in J. Bremmer, H. Roodenburg, *A cultural history of gesture: from antiquity to the present day* (Cambridge: Polity Press) 15–35.

Brommer F. 1959. *Satyrspiele: Bilder griechischer Vasen*, 2nd edn (Berlin: W. de Gruyter).

Brown A.L. 1984. 'Three and scene-painting Sophokles', *Proceedings of the Cambridge Philological Society* 210, 1–17.

Brown P. 2001. 'Introduction', *Menander. The plays and fragments*, ed. M. Balme (Oxford University Press).

Bundrick Sheramy D. 2005. *Music and image in classical Athens* (Cambridge University Press).

Burn L., Higgins R. 2001. *Catalogue of terracottas in the British Museum*, vol. III (London: British Museum Press).

Burnett A.P. 2003. 'The first tragic contest: revision revised' in G.W. Bakewell, J. Sickinger eds., *Gestures: essays in ancient history, literature, and philosophy presented to Alan L. Boegehold* (Oxford: Oxbow) 63–73.

Cambitoglou A., Aellen C., Chamay J. 1986. *Le Peintre de Darius et son milieu: vases grecs d'Italie méridionale* (Geneva: Association Hellas et Roma).

Campbell D.A. ed. 1992. *Greek Lyric*, vol. IV (Cambridge, MA: Harvard University Press).

Canarache V. 1969. *Masken und tanagra Figuren: aus Werkstätten von Callatis-Mangalia* (Constanza: Archäologisches Museum).

Caputo G. 1935. 'Palcoscenico su vaso attico', *Dioniso* 4, 273–80.

Catteruccia L.M. 1951. *Pitturi vascolari italiote di soggetto teatrale comico* (Rome: Bardi).

1965. *I tipi scenici dei protagonisti nelle commedie di Aristofane* (Rome: Bardi).

Ceccarelli P. 1998. *La pirrica nell'antichità greco-romana: studi sulla danza armata* (Pisa and Rome: Istituti Editoriali e Poligrafici Internazionali).

Ceccarelli P., Milanezi S. 2007. 'Dithyramb, tragedy – and Cyrene' in P. Wilson ed., *The Greek theatre and festivals: documentary studies* (Oxford University Press) 185–214.

Cesnola A.A. di. 1882. *Salaminia: the history, treasures and antiquities of Salaminia in Cyprus* (London: Trübner).

Charbonneau J., Martin R., Villard F. 1969. *Grèce classique: 480–330 avant J.-C.* (Paris: Gallimard).

Charitonides S., Kahlil L., Ginouvès R. 1970. *Les Mosaïques de la Maison de Ménandre à Mytilène, AntK-BH 6*.

Cipriani M., Longo F. 1996. *Poseidonia e i lucani: i greci in occidente* (Naples: Electa).

Connor W.R. 1990. 'City Dionysia and Athenian democracy' in W.R. Connor, M.H. Hanson, K.A. Raaflaub, B.S. Strauss eds., *Aspects of Athenian democracy. Classica et Mediaevalia*, vol. XL (University of Copenhagen Press) 7–32.

Costabile F. ed. 1991. *I ninfei di Locri Epizefiri: architettura, culti erotici, sacralità delle acque* (Catanzaro: Rubbettino).

Craik E.M. 1990. 'The staging of Sophokles' *Philoctetes* and Aristophanes' *Birds*' in E.M. Craik ed., *Owls to Athens: essays on classical subjects presented to Sir Kenneth Dover* (Oxford: Clarendon Press) 81–4.

Crosby M. 1955. 'Five comic scenes from Athens', *Hesperia* 24, 76–84.

Csapo E. 1986. 'A note on the Würzburg bell-crater H5697 ("Telephus Travestitus")', *Phoenix* 40, 379–92.

1993. 'A case study in the use of theatre iconography as evidence for ancient acting', *AntK* 36, 41–58.

1997. 'Mise en scène théâtrale, scène de théâtre artisanale', *Pallas* 47, 165–82.

1999–2000. 'Introduction' in E. Csapo ed., *Illinois Classical Studies* 24–5, 377–98.

2000. 'From Aristophanes to Menander? Genre transformation in Greek comedy' in M. Depew and D. Obbink eds., *Matrices of genre: authors, canons and society* (Harvard University Press) 115–33.

2001. 'The first artistic representations of theatre: dramatic illusion and dramatic performance in Attic and southern Italian art' in G.S. Katz, V. Golini, D. Pietropaolo eds., *Theatre and the visual arts* (Ottawa: Legas) 17–38.

2002. 'Kallipides among the floor-sweepings: the limits of realism in classical acting and performance styles' in P. Easterling, E. Hall eds., *Greek and Roman actors: aspects of an ancient profession* (Cambridge University Press) 127–47.

2003. 'The dolphins of Dionysos' in E. Csapo, M. Miller eds., *Poetry, theory, praxis: the social life of myth, word and image in ancient Greece; essays in honour of William J. Slater* (Oxford: Oxbow Books) 69–98.

2004. 'Some social and economic conditions behind the rise of the acting profession in the fifth and fourth centuries BC' in C. Hugoniot, F. Hurlet, S. Milanesi eds., *Le Statut de l'acteur dans l'antiquité grecque et romaine: actes du colloque qui s'est tenu à Tours les 3 et 4 mai 2002* (Tours: Presses Universitaires François-Rabelais).

2007. 'The men who built the theatres: *theatropolai, theatronai,* and *arkhitektones*' in P. Wilson ed., *The Greek theatre and festivals: documentary studies* (Oxford University Press) 87–115.

2008. 'The iconography of the *exarchos*', *MeditArch* 19/20, 55–65.

2010. *Actors and icons of the ancient theater* (Chichester, Malden MA: Wiley-Blackwell).

Csapo E., Miller M., eds. 2007. *The origins of theater in ancient Greece and beyond* (Cambridge, New York: Cambridge University Press).

D'Amicis A., Dell'Aglio A., Lippolis E., Maruggi G. 1991. *Vecchi scavi nuovi restauri* (Taranto: Scorpione).

D'Amicis A., Dell'Aglio A., Masiello L., Trombetta L. 2004. *Attori e maschere del teatro antico* (Taranto: Museo Nazionale Archeologico).

Davidson J. 2000. 'Gnesippus paigniagraphos: the comic poets and the erotic mime' in D. Harvey, J. Wilkins eds., *The rivals of Aristophanes: studies in Athenian Old Comedy* (London: Duckworth, Classical Press of Wales) 41–64.

Dearden C.W. 1976. *The stage of Aristophanes* (University of London, Athlone Press).

1990. 'Epicharmus, Phlyax, and Sicilian comedy' in J.-P. Descœudres ed., *EUMOUZIA: ceramic and iconographic studies in honour of Alexander Cambitoglou, MeditArch* supp. 1, 155–61.

1995. 'Pots, tumblers and phlyax vases' in A. Griffiths ed., *Stage directions: essays in ancient drama in honour of E.W. Handley, BICS* supp. 66, 81–6.

1999. 'Plays for export', *Phoenix* 53, 3–4, 222–48.

De Juliis E., Loiacono, D. 1985. *Taranto: il museo archeologico* (Taranto: Mandese).

De Juliis E. 2001. *Metaponto* (Taranto: Edipuglia).

Dinsmoor W.B. 1950. *The architecture of ancient Greece: an account of its historic development,* 3rd edn revised by W.J. Anderson and R. Phené Spiers (London, New York: Batsford).

Dörpfeld W., Reisch E. 1896. *Das griechische Theater: Beiträge zur Geschichte des Dionysos-Theaters in Athen und anderer griechischer Theater* (Athens: Barth, von Hirst).

Dover K.J. 1968. 'Greek Comedy' in *Fifty years (and twelve) of classical scholarship,* 2nd edn (Oxford: Basil Blackwell).

1972. *Aristophanic comedy* (London: Batsford).

1982. *The Greeks* (Oxford University Press).

Dover K., Arnott W.G. with Lowe N.J., Harvey D. 2000. 'Biographical appendix' in D. Harvey, J. Wilkins eds., *The rivals of Aristophanes: studies in Athenian Old Comedy* (London: Duckworth, Classical Press of Wales) 507–25.

Ede 1985. Charles Ede Ltd sale catalogue, *Antiquities* (London).

1996. Charles Ede Ltd sale catalogue, *Antiquities* (London).

2002. Charles Ede Ltd sale catalogue, *Greek pottery from southern Italy* (London).

Edmonds J.M. 1957–61. *The fragments of Attic comedy after Meineke, Bergk, and Kock,* 3 vols. (Leiden: Brill).

Eggebrecht A. ed. 1988. *Albanien: Schätze aus dem Land der Skipetaren* (Mainz am Rhein: P. von Zabern).

Else Gerald F. 1972. *The origin and early form of Greek tragedy* (New York: Norton).

Fedele B. *et. al.* 1984. *Antichità della collezione Guarini* (Galatina: Congedo).

Festa V. 1912. 'Une nouvelle représentation de phlyaque', *Revue Archéologique* 4th series 19, 321–39.

Fiechter E.R. 1936. *Das Dionysos-Theater in Athen: antike griechische Theaterbauten*, vol. VII (Stuttgart: W. Kohlhammer).

Foley H.P. 1981. 'The conception of women in Athenian drama' in H. P. Foley ed., *Reflections of women in antiquity* (New York: Gordon, Breach) 127–68.

2000. 'The comic body in Greek art and drama' in Beth Cohen ed., *Not the classical Ideal: Athens and the construction of the other in Greek art* (Leiden, Boston, Cologne: Brill) 275–311.

Forti L. 1965. *La ceramica di Gnathia* (Naples: G. Macchiaroli).

Fossey J.M. 1990. *Papers in Boiotian topography and history* (Amsterdam: J.C. Gieben).

Froning H. 2002. 'Masken und Kostüme' in S. Moraw, N. Eckehart eds., *Die Geburt des Theaters in der griechischen Antike* (Mainz am Rhein: P. von Zabern).

2009. 'Der Vogel*krater* ehemals in Malibu: Komödie oder Satyrspiel?' in S. Schmidt, J.H. Oakley eds., *Hermeneutik der Bilder* (Munich: C.H. Beck) 115–24.

Gebhard E.R. 1973. *The theater at Isthmia* (University of Chicago Press).

1974. 'The form of the orchestra in the early Greek theatre', *Hesperia* 43, 428–40.

Geddes A.G. 1987. 'Rags and riches: the costume of Athenian men in the fifth century', *CQ* 37 2nd series, 307–31.

Gerber D.E. ed. 1999. *Greek iambic poetry* (Cambridge MA, London: Harvard University Press).

Getty J. Paul, Museum. 1994. *A passion for antiquities: ancient art from the collection of Barbara and Lawrence Fleischman* (Malibu: J. Paul Getty Museum, Cleveland Museum of Art).

Ghiron-Bistagne P. 1976. *Récherches sur les acteurs dans la Grèce antique* (Paris: Belles Lettres)

Ginouvès R. 1972. *Le théâtron à gradins droits et l'odéon d'Argos* (Paris: J. Vrin).

Goette H.R. 2007. 'An archaeological appendix' in P. Wilson ed., *The Greek theatre and festivals: documentary studies* (Oxford University Press) 116–25.

Goldhill S. 1994. 'Representing democracy: women at the Great Dionysia' in R. Osborne, S. Hornblower eds., *Ritual, finance, politics: Athenian democratic accounts presented to David Lewis* (Oxford: Clarendon Press) 347–69.

Gomme A.W., Sandbach F.H. 1973. *Menander: a commentary* (Oxford University Press).

Grandjean Y., Salvat F. 2000. *Guide de Thasos* (Athens: École Française d'Athènes).

Green J.R. 1985. 'Drunk again: a study of the iconography of the comic theatre', *AJA* 89, 465–72.

1989. 'Motif-symbolism and Gnathia vases' in H.-U. Cain ed., *Festschrift für Nicholaus Himmelman: Beiträge zur Ikonographie und Hermeneutik* (Mainz am Rhein: P. von Zabern).

1995a. 'Theatre production: 1978–1995', *Lustrum* 37, 7–202.

1995b. 'Theatrical motifs in non-theatrical contexts on vases of the later fifth and fourth centuries' in A. Griffiths ed., *Stage directions: essays in ancient drama in honour of E.W. Handley*, BICS Supp. 66, 93–121.

1996. 'Messengers from the tragic stage', *BICS* 41, 17–30.

1997. 'Deportment, costume and naturalistic comedy', *Pallas* 47, 131–43.

1999. 'Tragedy and the spectacle of the mind: messenger speeches, actors, narrative, and audience imagination in fourth-century BCE vase-painting' in B. Bergmann, C. Kondoleon eds., *The art of ancient spectacle* (Washington, New Haven, London: Yale University Press) 37–63.

2001. 'Comic cuts: snippets of action on the Greek comic stage', *BICS* 45, 37–64.

2002. 'Towards a reconstruction of performance style' in P. Easterling, E. Hall eds., *Greek and Roman actors: aspects of an ancient profession* (Cambridge University Press) 93–126.

2006. 'The persistent phallos: regional variability in the performance style of comedy' in J. Davidson, F. Muecke, P. Wilson eds., *Greek drama III: essays in honour of Kevin Lee*, BICS supp. 87, 141–62.

2007. 'Let's hear it for the fat men: padded dancers and the prehistory of drama' in Csapo, Miller eds., 96–107.

2008. 'Theatre production: 1996–2006', *Lustrum* 50, 7–391.

Green J.R., Handley E. 1995. *Images of the Greek theatre* (London: British Museum Press).

Green J.R., Muecke F., Sowada K. N., Turner M., Bachmann E. 2003. *Ancient voices, modern echoes* (Sydney: Nicholson Museum, University of Sydney 2003).

Griefenhagen A. 1975. 'ΦΙΛΟΠΟΤΙΣ', *Gymnasium* 82, 23–32.

Haigh A. E. 1889. *Attic theatre: a description of the stage and theatre of the Athenians, and of the dramatic performances at Athens* (Oxford: Clarendon Press).

1896. *The tragic drama of the Greeks* (Oxford: Clarendon Press).

Hall E. 1999. 'Actor's song in tragedy' in S. Goldhill, R. Osborne eds., *Performance culture and Athenian democracy* (Cambridge University Press) 96–122.

2000. 'Female figures and metapoetry in Old Comedy' in D. Harvey, J. Wilkins eds., *The rivals of Aristophanes: studies in Athenian Old Comedy* (London: Duckworth, Classical Press of Wales) 407–18.

2002. 'The singing actors of antiquity' in P. Easterling, E. Hall eds., *Greek and Roman actors: aspects of an ancient profession* (Cambridge University Press) 3–38.

2006. *The theatrical cast of Athens: interactions between ancient Greek drama and society* (Oxford University Press).

Hammond N.G.L. 1972. 'Conditions of dramatic production to the death of Aeschylos', *GRBS* 13, 387–450.

Handley E.W. 1969. 'The conventions of the comic stage and their exploitation by Menander' in *Ménandre, Entretiens Hardt*, vol. XVI (Geneva) 1–26.

1985. *Cambridge history of classical literature*, vol. I part II, ed. P. Easterling, P.E. Kenney (Cambridge University Press).

1997. 'Some thoughts on New Comedy and its public', *Pallas* 47, 185–200.

2002. 'Acting, action and words in New Comedy' in P. Easterling, E. Hall eds., *Greek and Roman actors: aspects of an ancient profession* (Cambridge University Press) 165–87.

Harvey D. 2000. 'Phrynichos and his muses' in D. Harvey, J. Wilkins eds., *The rivals of Aristophanes: studies in Athenian Old Comedy* (London: Duckworth, Classical Press of Wales) 91–134.

Henderson J. ed. 1987. *Lysistrata* (Oxford: Clarendon Press).

1990. 'The *demos* and the comic competition' in J.J. Winkler, F.I. Zeitlin eds., *Nothing to do with Dionysos: Athenian drama in its social context* (Princeton NJ: University Press) 271–313.

1991. 'Women and the Athenian dramatic festivals', *Transactions of the American Philological Association* 121, 133–47.

2000. 'Pherekrates and the women of Old Comedy' in D. Harvey, J. Wilkins eds., *The rivals of Aristophanes: studies in Athenian Old Comedy* (London: Duckworth, Classical Press of Wales) 135–50.

Higgins R.A. 1954. *Catalogue of Greek terracottas in the department of Greek and Roman antiquities*, vol. 1 (London: British Museum).

Himmelman N. 1993. 'Some characteristics of the representation of the gods in classical art' in W. Childs ed., *Reading Greek art* (Princeton NJ: University Press) 103–38.

Hoorn G. van 1951. *Choes and Anthesteria* (Leyden: Brill).

Hordern J.H. 2004. *Sophron's Mimes: text, translation and commentary* (Oxford University Press).

Hourmouziades N.C. 1965. *Production and imagination in Euripides: form and function of the scenic space*. Greek Society for Humanistic Studies, 2nd series no. 5 (Athens).

Hughes A. 1987. 'Art and eighteenth-century acting style III: Passions', *Theatre Notebook* 41, 3, 128–39.

1991. 'Acting style in the ancient world', *Theatre Notebook* 45, 1, 2–16.

1996. 'Comic stages in Magna Graecia: the evidence of the vases', *Theatre Research International* 21, 2, 95–107.

1997. 'ΚΟΝΝΑΚΙΣ: a scene from the comic theatre', *EchCl* 41, new series 16, 2, 237–46.

2003. 'Comedy in Paestan painting', *OJA* 22, 3, 291–301.

2006a. 'The costumes of Old and Middle Comedy', *BICS* 49, 39–68.

2006b. 'The "Perseus Dance" vase revisited', *OJA* 24, 4, 413–33.

2008. '*Ai Dionysiazusai*: women in Greek theatre', *BICS* 51, 1–27.

Hunter R.L. 1985. *The New Comedy of Greece and Rome* (Cambridge University Press).

Jacoby F. 1904. *Das Marmor Parium* (Berlin: Weidmann).

Janko R. 1984. *Aristotle on comedy: towards a reconstruction of 'Poetics II'* (London: Duckworth).

Jones F. 1951. *The theater in ancient art* (Princeton NJ: University Press).

Jones N.F. 2004. *Rural Athens under the democracy* (Pittsburgh: University of Pennsylvania Press).

Kassel R., Austin C. 1989. *Poetae comici Graeci* VII (Berlin: W. de Gruyter).

2001. *Poetae comici Graeci* I (Berlin: W. de Gruyter).

Kerkhof R. 2001. *Dorische Posse, Epicharm und attische Komödie* (Munich: K.G. Saur).

Konstantakos I.M. 2002. 'Towards a literary history of comic love', *Classica et Mediaevalia* 5, 141–71.

Koster W.J.W. 1975. *Prolegomena de comoedia*, vol. III (Groningen: Bouma's Boekhuis) 7–10.

Kourouniotes K., Thompson H.A. 1932. 'The Pnyx in Athens', *Hesperia* I, 90–217.

Lada-Richards I. 2002. 'The subjectivity of Greek performance', in P. Easterling, E. Hall eds., *Greek and Roman actors: aspects of an ancient profession* (Cambridge University Press) 395–418.

Landels J.G. 1999. *Music in ancient Greece and Rome* (London, New York: Rout-ledge).

Laumonier A. 1921. *Catalogue de terres cuites du Musée archéologique de Madrid* (Bordeaux: Feret et fils).

Lawler L.B. 1964. *The dance of the ancient Greek theatre* (University of Iowa Press).

Lecoq J. 2000. *The moving body: teaching creative theatre* trans. D. Bradby (London: Methuen).

Lefkowitz M.R. 1981. *The lives of the Greek poets* (London: Duckworth).

Leskey A. 1966. *A history of Greek literature* trans. J. Willis, C. de Heer (London: Methuen).

Levi P. 1964. 'A Kabirion vase', *JHS* 84, 155 pl. 5–6.

Ley G. 1989. 'Agotharchos, Aeschylus and the construction of a *skene*', *Maia* 41, 35–40.

Leyenaar-Plaisier P.G. 1979. *Les Terres cuites grecques et romaines. Catalogue de la collection du Musée National des Antiquités à Leiden*, vol. III (Rijksmuseum van Oudheden te Leiden).

Libertini G. 1930. *Il Museo Biscari* (Milan, Rome: Bestetti e Tumminelli).

Lucas F.L. 1954. *Greek drama for everyman* (London: Dent).

MacDowell D.M. 1994. 'The number of speaking actors in Old Comedy', *CQ* 44, 325–35.

Marshall C.W. 1997. 'Comic technique and the fourth actor', *CQ* 47, 77–84.

1999. 'Some fifth-century masking conventions', *G&R* 46, 188–202.

2001. 'A gander at the Goose Play', *Theatre Survey* 53, 53–71.

Mastonarde D.J. 1990. 'Actors on high: the *skene* roof, the crane and the gods in Attic drama', *Classical Antiquity* 9, 247–94.

Matheson S.B. 1995. *Polygnotos and vase painting in classical Athens* (Madison: University of Wisconsin Press).

Mathieson T.J. 1999. *Apollo's lyre: Greek music and music theory in antiquity and the middle ages* (Lincoln: University of Nebraska Press).

Matt L. von, Zanotti-Bianco U. 1962. *La Magna Grecia* trans. H. Hoffmann (Geneva: Stringa).

Mayo M., Hamma K. 1982. *The art of south Italy* (Richmond VA: Virginia Museum of Fine Arts 1982).

Mertens D. 2001. 'L'architettura' in A. De Siena ed. *Metaponto: archeologia di una colonia greca* (Taranto: Scorpione), 45–70.

2004. 'Siracusa e l'architettura del potere: uno schizzo', *Sicilia Antiqua* 1, 29–34.

Mikalson J.D. 1998. *Religion in Hellenistic Athens* (Berkeley, Los Angeles, London: University of California Press).

Miller M. 1997. *Athens and Persia in the fifth century* BC: *a study in cultural receptivity* (Cambridge University Press).

Miller S.G. 2005. 'Architecture as evidence for the the identity of the early Greek *polis*' in M.H. Hansen ed., *Sources for the ancient Greek city-state*, Acts of the Copenhagen Polis Centre 2, Copenhagen, 201–44.

Millis B.W. 2001. Review of Harvey 2000, *BMCR* 17 (May).

Mitten D.G., Doeringer S. 1967. *Master bronzes from the classical world* (Mainz am Rhein: P. von Zabern).

Moretti J.-Ch. 1992. 'Les Entrées en scène dans le théâtre grec: l'apport de l'archéologie', *Pallas* 38, 79–107.

1997. 'Formes et destinations du *proskèneion* dans les théâtres hellénistiques de Grèce', *Pallas* 47, 13–39.

1999–2000. 'The theatre of the sanctuary of Dionysus Eleuthereus in late fifth-century Athens' in E. Csapo ed., *Illinois Classical Studies* 24–5, 377–98.

2004. 'Une scénographie à Delos', *MeditArch* 17, 173–84.

Morris D., Collett P., Marsh P., O'Shaughnessy M. 1979. D. Morris *et al.*, *Gestures: their origins and distribution* (London: J. Cape).

Münzen und Medeillen 1958. *Münzen und Medeillen sale catalogue* (Basle).

Nesselrath H.-G. 1990. *Die attische mittlere Komödie: ihre Stellung in der antiken Literaturkritik und Literaturgeschichte* (Berlin: W. de Gruyter).

1997. 'The polis of Athens in Middle Comedy' in G.W. Dobrov ed., *The city as comedy: society and representation in Athenian drama* (Chapel Hill, London: University of North Carolina Press).

2000. 'Eupolis and the periodation of Athenian comedy' in D. Harvey, J. Wilkins eds. *The rivals of Aristophanes: studies in Athenian Old Comedy* (London: Duckworth, Classical Press of Wales) 233–46.

Norwood G. 1931. *Greek comedy* (London: Methuen).

O'Connor J.B. 1966. *Chapters in the history of actors and acting in ancient Greece* (New York: Haskell House).

Orsi P. 1904. *Monumenti antichi*, vol. v, xiv.

Padgett J.M., Redmond A.E. 1993. *Vase-painting in Italy: red-figure and related works in the Museum of Fine Arts, Boston* (Boston: Museum of Fine Arts).

Palo F. di 1987. *Dalla Ruvo antica al Museo Archeologico Jatta* (Fasano: Schena).

Peredolskaja A. 1964. *Attische Tonfiguren aus einem südrussischen Grab, AntK Beiheft* 2 (Basle: Graf).

Pfrommer M. with E.T. Markus 2001. *Greek gold from Hellenistic Egypt* (Los Angeles: J. Paul Getty Museum).

Pickard-Cambridge A.W. 1948. Review of Anti 1947, *Classical Review* 62, 125–8.
    1949. 'South Italian vases and Attic drama', *CQ* 43, 57.
    1953. *The dramatic festivals of Athens* (Oxford: Clarendon Press).
Podlecki A.J. 1990. 'Could women attend the theater in ancient Athens? A collection of testimonia', *AncW* 21, 27–43.
Polacco L. 1987. 'L'evoluzione del teatro greco comico nel IV secolo', *Dioniso* 57, 267–79.
Polacco L., Anti C. 1969. *Nuove ricerche sui teatri greci arcaici* (Padua: CEDAM).
    1981. *Il teatro antico di Siracusa*, 2 vols. (Rimini: Maggioli).
Pollitt J.J. 1990. *The art of ancient Greece: sources and documents* (Cambridge University Press).
Pugliese Carratelli G. 1996. *The western Greeks: classical civilization in the western Mediterranean* (London: Thames and Hudson).
Pugliese Carratelli G. *et al.* 1983. *Megale Hellàs: storia e civiltà della Magna Grecia* (Milan: Credito Italiano, Libri Scheiwiller).
Putorti N. 1938. 'Museo Civico di Reggio Calabria', *Italia antichissima* fasc. 12.
Rehm R. 1992. *Greek tragic theatre* (London, New York: Routledge).
    2002. *The play of space: spatial transformation in Greek tragedy* (Princeton NJ: University Press).
Renier G. 1950. *History: its purpose and method* (Boston: Beacon).
Revermann M. 2006. *Comic business: theatricality, dramatic technique, and performance contexts of Aristophanic comedy* (Oxford University Press).
Riccioni G., Amorelli F. 1968. *La tomba Panatenaica di Vulci* (Rome: Lerici).
Richter G. 1966. *The furniture of the Greeks, Etruscans and Romans* (London: Phaidon).
    1987. *A handbook of Greek art* (London, New York: Phaidon).
Roberti M.M. 1976. *Museo teatrale alla Scala* (Milan: Electa).
Robertson M. 1989. 'A muffled dancer and others' in A. Cambitoglou ed., *Studies in honour of Arthur Dale Trendall* (University of Sydney Press 1979).
    1992. *The art of vase-painting in classical Athens* (Cambridge University Press).
Robertson N. 1998. 'The city center of ancient Athens', *Hesperia* 67, 255–83.
Rogers 1902. *The* Ecclesiazusae *of Aristophanes: acted at Athens in the year* BC *393* trans. B.B. Rogers (London: Bell).
Rohde E. 1968. *Griechische Terrakotten* (Tübingen: Wasmuth).
Romagnoli E. 1923. *Nel regno di Dioniso: studi sul teatro comico greco*, 2nd edn (Bologna: Zanichelli).
Romer F.E. 1983. 'When is a bird not a bird?', *Transactions of the American Philological Association* 113, 135–42.
Roselli D.K. 2009. '*Theorika* in fifth-century Athens', *GRBS* 49, 5–30.
Rosivach V. 2000. 'The audiences of New Comedy', *G&R* 47, 169–71.
Rothwell, K.S. Jr. 2007. *Nature, culture, and the origins of Greek comedy* (Cambridge University Press).
Ruffell I. 2002. 'A total write-off: Aristophanes, Cratinus, and the rhetoric of comic competition', *CQ* 52, 138–63.

2008. 'Audience and emotion in the reception of Greek drama', in M. Revermann, P. Wilson eds., *Performance, iconography, reception: studies in honour
of Oliver Taplin* (Oxford University Press) 37–58.

Rumpf A. 1947. 'Classical and post-classical painting', *JHS* 67, 10–21.

Russo C. 1994. *Aristophanes: an author for the stage*, revised edn (London, New
York: Routledge).

Rusten J. 2001. Review of Kerkhof 2001, *BMCR* 23 (December).

2006a. 'The four "new Lenaean victors" of 428–425 BC (and the date of the first
Lenaean comedy) reconsidered', *ZPE* 157, 22–6.

2006b. 'Who "Invented" comedy? The ancient candidates for the origins of
comedy and the visual evidence', *AJP* 127, 37–66.

ed. 2011. *The birth of comedy: texts, documents and art from Athenian comic
competitions, 486–280* trans. J. Rusten, J. Henderson, D. Konstan, R. Rosen,
N.W. Slater (Baltimore: John Hopkins University Press).

forthcoming 2011. 'A forgotten witness to comic art: the Phanagoria chous',
Hesperia.

Sandbach F.H. 1977. *The comic theatre of Greece and Rome* (London: Chatto and
Windus).

Schaal H. 1923. *Griechische Vasen aus Frankfurter Sammlungen* (Frankfurt am
Main: Frankfurter Verlags-Anstalt).

Schaps D. 1977. 'The woman least mentioned: etiquette and women's names', *CQ*
27, 323–30.

Schauenburg K. 1988. 'Kreusa in Delphi', *AA*, 644.

Scheithauer A. 1997. 'Les aulètes dans le théâtre grec à l'époque hellénistique',
Pallas 47, 107–27.

Scullion S. 1994. *Three studies in Athenian dramaturgy*, Beiträge zur Altertum-
skunde 25 (Stuttgart, Leipzig: Teubner).

Seeberg A. 1995. 'From padded dancers to comedy' in A. Griffiths ed., *Stage
directions: essays in ancient drama in honour of E.W. Handley*, BICS Supp. 66,
1–12.

2002–3. 'Tragedy and archaeology, forty years after', *BICS* 46, 43–75.

Shapiro H.A. 1989. *Art and culture under the tyrants in Athens* (Mainz am Rhein:
P. von Zabern).

1992. '*Mousikoi agones*: music and poetry at the Panathenaia' in J. Neils *et al.*
eds., *Goddess and polis: the Panathenaic festival in ancient Athens* (Princeton
NJ: University Press) 53–75.

Sidwell K. 2000. 'From Old to Middle to New: Aristotle's *Poetics* and the history of
Athenian comedy' in D. Harvey, J. Wilkins eds., *The rivals of Aristophanes:
studies in Athenian Old Comedy* (London: Duckworth, Classical Press of
Wales) 247–58.

Sieveking J. 1916. *Die Terrakotten der Sammlung Loeb* II (Munich: A. Buchholz).

Sifakis G.M. 1967. *Studies in the history of Hellenistic drama* (London: Athlone
Press).

1971a. *Parabasis and animal choruses: a contribution to the history of Attic comedy*
(London: Athlone Press).

1971b. 'Aristotle, *E.N.* IV, 2, 1123a 9–24, and the comic chorus in the fourth century', *AJP* 92, 410–32.

1979. 'Boy actors in New Comedy' in G.W. Bowersock, W. Burkert, M. Putnam eds., *Arktouros: Hellenic studies presented to Bernard M. W. Knox on the occasion of his 65th birthday* (Berlin, New York: W. de Gruyter) 199–208.

1995. 'The one-actor rule in Greek tragedy' in A. Griffiths ed., *Stage directions: essays in ancient drama in honour of E.W. Handley*, *BICS* Supp. 66, 13–24.

2002. 'Looking for the actor's art in Aristotle' in P. Easterling, E. Hall eds., *Greek and Roman actors: aspects of an ancient profession* (Cambridge University Press) 148–65.

Silk M.S. 2000. *Aristophanes and the definition of comedy* (Oxford University Press).

Sinn U. 1977. *Antike Terrakotten* (Kassel-Wilhelmshöhe: Thiele, Schwartz).

Six J. 1920. 'Agatharcos', *JHS* 40, 180–9.

Slater, N. 1986. 'The Lenaean theatre', *ZPE* 66, 255–64.

1988. 'Problems in the hypotheses to Aristophanes' *Peace*', *ZPE* 74, 43–57.

1990. 'The idea of the actor' in J.J. Winkler, F.I. Zeitlin eds., *Nothing to do with Dionysos: Athenian drama in its social context* (Princeton NJ: University Press) 385–95.

1999. 'Making the Aristophanic audience', *AJP* 120, 351–68.

2002. *Spectator politics: metatheatre and performance in Aristophanes* (Philadelphia: University of Pennsylvania Press).

Slater W. 2007. 'Deconstructing festivals' in P. Wilson ed. *The Greek theatre and festivals: documentary studies* (Oxford University Press) 21–47.

Small J.P. 2003. *The parallel worlds of classical art and text* (Cambridge, New York: Cambridge University Press).

Smith, T.J. 2002. 'Transvestitism or travesty? Dance, dress and gender in Greek vase painting' in L. Llewellyn-Jones ed., *Women's dress in the ancient world* (London: Duckworth, Classical Press of Wales).

2007. 'The corpus of *komast* vases: from identity to exegesis' in Csapo, Miller eds., 48–76.

Sommerstein A.H. 1980. 'The naming of women in Greek and Roman comedy', *Quaderni di Storia* 11 (June) 393–418.

1996. *Aeschylean tragedy* (Bari: Levante).

2000. 'Platon, Eupolis and the "demagogue-comedy"' in D. Harvey, J. Wilkins eds., *The rivals of Aristophanes: studies in Athenian Old Comedy* (London: Duckworth, Classical Press of Wales) 437–51.

Sourvinou-Inwood C. 2003. *Tragedy and Athenian religion* (Lexington: Lanham MD).

Stefani G. 1984. *Terrecotte figurate: materiali del museo archeologico nazionale di Tarquinia* 7 (Rome: G. Bretschneider).

Stephanis I.E. 1988. *Dionysiakoi Technikai* (Iraklion: University of Crete Press).

Stone L. 1981. *Costume in Aristophanic comedy* (New York: Arno Press 1981).

Storey I.C. 2003. *Eupolis: poet of Old Comedy* (Oxford, New York: Oxford University Press).

Sutton D.F. 1987. 'The theatrical families of Athens', *AJP* 108, 9–26.

Taaffe L. 1993. *Aristophanes and women* (London: Routledge).

Tanner J. 2006. *The invention of art history in ancient Greece: religion, society and artistic rationalisation* (Cambridge University Press).

Taplin O. 1977. *The stagecraft of Aeschylus: the dramatic use of exits and entrances in Greek tragedy* (Oxford: Clarendon Press).

  1987. 'Phallology, phlyakes, iconography and Aristophanes', *Proceedings of the Cambridge Philological Society* 33, 92–104.

  2007. *Pots and plays: interactions between tragedy and Greek vase-painting of the fourth century* BC (Los Angeles: J. Paul Getty Museum).

Thompson D.B. 1952. 'Three centuries of Hellenistic terracottas', *Hesperia* 21, 116–64.

Thompson H.A., Wycherley R.E. 1972. *The Athenian agora* XIV (Princeton: American School of Classical Studies).

Tillyard E.M.W. 1923. *The Hope vases* (Cambridge University Press).

Tomlinson R.A. 1983. *Epidauros* (London, New York: Granada).

Townsend R.F. 1986. 'The fourth-century *skene* of the Theater of Dionysos at Athens', *Hesperia* 55, 421–38.

Travlos I. 1971. *A pictorial dictionary of ancient Athens* (New York: Prager).

Trendall A.D. 1952. 'Paestan pottery supplement', *PBSR* 20, 1–53.

  1995. 'A Phlyax bell-*krater* by the Lecce Painter' in A. Cambitoglou, E. Robinson eds., *Classical art in the Nicholson Museum, Sydney* (Mainz am Rhein: P. von Zabern).

Vaio, J. 1973. 'Theme and action in *Lysistrata*', *GRBS* 14, 369–80.

Vervain C., Wiles D. 2001. 'The masks of Greek tragedy as point of departure for modern performance', *New Theatre Quarterly* 17, 254–71.

Webster T.B.L. 1948. 'South Italian vases and Attic drama', *CQ* 42, 15–27.

  1952. 'Chronological notes on Middle Comedy', *CQ* NS 2, 13–26.

  1953. *Studies in later Greek comedy* (Manchester University Press).

  1960. 'Greek dramatic monuments from the Athenian agora and Pnyx', *Hesperia* 29, 254–84.

  1970. *The Greek chorus* (London: Methuen).

  1974. *An introduction to Menander* (Manchester University Press).

Welles C.B. 1947. 'Archaeological news', *AJA* 51, 296–9.

West M.L. 1972. *Iambi et elegi Graeci ante Alexandram cantati*, 2 vols. (Oxford, New York: Oxford University Press).

  1989. 'The early chronology of Attic tragedy', *CQ* NS 39, 251–4.

  1994. *Ancient Greek music* (Oxford: Clarendon Press).

Westcoat B.D. ed. 1989. *Syracuse, the fairest Greek city: ancient art from the Museo Archeologico Regionale 'Paolo Orsi'* (Rome: de Luca).

Whitehead D. 1986. *The demes of Attica, 508/7 – ca. 250* BC (Princeton NJ: University Press).

Wilamowitz-Moellendorff U. von ed. 1927. *Lysistrata* (Berlin: Weidmann).

Wiles D. 1991. *The masks of Menander: sign and meaning in Greek and Roman performance* (Cambridge University Press).

1997. *Tragedy in Athens: performance space and theatrical meaning* (Cambridge University Press).

2000. *Greek theatre performance: an introduction* (Cambridge University Press).

2004. 'The use of masks in modern performances of Greek drama' in E. Hall, F. Macintosh, A. Wrigley eds. *Dionysus since 69: Greek tragedy at the dawn of the third millennium* (Oxford University Press).

2006. 'The poetics of the mask in Old Comedy' in M. Revermann ed., *Comic business: theatricality, dramatic technique, and performance contexts of Aristophanic comedy* (Oxford University Press) 374–94.

Williams R. 2004. 'New Comedy in performance: Menander and the mask', *Dioniso* NS 3, 148–53.

Wilson A. 1977. 'The individualised chorus in Old Comedy', *CQ* NS 27, 278–83.

Wilson P. 2000. *The Athenian institution of the khoregia: the chorus, the city and the stage* (Cambridge University Press).

2002. 'The musicians among the actors' in P. Easterling, E. Hall eds., *Greek and Roman actors: aspects of an ancient profession* (Cambridge University Press) 39–68.

2007. '*Khoragoi* and Sicilian choruses' in P. Wilson ed., *The Greek theatre and festivals: documentary studies* (Oxford University Press) 351–77.

Winkler J.J. 1990. 'The ephebe's song: *tragōidia* and *polis*' in J.J. Winkler, F.I. Zeitlin eds., *Nothing to do with Dionysos: Athenian drama in its social context* (Princeton NJ: University Press) 20–62.

Winter F.E. 1983. 'The stage of New Comedy', *Phoenix* 27, 38–47.

Wise J. 1998. *Dionysus writes: the invention of theatre in ancient Greece* (Ithaca: Cornell University Press).

Wolters P., Bruns G. 1940. *Das Kabirenheiligtum bei Theben* (Berlin: W. de Gruyter).

Zeitlin F.I. 1985. 'Playing the other: theater, theatricality, and the feminine in Greek drama', *Representations* 11, 63–94.

Zewadski W.K. 1995. 'The crooked staff motif', *Ancient Greek vases from south Italy in Tampa Bay collections* supp. 3 (Tampa) 90–117.

Index

0 1341 1463406 3